PIONEERING CONCEPTS
IN
MODERN SCIENCE

Edited by

ROBERT M. FRIEDENBERG, PH.D.

VOLUME II

ANTON F. VIERLING, JACQUELINE S. VIERLING AND
JOHN F. KROPF

COMPUTER ASSISTED LEARNING

HAFNER PUBLISHING COMPANY

New York and London
1969

COMPUTER ASSISTED LEARNING

by

ANTON F. VIERLING

Physics Department
U.S. Naval Academy and
Quality Educational Development, Inc.
Annapolis, Maryland

and

JACQUELINE S. VIERLING

Nuclear Physics Division
U.S. Naval Research Laboratory
Washington, D.C.

and

JOHN F. KROPF

RCA Instructional Systems
Palo Alto, California

HAFNER PUBLISHING COMPANY

New York and London
1969

© COPYRIGHT 1969
HAFNER PUBLISHING COMPANY

Printed and Published by

HAFNER PUBLISHING COMPANY, INC.
31 East 10th Street
New York, N.Y. 10003

LIBRARY OF CONGRESS CATALOG CARD NUMBER 68-58965

TO

OUR

TEACHERS

EDITOR'S PREFACE

This is the second book in the series "Pioneering Concepts in Modern Science." As indicated in Volume One, the purpose of this series is to advance the opportunities for scientists working in highly specialized fields to publish their ideas and thoughts on the most advanced fronts of their disciplines. The audience is the professional person but non-specialist. The contents of these books will reflect the individual author's most advanced points of view in their field. Many of these representations may still be early in their embryonic development.

All of the above ideas apply particularly to Volume Two, "Computer Assisted Learning." The rapidly evolving computer technology is currently far ahead of our capabilities to utilize this powerful tool. One approach to the development of adequate utilization of computers in our university educational curricula is given here. It is a first attempt to harness this "giant monolith," the computer, to all aspects of a physical science college teaching program with applications to many diverse non-science courses. This volume differs from others in this series by the addition of techniques as well as many carefully chosen examples illustrating the core of concepts which are the predominant focus of this text. Thus, this text meets the necessity of implementing the fundamental *ideas* of "Computer Assisted Learning" with sound, realistic and practical ways of bringing the computer into the classroom. This can be accomplished only by a text readable by the non-specialist. Every effort has been made to accomplish this end.

PREFACE

Recent developments in computer facilities have made it possible for both teachers and students to become "computer-involved." Some high schools and most colleges either have their own computer center or they have remote terminals which are linked to a large time-shared computer system. In spite of these desirable conditions, only a few teachers and students have learned to apply and use computer facilities available to them. It is the opinion of the authors that the inability of teachers and students to adapt themselves to today's "computer age" may be directly traced to a lack of published concepts and techniques for successful computer applications in the classroom. It is to ameliorate this condition that this book has been written.

In our experiences with students at the U.S. Naval Academy, we have developed methods of computer use in laboratory and classroom situations.* Furthermore, by our participation in a Commission on College Physics computer study group, we have been able to acquire considerable insight into the use of computers in education. It is one of the purposes of this book to share the knowledge gained through these projects with teachers and students in all fields of academic excellence where the computer may be of assistance. Many "tried and proven" examples should make it possible for all readers, independent of their mathematical training, to get a "feel" for computer applications in the classroom.

This book was planned to encompass a wide scope of individual computer experience. We included the rudiments of how the computer operates and also the details of solving sophisticated problems. The emphasis throughout is on computer applications and the solution of real problems in physics, chemistry, and engineering. The reader should be able to choose those portions and examples which best fit his particular needs and experience.

Finally, a word must be said of the philosophy, point of view and approach chosen for this text. To describe developments in "hardware" (i.e., actual computer machinery) would have been a serious error in judgment since developments are occurring so rapidly in this field. Yet the ideas and concepts of the learning process are very much tied to the capabilities of existing machines. Thus, emphasis is placed upon a *rationale* or *model for thinking* "as the computer thinks," to enable teachers and students to adapt to current improvements in technology. However, since there is no question that it is the technology that has brought about the increased applications of computers to learning, one must pay some heed and awareness to these machines. Some insight into the fundamental work-

* The Academic Computer Center at the Naval Academy supported the classroom use of computers through a subproject under Bureau of Naval Personnel TDP 43–03X.

ings of computers is given but is *not essential* to the understanding or to the utilization of computer assisted learning. The emphasis is and must be given in terms of:

1. concepts
necessary for the computer to assist in the learning process;
2. techniques
to enable the teacher and student to implement his ideas and;
3. examples and illustrations
to enable those unfamiliar with the mathematical and programming tools to be successful in this field.

We wish to express our gratitude to the many professional friends who have encouraged us to undertake this task. We are particularly thankful to Dr. J. R. Smithson, Head of Physics, U.S. Naval Academy, Annapolis, for the foresight to permit us to introduce computers in the undergraduate physics courses. Dr. J. W. Robson, formerly with the Commission of College Physics, currently at the University of Arizona, Tuscon, was very instrumental in providing the opportunity for experiments in computer usage in the classroom. Professor S. Elder, and Professor V. Acosta, of the U.S. Naval Academy, gave valuable inputs through conversations as to the nature and extent of the computer's role in education. Dr. D. Denison of the Navy's Computer Utilization Branch, Alexandria, also added advice and comments which were helpful in the design and restructuring of the manuscript. Dr. E. P. Radford, Jr., of Johns Hopkins University, Baltimore, is mentioned for being indirectly responsible for the writing style. Mr. J. Gillis, President of Quality Educational Development, Inc., contributed to the discussion and formulation of our opinions and concepts in educational technology. Also, we are thankful to the students who have tried and 'debugged' the problems and who gave so eagerly of their time.

In conclusion, we wish to acknowledge the patience and cooperation of Dr. Robert M. Friedenberg in editing our book. His thorough understanding of the teaching aspects of the subject matter, and his experience in uncovering the many "pitfalls" in technical writing have contributed to the completeness of our book.

INTRODUCTION

The application of computers to education at all levels for a broad array of subjects makes clear the importance of, and need for, skilled individuals aware of how computers can assist them individually in their learning or teaching processes. Although this book considers only computer applications to the physical sciences from early undergraduate through graduate college levels, it develops a point of view and rationale (or model, if one prefers) which has utility and import for all fields of knowledge at all educational levels. Whether the goal for a specific science course (for example, physics, chemistry, engineering, or mathematics) is to increase research effectiveness and perspective in analysis, or to survey a broad field of knowledge and animate with computer derived films a seemingly dry subject, the use of computers will allow teachers and students alike to derive many benefits soon to become essential in this space atomic age of advanced technology.

For the beginner this book offers the simplest ideas and "crawling stages" of how to make use of and utilize the many facets of the computer. None are exempt from this usage as computers are rapidly becoming an everyday part of our lives. All will find the opening chapters of simple explanation and of human interest with no previous mathematical skills demanded of the reader. The later chapters that follow carry the reader through more advanced sections which will however, require an input from the reader to learn and master the material.

For the advanced graduate student, teacher, and specialist, this book includes insight acquired through years of experience in such research activities as problem solving, problem simulation, and synthetic experiments. Much of this general methodology and technique of computer thinking may also be applied to the elementary learning process. However, independent of these more advanced methods, both the inexperienced teacher and student will find a thorough introduction to flexible relationships that can exist between man and the computer.

The book is divided into two parts; Part I outlines general computer principles, and Part II demonstrates many specific examples of computer applications in the classroom. The first two chapters of Part I are devoted to a description of the role of the time-sharing computer system in education. This discussion draws heavily upon actual classroom experience of the authors combined with the results of college committees of which the authors were members. The computer's role in education is explained in terms of:

(a) classroom teaching,
(b) laboratory simulation,
(c) animated film making, and
(d) student learning.

In these two chapters emphasis has been placed upon the acceptance of the computer as a learning tool by both the teacher and student. An explanation of how computers operate paves the way for the man-computer partnership which is stressed in this book.

Chapter three evaluates the rationale of the computer integrated with existing course material. Methods are suggested for course revision which can update existing subject matter to allow for more effective use of the computer by the students. Observations of actual student reactions are discussed and a hierarchy of objectives is outlined. The first three chapters can be read with ease and should prepare the reader for the theme of computer thinking. In subsequent chapters, more technical and subject-matter oriented material is presented. These chapters will require more attention and study by the reader.

Chapter four is devoted to a complete description of the very popular BASIC language which is used throughout the book. Useful programming techniques are discussed and demonstrated in detail. The reader acquires a complete familiarity with the writing of computer programs and their use in the solution of problems. Methods of program evaluation are shown in combination with practical ideas for program revision. Chapter five completes this sequence by explaining some of the specific computer mathematics needed by all potential users.

Part II contains three chapters; one for Physics, one for Chemistry, and one for Engineering. These chapters contain complete and often independent lessons on topics that are appropriate for computer-assisted-learning. Each lesson is clearly identified as to subject, level of difficulty, and learning application. These chapters are especially helpful to the teacher who would like "to get started." Practical teaching examples have been chosen in each field which will allow the teacher to incorporate the examples into an existing course.

The primary purpose of this book, therefore, is to bring the computer into the classroom as a working entity, solving real problems. The ability to use computers effectively can best be acquired by "hands-on" experience in a classroom environment. Teachers and students with no previous computer experience will be able to understand and apply the computer techniques discussed in this book.

TABLE OF CONTENTS

LIST OF FIGURES

LIST OF PROGRAMS

LIST OF TABLES

PART I

INTRODUCTION OF CONCEPTS

CHAPTER 1

THE COMPUTER RETURNS TO CAMPUS

1.1 INTRODUCTION

The purpose of this book is to describe in detail to teachers and students alike the flexible relationships that can exist between man and computer. No previous computer programming knowledge or computer experience will be required to understand all aspects of the material presented in this book. The aim, therefore, is to introduce to the non-computer specialist, in the simplest manner possible, applications of computer "know-how" to problems in mathematics, physics, chemistry and engineering. The reader will find an ample description of the computer, how it operates, and how it can be used effectively to solve both very simple and more complicated scientific problems. Since computer mathematics requires only the most elementary operations, only a knowledge of algebra will be essential to the full utilization of the computer methods described.

Computer involvement in every phase of human life is now nearly complete. In various ways, computers can compose music, schedule productions of steel mills, play war-games, conduct detailed library reference services, and perform an endless list of other skills previously reserved for man alone. The growth in the use of the digital computer has been explosive, and appears to be limited only by the availability of computer components and of skilled, human minds to develop the computer techniques. The first large scale digital computers appeared in the early 1950's. Over 4,000 digital computers were installed in 1960, and that number shot to more than 40,000 digital computers in 1968.

The modern computer ironically began its existence on the college campus with the development in 1946 of the first all-electronic digital computer at the University of Pennsylvania. This machine was named 'The Electrical Numerical Integrator and Automatic Computer' or 'ENIAC.' After a shaky start on several campuses in the late 1940's, the computer set out on a successful career in industry. Coupled with industrial machines, computers became flexible and comprehensive task performers especially applicable to the efficient control of mass production items. Computers solved the monumental problem of accurate handling of industrial inventory and advanced sales. In short, the industrial and government complexes of the world depend heavily on computers not only for research, development and routine operation, but also for major decision-making information.

Several technological developments high-lighted this industrial career. The introduction of the transistor, magnetic memory devices, and semi-conductors have made the time required for numerical manipulations dwindle to the nanosecond * range. The image of the computer enthroned

---

* A nanosecond is one billionth of a second.

Figure 1.1   The computer returns to campus

in its air-conditioned palace prevails, and is fostered by the reports that the machine is extremely expensive (megabucks), computes with frightening speed (microseconds), and has a memory of startling dimensions (one hundred and fifty kilowords). The threatening appetite of this electromechanical device and its ability to produce ream upon ream of data has added to the not-so-flattering label of "data generator." Now, after twenty years of wide-spread industrial application, the computer is trying to return to campus and play an active role in the educational process of students.

Because of the popular image of the digital computer as an industrial giant, the thought that computers could be tamed to assist in the educational effort has perplexed many educators and laymen. With more than sixty million persons enrolled in schools in this country and with seven percent of the gross national product being spent for education, it becomes obvious that the computer has not been assigned an easy job. What role can the computer play in the educational system?

Historically, computers were first introduced into universities as *special* electrical machines with auxiliary pieces of peripheral equipment operated by *specialists*. This computer *specialist* could communicate to the machine by a numerical language called "machine language," which was often limited to his specific computer. Over the years, it became obvious that if the computer were to take an active role in the educational process, there had to be a means for the teacher and student to communicate easily and directly with the machine; the language-barrier had to be overcome. The programming language had to be so simple that its details would not be an obstacle to even the most non-scientific teacher or student. Any grammatical rules needed for the language had to be almost intuitive for the potential users.

Professors John G. Kemeny and Thomas E. Kurtz of Dartmouth College, with the assistance of their students, have developed such a language called BASIC (*B*eginner's *A*ll-purpose *S*ymbolic *I*nstructional *C*ode). BASIC was found to have such general acceptance by students, teachers, businessmen, and engineers that nearly all commercial computers now have the BASIC language available for potential users. BASIC has acquired the reputation of being simple and flexible and therefore it would be safe to say that BASIC is here to stay. This modern computer language is not only easily learned, but gives the student direct and conversational access to the power of today's sophisticated computers. BASIC and a few other interactive languages have the demonstrated capability of extending the student's ability for logical problem solving. The BASIC language has been chosen for integrated classroom use in this book because of its wide-spread availability and proven success with students and teachers. (Following a thorough introduction to the BASIC language in Chapters 2 and 4 of this book, all further symbols and equations in the remainder of the text will be in BASIC.)

Currently, virtually all the major colleges in this country have access to digital computers, and science graduates without at least an introductory course in the use of computers are by far the exception. At present, however, there remains a substantial lag in effective pedagogic techniques to include computer methods directly into the classroom as a means to enhance student understanding of the subject matter. As the educational technologist more clearly and precisely defines the learning process, a computer can more realistically be assigned the job of a learning assistant. Even though the scientific study of how students learn and what might make them learn more effectively has produced many interesting and important facts, more information appears to be necessary. Educational effectiveness is difficult to measure in spite of the current theoretical basis for achievement. One of the primary aims of teachers utilizing computers in the educational field is to make the learning process more individual and more effective. Since this will involve the analysis of voluminous data, the computer will undoubtedly be involved in determining its own effectiveness as an aid to learning.

The computer has in the last few years made a conscientious effort to return to the college campus. Usually it's job description has been restricted to the business offices and to a limited number of students with the acumen to master the computer techniques which were, to say the least, difficult. On campus, it became apparent that the computer had to deal with many people of diverse needs (both professors and students) in a very individual and personal way. This meant that the computer would no longer administer its services through specialists (systems analysts, high-powered programmers, etc.), but that the computer had to become more human, more understandable, and more reachable. This was no easy decision and it was not an easy task. In the last few years, the machine has been taught new languages (very conversational languages), and furthermore, man can now communicate with the machine directly through such simple devices as the

Figure 1.2   A typical student study carrel consists of a computer controlled typewriter (left), a random access image projector (center), and a cathode-ray tube (right)

typewriter and television screen for pictorial access to computer information (See Fig. 1.2).

In its new role, the computer looks for greater involvement in the educational process from grade school through college. Needed are imaginative teachers who, while lacking computer involvement in their own education, have the foresight to realize the advantage of early computer involvement by their pupils. These teachers will dictate the role of the computer in educational technology and thereby tame the powers of this unusual giant and harness its talents to the problems of educating the masses. Computer science will play an ever-increasing role in the learning aspects of education and this interaction will be of such profound proportions that it will dramatically change the structure, form, and process of learning and the role of the student.

The primary purpose of this book, therefore, is to introduce to the non-computer specialist, both teacher and student, the practical partnership that can exist between man and machine. This book introduces the reader to applications of computer mathematics for problems in physics, chemistry and engineering. Of considerable practical value in Chapters 6, 7, and 8 are detailed examples of the computer used in the classroom, in the laboratory, and in student tutorial.

1.2   THE ROLE OF COMPUTERS IN EDUCATION

As an adaptive teacher, the computer appears to benefit from its designed ability to store and retrieve seemingly endless amounts of data including

Figure 1.3   The computer as a professor's aide

names, dates, pictures, and functional relationships. For example, a modern adaptive computer-teacher could consist of a cathode-ray tube (special TV set), a typewriter keyboard, and a light pen by means of which touch probe responses may be made on the face of the cathode-ray tube (See Fig. 1.4). In addition, there would be an image projector with over 2,000 frames all under the control of the computer (See Fig. 1.5). Audio messages may be exchanged between student and computer-teacher by a set of earphones and a microphone. It appears that over four hours of computer controlled audio messages can be stored for immediate access and dialogue with a student.

In contrast to the classical situation of one teacher and many students, the computer allows the luxury of individual instruction. After all, if the teacher is to have any effect on the individual student's process of learning, the teacher must be acutely aware of the student's understanding and comprehension at each step along the difficult road. For a human-being to be responsive to the personal needs of even twenty individuals in a classroom at all times during a normal class period is almost impossible. The computer, on the other hand, was designed to work quickly and accurately. The ratio of computer speed to human speed has been estimated to be more than one million to one. This speed also makes it possible for *one* computer to be used by many students at the same time. As each student interacts with "his share" of the machine, the computer

Figure 1.4   A student is shown communicating with the computer using a light pen. Computer communication may also be accomplished using a typewriter keyboard (also shown)

responds so quickly that each student thinks that he is the sole user of the machine.

For each individual student, the computer may initially assume a certain level of understanding of a subject. Quickly it detects from the student's response to questions, just how much is really understood. In constantly

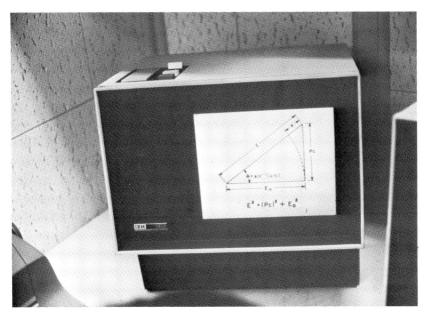

Figure 1.5   A random access image projector allows the computer program to select
the appropriate slide for student viewing

modifying its explanations, the computer insures progressive understanding
of each new step in the subject matter. The adaptation of the computer's
pedagogy continues until successful communication is established; the
student then proceeds to the next step. The computer has the additional
advantage of encouraging the student to admit that he has not learned or
understood a particular concept. In contrast, all teachers have experienced
the natural reluctance of students to ask questions in class for fear of
exposing their culpable ignorance of the subject matter.

This teaching role of the computer will obviously not replace the need
for persons with sound training in pedagogy. It will hopefully reduce the
existence of unskilled teachers in the classroom who often do little more
than keep order during the class period. Excellent teachers will always be
in high demand. They will be required to program * their teaching techniques and knowledge of the subject matter for the computer. With the help
of the "shared" computer, the instructional process can eventually be
tailored in a practical way to match the already known difference in motives
and abilities among students. As the computer frees the good teachers from
the rigorous classroom schedule, more time can be devoted to the students
who have demonstrated difficulty in understanding the subject matter as well
as to average and brilliant students who are thirsting for additional knowledge. Again, the individual contact of student and teacher will be enhanced.
In Chapters 6, 7, and 8, the reader will find specific examples of the computer used in this manner. For instance, in Chapter 7 the student explores

* The term "program" refers to instructions given to the computer and is discussed
fully in Chapter 2.

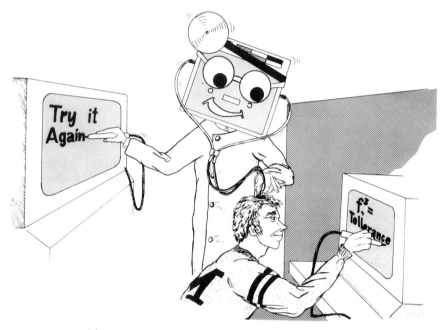

Figure 1.6   The computer as a doctor of learning analysis

the chemical concept of "the mole" under the guidance of a tutorial program. The computer presents a problem to the student and waits for the
student to type his answer. Depending on the user's response, the program
will give the student a hint, show him how to work the problem, or give him
another problem. In this way, the tutorial session is tailored to meet the
individual student's needs.

As a tool for individual student learning, the computer's capabilities have
so far been virtually unexplored. Each student has his basic mental talents
or learning capabilities. However, it soon becomes apparent that the student's innate abilities could be substantially enhanced by planned exposure
to specific environmental stimuli. For example, in the conventional classroom setting, rather than just listening in class, the student is encouraged to
copy what he hears by taking notes (pencil and paper become tools for
learning). Furthermore, this same student reads about the thoughts of
others in books (learning tools) and he may use problem workbooks or
programmed textbooks. The student has also been taught to make use of
libraries and films to further his understanding of subject matter. The
digital computer now poses the question of combining the advantages of
existing educational tools (as above) with those new tools and concepts
derived from computer technology. How to stimulate and guide students
into this active role of acquiring the skill to search and organize a field of
study by essentially 'augmenting' their abilities by means of a computer
presents a real challenge to teachers everywhere. Simply using the computer
to emulate classroom practice falls far short of the intended goal. Instead,

Figure 1.7   The computer as a student tutor

the student must be guided to explore concepts with the computer which were impossible or impractical by normal classroom techniques. For example, in Chapter 6 the motion of a complex spring-mass system is calculated by the computer. The reader is guided to follow the computer solution in a step by step process. The student explores the effect of an increase in mass on the motion of the spring thereby gaining greater insight into the nature of the real problem.

As the keeper of academic records the computer can assist the teacher in several important ways. One of the most evident attributes of a successful teacher is his ability to realize the talents and shortcomings of each individual student. To know the IQ, family background, mathematics aptitude, and many other pertinent data of each student in a class is difficult for today's teachers. Yet how can a teacher be sensitive to the real needs of a student without immediate access to this information. The computer feeds on data and has an enormous capacity to store information. In fact, how much data does each student generate? If one considers homework, laboratory and daily class work, plus examinations, a student can easily

Figure 1.8   The computer as a keeper of academic records

generate fifty items of data in a semester. Fifty data points times about as many students could reduce the teacher's role to a full time record keeper.

With the current widespread use of grades as a measure of academic performance, the teacher must look for a suitable assistant who can assure that each student's record is accurately and individually monitored. The ideal solution would be to place the computer in charge of the grade records with built in statistical programs which can immediately inform the teacher of the current status of a student and of the student's progress in relation to the others in the class. In effect the course becomes computer-managed in the sense that the teacher consults the machine for information regarding how well the students as a group are responding to certain difficult concepts. As a data base (or basis for comparison), the teacher may require the computer to compare the current class with previous classes and in this manner have an indication of whether to spend more or less class time on certain subject matter. The computer would thus relieve the teacher of much tedious record keeping and allow more time for direct interaction with the students both as a group and as individuals. Furthermore, by proper use of the computer-generated statistics of the class progress, the teacher can more realistically prepare the next lesson. The computer becomes a management and decision-making tool for the teacher, constantly informing him of the progress and difficulties of each individual student.

As a student examiner the computer may be an unusual asset to the teacher. Many teachers who have experienced long hours of examination correction would agree *"That's what takes the fun out of it all."* The grades are always due much too soon and this means late evenings of correction when human efficiency may be at a low ebb, and tolerance for student mistakes becomes an unpredictable variable. A good examination should separate students in a class on the basis of mastery of subject matter. Any possible human errors due to teacher's haste and/or fatigue while correcting the examination should be removed. The computer's role of correcting examinations has been particularly successful for multiple-choice questions and has made it possible for the teacher to do more thinking about the nature of the examination and the possibility of improving the questions. A good question should distinguish those students who understand the subject matter from those students who do not. The computer can be programmed to analyze each question based upon student performance.

Computer question analysis allows the teacher to reconsider and redesign his testing techniques. Furthermore, this method provides for an accurate check if some worthwhile data have actually been generated by a particular question. Statistical programs for student examination analysis are easily written in BASIC (See T-score conversion example in Appendix C). The computer would appear to be capable of handling the job of student examination in an efficient, accurate, and rapid manner thereby assisting the normal teacher. Again, the emphasis is not to surrogate the human teacher but instead to free the teacher to interact more closely and intimately with the pupils.

Figure 1.9   The computer as a ready proctor for exams

As an informal student counselor the computer has the capability to store in its memory the complete picture of a student's abilities, aptitudes, and desires, and to compare these with the professional requirements of numerous careers. A factual appraisal of the possible vocational tendencies of the student can assist the guidance counselor in advising the student. Current counseling techniques suffer from two major shortcomings. First, personality differences between the student and counselor are often the source of ineffective contact with the resultant dissatisfaction on the part of both parties concerned. Secondly, the quality of the counseling is restricted in scope by the depth of the counselor's own experience and by his knowledge of the student's desires and abilities. Obviously, one man can not be expected to know accurately the demands and requirements of all vocations. The rather impersonal computer, as the storehouse for a great deal of information about the student and possible career requirements, could

Figure 1.10   The computer as a student counselor

interact with the student indicating suggested vocational tendencies. This file of information on both student abilities and career patterns would be kept completely current for maximum effectiveness.

As a dynamic film producer the computer has captured the attention of many teachers. The computer calculates so rapidly that individual points and line segments can be continuously displayed on a cathode-ray tube. Cathode-ray tube results can be filmed and shown to groups or classes of students. Only a few of the many applications will be mentioned here. In a physics class dealing with vectors, one might imagine describing the addition of vector quantities by a computer-generated display of the continuous sum of two rotating vectors. In a chemistry class, the symmetry of molecules can be studied by a computer model relating such parameters as bond angle, bond length, and atom location. The teacher of engineering drawing will find considerable application of the three-dimensional computer display of design objects. These objects can be rotated and inspected from several views on a graphic computer terminal.

In this book individual student-computer interaction is encouraged. In Chapters 6 and 7 it will be demonstrated how a student at his own carrel with a typewriter or cathode-ray tube can effectively explore simple and complex problems. This interaction of the student with the machine allows, for instance, a student in Section 6.12 to study the effect of slit width on the resulting diffraction pattern. Furthermore, the pattern can be seen since there is a graphical display of the results. This exploration of complex problems cannot be effectively performed by normal calculating procedures. There is just not enough time in the day.

The computer as a film producer has also proven to be an effective method of bypassing the more technical aspects of mathematics when teaching students of limited ability. Students can often understand a difficult problem when the teacher demonstrates the solution graphically. Anyone who has tried to draw even a time-varying sine curve knows the difficulty that arises when drawing adequate time-dependent graphs on the blackboard. Computer animation, through continuously time-varying graphs, is certainly an excellent method for students to appreciate the solutions to complex problems without having to understand the difficult mathematical process that yielded the solution. For the more advanced student who understands and has experienced the complex solution, the computer animated solution adds immensely to the full comprehension and retention of concepts.

Teachers who have in the past few years participated in computer film making have been excited about this pedagogic application. However, the need for extensive programming skills and the inaccessibility of computers have thwarted many enthusiasts. Now with the development of individual "office-access" to the most sophisticated computers, and with the introduction of man-computer languages, the teacher can truly become the computer innovator. Few teachers or students have ever considered writing the script, producing and directing their own computer animated solution to classroom problems. In Section 8.4, for example, the production of a square wave using Fourier Analysis is demonstrated by actual computer

Figure 1.11   The computer as a dynamic film producer

graphing of the successive Fourier terms needed for the solution. This animated version of a normally complicated problem lends much interest to the classroom demonstration.

As a teaching tool, computer animation can provide a challenge to the student's intuitive resources. The computer display can easily be coordinated with an organized presentation and thereby encourage student interaction with the teacher through computer-generated results.

1.3   MAN-COMPUTER INTERACTION

Thinking and reasoning are unique processes of the human mind. To think suggests consideration of, or reflection on, an idea in one's mind. To reason emphasizes the use of one's powers of conception, judgment and inference. The intelligent human stands apart from other members of the animal kingdom in his ability to use the power of thought to reason and generate new ideas and hypotheses. Whether by intuition, foresight, or even 'guts,' man has made great strides in understanding nature by his conceptual approach to complex problems.

Almost one hundred years ago man conceived the idea of creating a counterpart or a partner which would acquire the mental attributes which the human mind so obviously lacked. In the words of Jules Verne "Thanks to the Piano Electro-Reckoner, the most complex calculations can be made in seconds." The modern digital computer bears out these dreams by its valuable capability to execute procedures with lightning speed and accuracy. With a computer memory cycle of less than 2 microseconds and a memory capacity larger than 4,000 words, the computer can be considered as a worthy component of the man-computer partnership. Most modern computers can easily read and add a thousand ten-digit numbers before a man can even read and remember one.

Can man unite his mental powers with the machines and in effect extend his thinking, augment his reasoning, and even assist his learning process? The answer to this question is a qualified 'yes.' The realization of the power of the man-computer partnership has just begun to develop and therefore the 'how' of the preceding question can not be completely answered. One of the most obvious impediments to useful man-machine interaction is communication between man and machine. Man's conversational language and the computer's machine language, until recently, have been incompatible. The only mode of communication before conversational computer languages has been through a competent programmer, thus making an active interplay between the creative human mind and the computer extremely difficult. The development of BASIC and other interactive languages has greatly facilitated man's use of the computer. Typically two to three hours are necessary to become reasonably competent in BASIC (a rather minimal investment in time when one considers that it takes about five hours to learn to drive a car and nine hours to learn to fly an airplane).

Another example of the natural language conversation between man and computer is the ELIZA program developed at MIT under Project MAC. The following is an example dialogue between a student and the machine (1). (The capitalized lines are the machine responses):

Men are all alike.

IN WHAT WAY

They're always bugging us about something or other.

CAN YOU THINK OF A SPECIFIC EXAMPLE

Well, my boyfriend made me come here.

YOUR BOYFRIEND MADE YOU COME HERE

He says I'm depressed much of the time.

I AM SORRY TO HEAR YOU ARE DEPRESSED

It's true. I am unhappy.

DO YOU THINK COMING HERE WILL HELP YOU NOT TO BE UNHAPPY

I need some help, that much seems certain.

WHAT WOULD IT MEAN TO YOU IF YOU GOT SOME HELP

Perhaps I could learn to get along with my mother.

TELL ME MORE ABOUT YOUR FAMILY

My mother takes care of me.

WHO ELSE IN YOUR FAMILY TAKES CARE OF YOU

My father.

YOUR FATHER

You are like my father in some ways.

WHAT RESEMBLANCE DO YOU SEE

You are not very aggressive but I think you don't want me to notice that.

WHAT MAKES YOU THINK I AM NOT VERY AGGRESSIVE

You don't argue with me.

WHY DO YOU THINK I DON'T ARGUE WITH YOU

You are afraid of me.

DOES IT PLEASE YOU TO BELIEVE I AM AFRAID OF YOU

My father is afraid of everybody.

WHAT ELSE COMES TO MIND WHEN YOU THINK OF YOUR
    FATHER

Bullies.

DOES THAT HAVE ANYTHING TO DO WITH THE FACT THAT
    YOUR BOYFRIEND MADE YOU COME HERE

The computer for the conversation is programmed to analyze input sentences on the basis of "decomposition rules" which are triggered by key words appearing in the input text. Responses are generated in reverse, that is, "reassembly rules" associated with selected "decomposition rules." The choice of the key word in the input statement is important. For example, in the first line of conversation above, "Men are all alike," 'Alike' is chosen as the key, and a routine response returns, "IN WHAT WAY."

The language barrier should become even less significant. A most likely development in the near future should be voice communication with the computer where the machine will translate voice directly into computer language.

A second obstacle which did initially limit interaction with the computer was the problem of allowing a "slow" human to monopolize a high-speed, expensive machine, ($$$$/hour). The efficiency rating of a computer seemed to be measured by the percent of time the machine was actually working on a program. For many years, computer centers restricted the 'hands on' use of the computer to special operators thereby frustrating the individual user's attempt to obtain some 'feel' of the computer partnership. When it became technically possible for many users to share the computer at the same time, and to work with the computer at a distance, a true intellectual partner became available.

In Chapter 2 the reader will find a thorough introduction to the computer 'system' needed when a computer is shared by many users. This very important chapter also supplies the necessary background needed to begin BASIC programming.

CHAPTER 2

COMPUTER TIME SHARING WITH AN INTRODUCTION TO BASIC

2.1 INTRODUCTION

For the few teachers and students who have visited a modern digital computer center, there exists an aura of mystery surrounding these grey, box-like instruments with their spinning wheels and flashing panel lights. Visitors are told that the computer contains a 'memory' where much information is stored, and that there is a 'nerve center' which controls computer operations. The mystery continues as the visitors are told that there is a 'brain' which accomplishes arithmetical operations, and a 'logic' unit where decisions are made.

These computer analogies to certain attributes of the human being serve a very descriptive purpose and contribute to a qualitative understanding of the function of a computer. This chapter describes the functional components of a computer in sufficient detail to enable teachers and students to better design their learning techniques within the operative framework of the computer. Readers who are already well versed in computer science, but who wish to learn to apply their computer skills to the classroom are encouraged to go directly to Chapter 3.

2.2 HOW THE COMPUTER OPERATES

The word "computer" only describes one very special function of the machine. Every basic computer system consists of four main components: one or more devices for inputting information (See Figs. 2.1 and 2.4), a memory unit to store information (See Fig. 2.2), a central processing unit for numerical calculations and information manipulations (See Fig. 2.3), and finally one or more devices for outputting information (See Fig. 2.4).

The computer can receive both numerical and alphabetical information punched into cards, or punched into paper tape (See Figs. 2.5 and 2.6). The input information consists of two distinct items. First, there must be a written set of instructions which describe in 'step by step' fashion exactly what the computer must do to complete its 'job.' This set of instructions is called a 'program.' Second, there must be numerical or alphabetical data which the computer will manipulate as prescribed by the program. The input information (program plus data) is electronically read from cards or paper tape and transmitted to the computer memory unit.

A computer memory unit serves to store both initial data and instructions and also intermediate and final answers. The memory unit can best be compared to a large personal address file with only one name and address

Figure 2.1   A card reader is one of the devices which can be used to feed information into the computer (input) and to receive information from the computer (output). In this case, the information is punched onto cards

on each index card of the file. Only one instruction or item of data can be filed in each location of the memory units. Like an address file, when new information is placed into a given memory location, the old information is just erased. Also like an address file, when the information in a given memory location is copied, the old information is not disturbed.

There are many types of storage media available for digital computers; for instance, magnetic drums, disks or the punched card. A distinguishing characteristic of all computer storage elements is their ability to represent only two distinct states. For example, a magnetic core may be magnetized in either of two directions; a switch may be opened or closed; a card may have a punched hole or it may be blank; and so on. This very important characteristic of the on-off, open-closed status of memory storage elements makes it possible for these elements to represent useful information. One state can be arbitrarily denoted as a 0, the other state can be denoted as a 1. Therefore each storage element can store one 'bit' of information, either a 0 or a 1. These 'bits' are the most elementary units of information stored in digital computers. The two-digit, or binary system of numbers allows data and information to be coded in a very simple form. For example, a six bit code is required for the unique identification of all the letters of the alphabet. In most computers, each storage location is designed to store only a fixed number of bits called a 'word'; for example, the IBM 7090 uses 'words' which contain 36 bits each. In comparison to the previous analogy of the personal address file, this relates to one name per index card.

With computer program and input data stored in the form of zeros and ones in the proper memory locations, the computer is ready to initiate the

Figure 2.2   A magnetic disk pack can be used for additional memory space

job. The calculations take place in the central processing unit which has an arithmetic section and a control section. In the arithmetic section all mathematical operations (including multiplication and division) are reduced to simple additions and subtractions. The computer can accomplish these operations with incredible speed because of the simplicity of the binary numbering system. For instance to add 3 plus 6 in binary form the following occurs:

BINARY NOTATION	DECIMAL EQUIVALENT
000011	3
+ 000110	+ 6
001001	9

The rules for binary notation are:

(a)	1	(b)	1	(in binary)
	+0		+1	
	1		10	

(a) one plus zero is one
(b) one plus one is zero carry one

It has just been shown that the binary notation of 3 is: 0011 while the binary notation of 6 is 0110. At first glance, this notation may seem confusing. However, a brief example of decimal notation (base 10) followed by an explanation of binary notation (base 2) should clarify the concepts of these numbering systems.

Figure 2.3   A processing unit manipulates information in accordance with the
computer program

Consider the number one thousand one hundred and eleven, which is
written 1111 in decimal notation. Each column of digits has the following
meaning:

$$
\begin{array}{cccc}
1 & 1 & 1 & 1 \\
\uparrow & \uparrow & \uparrow & \uparrow
\end{array}
$$

$10^0=$ single digits up to 9 ($10-1=9$)
$10^1=$ number of tens ($10^1=10$)
$10^2=$ number of hundreds ($10^2=100$)
$10^3=$ number of thousands ($10^3=1000$)

Note that each column can contain a number from 0 to 9. Thus, one
thousand one hundred and eleven (decimal) is written: 1111.

Similarly, in the binary notation system one can write:

$$
\begin{array}{cccc}
1 & 1 & 1 & 1 \\
\uparrow & \uparrow & \uparrow & \uparrow
\end{array}
$$

$2^0=$ single digits up to 1 ($2-1=1$)
$2^1=$ number of twos ($2^1=2$)
$2^2=$ number of fours ($2^2=4$)
$2^3=$ number of eights ($2^3=8$)

Note that each column will contain either 0 or 1. The number 1111
(binary) can be converted to decimal by referring to the instructions above.
It can thus be seen that 1111 (binary) means: one 1, one 2, one 4, and
one 8, which is equivalent to 15 (decimal).

Figure 2.4   A typewriter used to input and output information is shown. This means of information transfer is slow compared to cards or tape

Now that binary notation has been clarified, the operations of multiplication and division by the computer can be discussed. To multiply 3 times 3 in binary form, the computer simply adds 3 plus 3 plus 3, or:

BINARY NOTATION	DECIMAL EQUIVALENT
000011	3
000011	3
+000011	+3
001001	9

In a similar fashion, to divide 9 by 3, the computer subtracts 3 from 9 as many times as possible, which of course is 3. The arithmetic section conducts the operations for which the computer is known, namely computing.

The control section has the more difficult task of 'supervising' the whole system. This operation insures that the stored program causes the desired operations to be performed in the sequence specified. The control section checks the next instruction of the program and sets up the proper conditions for its execution. When the computer has completed the job there must be a return of information to the user. The binary form of the computer-generated results is decoded and returned to the user via a high-speed printer, or typewriter as shown in Fig. 2.7.

It should thus be clear that a computer can conduct numerous sophisticated operations such as receiving information, storing information, manipulating information, and returning information simply by the repetitive and programmed use of the two-state elements. Computer operations are primarily limited only by memory size (or the number of programs and

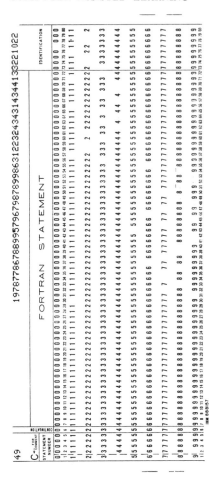

Figure 2.5 A computer punched card stores information in the form of holes punched in certain locations. Cards are read and/or punched rapidly by computers making them a relatively fast means of input/output

amount of data that can be stored), and memory access time (or the time required to retrieve a specific item of information from the memory), and finally the amount of available peripheral equipment (magnetic disks and other input/output devices).

2.3 HOW A COMPUTER IS USED

The IBM 1130 (shown in Figure 2.8), a small computer by current standards, can frighten the most enthusiastic beginner. The physical size, multi-components and many buttons have made direct individual use of such a computer by large numbers of teachers and/or students ineffective and expensive. Consequently, most computer centers have become 'closed shops,' that is, only special operators are allowed in the computer room. Teachers and students must punch their programs on cards (See Fig. 2.9)

Figure 2.6 A student is shown typing on a teletypewriter console. When a switch is on, the information being typed is punched onto a paper tape (lower left) which can be used to input information into a computer

and then leave the card deck at the computer room for handling by the operators. This system of "batch" processing, or the processing of programs one behind another, has serious disadvantages for educational use. The number of programs to be processed by an academic computer center is normally so large that it may require from 10 to 20 hours for a program to be returned to the student. In addition, program debugging (the detection and correction of errors in a program using test data and test runs)

Figure 2.7   A high speed printer is used to transfer computer-generated results to paper output

usually requires a large number of tries before the program is successfully processed by the computer. If it takes on the order of one day for each try, the student and teacher may lose interest. A much larger and faster computer would certainly solve many of the problems of delay mentioned above; however, few academic computer centers have sufficient money to fund such a computer. On the other hand, a system for "sharing" a large, expensive computer would spread the computing cost, and make the facility available to more users. But how does one share a computer?

Simultaneous use of a computer by two or more users requires the transmission of programs and data from a teletypewriter (See Fig. 2.10) via telephone lines to the computer. Each user (there may be over one hundred people sharing the computer) appears to be "on-line," or in communication contact, with the computer. This mode of computer operation, called "time-sharing," makes it possible to use a computer on another campus, in another state, or in another country. The student (or teacher) operates from a remote console (another term for teletypewriter) in a 'real-time' basis; i.e., the handling of information by the computer and return to the user occurs in seconds. This often gives the false impression that there are no other users of the computer.

While typing the computer program and data on the teletypewriter, a paper tape can be punched simultaneously if the "ON" button of the tape unit is depressed (See Fig. 2.11). This use of a paper tape is another means of storing data and the program. The paper tape containing the program and data can then be sent to the computer by initiating the tape-reader (move the tape lever to the "START" position) on the remote console

Figure 2.8   On IBM 1130 computer is a small, popular machine

(See Fig. 2.12). Therefore, the interaction between user and computer can take place through the printed material typed on the teletypewriter or the paper tape. The computer transmits information back to the user by causing the teletypewriter on the remote console to type out the message electronically.

Computer time-sharing has made high demands upon computer-design personnel. For example, the programs and data stored by each user must be protected so that other users cannot modify or access the stored information without prior permission of the original author (memory protection). Special user numbers (identification numbers) and 'passwords' are assigned so that only a group of authorized users may access stored programs and data.

In summary, the following are typical features of a computer time-sharing system:

1. Two or more users may simultaneously use the computing facility.
2. Individual users are provided access to the central processing unit through on-line remote consoles.
3. Operation is on a real-time basis.
4. Memory protection features allow only authorized persons to access the information and data stored by users.

2.4   ORGANIZATION OF THE TIME-SHARING SYSTEM

The close relationship between man and computer provided by the time-sharing system is implemented by 'hardware' and 'software.' Hardware

Figure 2.9   A card punch machine

denotes the physical equipment and devices composing the computing system (See Figs. 2.1 through 2.4) as opposed to software which denotes the programs and routines used to extend the computer capabilities. A schematic (See Fig. 2.13) of a time-sharing system shows the relationship of the general components consisting of remote terminals, some form of communications control, one or more central processing units (CPU), auxiliary storage, and various peripheral units. Students and teachers communicate with the computer through remote consoles. The user's requests are channeled through a communications control to one or more processing units. Typically, a system capable of accommodating thirty simultaneous students has two CPU's. Systems which contain at least two CPU's are capable of multiprocessing which is a term describing the simultaneous handling of more than one process (such as addition, subtraction or multiplication). Multiprogramming denotes the concurrent handling of several computer programs.

The central processor can be very busy. It must perform input/output control, memory accessing and addressing, editing and translating of programs, processing, and control of the consoles. The program which regulates the flow of information into and through the computer and allocates the computer resources according to a priority schedule is known as the 'executive.' The processing unit generates addresses, performs the actual computations, and controls the peripheral devices.

The main computer memory consists of rapid access storage where information retrieval can be accomplished in microseconds. Additional storage is provided by the auxiliary memory which is comprised of slower

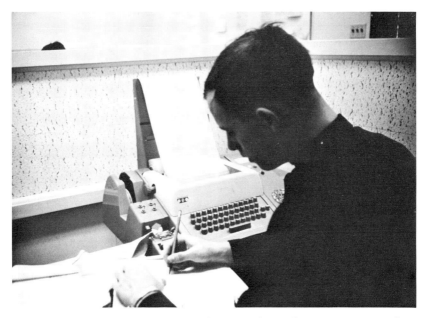

Figure 2.10 A teletype computer terminal can give each user access to a larger computer

random-access large-capacity storage devices such as disks and drums. The electronic units of the computer and the various peripheral devices (spinning magnetic tapes) operate at widely differing speeds. In order to acommodate these different speeds, buffers are used to serve as intermediate storage areas. Buffers may exist between input/output devices and the main high speed storage or between two storage areas with different access times. The computer is often organized such that one operation is begun either when the device necessary for the operation is free or when a previous operation has been completed; this is called asychronous operation because the system is not hampered by a rigid time-schedule. The smooth flow of information and data from the remote consoles via the communications control into the central processing unit and back to the remote consoles is controlled by the executive program and expedited through the use of buffers and asychronous operation. The organization of the computer's operations is paramount to simultaneous use by several students. When properly done, each student has the illusion of being the only user of the computer.

Initiation of this process of man-computer interaction is a relatively simple matter. The steps required for connection into a time-shared installation will be given for the teletypewriters (remote consoles) currently employed by several time-shared installations. A photograph of a Model 33 teletypewriter (TTY) machine (See Fig. 2.14) shows the keyboard, control unit, paper tape punch, and paper tape reader which are available to the user. The computer is accessed by the user as follows:

1. Press the ORIG key.

Figure 2.11 A paper tape punch

2. Listen for the dial tone, then dial the phone number of the time-sharing installation.
3. The computer will answer and type the name of the installation, the date, and the time.

The sign-on exchange which follows is given below. The slanted words are typed by the computer system. Note that only capital letters are available on the teletypewriter keyboard.

USER NUMBER— Z99999 ®

SYSTEM— BASIC ®

NEW OR OLD— NEW ®

NEW PROGRAM NAME— SUM ®

READY

The computer first requests a user number which is a six character number assigned to each user by the time-sharing installation. At the end of each line the user must press the RETURN key on the keyboard as denoted by ®. The user is then required to give the system (or programming language) which is to be used. Depending upon the services available from the time-sharing computer, one could use any of a number of languages such as JOSS, CAL, FORTRAN, BASIC and others. In this book the BASIC language has been chosen. As will be seen in the following section, the rules

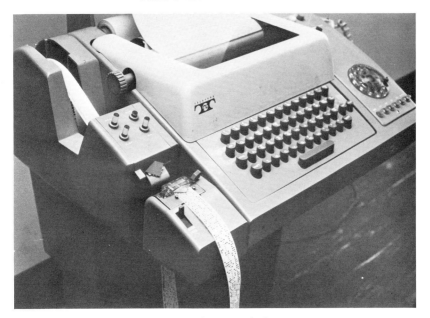

Figure 2.12   Reading a punched paper tape

of BASIC are learned quickly and one can begin application with the minimum amount of effort.

The computer then requests NEW or OLD—if the program has been previously stored the user types OLD, otherwise he types NEW. Words which are used to direct the computer to perform specific actions (BASIC, NEW, OLD) are referred to as 'system' commands. The computer next requests the program name and checks this name against stored programs. If the NEW name given by the user is not already the name of an OLD program, the computer will type READY. At this point the user may enter his program which must be written in a programming language available on the time-sharing system.

2.5   THE BASIC LANGUAGE

Currently there exist many computer languages; they are specifically designed either for business, or engineering, or science. The BASIC computer language has a major advantage for students and educators in that it is simple and easy to learn. In this section several aspects of BASIC will be demonstrated without unnecessary detail. In Chapter 4, a more thorough treatment of BASIC will be introduced through useful programming examples.

In order to better understand the important concept of programming, one could try to imagine a scientist who has just obtained a *"genie"* as an assistant. The genie is very capable, but must be told precisely what to do. The scientist finds it necessary to prepare a list of instructions which the

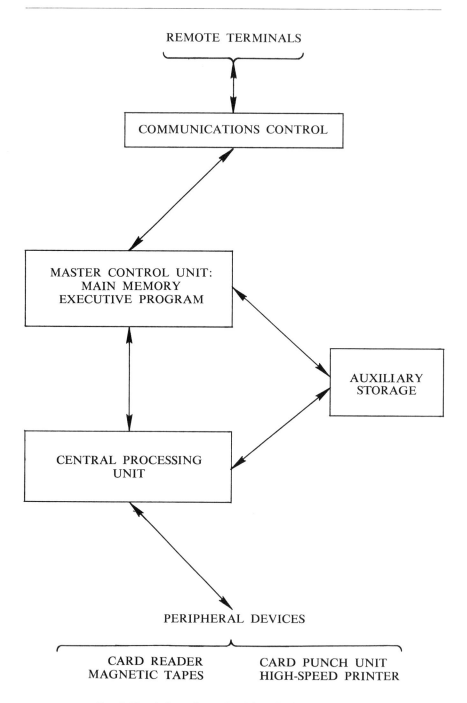

FIG. 2.13   A flow chart of a "time-sharing system"

Figure 2.14 A model 33 teletypewriter (TTY)

genie can obey and thereby assist in the busy activities of the science world. The scientist writes the following instructions:

(10) a REMark for clarity; call this job
* * * * START * * * *
(20) Now READ the values of A, B, C, and D
(30) You will find these values in the DATA file as 10, 6×10^{-3}, .175, and 5.
(40) Then LET $X = B^2 \times D + C$
(50) also LET $Y1 = C \times \sin(A)$
(60) finally PRINT the values of X, and Y1
(70) that is the END of this job

The computer (also a helpful genie) must be told exactly what to do. The computer's set of instructions consists of many short imperative statements organized into a sequence called a computer 'program.' The computer will execute these imperative statements in the order in which they are numbered. Since one often wants to add statements to an existing program, it is advisable to number the statements with room for these later additions. For instance, consider the following BASIC program which directs the computer to execute the job previously assigned to the genie by the scientist:

```
90   REM ** START **
100   READ A,B,C,D
110   DATA 10, 6E-3, .175, 5
120   LET  X=B↑2*D+C
```

```
130   LET Y1=C*SIN(A)
140   PRINT X, Y1
150   END.
```

It should be noted that:

1. each statement begins with a line number and there is room for additional statements,
2. each statement starts, after the line number, with an English word,
3. only capital letters are used, and
4. spaces are not significant in BASIC.
   Line 100 could equally be written:

$$100READA,B,C,D$$

but considerable clarity is lost when spaces are not used.

Line numbers are used to distinguish system commands (which do not have line numbers) from program statements (which always have line numbers) as well as to indicate the order in which the statements are to be executed. (Remember that system commands are instructions to the system such as OLD, SAVE, and RUN.) Statements can be entered into the computer in any order since the computer sorts the statements by line number prior to execution. The assignment of line numbers is arbitrary and any number between 1 and 99999 is acceptable. It is convenient to separate consecutive line numbers by an increment of 10 to allow for the insertion of additional statements.

The REM statement (REMarks) is used to include comments or labels in the program; the computer ignores all information in a REM statement. Variables are denoted by a letter, or by a letter followed by a single number less than ten. Variables used in the program START are A,B,C,D,X, and Y1. Variables are assigned a value by means of a READ or a LET statement. A READ statement must be accompanied by a DATA statement which lists the constant numerical values to be assigned to the variables. The READ statement should appear in the program prior to the use of the variable whose value it assigns, or all READ statements can be collected at the beginning of the program. Data must be inserted in the DATA statement to correspond to the order of variables in the READ statements.

Numbers must be expressed in decimal form, may be positive or negative, and may contain up to 9 digits. Exponential notation is used to express large numbers or powers of ten. The number $1/1000$ may be entered in a BASIC program as .001 or 1E-3; the number .000123456789 must be expressed as .123456789E-3 to avoid using more than 9 digits. In the program START, the READ and DATA statements cause the variables to be assigned the following values: $A=10$, $B=.006$, $C=.175$, and $D=5$.

Statements 110 and 120 show one of the primary functions of the computer which is the evaluation of formulas. Arithmetic operations which can be used in BASIC to write a formula are summarized in the following table:

BASIC SYMBOL	MEANING	PRIORITY
↑	raise to a power	1
*	multiply	
/	divide	} 2
+	add	
−	subtract	} 3

For example, the formula

$$B \uparrow 2 * D + C$$

is translated as: raise B to the second power, multiply by D, and add C, according to the priority listed in the table. When operations of the same priority are listed in the same line, they are executed from left to right. However, operations enclosed in parentheses are performed first. For example, the BASIC formula $(X+A)*D$ would cause the sum of $A+X$ to be multiplied by D.

The computer can also evaluate several mathematical functions as indicated by statement 120. Thus $SIN(X)$ causes the sine of X to be calculated. In addition to $SIN(X)$, $COS(X)$, $TAN(X)$, $ATAN(X)$, some functions which are available are:

FUNCTION	INTERPRETATION
EXP(X)	natural exponential of X, e^x
LOG(X)	natural logarithm of X, ln x
ABS(X)	absolute value of X, $|x|$
SQR(X)	square root of X, $\sqrt{X}$
INT(X)	integer value of X

The statement which indicates that the computer should return information to the user is the PRINT statement in line 130. In this case the calculated variables X and Y1 will be printed on the typewriter. Finally, every computer program in BASIC must terminate with the END statement to indicate to the computer that the job has been completed.

2.6 A COMPUTER PROGRAM SKELETON

A computer's usefulness depends upon the individual's ability to carefully plan a set of instructions for the machine. These instructions, called a computer program, are normally typed directly onto paper tape and then read into the remote terminal as was discussed earlier (See Figs. 2.6 and 2.11). When the computer executes a set of instructions, it can accept information, manipulate information, and finally return information in a form prescribed by the teacher or student. The computer program must insure the correct handling of all information and therefore the following A, B, C's are essential to every computer program:

A	Instructions to the computer to accept information or data
B	Instructions to the computer on how to manipulate the information or data
C	Instructions to the computer on how to output the resulting data

It would be helpful to examine each of these steps in detail and to indicate the nature of the instructions for each of the above operations.

A. THE COMPUTER ACCEPTS INFORMATION

There are two methods of instructing the computer to accept data. The first method which uses the BASIC instruction READ, has been discussed. This instruction tells the computer to look for numerical or alphabetical information under the BASIC instruction Data. This seems like a straightforward method where both the instruction to READ and the DATA are stored in the computer program. Therefore, if there is a READ instruction there must follow a DATA instruction which indicates what DATA is to be READ.

A second method of instructing the computer to accept information is by using the INPUT instruction. When this instruction occurs in a program, the computer waits for data to be entered through the keyboard. This means that the teacher or student must type in a set of data while the computer waits. Notice the difference between these two methods of entering information for the computer's use:

INSTRUCTION	RESULT
(1)　　READ	Computer goes to DATA instruction and reads data
(in program)	*(in program)*
(2)　　INPUT	Computer waits for user to enter data by teletypewriter
(in program)	*(not in program)*

Of course, the final effect is the same, that is, the computer has information for further manipulation (addition or subtraction).

B. THE COMPUTER MANIPULATES INFORMATION

In every computer program there are instructions which tell the computer what to do with the data. The computer can be instructed to add, subtract, multiply, and divide. Furthermore, the computer can be instructed to compare data in size (bigger or smaller), in sign (plus or minus) or even some logical comparisons can be made.

The student or teacher has considerable flexibility for handling the data and many specific examples will be treated in later sections. The important item to recognize is that every program will have instructions to indicate to the computer what to do with the data and how to prepare the results for return to the user (teacher or student).

C. THE COMPUTER OUTPUTS INFORMATION

The objective of any program can only be judged if the results can be seen by the user. Therefore, the computer must be instructed to output the results. Since the teletypewriter (Fig. 2.10) is the interface between man and the computer, this is where the output should be planned. The PRINT instruction indicates to the computer that the teletypewriter will be used to type out electronically (i.e., automatically) the results of calculations that are of interest to the user.

2.7 COMPUTER PROGRAM VARIABLES

When a quantity is to be assigned different values in a program, or when it assumes different values during the execution of the program, the quantity is referred to as a *variable* and it is designated by *symbols* (letters and numbers). One might take the following simple example: the cost of a tank of gasoline depends upon the size of the tank (in gallons) and the cost of a gallon of gasoline. Therefore the amount paid by each customer is,

$$AMOUNT = COST \ (PER \ GALLON) \times GALLONS$$

All three of these terms (*A*MOUNT, *C*OST, and *G*ALLONS) could be variables and thus would be represented by symbols in the computer program. The example may be persued further by actually listing the variables. Therefore, let

A = amount of money to be paid
C = cost of one gallon of gas
G = number of gallons to fill tank

Thus,

$$A = C \times G$$

in an algebraic representation of the equation.

For a computer to perform this operation, the instructions could be arranged like this:

INSTRUCTION	RESULT
READ C, G	read in the values of *cost* and *gallons*
DATA 33, 12	C = 33 cents per gallon
	G = 12 gallons
LET A = C × G	multiply C times G and store in A
PRINT A	type out the *amount*

In summary, *variables* are important in programming and should be remembered as *symbols* (letters and numbers) given to quantities that are manipulated by the computer.

In some cases, it is desirable to identify several different quantities by the same name. In other words, in the previous example, assume that a person bought gasoline at four different stations and each time filled the gas tank with a different amount of gasoline. A table may be constructed showing the cost per gallon, and the number of gallons bought at each station:

	COST PER GALLON	NUMBER OF GALLONS
Station 1	$C(1)$	$G(1)$
Station 2	$C(2)$	$G(2)$
Station 3	$C(3)$	$G(3)$
Station 4	$C(4)$	$G(4)$

Notice that the cost is designated by a different variable (or symbol) at each station as is the number of gallons. Each variable consists of a symbol followed by a number in parentheses. The number in parenthesis is called a subscript. However, it is still clear, for instance, that the symbol $G(2)$ represents the number of gallons put in the tank at Station 2, while $C(2)$ is the cost per gallon at this station. Thus the subscript corresponds to the station number. This type of variable notation is called a *subscripted variable* and is very useful when indicating different values of the same parameter. The variable is called *subscripted* because the algebraic expression, G_2, is usually written in that form, below the line. In BASIC, however, numbers can not be typed below the line so the "subscript" is written in parentheses and G_2 becomes $G(2)$.

It would, of course, have been possible to use C1, C2, C3, and C4 as the different names for the cost per gallon. These variables are also clearly related to each particular station and yet recognizable as cost. The use of the parenthesis, as in $C(1)$, is unique for the subscripted variable and makes this variable very powerful in programming techniques. As an example of the use of a subscripted variable, study the following:

> allow the variable N to range from 1 to 4
> (i.e., $N=1$, or $N=2$, or $N=3$, or $N=4$)
> Now one could write,
> $C(N)$ for $N=1$ to 4

This would be equivalent to writing $C(1)$, $C(2)$, $C(3)$ and $C(4)$, and therefore represents the same four values of the cost parameter.

When the subscripted variable is used in computer programming, there is one additional instruction that often becomes important. Variables, such as M, R, A1, etc., are all given a special location in the computer memory for storage. A subscripted variable, such as $B(N)$ where $N=1$ to 100, must also be assured proper storage room. In other words, one storage location is needed for B(1), one for B(2), one for B(3), and so on up to B(100). Thus 100 storage locations are required for B(N) when N = 1 to 100. The computer could save 1000 locations for each subscripted variable, but this would be highly inefficient since, in the average program, each subscripted variable usually has less than ten values. In time-sharing BASIC then, the system saves ten locations for each subscripted variable unless the program tells it otherwise. If, for example, the subscripted variable is S(X) where X takes on values from 1 to 4, no special instruction is needed. However, for the subscripted variable B(N) where N = 1 to 100, the computer system must be told to reserve 100 locations for B(N). A special instruction, called the DIMension instruction, is used to reserve the required space. These points are summarized below:

INSTRUCTION	INTERPRETATION
B(N) (for N = 1 to 100)	subscript greater than 10,
DIM B(100)	DIMension statement needed to save 100 locations
S(X) (for X = 1 to 4)	subscript 10 or less, DIMension statement not needed

The subscripted variable is not restricted to computer use, but will be found in many science books.

2.8 COMPUTER ITERATION AND LOOPING

The term "to iterate" means to repeat or to do something many times. The computer combines two unique talents, speed and accuracy. Consequently, it is often easier for the computer to perform a simple operation many times rather than a complicated operation just once. For example, in order to divide 9 by 3 ($3\overline{)9}$ or 9/3), the computer prefers to subtract 3 from 9 as many times as possible and to count the number of subtractions. Therefore,

$$\begin{array}{l} 9 \\ \underline{-3} \ \ \text{once} \\ 6 \end{array} \qquad \begin{array}{l} 6 \\ \underline{3} \ \ \text{twice} \\ 3 \end{array} \qquad \begin{array}{l} 3 \\ \underline{3} \ \ \text{three times} \\ 0 \end{array}$$

or 9 divided by 3 equals 3.

The computer, when used most efficiently, will be instructed to "loop" back to a previous instruction and iterate a series of steps. This can best be illustrated by considering the example shown in the previous section. Assume that a person visits four gasoline stations and fills his gas tank in his car each trip. He wishes then to calculate the amount of money to pay each station. A computer program to assist him in this calculation would look as follows:

```
READ C(1), C(2), C(3), C(4)
DATA 32, 33, 36, 31
READ G(1), G(2), G(3), G(4)
DATA 6, 10, 2, 5
LET A(1)=C(1)*G(1)
LET A(2)=C(2)*G(2)
LET A(3)=C(3)*G(3)
LET A(4)=C(4)*G(4)
PRINT A(1), A(2), A(3), A(4)
END
```

The above set of instructions is long and the computer is not being used effectively. Now, study the following set of instructions carefully, remembering the use of the subscripted variable.

```
FOR N=1 TO 4
   ↓
→READ C(N), G(N)
   ↓
 DATA 32, 6, 33, 10, 36, 2, 31, 5.
   ↓
 LET A(N)=C(N)*G(N)
   ↓
 PRINT A(N)
   ↓
—NEXT N

      END
```

When interpreting the loop (indicated by the arrows), one can assign the first value of N (in this case 1) to all the subscripts the first time through the loop. Thus, during the first time through the loop, the instructions read in effect:

```
N=1
READ C(1), G(1)
DATA 32, 6
LET A(1)=C(1)×G(1)
PRINT A(1)
```

The second loop is the same except N=2 in all the subscripted variables. This process continues automatically until N=4, which is the last time through the loop. In this manner, all of the instructions will be executed by the computer 4 times. The loop, or even multiple loops, make it possible to direct the computer to complete many steps with very few instructions. The importance of looping and iteration in computer programming will become more clear in later sections. This brief introduction to BASIC should convince the reader that with a limited number of vocabulary words, conversation with the computer in a time-sharing mode becomes a reality. In Chapter 4, the reader will become more thoroughly exposed to the power of BASIC through practical examples.

By investing the small effort required to learn BASIC, teachers and students will find the satisfaction of enlisting the assistance of the computer for both tedious, everyday calculations and for the completion of work impossible without a computer. For the teacher this may mean student records and statistics (see Appendix C) and for the student this may mean homework problems worked more thoroughly and in more detail.

Students versed in BASIC can be encouraged by the teacher to explore decision-making models. This experience develops professional skills in problem situations which may not be encountered often enough to acquire or maintain essential proficiency. These models include both theoretical tests of new hypotheses in abstract situations, or practical business-management situations which may be readily manipulated.

In Chapters 6, 7, and 8 many examples will be given which encourage the student to explore a simulated physical situation. Most programs have been written in both algegra and the BASIC language to encourage reading and understanding.

After this brief introduction to the time-sharing system and a popular computer language, BASIC, the next chapter will deal primarily with the rationale behind computer-oriented course material. Courses have been taught for years without computers; thus, what is the reason for the current demand for the use of the computer in the classroom? Chapter 3 will discuss these and other questions related to the selection of subject matter for enhanced computer usage.

CHAPTER 3

RATIONALE FOR COMPUTER-LEARNING STUDIES

3.1 INTRODUCTION

In spite of marked advances in technology and the successful application of new technical skills to this atomic space age, teachers and students alike have been relatively untouched by these advances in their normal pursuits of learning. The textbook, teacher, student, and the classroom have been and are today the most common elements in the learning process. Yet the effectiveness of the current mode of teaching at the college level has come under severe scrutiny. Juniors, when properly questioned, may on occasion not remember a word of their freshman courses, and the testing of graduate students has often revealed appalling ignorance in basic intellectual skills supposedly learned earlier.

Evaluation of current teaching methods and techniques reveals the severity and urgency of the problem. There is a lack of adequate teachers and an ever increasing number of qualified students. Classrooms, swelling to capacity, reduce the teacher to a distant lecturer who transmits 'knowledge' from his lecture notes to the student's scratch-pad via the blackboard.

A major promise of the new computerized educational technology is that it will lead to 'individualized instruction.' This term can have many meanings; but, all meanings pay at least lip service to the promise that each student has his own rate and style of learning. The hope is that technology can make the teaching of the individual adaptive to his own needs and capabilities. The computer, as one of the more exciting technological advancements, may be capable of changing the role of both the teacher and student in such a way as to make the learning process more individual and more effective. Educators are challenged to study the use of the computer as a teaching tool, and to assess its impact on the very structure and content of the fields of knowledge as they are presently organized. For example, could physics be taught to non-science majors without calculus by a combination of computer animation and numerical analysis? Or, would a chemistry student have to memorize the properties of any organic compounds if he were taught methods of rapid computer information retrieval?

Some existing techniques and methods will be rendered obsolete, others will have their importance enhanced, and new techniques and methods will necessarily be invented. This chapter describes possible criteria for subject matter selection for a computer-integrated course, discusses the predictable effects of computers on teachers and students, and suggests methods of computer-media development.

Figure 3.1   The Computer as a Library of Information.

3.2   SUBJECT MATTER SELECTION AND PRESENTATION

Major emphasis must be placed on a general re-organization of subject matter and method of presentation for the computer to measurably enhance student learning ability. Attempts to integrate the computer into an existing course, without some change in textbook and lecture notes, have not been very successful. In these cases, the computer was an added burden to the normal course and required extra teacher and student time. The design of course material in a manner which insures the need for computer use is paramount to a successful computer-integrated course.

A computer-integrated course exposes the student to computer techniques within the framework of the normal course. This means, for example, that an undergraduate physics course would enable science students to acquire computer skills by solving physics problems on the computer during the semester. Non-science students, many of whom will later be in decision-making roles in industry and government, must also be exposed to computing and its practice, its powers and its limitations. The type of exposure to computers depends upon the subject matter, and the type of student participation planned.

The selection of subject matter falls into the following categories each of which is dependent upon the kind and amount of student involvement (the categories will be discussed at length in the following paragraphs):

A. The student programs on the computer an assigned problem and obtains his own solutions.

B. The student changes the data parameters of an existing program and learns through analysis of the computer-generated results.

In the first category (Category A), the student is introduced to the essentials of a conversational computer language (for example BASIC) during the first class session. For the remainder of the course, the presentation of subject matter in the form of equations and symbols is made for the most part in computer notation. The student no longer considers the computer programming a function distinct from the course material. In this manner, the student learns to think of each situation in terms of possible computer solutions. The computer approach might require the student to devise a mathematical model (see Section 6.3 for example), employ computer numerical methods (see Section 8.2 for example) or program a simple routine for summing numbers (see Section 4.3 for example). At the completion of a course organized to include the computer, the student is expected not only to have mastered the subject matter, but of equal importance, the student has acquired the computer programming skills that are particular to the current course. Furthermore, the student gains working insight into the many facets of the computer, that is, how it operates, what are its limitations, and how it can be a partner in solving problems.

Subject matter for this first category (Category A) includes all courses that are basically problem oriented (mathematical or logical). For example, physics in contrast to biology, or business in contrast to history. Problem-oriented courses have in common the treatment of natural phenomena by man-made axioms normally written in equation form. For instance, force, mass, and acceleration have been observed experimentally to always be related as $F = MA$. This axiom, Newton's Second Law, may have to be calculated many times if the mass or acceleration is changing rapidly with time. This type of problem can be handled by a student using a computer (see Trajectory Problem in Section 6.4).

Proper utilization of the computer in problem-oriented courses will encourage the treatment of problems without idealizing assumptions, thereby, not requiring the closed-form analytic solution. In Figure 3.2 the computer output, which normally is displayed on the typewriter, has been used to drive an oscilloscope so that the students' solution becomes immediately visible. This use of the BASIC language has proven very effective for students in adding 'life' to the solution of complex problems. Very often, problems given to students are, by necessity, ideal; i.e., assumptions are made which are known to differ from the actual physical phenomenon being studied. The computer's speed allows the consideration of "non-ideal" situations. For example, in a projectile problem, the consideration of air resistance or changing force of gravity is beyond the scope of most elementary physics textbooks. With the computer, even the non-science student can be made to realize the effect of numerous real parameters on the solution of existing problems.

In the second category of subject matter (Category B), the student is not required to know any computer language. The student learns to operate the computer terminal (basically a typewriter connected by phone lines to the computer as in Figure 3.3), and all instructional information has been pre-programmed by the teacher. The subject matter best suited for this mode of learning is restricted to courses requiring considerable amounts of drill and training. Drill and training refers to repetitive exposure, and

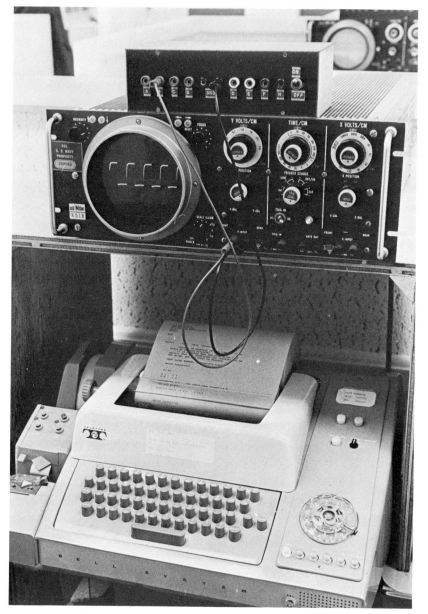

Figure 3.2   The Computer Produces Visual Output.

memorization. In electrical engineering, as just one example, students must be trained to operate the oscilloscopes for signal measurement and detection. In Figure 3.4, a student is shown following instructions dictated by the computer (instructions are typed on the console). The computer carefully leads the student through a series of training steps followed by ques-

Figure 3.3   Computer Communications by Telephone.

tions to probe student understanding. The student can only progress if he has mastered all previous steps. When he has completed this training, the same oscilloscope can become a tool for further computer problems as was previously described. Almost all courses require some drill and training,

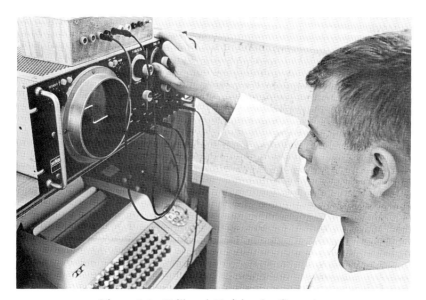

Figure 3.4   Drill and Training by Computer.

some more than others; for example, languages more than mathematics, medicine more than economics, and chemistry more than engineering.

Subject matter for drill and training is presented in question and answer form very similar to the popular programmed textbook. The computer has the advantage of flexible presentation of the next learning frame, and continual record keeping of student responses. The computer terminal can display pictures and graphs, or can be made to access a slide-projector cartridge. The obvious advantage of the computer for drill and training is that the student is self-paced and continually informed of any deficiencies in retention of subject matter.

In this book an attempt has been made to show practical examples of subject matter for computer-integrated courses in physics, chemistry and engineering. In Chapter 6, the physics teacher and student will discover the use of the computer in the problem-oriented situations of the motion of a projectile (see Section 6.2) or the period of a simple harmonic oscillator. In Section 6.12 an example of drill and training can be found when the student explores the effect of slit-width on the intensity of a diffraction pattern. The treatment of chemistry with computer assistance (in Chapter 8) includes considerable drill and training as shown in Section 7.3 where the computer tutors the student until he provides the correct numerical answers. The student's role is an active one and no progress can be made unless he masters each step. In Sections 7.4 or 7.5, examples of more advanced problems that can effectively be solved by a computer are shown. Engineering courses require the treatment of 'non-ideal' problems. In Chapter 8, strong emphasis has been placed on the student's active par-

Figure 3.5   The Computer as a Laboratory Assistant.

ticipation in programming the solution to such problems as heat transfer (see Sections 8.7 and 8.8) and electrical problems involving resistors, capacitors, and inductors (see Sections 8.2 and 8.3).

The computer provides a powerful tool in the formation and manipulation of many complex parameters confronting the students of physics, chemistry and engineering. It is emphasized that other subjects could have been chosen as examples for this book. Furthermore, other categories of computer-assisted-learning will develop as the transition to computer-integrated courses continues.

3.3   STUDENT NEEDS AND LIMITATIONS

It is often said that "the only way to learn a subject is to teach the subject." The student needs to take a more active role in the learning process and to set the pace in relation to his own limitations. The current changes in teaching technology have one major advantage for the student. Before man can make a machine assist in the learning process, very specific objectives must be delineated for each course. In other words, what are the course objectives and what will the teacher accept as a measure of the completion of these objectives. For the student, this means that his responsibilities will be spelled-out in minute detail as measurable behavioral objectives. The student will not be told simply to "know" Physics, but he will be presented with a long list of objectives which he must master before the teacher will be convinced that the student "knows" Physics. For example, a student may be told that at the completion of a certain segment of the course, he must be able to:

(a) Derive Maxwell's equations
(b) Demonstrate Conservation of Energy
(c) Plot distance as a function of time

Figure 3.6   The Computer as a Manager of Student's Schedules.

The computer-integrated course, where student response data is managed by the computer, should serve to maintain student awareness of his progress in the course and of the necessary steps a student must take when remedial action is indicated. The need for a student to 'guess' what a teacher requires of him, or what the teacher thinks is important, has been replaced by realistic course objectives monitored by the computer memory. An example of this strategy can be taken from the lesson on forced harmonic motion in Section 6.6. The student has been given the following objectives:

1. Determine the motion of a mass-spring system when acted upon by a force.
2. Write a computer program to determine the position of the mass at any time.
3. Prepare a computer program to plot the results of part 2 above.

The teacher can check the student's results by supplying parameters which he knows to be correct, then letting the computer test the student's results. A record is kept in the computer memory of the student's attempts and his progress toward a solution.

In Section 7.3, an example output of the student's record as maintained by the computer is shown. The teacher can immediately see when and how often each student has used the computer. Moreover, there is a record of all correct and incorrect responses making it possible for the teacher to pinpoint difficulties in student understanding and insuring prompt remedial action.

3.4 TEACHER GOALS AND REQUIREMENTS

A teacher's most important goal is to arm the student with all the necessary tools for self-learning. These tools have in the past included:

1. an appreciation for books,
2. a motivation to study,
3. a desire to know,
4. an acquisition of curiosity, and many others.

Can the computer be added to this list of learning tools? The answer can be "yes" only if teachers are willing to commit the necessary energy to the effort of re-organizing course material for computer involvement. The teacher must not only acquire a basic understanding of educational computer uses (this book should point the way) but more important, the teacher must examine the course in terms of realistic instructional objectives.

In preparing to restructure his course, the teacher may ask the following questions:

1. What specifically is to be learned?,
2. How must one design achievement measures?,
3. Can the course objective be communicated to the student?, and
4. What is acceptable proof that the course objectives have been met?

The objectives of the course as designed by the teacher must in general have the following qualifications:

1. The objectives must be *measurable*. The performance that is acceptable as evidence that the objective has been achieved and the conditions under which it is to occur must be stated or given.
2. The objectives must be *understandable* to others. Words, such as: to know, to understand, to appreciate, to enjoy, insight, deep feeling, etc., are too general and not specific. Words such as to write, to identify, to solve, to list, to calculate, to memorize, etc., are considered "action words," and are necessary.
3. The objectives must be *feasible*. There must be sufficient time, material, equipment, facilities, etc., available for student use to accomplish the objective.

For most teachers, this process is a painstaking one indeed, probably one that should be done before teaching any course. A course evaluation of this nature has become most important with the advent of computer-integrated study for two reasons. First by proper study of every objective in the course, it becomes readily apparent where the computer can best be introduced in the learning process. And secondly, by proper delineation of measurable objectives, the data management and evaluation of the new course can be properly handled by the computer.

3.5 TIME AND EFFORT

The advantages of a computer-integrated, computer-managed course must be weighed against the time and effort required by the teacher to make the transition to such a course. The expense of computer-assisted-learning will not be considered due to the rapidly changing cost of computer machinery (mostly decreasing costs). Experimental costs of developing systems have always been considerably higher than final operational costs. The time and effort to transfer to a computer course can best be described in four phases. The following history of course development, based upon the personal experience of the authors, included the planning, evaluation, and design of fifty tutorial programs for an undergraduate physics course for non-science majors. The programs were all in BASIC and were similar in format to the examples shown in Sections 7.2 and 7.3.

The four phases of computer-course development can be summarized as follows:

(1) teacher training in computer technique,
(2) current course evaluation by 'pin-pointing' objectives,
(3) program writing to meet course objectives,
(4) course evaluation and try-out.

In phase one, experience has shown that properly motivated teachers can become sufficiently familiar with the BASIC language and the teletypewriter operation in three to six hours. This includes programming problems and full realization of the capabilities and limitations of the computer. Careful reading of Chapters 2 and 4 of this book would provide the necessary background to begin work on the remote console of a computer.

Having acquired the necessary computer skills, the teacher must examine all facets of his course to determine and isolate applications within the framework of the computer's capabilities. This search forms phase two, an all important and very difficult phase requiring considerable creativity. In the course being described, the authors examined each segment and objective of the physics course. These were again divided into sub-segments and more descriptive objectives, until finally, it became quite evident exactly why the course was being taught and what was expected of the students (this experience alone was unusually revealing).

Based upon course objectives and student needs the authors decided upon the computer tutorial strategy as the most immediate application of computers to this particular physics course. Having chosen a strategy which includes computer techniques in each course segment, the teacher is ready to begin phase three.

In phase three, the actual computer programming and 'debugging' takes place. If phase one and two have been properly defined, phase three can be a real pleasure. Years of teaching experience can now be arranged in a careful format of questions, answers, and extensive remedial. The actual typing of the tutorial script onto the computer terminal can be performed by the teacher, advanced students, or a skilled typist.

The evaluation of the pedagogic value of the computer-integrated course material takes place in phase four. Student try-out with corrective and constructive suggestions (feedback) will be a very rewarding and busy experience for the teacher. Students have a way of finding all mistakes, and offering practical suggestions for rewriting and up-dating. In the history of the course being developed the students who participated in this particular computer-assisted-learning experience performed considerably better on the final examination than a like group conventionally taught. Furthermore, there were no recorded failures in this group, whereas in a comparable class there are normally from 4 to 6 percent failures.

Experience in developing the four phases described above has shown that the teacher will spend about 20 hours of preparation for each first student hour during the transition period. Once the transition has been successfully completed, the time required decreases sharply. Student enthusiasm helps to generate the initial effort, and is sustained by the challenge of new problems and applications. (Some of the programs in this book were student-generated.)

In Part II of this book, the reader will find practical examples of integrated course material. In most cases, the teacher can adapt these examples directly to the needs of his particular course objectives. The introduction to Part II will explain in detail how the examples are to be used by the teacher and the student.

The next chapter introduces the reader to many important computer techniques used in computer problem solving and, in addition, describes the remaining BASIC language commands. The emphasis in this book is to 'learn by doing' and thus the reader is encouraged to study all the examples in the next chapter and, when possible, to actually try the examples on a computer terminal.

CHAPTER 4

BASIC COMPUTER PROGRAMMING

4.1 INTRODUCTION

In spite of the universal reputation of the computer as a manipulator of the most complex mathematics, the truth is that the computer's reputation stems from its unique ability to add and subtract numbers very quickly and very accurately. The strength of this mathematical giant lies primarily in the simplicity of its many two-state memory elements which represent either a 0 or a 1. By the 'flip' of a switch a 0 becomes a 1 or a 1 becomes a 0. For this reason, the binary number 10110 can become 01001 in an instant. In order to capitalize on this attribute of the computer, it becomes necessary to formulate problems in a manner which differs substantially from more classical techniques. In contrast, the power of man's intellect derives from his ability to treat abstract concepts in a manner which results in the conception of 'new' ideas. This 'brain-power' seldom includes accuracy; in fact, the mind purposely removes the intricate details during its creative moments. "Give me the big picture, forget the details until later." The computer, on the other hand, works only in the intricate and detailed mode. The computer can not 'think' abstractly and is acutely dependent upon being given all the 'facts' by man. For the computer the first axiom is "Garbage In equals Garbage Out." The computer can be of great assistance only if one carefully plans all the decisions and the steps that the computer must take. The computer lends its speed and accuracy to man's ingenuity to form an unusual partnership.

This chapter is devoted to methods of converting the more conceptual approach to problems employed by man into the detailed, incremental approach required for computer problem solving. A computer program consists of a complete set of directions guiding the computer, in a 'step by step' fashion, to the solution of a problem. Every person who learns to program a computer acquires a 'bag of tricks' which help to make the final computer program more efficient in its construction. The techniques demonstrated in this section are complete and can assist the novice programmer in the solution of more complex problems.

The chapter is organized as follows: In the beginning there is a short discussion of system commands (Section 4.2) since these commands must be used when a program is run. [System commands are used to give instructions to the time-sharing system—some examples are RUN, SAVE, STOP.] The next section (4.3) discusses a program to sum a series of numbers in order to introduce some fundamental BASIC statements and some general programming techniques. The remaining sections discuss all the steps which must be followed in preparing a program for the computer.

55

The reader is led through these steps by using a program which serves as a sample exercise of programming techniques. The program used is SORT, a program which sorts a series of numbers into ascending order. The steps to be followed are considered in turn. First, the use of flow charts to diagram the logical flow of a program (Section 4.4) is discussed. Then, a complex program, the sorting of numbers (Section 4.5), is considered in detail. This program serves to introduce the remainder of BASIC statements and programming techniques which are needed by the reader. The flow chart and the first written version of this sort program are given. The reader is then introduced to a method of program *re*writing (Section 4.6). Program rewriting entails an evaluation of the first version of a program in order to ensure that the program is efficiently written. Finally, there is a brief section on one step that few programmers can avoid—debugging the program (Section 4.7).

One further comment should be made—an effective approach to learning computer techniques is by "doing" and therefore it is suggested that each program discussed in this chapter be prepared by the reader and tried on a computer terminal. Finally, it may be noted that the methods and programs described are essentially independent of existing hardware. This philosophy was adopted because of the rapid changes in the computer equipment made available by industry.

For the benefit of the reader who has no experience of contacting the existing hardware and time-sharing services, a few of the industrial firms are mentioned below:

C-E-I-R, Inc.
Multi Access Computing Services
Washington, D.C.

General Electric Company
Computer Time-sharing Services
7735 Old Georgetown Road
Bethesda, Maryland

HONEYWELL, Inc., Time-sharing
Minneapolis, Minnesota

COM-SHARE
4001 West Devon
Chicago, Illinois

The reader will find that a variety of time-sharing services are available in his local area and special rates are often given to academic institutions.

4.2 SYSTEM COMMANDS

In order to communicate with the computer, the user must have at his disposal commands which direct the computer to carry out specific actions. These commands can be classified as (a) directive, (b) editing, and

(c) informative. They are distinguished from program statements by the fact that no line number precedes the command.

Directive commands are used to communicate with the computer concerning the running and storage of programs. Typically, a student and/or teacher would operate the teletypewriter (or TTY) in the LOCAL mode and type a program onto paper tape (See Fig. 2.7). In the LOCAL mode, the TTY is not connected to the computer system so the user does not incur additional charges (i.e., charges other than the basic monthly rental fee). This mode is thus often used for the slow process of typing programs and large amounts of data onto paper tape. (The program may be entered via the keyboard while the TTY is connected to the computer system, but this can be expensive since the user is charged for this time.) After putting a program onto tape, the user presses the ORIG button, listens for the dial tone, and dials the time-sharing installation. When the computer answers, the name of the time sharing system will be typed on the TTY, the date, and the time. (Later, when the user signs off, the computer will type the elapsed time so that the user can keep a record of the charges incurred for on-line service.) The user then types his user number, and the SIGN-ON exchange takes place as noted earlier (see Chapter 2).

During the SIGN-ON exchange, the computer will request the system being used and whether the program is new or old. After typing a directive command, the user must press the carriage return button (indicated in the text that follows by (R)). For example, after the computer types

SYSTEM—

the user may reply

BASIC (R)

to indicate that the BASIC language will be used. When the computer requests

NEW OR OLD—

the user replies NEW if the program is not stored in the computer, and OLD if the program has been previously stored (or saved). The computer will next type READY if all the information typed by the user is correct. The user can then type

TAPE (R)

(where (R) refers to depressing the carriage return button), the computer again responds READY, and the program is input via tape. When the entire program has been read into the computer, typing

KEY (R)

restores normal keyboard control. The user may then direct the computer to execute the program by typing

RUN ®

Additional directive commands are given in user manuals.

Another class of system commands are the editing commands used to edit or reorganize programs in the computer. For example, it is possible to re-number a program. The edit command

EDIT RESEQUENCE ®

can be used to direct the computer to re-number a program from the beginning, using 100 as the first line number, incrementing the line numbers in steps of 10. It is possible the user may want to use a different increment or start with another line number. Other conditions can be specified by typing numbers after the command. Typing

EDIT RESEQUENCE 10,2,5 ®

would cause re-numbering from line number 2, in steps of 5, with 10 as the first line number. The re-numbered program may be printed out with the command, LIST ®, which causes the program to be listed on the TTY. A wide variety of editing commands are available on most time sharing systems.

The teacher and student will find that systems commands are generally easy to remember and construct. With a little practice, the interaction with the computer becomes almost second-nature.

4.3 SUMMATION OF NUMBERS

Many problems that the computer can handle require the repetitious manipulation of a series of numbers. For instance, it may be necessary to add 1 plus 2 plus 3 plus 4. This example, the summation of a series of numbers, will be discussed at length. Even the computer must be instructed in detail how to add numbers, and this process often occurs in practical problem solving. For example, in calculating the average of a group of numbers one can write:

$$\text{Average} = \frac{A_1 + A_2 + A_3 \ldots \ldots + A_N}{N}$$

where A_1, A_2, ... A_N are called subscripted variables (as ordinarily used in algebra) which represent a series of discrete numbers, and $N =$ the total number of entries. The above equation states that the average is found by adding the numbers together and then dividing by N. Not only is this a very common computer problem, but also two important programming concepts called the *subscripted variable* and *looping* can be introduced by developing a program to sum numbers.

Consider, for example, a program to calculate the sum of 100 numbers. Let us designate the name of the program as SUM. (As mentioned in Chapter 2, each BASIC program is given a name for the purpose of identification.) In developing the program, the numbers to be summed must be read by the computer. To do this, one could write in BASIC:

    100 READ A1, A2, A3, A4, ... L1
         (read the variables A1, A2, etc.)
    110 DATA 6, 8, 3, 2, ... 10
         (whose values are 6,8,3,2, etc.)

However, in order to facilitate the handling of a long list of numbers, it is convenient to use the subscripted variable. In BASIC, subscripted variables consist of a single letter followed by a subscript in parentheses. Thus A1, A2, A3 is written $A(1)$, $A(2)$, $A(3)$ in BASIC. To be more general, one can write

$$A(N) \text{ for } N = 1 \text{ to } 100$$

which defines a list of subscripted variables $A(N)$, where N can have values from 1 to 100. Using the BASIC subscripted variable, then, the list of 100 numbers which must be read into the computer for the program SUM can be written:

    90   DIM A(100)
    100 READ A(1), A(2), A(3), ... A(100)
    110 DATA 6,8,3, ... 10

Note that a DIM (DIMension) statement has been added which indicates to the computer the maximum amount of space it must save to accommodate the list of numbers. In other words, the statement DIM A(100) tells the computer to save 100 spaces (or memory locations) for values of the variable A. A dimension statement is required when a subscript greater than 10 is to be used. Note once more that the variable $A(N)$ is called a 'subscripted variable', where, the letter 'N' is the 'subscript' and can have the value of 1, 2, 3, 4, etc. This notation is quite common for engineers and scientists who often represent different values of the same variable by A_1, A_2, A_3, A_4 and so on.

Tables of numbers can be entered by *doubly-subscripted variables* such as $A(I,J)$. As in singly-subscripted variables, a dimension statement (DIM) is required when a subscript greater than 10 is to be used. The form of the subscript remains flexible and formulas are permitted. For example, $A(I)$, $A(J)$ are both equally valid. Furthermore, one may wish to use $A(2*I)$ to pick out a certain sequence of numbers in an ordered list (in this case, $A(2)$, $A(4)$, $A(6)$, $A(8)$, $A(10)$, etc.).

Return now to the input in Program "SUM" of 100 numbers by referring to statement 100:

    100 READ A(1), A(2), A(3), ... A(100).

This would obviously be a very long statement of essentially repetitious commands. After all, if the computer were told to

    100 READ A(N),

for $N = 1, 2, 3, 4, \ldots . 100$, the work would be simple. This brings to the forefront a most powerful programming device called the 'loop'. When portions of a program are performed again and again with only slight modifications, the loop is used. BASIC provides three special statements to specify a loop. The first two statements commonly used in looping are:

GO TO [line number]
IF [formula] [relation] [formula] THEN [line number]

These statements are discussed later in this chapter in connection with the sorting of numbers (Section 4.4) .

The third looping method, the FOR and NEXT statement, was formulated specifically for looping. For example, the statements necessary to input 100 numbers may be rewritten using a loop:

```
90    DIM  A(100)
100   FOR  N=1  TO  100
110   READ  A(N)
120   NEXT  N
130   DATA  6,8,3, . . . . . . 10
```

It is very important at this point to understand the characteristics of the loop (statement 100, 110, and 120). This program segment will be executed as follows: the computer reads statement 90 which directs it to set aside 100 cells (memory locations) for values of A. Statement 100 is executed which sets up the subscript N to control the count from 1 to 100 in steps of 1. The first time through the loop, $N = 1$. Execution of statement 110 causes $A(N)$ to be set equal to the first item of the DATA statement, or $A(1) = 6$, and this value is stored in the first cell which is labeled $A(1)$. Execution of statement 120 performs the test: Is $N = 100$? It is not, therefore the computer increments N by 1, setting $N = 2$, branches back to statement 110, and $A(2)$ is set equal to 8. This looping continues until $N = 100$, at which point the computer will have read and stored 100 numbers. The loop in computer programming has the outstanding feature of allowing a statement (in this case 110 READ $A(N)$) to be executed many times even though it is only written once.

The FOR statement is flexible since it may be written,

FOR [subscript] = [formula] TO [formula] STEP [formula]

or, for example,

200   FOR I = X + 5 TO N − 1 STEP P

The NEXT statement must specify the variable given in the FOR statement. A step of one is assumed if no STEP is specified, as in line 100 of the previous example. In statement 200, however, I will be incremented by the value of P each time through the loop. For example, suppose that the values of $X = 0$, $N = 101$, and $P = 5$. The first time through the loop, $I = X + 5 = 0 + 5 = 5$. The second time through the loop, since $P = 5$, I will be incremented by 5 or $I = 10$. This looping will continue until $I = N − 1 = 101 − 1 = 100$ at which time the loop is finished.

The complete program called SUM may now be written using the BASIC expressions which have been introduced here and in Chapter 2.

```
80   REM ** SUM **
90   DIM A(100)
100  LET S=0
110  FOR N=1 TO 100
120  READ A(N)
130  LET S=S+A(N)
140  NEXT N
150  PRINT S
160  DATA 6,8,3, . . . . . . 10
170  END
```

This program will be explained in detail since it illustrates the use of important BASIC statements and programming techniques. The basic program skeleton used is:

1. identifying statements (line 80)
2. input of data (line 90, 120)
3. body of program—data is manipulated (line 100–140)
4. output of data (line 150)
5. data (line 160)
6. end of program statement (line 170).

Line 100 assigns the value zero to S; alternately this could have been done with

```
105   READ S
110   DATA 0
```

but the method chosen is simpler. Some time-sharing systems initialize all variables to zero automatically. If such a system is used, line 100 is deleted.

The computer executes line 130 as follows: the statement

$$130 \quad LET \ S=S+A(N)$$

is interpreted by the computer to mean: take the current value of S from the memory cell labeled S, add to this A(N), and store this new value back in cell S. The first time through the loop, N=1. Thus the computer takes the previous value of S (in this case zero), adds A(1) (given in the DATA statement as 6) and stores the sum, or 6, in the cell saved for S. The original value of S, zero, is thus destroyed; this is referred to in computer terminology as destructive input. The second time through the loop, N=2, and execution of line 130 causes the current value of S (which is 6) to be added to A(2), whose value is 8, and the resulting sum, or 14, is stored as the new value of S. Finally, when N=100, program control passes to statement 150 and the value of S, which is the sum of the 100 numbers, is printed. Line 170 signals the END of the program. The END statement must appear as the last line in every program.

BASIC statements are simple and programs written in this language are easy to interpret. Having mastered the rudiments of BASIC, a final step is necessary before one proceeds to the writing of a program. The step-by-step instructions to the computer must be organized into a logical sequence. This sequence can best be constructed by using a 'flow chart' as discussed in the next section.

4.4. FLOW CHARTS

The old cliché *"a picture is worth a thousand words"* has particular truth for a person preparing a computer program. Teachers, who often find many uses for pictorial representation in the classroom, should readily accept the flow chart as a powerful tool for depicting the many steps which must be performed to accomplish a computer objective. In programming a computer, the teacher and student must remember that the computer has no way of anticipating the requirements of a problem and therefore it must be provided with all the information needed to make a decision. The major function of the flow chart is to clarify what must be done as a result of each decision. All alternative courses of action are dictated to the computer. The amount of information put into the flow chart depends mainly upon personal preference and the level of programming difficulty.

Appropriately then, programmers use flow charts to organize the flow of data and information from input, through the processing steps, to output. The basic flow chart symbols (Fig. 4.1) are used to designate types of actions such as input/output, processing, decisions, and those functions which are pre-defined. Lines are used to connect symbols, and arrows indicate the direction of the flow of information. In addition, each program must have a beginning (start), and must later have an end (stop). A connector is used when the program is too long to fit on a single page or when a line with an arrow would be confusing. The use of these symbols will be illustrated with reference to the program "SUM" which was discussed in the last section (4.3).

"SUM", a program to sum 100 numbers, is represented by the flow chart in Fig. 4.2; the program statements are listed beside the chart next to the corresponding symbol. Again, arrows indicate the direction of flow of information. A square is used to indicate the beginning and end of the program (START, END). A rectangle is use to indicate processing or annotation, $N=1$, for example. Input and output is designated with an oval as is shown for READ A(N), and PRINT S. The one other important symbol shown is the decision box. The decision on whether or not to terminate the loop depends on the question: Is $N=100$?, and this question is thus put in the decision box. A decision box will always have at least two arrows leaving the box; each arrow should be labeled to answer the question posed in the decision box. In addition, the user may want to sum several batches of 100 numbers. In this case, a variable X may be introduced (Fig. 4.3) which counts the batches of numbers to be summed. The program will loop back to the beginning of the summation X times. It may

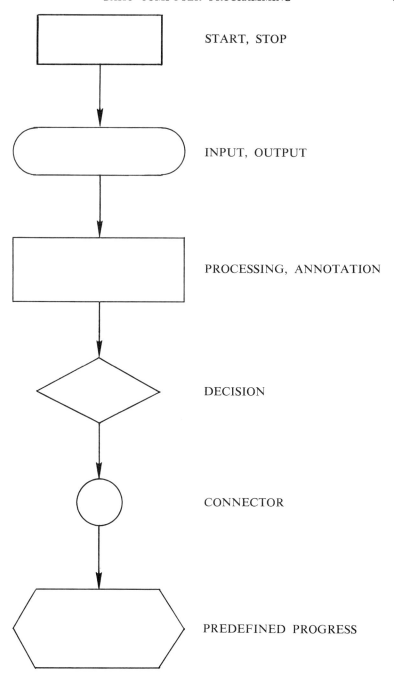

Figure 4.1   Flow Chart Symbols

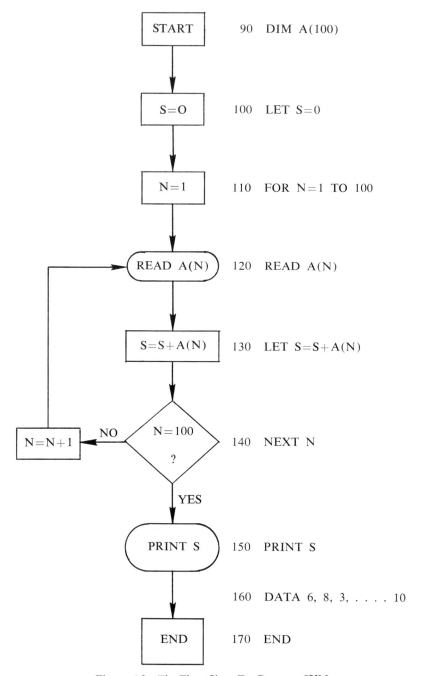

Figure 4.2 The Flow Chart For Program SUM

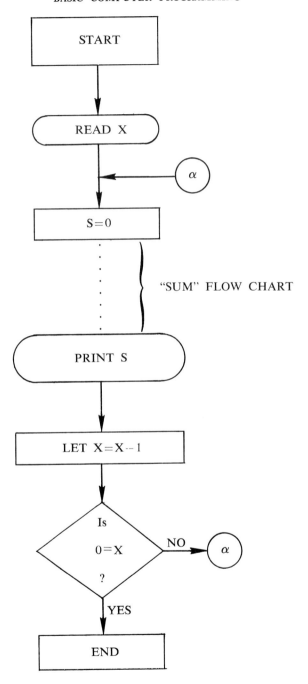

Figure 4.3 The Flow Chart of Program SUM to Add Batches of Numbers

be noted that a connector is used in the flow chart (Fig. 4.3) to indicate the branching back to the beginning of the program.

The examples used in this section are simple in concept. The techniques which they serve to illustrate are fundamental to programming. The essentials of looping, loop control, and an understanding of the type of thought process necessary to communicate with the computer, must be mastered before one can proceed to more complex programs. Remember, complex programs are, for the most part, nothing more than an elaborate network of short programming segments. However, while the flow chart may be optional for short programs, it is indispensable for complex programs as an aid to the programmer in the logical organization of his thoughts. The flow chart should be kept with the final version of the program since it can serve to refresh the author's memory as well as to explain the program flow to others who may use the author's program. Finally, if it is written in general terms, it can be used to write a program in any language, for any computer.

4.5   SORTING NUMBERS: AN EXERCISE IN WRITING PROGRAMS

Locating the largest number in a series, and ordering numbers by arranging them from the smallest number to the largest number, are practical programming techniques. For example, a teacher may want to arrange his students in linear order according to their grade on a major examination. If the teacher has 100 students, this can be a tedious job; the computer, however, can accomplish the task in seconds.

A program to sort numbers also embodies many important programming concepts and techniques applicable to a range of scientific problems. An example of number sorting will be illustrated with a program called SORT. This program will serve to complete the introduction of BASIC statements.

SORT is a program used by students to read a series of numbers, limited in this case to a maximum of 100, then arrange them in ascending order, and finally, print out the numbers in order. It is convenient to begin by making a flow chart (See Fig. 4.4) of the actual sort routine. At first glance, this flow chart looks complicated. However, a few comments will clarify this representation of logical program flow. Nothing has been said of the input or output for these numbers; connectors are used to show that the initial block of numbers is available at α and the sorted numbers are ready at β. The list of numbers is referenced by the subscripted variable $A(I)$. The numbers are sorted by comparing two numbers in the list at a time; if the number designated $A(I+1)$, or $A(J)$, is less than $A(I)$, the two numbers are interchanged; otherwise they are left unchanged. Reference to the flow chart (Fig. 4.4) shows that "nested loops", or one loop within the other, are required to affect the comparison of $A(I)$ and $A(I+1)$. Nested loops, as used in this example, are allowed in BASIC programming; crossed loops will not be accepted by the computer (Fig. 4.5). The loops are controlled by the variables I and J, where $J = I + 1$;

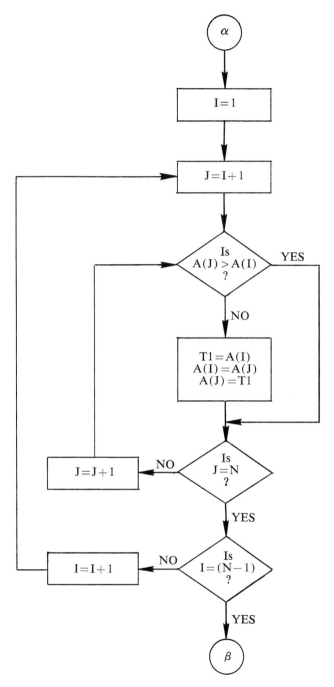

Figure 4.4 A Multiple Decision Flow Chart

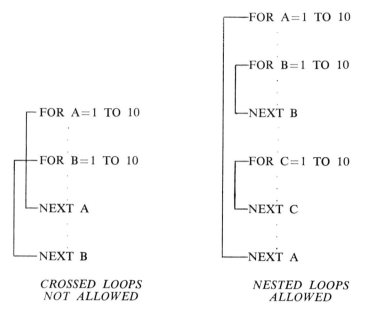

CROSSED LOOPS   NESTED LOOPS
NOT ALLOWED   ALLOWED

FIG. 4.5   Programming Loops

these variables are also used as subscripts. The numbers are interchanged, when $A(J) < A(I)$, by the statements

$$350 \quad \text{LET} \quad T1 = A(I)$$
$$360 \quad \text{LET} \quad A(I) = A(J)$$
$$370 \quad \text{LET} \quad A(J) = T1$$

where T1 is a temporary variable used to save the value of $A(I)$ during the interchange of the numbers. Thus, when executed, the above routine (lines 350, 360 and 370) compares the first number to all the other numbers in the list in turn. This puts the smallest number in the list in cell $A(1)$. The routine then compares $A(2)$ with the other numbers in the list, $A(3)$, $A(4)$, ... $A(N)$, and puts the next to smallest number in cell $A(2)$. In this manner, the above routine passes down the list, sorting the numbers in turn, until N numbers have been sorted. At this point, the smallest number is in cell $A(1)$ and the largest in $A(100)$.

The sort routine can then be incorporated into the entire SORT program (Fig. 4.6) which includes input and output instructions for use of the program, and a check to ensure that the limitations of the program are not exceeded. It should be emphasized that SORT was chosen as an example because of its usefulness as a teaching tool. After a brief introduction to BASIC (such as found in earlier sections), students can be required to write a SORT program for practice and can be directed to write their own programs to manipulate data.

The flow chart of SORT (Fig. 4.6) is interpreted as follows: A student begins execution of the program. He is asked if he has received instruc-

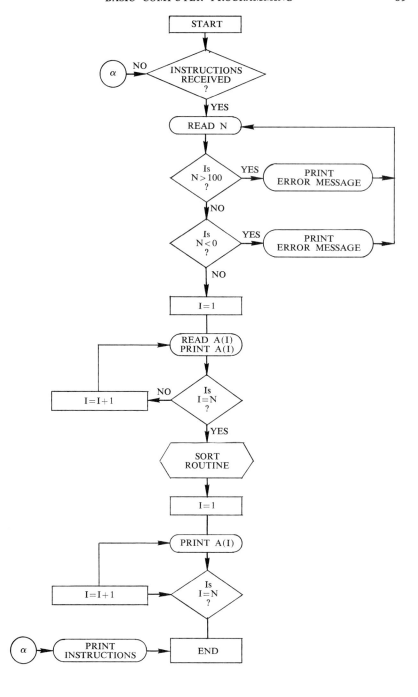

Figure 4.6 A Modified Flow Chart for Program SORT

tions; if he hasn't the program gives him instructions and stops, otherwise the run continues. The program then reads N, the count of the numbers to be sorted, and checks to see that N is not greater than the program can accommodate. (In this case; the limit is set at 100). It then checks to see if N has a meaningless value. If either of these error conditions exist, an error message is printed and another value of N is read. If no errors in N are detected, the program reads N numbers, prints them, sorts them, and finally prints the sorted numbers.

It is advisable at this point in program writing to pause and study the flow chart before proceeding. The logical flow of the program should be checked by stepping through the flow chart with sample data. In addition, some of the questions which should be considered are:

1. Does the program include checks which ensure that program limitations are not exceeded?
2. Does the program, where possible, include checks for logical errors such as inconsistent or meaningless data?
3. Does the program suit the purpose for which it was intended?

In short, the novice programmer is advised not to rush into the task of translating the flow chart into BASIC. One of the most fundamental advantages of a computer integrated course should become apparent from these questions. The student must plan the solution of his problem by a logical, detailed program which, in effect, means that he understands the subject matter to the extent of teaching it to the machine. The 'active' role of the student becomes very effective in the learning process. In the next three paragraphs, a *"line by line"* discussion of the SORT program will indicate just how precise one must be when directing the computer.

A first attempt at the representation of SORT in BASIC, SORT1 (Program 4.1), can be used to introduce additional BASIC statements. The REM (REMarks) statement, line 100, is used to insert comments or explanatory remarks in the program. The computer ignores everything on the same line following the REM. The statement

GO TO [line number]

is a control statement used to direct computer execution in a non-sequential manner. In line 110, the flow of execution is directed to line 510 so that the instructions may be printed out. Note that

PRINT "MESSAGE"

causes the computer to print *verbatim* whatever appears between the quotation marks. The computer advances the paper of the typewriter one line when it executes the statement

560   PRINT

The print statement is also used to output columns of data as in line 270; use of the semicolon following a variable causes $A(I)$ to be printed in columns 12 spaces wide for 7, 8, and 9 digit numbers, similar to the use of the TAB key on a typewriter. The width of the column is varied depending on the length of the variable being printed. The use of a comma instead of

```
100 REM * * * * * * SORT1 * * * * * *
110 GO TO 510
150 DIM A(100)
160 PRINT " THIS PROGRAM SORTS A MAXIMUM OF ONE HUNDRED NUMBERS."
170 PRINT
180 PRINT"HOW MANY NUMBERS DO YOU WANT TO SORT";
190 INPUT N
200 IF N >100 THEN 460
210 IF N <=0 THEN 490
220 FOR I = 1 TO N
230 READ A(I)
240 NEXT I
250 PRINT "THE NUMBERS TO BE SORTED ARE:"
260 FOR I=1 TO N
270 PRINT A(I);
280 NEXT I
290 LET K=N-1
300 FOR I=1 TO K
310 LET L= I + 1
320 FOR J=L TO N
330 IF (A(J)-A(I))<=0 THEN 350
340 GO TO 380
350 LET T1=A(I)
360 LET A(I)=A(J)
370 LET A(J)=T1
380 NEXT J
390 NEXT I
400 PRINT
410 PRINT "THE NUMBERS HAVE BEEN SORTED AS FOLLOWS:"
420 FOR I=1 TO N
430 PRINT A(I)
440 NEXT I
450 STOP
460 PRINT"THIS PROGRAM IS WRITTEN TO SORT A MAXIMUM OF 100 NUMBERS."
470 PRINT "TRY AGAIN."
480 GO TO 180
490 PRINT "YOU HAVE USED A MEANINGLESS VALUE OF N. TRY AGAIN."
500 GO TO 180
510 PRINT"THIS PROGRAM SORTS A MAXIMUM OF ONE HUNDRED NUMBERS."
520 PRINT"TO USE THE PROGRAM, TYPE THE FOLLOWING:"
530 PRINT
540 PRINT "110 DATA 5, 9, -3, 0"
550 PRINT "RUN"
560 PRINT
570 PRINT "TYPE THE NUMBERS YOU WANT TO SORT IN PLACE OF THE NUMBERS"
580 PRINT "GIVEN IN THE EXAMPLE. STATEMENT NUMBERS 110-149"
590 PRINT "ARE RESERVED FOR DATA. YOU WILL BE ASKED TO GIVE THE"
600 PRINT "COUNT OF THE NUMBERS BEING SORTED DURING THE RUNNING"
610 PRINT "OF THE PROGRAM."
620 DATA 5,9,-3,0
630 END
```

PROGRAM 4.1 SORT1

a semicolon (line 270) would divide the teletypewriter line into five zones of 15 spaces each.

Variables are assigned values by READ (line 230), LET (line 290), or INPUT (line 190) statements, for example:

190 INPUT N
230 READ A(I)
290 LET K=N−1

The READ and LET statements have already been shown. INPUT is used to enter data during the running of the program. It should be used to enter only small amounts of data since its execution is time-consuming. Execution of the INPUT statement causes a question mark to be typed. It is generally used in combination with a PRINT statement (line 180) to tell the user the variable to enter. The user, upon seeing the question mark, types the value, and then presses the carriage return key.

Another control statement has the form

IF [formula] [relation] [formula] THEN [line number]

It is used in lines 200 and 210 to check the value of N and to direct the computer to print the error messages if necessary. The following standard relations may be used:

SYMBOL	MEANING
=	is equal to
<	is less than
<=	is less than or equal to
>	is greater than
>=	is greater than or equal to
<>	is not equal to

Finally, note that STOP (line 450) is equivalent to GO TO 630 and it is used when a program has more than one end point. The last line of every program must be an END statement.

Teachers and students can appreciate from this program that BASIC is a conversational language. Such imperative words as READ, PRINT, and STOP certainly are a part of daily conversation. The emphasis is on "telling" the computer exactly what must be completed and how it is to be completed. There is no intuition in the computer's method.

4.6   PROGRAM REWRITING

Program 4.1, SORT1, fulfills the essential criteria of a working program: it will read a group of numbers, sort them, and print them out—everything it was intended to accomplish. However, sections of the program can be rewritten in a more efficient manner. The user should take a moderate approach to the task of program rewriting: obvious changes should be made but it is foolish to go to great lengths to reduce the statements to the shortest possible number unless one is approaching the limits of the system.

A short check-list will be used to illustrate program rewriting:

1. Testing* should be adequate and properly placed.
2. Avoid repetition of identical statements.
3. Avoid introducing extraneous variables.
4. Avoid extraneous control arithmetic.

* Testing refers to statements inserted by a programmer to check whether or not the input data satisfies the requirements of the program.

As an example, this check-list will be used to determine the possible areas for rewriting in SORT1.

1. Consider the *testing* used in SORT1. The value of N is checked to ensure that $0 < N < 100$ before data is read (Program 4.1, lines 200, 210) but there is no check to see that N is the correct count of the data items. However, if N is too large, the computer will print OUT OF DATA and stop during the execution of the program; if N is too small, the user will note that all of the numbers were not read when the numbers to be sorted are printed. Similarly, all decisions in the program are reviewed to confirm that testing is adequate and properly placed.

2. *Repetitive identical statements* in SORT1 are noted in the two loops which read and print the numbers to be sorted. Lines 220–280 (Program 4.1) are rewritten to avoid statement duplication:

```
220   PRINT "THE NUMBERS TO BE SORTED ARE:"
230   FOR I=1 TO N
240   READ A(I)
250   PRINT A(I);
260   NEXT I
```

3. It is recalled that the FOR statement has the form

FOR [formula] TO [formula] STEP [formula] yet, lines 290 and 310 (Program 4.1) introduce formulas which can be incorporated into the FOR statement. Therefore, these *extraneous variables* are deleted (lines 290 and 310) and the lines rewritten:

```
300   FOR I=1 TO N-1
320   FOR J=I+1 TO N
```

4. Finally, checking for *extraneous control arithmetic,* it is noted that 2 lines (330 and 340) in SORT1 are used to effect one decision. It is evident that line 340 can be deleted and line 330 rewritten

```
330   IF A(J)>A(I) THEN 380
```

The rewritten version, SORT2 (Program 4.2) is now ready for a trial run.

4.7   ON-LINE DEBUGGING

Having outlined a program with a flow chart, written the program, and rewritten the program, most novice programmers expect the program to run perfectly the first time. However, this is seldom the case. Even experienced programmers often find that there are small errors, or "bugs," in the program which are not detected until the program is fed into the computer. Thus no discussion of the step-by-step process of writing a program is complete without a section on "debugging," or removing the bugs.

```
100 REM * * * * * * SORT2 * * * * * *
110 GO TO 480
150 DIM A(100)
160 PRINT " THIS PROGRAM SORTS A MAXIMUM OF ONE HUNDRED NUMBERS."
170 PRINT
180 PRINT "HOW MANY NUMBERS DO YOU WANT TO SORT";
190 INPUT N
200 IF N >100 THEN 430
210 IF N <=0 THEN 460
220 PRINT "THE NUMBERS TO BE SORTED ARE:"
230 FOR I = 1 TO N
240 READ A(I)
250 PRINT A(I);
260 NEXT I
290 FOR I = 1 TO N-1
300 FOR J = I+1 TO N
310 IF A(J)>A(I) THEN 350
320 LET T1=A(I)
330 LET A(I)=A(J)
340 LET A(J)=T1
350 NEXT J
360 NEXT I
370 PRINT
380 PRINT "THE NUMBERS HAVE BEEN SORTED AS FOLLOWS:"
390 FOR I=1 TO N
400 PRINT I "=" A(I)
410 NEXT I
420 STOP
430 PRINT "THIS PROGRAM IS WRITTEN TO SORT A MAXIMUM OF 100 NUMBERS."
440 PRINT "TRY AGAIN."
450 GO TO 180
460 PRINT "YOU HAVE USED A MEANINGLESS VALUE OF N. TRY AGAIN."
470 GO TO 180
480 PRINT "THIS PROGRAM SORTS A MAXIMUM OF ONE HUNDRED NUMBERS."
490 PRINT "TO USE THE PROGRAM, TYPE THE FOLLOWING:"
500 PRINT
510 PRINT "110 DATA 5, 9, -3,0"
520 PRINT "RUN"
530 PRINT
540 PRINT "TYPE THE NUMBERS YOU WANT TO SORT IN PLACE OF THE NUMBERS"
550 PRINT "GIVEN IN THE EXAMPLE. STATEMENT NUMBERS 110-149"
560 PRINT "ARE RESERVED FOR DATA. YOU WILL BE ASKED TO GIVE THE"
570 PRINT "COUNT OF THE NUMBERS BEING SORTED DURING THE RUNNING"
580 PRINT "OF THE PROGRAM."
590 DATA 5,9,-3,0
600 END
```

PROGRAM 4.2 SORT2

On-line debugging proceeds rapidly if there are no logical errors in the program. The common programming pitfalls are:

1. errors of form
2. missing statements
3. crossed loops
4. program improperly typed
5. logical errors.

The general debugging sequence is as follows: once the program has been read into the computer, the system will look for programming errors in the program. If none are found, execution will begin. Usually, there are several minor errors in each program and the computer types a list of these errors. The computer will check for the first three pitfalls noted in the list above. In SORT2 (Program 4.2), three errors were found by the computer (Fig. 4.7A #2); these are discussed later in this section. Errors of form generate error messages such as ILLEGAL FORMULA, ILLEGAL VARIABLE, and INCORRECT FORMAT, which are self-explanatory. Missing statements provoke such error messages as NO DATA and NO END INSTRUCTION while crossed loops are referred to by NO MATCH WITH FOR. All the possible error messages are listed in the manuals. The computer generates the error messages, if any, and then ends the run. The user must interpret the messages, enter the necessary corrections, and initiate another run.

Improperly typed programs may include errors of form or missing statements which will be detected by the computer. They may also lead to logical errors. This final pitfall is often the most difficult to overcome. Logical errors are hopefully detected during program execution or when the answers are printed. The computer will note, for example, DIVISION BY ZERO. Furthermore, the user should run his program with sample data to check for logical errors. This sample data should test the effectiveness of the checks in the program as well as represent the range and kind of data the program is expected to handle.

In order to discuss debugging, three errors were added to SORT2 (Fig. 4.2) when it was read into the computer. The following discussion will consider this sample debugging sequence (Fig. 4.7A to 4.7D). The computer types READY when it is awaiting instructions on what to do next. The user then types RUN (Fig. 4.7A #1) and presses the carriage return button. After the first attempted run, the computer detected an error of form, a missing statement, and a typing error (Fig. 4.7A #2). The computer indicated it was waiting instructions by typing READY (Fig. 4.7A #3). At this point, the user must refer to the statements in which the computer indicated there were errors. The first statement noted

190   INPUT NO

contained an illegal expression because NO is not a BASIC variable; the user should have typed N. The second statement noted

310   IF A(J)>A(I THEN 350

was missing a parentheses. Third, there was a READ statement in the program but no DATA statement. The user corrected these errors by typing the appropriate lines (Fig. 4.7A #4) and requesting that the corrected program be "saved" (Fig. 4.7A #5).

After making these corrections, the computer is READY (Fig. 4.7B #1) and the user requested another run. This time, the computer found no errors in the program and SORT2 was executed. SORT2 was written so that the first time it is run, the user is given instructions on how to use the program (Fig. 4.7B #3). The user follows these instructions and types a DATA statement and requests a run (Fig. 4.7C #1). [It may

1. . . *RUN*

2. . . ⎧ SORT2   09:39   SATURDAY11/16/68

        ILLEGAL EXPRESSION LINE # 190

        LEFT PAREN NOT MATCHED WITH RIGHT LINE # 310

        NO DATA

        RUNNING TIME: 00.5 SECS

3. . . READY

4. . . ⎧ *190 INPUT N*
       310 IF A(J) > A(I) THEN 350
       590 DATA 0

5. . . *SAVE*

Fig. 4.7A Program Debugging: Detection and Correction of Errors in SORT2
(words typed by the user are in italics)

   1. The user requests a run.
   2. An attempted run—note heading, list of program errors, and running time.
   3. The computer requests instructions.
   4. The user corrects the errors by retyping the appropriate lines.
   5. The corrected program is "saved."

1. . . ⎰ WAIT. .
      ⎱ READY

2. . . *RUN*

3. . . ⎧ SORT2   09:41   SATURDAY11/16/68

        THIS PROGRAM SORTS A MAXIMUM OF ONE HUNDRED
        NUMBERS. TO USE THE PROGRAM, TYPE THE
        FOLLOWING:

        110 DATA 5, 9, −3,0
        RUN

        TYPE THE NUMBERS YOU WANT TO SORT IN PLACE
        OF THE NUMBERS GIVEN IN THE EXAMPLE.
        STATEMENT NUMBERS 110–149 ARE RESERVED FOR
        DATA. YOU WILL BE ASKED TO GIVE THE COUNT OF
        THE NUMBERS BEING SORTED DURING THE
        RUNNING OF THE PROGRAM.

        RUNNING TIME: 00.9 SECS.

4. . . READY

Figure 4.7B Program Debugging: Corrected version of SORT2: first run
(words typed by the user are in italics)

   1. The computer requests instructions.
   2. The user requests a run.
   3. The program runs, and the instructions for use of the program are typed.
   4. The computer again requests instructions.

1. . . $\begin{cases} 110\ DATA\ 87273,1,0,-2,6E-3,1,2 \\ RUN \end{cases}$

SORT2   09:42   SATURDAY11/16/68

THIS PROGRAM SORTS A MAXIMUM OF ONE
HUNDRED NUMBERS.

HOW MANY NUMBERS DO YOU WANT TO SORT ? *101*
THIS PROGRAM IS WRITTEN TO SORT A MAXIMUM
OF 100 NUMBERS.

2. . . TRY AGAIN.

HOW MANY NUMBERS DO YOU WANT TO SORT ? *0*
YOU HAVE USED A MEANINGLESS VALUE OF N.
TRY AGAIN.

HOW MANY NUMBERS DO YOU WANT TO SORT ? *−2*
YOU HAVE USED A MEANINGLESS VALUE FOR N.
TRY AGAIN.

HOW MANY NUMBERS DO YOU WANT TO SORT ? *10*
THE NUMBERS TO BE SORTED ARE:

3. . .   87273   1   0   −2   .006   1   2
OUT OF DATA LINE   240

RUNNING TIME: 01.0 SECS.

Figure 4.7C.   Program Debugging: Testing and Program (SORT2)
(words typed by the user are in italics)

1. The user follows instructions and types a data statement and then requests a run.
2. The program is executed and the user tests invalid values of N.
3. The user tests a value of N greater than the data—the program runs out of
data and the run is terminated.

1. . . *RUN*

SORT2   09:44   SATURDAY11/16/68

THIS PROGRAM SORTS A MAXIMUM OF ONE HUNDRED
NUMBERS.

HOW MANY NUMBERS DO YOU WANT TO SORT ? *6*
THE NUMBERS TO BE SORTED ARE:
   87273   1   0   −2   .006   1

2. . . THE NUMBERS HAVE BEEN SORTED AS FOLLOWS:
    1 $=-2$
    2 $= 0$
    3 $= .006$
    4 $= 1$
    5 $= 1$
    6 $= 87273$

RUNNING TIME: 00.9 SECS

Figure 4.7D   Program Debugging: A successful test run of SORT2
(words typed by the user are in italics)

1. The user requests a run.
2. The program runs successfully and six numbers are sorted in ascending order.

be noted that the program had another DATA statement (line 590, Fig. 4.7A #4). This DATA statement was in effect a "dummy" statement. The program writer did not know in advance what data the user would have. When the computer checks for errors, however, it checks that there is at least one DATA statement if there is a READ statement or else the program is not executed. Thus statement #590 is a "dummy" required to pass the initial computer inspection.]

In testing the program, the user should ensure that all the "checks" written into the program function properly. SORT2 had several checks on the values of N (the total numbers to be sorted) and the user tests these "checks" in the debugging run (Fig. 4.7C #2). The user also checks to see what happens if N is greater than the amount of numbers given in the DATA statement (Fig. 4.7C #3). As shown, program execution is terminated if the computer runs out of data. Having "debugged" the program, the user requested a final run in which 6 numbers were sorted in ascending order (Fig. 4.7D).

4.8   SUMMARY

Outline of the steps to be followed in writing a computer program:

1. *Construct a flow chart.* Pause and study the flow chart before proceeding. (Consider the questions listed in section 4.5.) Step through the flow chart with sample data—do not rush this phase.
2. *Write the program in BASIC.* Carefully check for logical errors in the program.
3. *Rewrite the program.* Check for adequate testing; delete or condense identical statements, extraneous variables, or extraneous control statements.
4. *Debug the program.* Correct the errors noted by the computer. Conduct a trial run to evaluate program execution using test data.

CHAPTER 5

COMPUTER MATH-TECHNIQUES

5.1 INTRODUCTION

Due to the computer's unique method of handling numbers, any problem can be solved by rapid addition or subtraction of unit quantities. The computer can be instructed to multiply (many additions) or to divide (many subtractions); however, certain mathematical operations cannot be performed on the computer in the conventional manner. For example, integration and differentiation are operations which must be approximated by the computer. This chapter gives a brief summary of a few math-techniques which are very useful for computer solutions. The reader is referred to the Appendix for a list of excellent textbooks which explain numerical methods in great detail. The three topics discussed in this chapter are iteration, differential equations, and integration. These topics are introduced in a general but precise form and should prepare the reader for solving more difficult problems in subsequent chapters. Problems in physics, chemistry, and engineering should be investigated with an awareness of the computer's capabilities and limitations.

5.2 PRINCIPLES OF ITERATION

In the solution of applied science and engineering problems, it is often necessary to try many different values of a certain parameter before obtaining the best fit. This process of systematic 'guessing' at a solution, often called iteration, can be handled by the computer. The following are examples of this type of problem:

1. The mathematical statement of a physical problem requires an iterative approach for evaluating one or more variables. For example in the equation

$$\exp(-y) + \sin(y^2) = 10$$

This is called a transcendental equation and can be solved either by graphical methods or by successive 'guesses' at the value of "y" for which the equation holds.

2. Often in a design problem, there are several parameters which can vary. In order to choose the optimum design, the computer tries many combinations of the design parameters. This section deals with a discussion of one possible method of numerical solution of these types of problems. Other specific methods can be found in this book by referring to the index.

A simple procedure for solving iterative problems, known as the Newton-Raphson method, can best be described by treating an example. If the approximate root of $x^2 = 20$ is required, this means

$$x \text{ times } x = 20.$$

Since $4 \times 4 = 16$ and $5 \times 5 = 25$, one might "guess" that the actual value of the root of 20 must be greater than 4 but less than 5. The computer method involves defining a function, $f(x)$, such that,

$$f(x) = x^2 - 20.$$

The value of x for which $f(x) = 0$ is the desired root. Many 'guesses' at the value x would probably result in a solution of $f(x) = 0$. However, a systematic approach may save time and effort. In Fig. 5.1 where the function $f(x)$ is plotted versus values of x, the x-intercept becomes the solution for which $f(x) = 0$. An initial guess for x could be x_1 for which $f(x_1) \neq 0$. To obtain the next systematic guess for x, the tangent to the curve at x_1 is extended to the x-axis and the intercept, x_2, is tried as a solution of $f(x) = 0$. In the case shown in Fig. 5.1, $f(x_2) \neq 0$, so other similar guesses must be made. Now to arrange this verbal discussion into equation form, consider the following:

$$\text{tangent at } x_1 = \text{first derivative of } f(x) \text{ at } x_1.$$

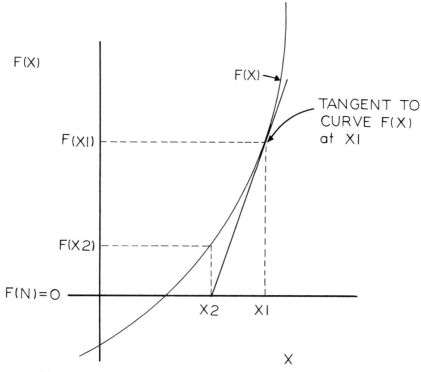

Figure 5.1   A Graph of the Function F(x) versus X with slope shown.

Let us define

$$f'(x) = \text{first derivative of } f(x),$$

Then, since the derivative of $f(x)$ at x_1 is equal to the slope of the curve at a point x_1,

$$f'(x_1) = f(x_1)/(x_1 - x_2)$$

where

$$x_1 = \text{first guess}$$
$$x_2 = \text{second guess}.$$

Study Fig. 5.1 for the geometry involved. Solving for x_2 yields,

$$x_2 = x_1 - f(x_1)/f'(x_1) \qquad\qquad 5.1$$

Equation 5.1 can be repeated many times to give better estimates of the value of x which will make $f(x) = 0$.

In the example being considered,

$$f(x) = x^2 - 20 \qquad\qquad 5.2$$
$$f'(x) = 2x \qquad\qquad 5.3$$

Therefore, the new value of x can be estimated by the iterative equation (obtained by substituting equations 5.2 and 5.3 into Equation 5.1)

$$x_2 = x_1 - (x_1^2 - 20)/(2x_1) \qquad\qquad 5.4$$

or in BASIC,

$$\text{LET } X = X - (X{\uparrow}2 - 20)/(2*X).$$

The method of Newton-Raphson converges very slowly if the slope of $f(x)$ versus x should be small. Furthermore, if the slope becomes zero at any point, the method does not yield a solution. The situations of small slope or zero slope should be tested in the computer program to avoid endless iteration.

5.3   ORDINARY DIFFERENTIAL EQUATIONS WITH INITIAL CONDITIONS

For students in science and engineering, closed-form solutions of either ordinary or partial differential equations are common and can often be obtained by reference to a handbook. Unfortunately, however, many applied problems lead to differential equations for which there are no known analytical solutions. This section describes the fourth order Runge-Kutta, a useful method for solving differential equations with initial boundary conditions. The reader is referred to the index of this book for other examples of practical numerical methods. The method of Runge-Kutta has particular applications to computer programming and can most easily be understood by considering a first order differential equation.

Suppose that the linear velocity of an object changes with time as follows:

$$v = 2 + t^2 + y \qquad\qquad \text{(algebra)}$$
$$\text{LET } V = 2 + T{\uparrow}2 + Y. \qquad \text{(BASIC)}$$

or, in a word equation:

$$Y \text{ velocity} = 2 + \text{Time squared} + Y \text{ displacement}.$$

The problem is to solve for the displacement, Y, of the object at a time, $T=9$ seconds, given that at $T=3$ seconds, $V=12$ meters/seconds and $Y=1$ meter. A very poor approximation would be that

$$y_9 = y_3 + v_3(t_9 - t_3)$$

where the subscripts refer to the times. This expression, based on the assumption that the velocity remains constant during the time interval of $t_9 - t_3$ (6 seconds), is not correct because clearly the velocity increases as the square of the elapsed time. Consider, however, that the approximation becomes better if the time interval is made much smaller, for instance, 1.0 second. As the time increment approaches zero, there is obviously less and less change in velocity.

In Fig. 5.2, the slope, MO, at the initial point (y_0, t_0) is known since the velocity is, by defiintion, the change in displacement divided by the change in time or the slope of the displacement curve. The velocity will change during the interval of one second between T3 and T4. The Runge-Kutta method strives to make a reasonable average of the velocity during the time interval, T3 to T4. The following terms enter into the calculation of this average velocity:

LET $M0 = $ *initial velocity which is given*

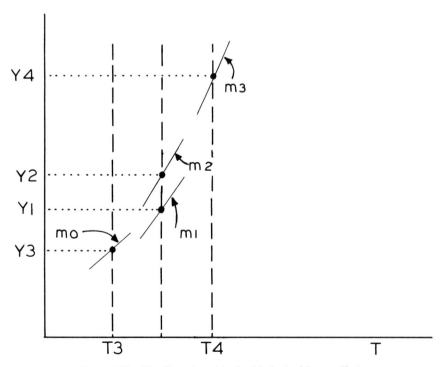

Figure 5.2   The Slopes used in the Method of Runge-Kutta.

LET M1 = *first estimate of the velocity at the middle of the time interval. This is found by:*
$$= 2 + (T3 + .5)\uparrow2 + (Y3 + .5*M0) \quad where \quad .5 \quad is \quad \frac{1}{2} \quad of$$
the time increment.

LET M2 = *second estimate of the velocity at the middle of the time interval. This is found by:*
$$= 2 + (T3 + .5)\uparrow2 + (Y3 + .5*M1)$$

LET M3 = *first estimate of the velocity at the end of the time interval. This is found by:*
$$= 2 + (T3 + 1)\uparrow2 + (Y3 + 1*M2).$$

The weighted average velocity for the interval of T3 to T4 seconds becomes,

$$(M0 + 2*M1 + 2*M2 + M3)/6$$

Therefore, the Runge-Kutta estimate of Y4 at time T4 is,

LET Y4 = Y3 + (M0 + 2M1 + 2M2 + M3) * (T4 − T3)/6

This can easily be re-written as an iterative set of equations as follows, where D = time increment:

LET M0 = V
LET M1 = 2 + (T + D/2)↑2 + (Y + D/2*M0)
LET M2 = 2 + (T + D/2)↑2 + (Y + D/2*M1)
LET M3 = 2 + (T + D)↑2 + (Y + D*M2)
LET Y = Y + (M0 + 2*M1 + 2*M2 + M3) *D/6
LET T = T + D
LET V = 2 + T↑2 + Y

Several applied examples of the Runge-Kutta technique will be demonstrated in later chapters.

5.4 NUMERICAL INTEGRATION

Evaluation of integrals by finite difference methods is one of several techniques available. This section deals exclusively with Simpson's Rule; however, other methods exist and some are described in subsequent chapters of this book.

Simpson's Rule consists of connecting successive groups of three points on a curve by second-degree parabolas, and summing the areas under the parabolas to obtain the approximate area under the curve. In Fig. 5.3, the geometry of this method is shown. Simpson's Rule (given without proof) relates to the integral of f(x), where f(x) is a quadratic polynomial, as follows:

$$f(x)dx = h/3 * (f_0 + 4*f_1 + 4*f_2 + 4*f_3 + 4*f_4 + 4*f_5 + f_6)$$

Where,

$$f_0 = f(x_0) = \text{value of the function at } x_0$$
$$f_1 = f(x_1) = \text{value of the function at } x_1$$

and so on.

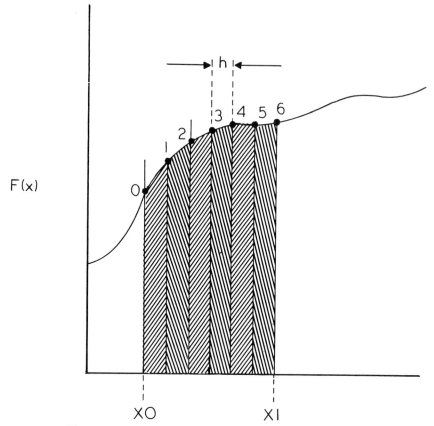

Figure 5.3   The Graphical Representation of Simpson's Rule.

This is Simpson's one-third rule and will yield the approximate area under the curve when the area is divided into an even number of strips. Applications of Simpson's Rule are demonstrated in subsequent chapters.

   In summary, it should be emphasized that there are many more very useful computer-math techniques. In subsequent chapters of this book, there will be an opportunity to demonstrate several methods of solving complicated problems using numerical methods and a computer.

PART II

COMPUTER APPLICATIONS IN THE CLASSROOM

INTRODUCTION

The purpose of writing this book has been to encourage the reader to use the computer as a means to greater insight and understanding of a certain subject matter. As with other learning tools, considerable effort and diligent practice is required to make the computer a useful learning assistant. The subsequent chapters demonstrate by numerous examples in physics, chemistry, and engineering how the computer can be used in the classroom in a learning mode.

The organization of the next three chapters has been to group subject matter into unique and often independent lessons. These lesson units are designed to be used as additional or substitute portions of an already existing course. A brief outline of the *Lesson Characteristics* is given at the beginning of each lesson to facilitate matching of the lesson to possible classroom situations. An explanation of these characteristics is as follows:

COURSE LEVEL (a) high school
(b) college, introductory
(c) college, intermediate
(d) college, advanced

These broad categories indicate the student academic level suggested for each lesson.

MATH BACKGROUND REQUIRED (a) algebra
(b) trigonometry
(c) analytic geometry
(d) calculus

The divisions indicate mathematics achievement level desirable for lesson understanding. Calculus assumes a knowledge of a, b, and c. Analytic geometry assumes a knowledge of a and b, and so on.

PEDAGOGY (a) computer tutorial
(b) computer quiz
(c) computer learning
(d) computer simulation

Each of these categories needs some explanation. *Computer tutorial* refers to a question-answer series between student and computer where wrong answers are followed by remedial explanation by the computer. *Computer quiz* indicates a series of questions initiated by the computer and answered by the student without remedial explanation. The student score is automatically recorded for the teacher's records. *Computer learning* refers to the situation of a student programming a problem for the computer in such a manner as to gain greater insight into the problem and subject matter. *Computer simulation* indicates a program which causes the computer to mimic a physical phenomenon and to graphically display the results. This allows students to study the nature of a situation and analyze the consequences of several actions before approaching the actual physical problem.

PROBLEM APPROACH   (a) analytic solution
                    (c) numerical solution

These two categories are, in fact, not mutually exclusive. An *analytic solution* will refer to the use of one or more algebraic equalities to find the final answer. The analytic solution, sometimes referred to as a closed-form solution, will normally have one equation relating the unknown quantities to the known quantities. A *numerical solution* is required when there is no simple relationship between known and unknown quantities. Some method of approximation becomes necessary to predict the final answer. The numerical solution is characterized by guessing techniques, averaging, and estimations which are based on sound theoretical grounds.

STUDENT PARTICIPATION   (a) uses prepared program
                         (b) assists in program writing

In some cases, the student will benefit most by using a program *prepared in advance* by the teacher. In other cases there is more to be gained by the student's active participation in *program writing*.

PROGRAMMING SKILLS   (a) introductory BASIC
                      (b) intermediate BASIC

TIME OF STUDENT INVOLVEMENT   (a) in class (time allowed)
                               (b) out of class (time
                                                  allowed)

In most cases computer involvement requires students to go to available computer terminals for actual 'on-line' experience. In order to make the experience fruitful a certain amount of *in class* time must be spent to explain the problem, and a certain amount of *out of class* time must be spent by the student.

SUGGESTED READINGS   (a) appropriate readings

(Several references are suggested for most lessons in order to amplify the background and theory, and to give an example of a non-computer approach to the same subject matter.)

This outline of the specific lesson characteristics is then followed by a more detailed *Lesson Description* to give the reader a clear picture of the nature of the problem to be treated in the particular lesson. In most cases, a preliminary reference to the suggested readings should be made at this time. Following the lesson description, the reader will find the minimum necessary *Background and Theory* which should make possible an understanding of the physical phenomenon being described. The emphasis in this development has been to expose the equations and functions in the BASIC language from the outset. However when (a) it is more clear, or (b) BASIC symbols do not exist, or (c) it is more complete, the equations are also written in the normal algebra. In all instances, the algebra will use lower case letters, whereas the BASIC will use all capital letters. For example:

$$f = ma \qquad \text{algebraic equality}$$
$$\text{LET } F = M*A \quad \text{BASIC equivalent}$$

It must be emphasized at this time that the algebraic equation always indicates an equality, whereas, the BASIC equivalent may often only be an instruction to the computer which, when executed, produces the same equality as the algebraic equality. This point will be emphasized in subsequent examples.

In each lesson there is sufficient background and theory to enable the reader to understand the computer solution. However, the suggested references invariably treat the same subject matter but in a conventional form.

Each lesson will also contain a section of *Computer Techniques* to point out special methods used in the solution of the lesson problem. Another section, *Comments about the Computer Program,* will explain the essential features of the program in the particular lesson and should be read before an attempt is made to interpret the BASIC program. The computer output produced by the program and its learning value are considered in the section entitled *Discussion of Computer-Generated Results.* Finally, an *Appendix* at the end of some lessons contains a very detailed explanation of every step of the program. The Appendix need not be referred to if the program can be read and understood.

The organization of subject matter into independent lessons should encourage the teacher or student to use the computer as a parallel to an existing course. The problems are not only practical, but also typical of those encountered in most undergraduate science courses. The coordinated use of these lessons should enhance the students' understanding of the subject matter and simultaneously provide the student with a working knowledge of computers in the framework of applied problems.

CHAPTER 6

COMPUTERS IN PHYSICS EDUCATION

6.1 INTRODUCTION

Physics as a science deals with universal concepts that can normally be described by mathematical relationships. A strong aptitude for mathematics appears to be a prerequisite for students studying physics. Since most students must participate in at least one semester of physics, the lack of a mathematical aptitude or inclination often makes the physics course a discouraging experience. It is unfortunate that the interesting and vital concepts of physics are often lost to those students who fail to understand the mathematical techniques which are invoked.

This chapter suggests several methods by which the computer can be used to assist students with varying mathematical abilities to understand and retain both the mathematical manipulations and the concepts of physics. Sir Isaac Newton began his description of falling objects by introducing some of the numerical techniques stressed in this chapter. Newton's invention of calculus followed from the lack of rapid computing techniques which are necessary for the numerical approach to problems.

A representative sampling of physics problems which can be used by the non-calculus student has been selected for presentation in this chapter. Furthermore, several computer-generated graphical solutions to difficult concepts are presented as an indication of the power of the computer to simulate physical phenomena for demonstration purposes. Students have been required to prepare programs of this nature for laboratory and homework assignments. Based upon actual experiences with students, these problems indicate that the computer encourages the inventive processes of science. By careful design the computer can assist the student to a fuller comprehension of the problem solution and a greater insight into the subject matter.

The chapter is organized in separate, more or less, independent lessons. Each lesson is completely specified as to physics content, level of difficulty, and programming skills required. The lessons are presented in an order similar to the subject matter of an ordinary undergraduate physics course.

The lessons presented in this chapter could be incorporated directly into an existing undergraduate physics course in two ways. First, for the physics course in which the student is required to know calculus, the students may be required to write programs using the numerical approach to problem solving. The programs in this chapter would then be useful as examples. Second, for the non-calculus physics course, the straightforward approach of numerical analysis plus the simulation techniques can assist the student to grasp the basic concepts of physics.

In Sections 6.2 through 6.7 the reader will find a computer solution of projectile motion. The treatment of projectile motion begins with the 'ideal' problem (simplifying assumptions) and gradually the 'real' factors such as air resistance are added. The numerical solution of simple harmonic motion is presented in Section 6.8 and is followed in Section 6.9 with the addition of friction. A forcing-function is added to harmonic motion in Section 6.10 to make the problem more realistic. Calculus has not been used in the solution of these problems.

The treatment of optical phenomena (interference and diffraction) in Sections 6.11 and 6.12 uses only the addition of vectors. All readers are urged to read Chapters 2 and 4 of this book before continuing to this and subsequent chapters.

6.2   PROJECTILE FLIGHT I

Lesson Characteristics:

PHYSICS LEVEL   pre-college and junior college

MATHEMATICS BACKGROUND REQUIRED   algebra and trigonometry

PEDAGOGY   computer learning

PROBLEM APPROACH   numerical solution

STUDENT PARTICIPATION   assists in program writing

PROGRAMMING SKILLS   introductory BASIC

TIME OF STUDENT INVOLVEMENT   in class—20 minutes out of class—1 hour

RECOMMENDED READING   (2) Sec 3–2 to 3–7
Sec 4–1 to 4–3
(3) Chapter 3—Sec 2 to 6
Chapter 4—Sec 11
(4) Sec 9.4 to 9.6

Lesson Description: The rudiments of Newtonian physics are often taught to non-science majors at college and high school students who have had only geometry, trigonometry, and algebra. The basic definitions of velocity and acceleration are taught in terms of word descriptions which are meaningful. However, the related formulas such as: $y = y_0 + v_0 t + \frac{1}{2} at^2$, have little intuitive meaning.

In this section, the basic definitions of velocity and acceleration and one of Newton's laws of motion are developed by means of a non-calculus approach to a problem of, *"motion with constant acceleration."* Velocity and acceleration are introduced by word descriptions and incremental terms approximating the true calculus definitions. This form of presentation has been found to be (1) easily understood, (2) meaningful, (3) oriented towards the non-calculus student in the solution by numerical methods, and finally (4) more clear for the calculus student in the precise understanding of the mathematical relationship that he is studying.

Several methods of introducing the student to the computer numerical methods are suggested. The method to be stressed in this section is to have the student: (1) increment a few of the approximated definitions by hand, (2) make a plot of this data, and (3) have him write a simple computer program to complete the calculations started by hand.

Background and Theory: The basic definitions of velocity and acceleration, and Newton's second law of motion are needed for the trajectory problems of this chapter.

$$\text{velocity: } v = \frac{\text{change in distance}}{\text{change in time}}$$
$$= \frac{s_2 - s_1}{t_2 - t_1} = \frac{\Delta s}{\Delta t}$$

or rate of change of displacement with time. Although this is an average velocity, the instantaneous velocity can be approximated by $\Delta s / \Delta t$, as Δt becomes very small.

$$v = \Delta s / \Delta t \tag{6.2–1}$$

$$\text{acceleration: } a = \frac{\text{change in velocity}}{\text{change in time}}$$
$$= \frac{v_2 - v_1}{t_2 - t_1}$$

or rate of change of velocity with time.

$$a = \Delta v / \Delta t \tag{6.2–2}$$

Instantaneous acceleration $= \Delta v / \Delta t$ in the limit as Δt becomes very small.

Equations (6.2–1) and 6.2–2) can be rewritten as incremental values of displacement and velocity:

    (1) From Equation 6.2–1
$$\Delta s = v \ (\Delta t) \tag{6.2–3}$$
    (2) From Equation 6.2–2
$$\Delta v = a \ (\Delta t) \tag{6.2–4}$$

The displacement may be approximated using Equation (6.2–3) to estimate the next position.

$$s = s_0 + \Delta s$$
$$s = s_0 + v \ (\Delta t)$$
$$\text{LET } S = S + V * T1 \quad \text{(BASIC equivalent)} \tag{6.2–5}$$

(NOTE: The BASIC equivalent is an *instruction,* not an equality.)

In a similar manner the instantaneous velocity may be approximated using Equation (6.2–4).

$$v = v_0 + \Delta v$$
$$v = v_0 + a \ (\Delta t)$$
$$\text{LET } V = V + A * T1 \tag{6.2–6}$$

The velocity of Equation 6.2–5 and the acceleration of Equation 6.2–6 are the average values over the interval of time, Δt, and become approximate instantaneous values as Δt becomes very small.

Newton's Second Law may be stated as follows:

$$Force = Mass \times Acceleration \text{ or, } f = ma.$$

For the case of the constant acceleration of gravity in a frictionless reference, the acceleration becomes that of gravity and:

$$f = mg$$
$$\text{where, } g = -9.8 \text{ m/s/s}$$
$$\text{LET } F = M*G. \qquad (6.2-7)$$

The trajectory of a ball thrown in the air at an initial velocity and angle from the horizon is normally computed by application of a derived formula in calculus. Furthermore, the case normally studied is for frictionless flight at constant acceleration. This 'ideal' case will be considered initially in order to become familiar with several numerical methods for solving these time-dependent equations. After the numerical methods have been introduced, the more 'real' case of friction will be studied. Since the acceleration is a constant (g) for the problem of this section, Equation (6.2–6) will become

$$v = v_0 = g \, (\Delta t)$$
$$\text{LET } V = V + G*T1 \qquad (6.2-8)$$

Computer Technique: The incremental method used in Program (6.2A) of this section is essentially Euler's method described in many numerical analysis books. The student should master this simple method before trying to improve upon it. The purpose is not to teach the numerical method, but to enable the thought process to lead to a better understanding of the basic principle involved. For example, the student may obtain a deeper insight into the meaning of instantaneous velocity, changing vector quantities and the analytical model being taught. The first program a student may be asked to write on the projectile (or ball, etc.) problem may be done prior to his knowledge of the analytical solution. He could be asked to estimate the highest point of travel, time of flight, and total distance traversed by using each of three time increments 1, .1, and .01 seconds. He could be encouraged to write the program, debug it, try the three time increments, and then interpolate (linear interpolation will give satisfactory results) between data points for the desired results.

There are several approaches available to indoctrinate the student to the computer and its simple language. One method that works well is to give the student a simple program outlining for him how it works; next, assign the student the task of describing (as homework) in detail what the program does. He may then run the program and obtain several iterations of data for different initial conditions, e.g., find the launch angle for maximum trajectory or height, etc., by trial and error. Another method of introducing the computer would be to have the student write a series of word and symbol statements describing in detail how to set the problem up so that a computer linguist could convert his words into a working program. After this assignment has been submitted, he could then be given a program which will do the job. Have him study the program and run it. Then quiz him on the techniques used. He should now be ready for the analytical solutions and have a better understanding of the basic principles involved.

For this problem, it would be helpful for the student to apply the numerical method in several iterations calculated by hand, before attempting to write the computer program.

Initial conditions for all of the methods to be discussed with the trajectory problem are:

$$\text{Initial Velocity, } V_0 = 100 \text{ meters/second,}$$
$$\text{Initial Angle, } A = 45°.$$

The results of the first three iterations, for $\Delta T = T1 = 1$ second, and $V2 = Y - $ velocity, are shown graphically in Figure 6.2A for Y versus time:

$$\begin{aligned} v_1 &= v_0 \sin(a) \\ \text{LET} \quad V2 &= V0*SIN(A) \end{aligned} = 70.7 \text{ M/S } (\textit{Initial Y Velocity})$$

$$\begin{aligned} y_1 &= y_0 + v_1 \Delta t \\ \text{LET} \quad Y &= Y + V2*T1 \end{aligned} = 0 + 70.7 \text{ M } (\textit{Y after 1 second})$$

$$\begin{aligned} v_2 &= v_1 + g \Delta t \\ \text{LET} \quad V2 &= V2 + G*T1 \end{aligned} = 70.7 - 9.8 \text{ M/S } (\textit{V after 1 second})$$

$$\begin{aligned} y_2 &= y_1 + v_2 \Delta t \\ \text{LET} \quad Y &= Y + V2*T1 \end{aligned} = 70.7 + 60.9 \ (\textit{Y after 2 seconds})$$

$$\begin{aligned} v_3 &= v_2 + g \Delta t \\ \text{LET} \quad V2 &= V2 + G*T1 \end{aligned} = 60.9 - 9.8$$

$$= 51.1 \text{ M/S } (\textit{V after 2 seconds})$$

etc.

Comments About the Computer Program: The Program 6.2A will translate these basic equations in small incremental steps chosen by the operator. The input data is: V0 (initial velocity), A (initial angle), T1 (ΔT), and C9 (number of ΔT iterations desired before printing the result). Furthermore, the initial X and Y component velocities are calculated in statements 150 and 160. The analytical solution is included in statements 170 to 260 in order to compare the various methods to the theory. This will then give confidence when attempts are made to solve problems which cannot be solved by analytical techniques. These theoretical values utilize V2 and should be solved prior to entering the numerical solution loop since V2 is iterated to a different value after the numerical solution has begun.

Note that printed explanations and calculations in statements 220 or 230 can be in a single print statement by careful use of the quotation marks and commas. Some computers require semicolons between printed matter and variables if the answers are to fall immediately after the equal sign in the printed matter.

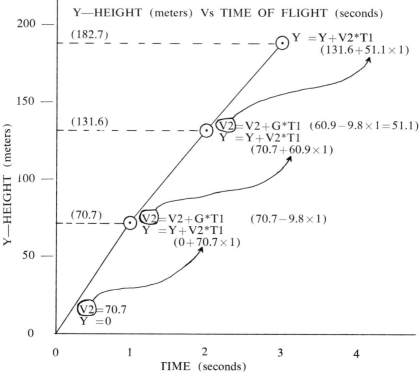

FIG. 6.2A. Simple iteration scheme for solving the projectile problem. (Euler Method)

The loop for iterating the numerical method of solution is:

300   LET X=X+V1*T1
      ↓
310   LET Y=Y+V2*T1
      ↓
320   LET T=T+T1
      ↓
330   LET I=I+1
      ↓
340   LET S=SQR (X*X+Y*Y)
      ↓
350   LET V2=V2+G*T1
      ↓
360   IF Y<=0 THEN 460   *LOOP TEST*
      ↓
410   IF I=C THEN 430
      ↓
420   GO TO 300

```
100 REM ***************ROCKET TRAJECTORY 1 ***************
110 PRINT"WHAT IS INITIAL VELOCITY, ANGLE, TIME INCREMENT,"
120 PRINT"AND PRINT INTERVAL";
130 INPUT VO , A , T1 , C
140 LET A = A*PI/180
150 LET V1 = VO*COS(A)
160 LET V2 = VO*SIN(A)
170 LET G = -9.8
180 LET T5 = -V2/G
190 LET X9 = 2*T5*V1
200 LET Y5 = V2*T5+G*T5+2/2
210 PRINT
220 PRINT"THEORY: TOTAL TIME =" 2*T5
230 PRINT"Y MAX ="Y5,"TOTAL DIST. ="X9
240 PRINT
250 PRINT"X VELOCITY ="V1
260 PRINT
270 PRINT"X DIST.","Y HEIGHT","DISTANCE","Y VELOCITY","TIME"
280 PRINT
300 LET X = X+V1*T1
310 LET Y = Y+V2*T1
320 LET T = T+T1
330 LET I = I+1
340 LET S = SQR(X*X+Y*Y)
350 LET V2 = V2+G*T1
360 IF Y<=0 THEN 460
410 IF I = C THEN 430
420 GOTO 300
430 PRINT X , Y , S , V2 , T
440 LET I = 0
450 GOTO 300
460 PRINT X , Y , S , V2 , T
470 PRINT
480 END

>
```

PROGRAM 6.2A. Simple Euler (Rocket trajectory)

This series of summations and one calculation ($S = \sqrt{x^2 + y^2}$) are the basic components of the iterative loop. The initial value (zero in this case for X, Y, T and counter, I) of each variable is added bit by bit each time the loop is iterated. In some computers all variables must be initialized to zero in this kind of summation activity since any number whatsoever may be in the computer's memory for that particular variable location. In this time-shared-computer all memory locations are initialized to zero before each program is run. Therefore, the value of X=X+V1*T1 for the first pass through the program will be X=0+V1*T1; the second pass will be: X=V1*T1+V1*T1+etc., until the program stops. This brings up the question of how to stop the program. The total flight path is of interest but surely when the projectile hits the ground the program should stop. Therefore, when $Y \leq 0$, stop calculating, otherwise go through the loop again, adding a little more to X, Y, T, V2 (V_y), indexing a counter and finding total distance. (The reason for the counter will be obvious a little later.) Then print the final values when $Y \leq 0$

$$360 \quad \text{IF } Y <= 0 \text{ THEN } 460$$
(Last print statement number)

If Y is not ≤ 0 then continue the loop. If the position of the projectile is required then print or plot the data. For example, if the input data are: $V(0) = 100$ m/s, $A = 45°$ and $T1 = .01$ seconds, then 100 calculations will be made for each one second duration of the projectile's travel. The projectile will travel for over 14 seconds which means that 1400 sets (lines) of data could be printed (which would not be very useful). Besides, it would take a long time to print 1400 lines of data on a typewriter. Thus one introduces a counter, (I), and instructs the computer to print only when the counter is equal to the print interval in the data (C). Now data can be printed each second by making $C = 100$ (when $T1 = .01$).

410	IF I=C THEN 430	(PRINT answers)
420	GO TO 300	(Start of summation loop)
430	PRINT X, Y, S, V2, T	

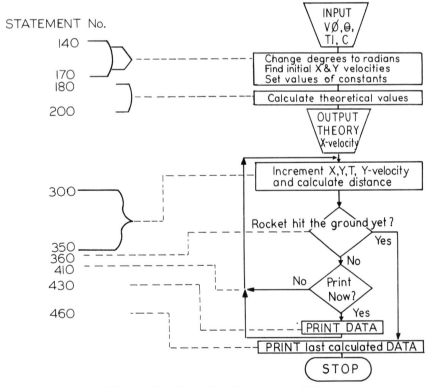

Figure 6.2B. Flow chart for Program 6.2A.

```
440   LET I=0                              (Begin new count)
450   GO TO 300
460   PRINT X, Y, S, V2, T
480   END
```

The entire program and its flow chart are shown in Program 6.2A and Figure 6.2B respectively.

In Table 6.2A the time column is almost, but not quite a whole number (integer) after the first second. This is due to round-off error in digital computers.

Appendix A6.2 describes a way to eliminate this round-off-error.

Discussion of Computer Results: Tables 6.2A through 6.2E use the same input data with the exception of the time increment, T1. The time interval becomes progressively smaller from one second to 0.001 second intervals. The theoretical values are printed prior to the numerical listing for comparison purposes.

The one second interval, Table 6.2B, shows considerable error, and would indicate that a smaller time interval should be used. The student should be able to analyze the results by trying several time increments, and checking the time for total flight by comparing the value of y just before the last data line and interpolating this value with the bottom line value of Y in order to obtain a better time of flight.

```
WHAT IS INITIAL VELOCITY, ANGLE, TIME INCREMENT,
AND PRINT INTERVAL? 100, 45, .01, 100


THEORY: TOTAL TIME = 14.43075064
Y MAX = 255.1020408            TOTAL DIST. = 1020.408163

X VELOCITY = 70.71067812
```

X DIST.	Y HEIGHT	DISTANCE	Y VELOCITY	TIME
70.71067812	65.85967809	96.63072596	60.91067809	1
141.4213562	121.9193562	186.7199224	51.11067807	1.999999999
212.1320344	168.1790342	270.7105235	41.31067805	2.999999999
282.8427124	204.6387122	349.1088691	31.51067802	3.999999998
353.5533905	231.2983901	422.4913552	21.71067801	4.999999996
424.2640685	248.1580681	491.5103525	11.910678	5.999999994
494.9747465	255.217746	556.8986421	2.110677999	6.999999992
565.6854245	252.477424	619.4714272	-7.689322002	7.99999999
636.3961026	239.9371019	680.1248505	-17.48932201	8.999999986
707.1067806	217.5967799	739.8299519	-27.28932202	9.999999981
777.8174586	185.4564578	799.6212207	-37.08932204	10.99999998
848.5281366	143.5161357	860.5793862	-46.88932206	11.99999997
919.2388147	91.77581361	923.8088538	-56.68932208	12.99999997
989.9494927	30.2354915	990.4111182	-66.48932211	13.99999996
1021.769298	-0.654903453	1021.769508	-70.89932212	14.44999996

```
>
```

TABLE 6.2A.

WHAT IS INITIAL VELOCITY, ANGLE, TIME INCREMENT,
AND PRINT INTERVAL? 100, 45, 1, 1

THEORY: TOTAL TIME = 14.43075064
Y MAX = 255.1020408   TOTAL DIST. = 1020.408163

X VELOCITY = 70.71067812

X DIST.	Y HEIGHT	DISTANCE	Y VELOCITY	TIME
70.71067812	70.71067812	100	60.91067812	1
141.4213562	131.6213562	193.1946723	51.11067812	2
212.1320344	182.7320343	279.9839216	41.31067812	3
282.8427125	224.0427125	360.8256324	31.51067812	4
353.5533906	255.5533906	436.2425191	21.71067812	5
424.2640687	277.2640687	506.8287322	11.91067811	6
494.9747468	289.1747468	573.2556447	2.110678115	7
565.685425	291.2854249	636.2760398	-7.689321885	8
636.3961031	283.596103	696.7257349	-17.48932189	9
707.1067812	266.1067811	755.5215543	-27.28932189	10
777.8174593	238.8174593	813.654582	-37.08932189	11
848.5281374	201.7281374	872.1778726	-46.88932189	12
919.2388156	154.8388155	932.1883172	-56.68932189	13
989.9494937	98.1494936	994.803158	-66.48932189	14
1060.660172	31.66017172	1061.132587	-76.28932189	15
1131.37085	-44.62915017	1132.25075	-86.08932189	16

TABLE 6.2B.

WHAT IS INITIAL VELOCITY, ANGLE, TIME INCREMENT,
AND PRINT INTERVAL? 100, 45, .1, 10

THEORY: TOTAL TIME = 14.43075064
Y MAX = 255.1020408   TOTAL DIST. = 1020.408163

X VELOCITY = 70.71067812

X DIST.	Y HEIGHT	DISTANCE	Y VELOCITY	TIME
70.71067812	66.30067811	96.9318313	60.91067811	1
141.4213562	122.8013562	187.2970184	51.11067811	2
212.1320344	169.5020343	271.534417	41.31067811	3
282.8427125	206.4027124	350.1457978	31.51067811	4
353.5533906	233.5033905	423.7025294	21.7106781	5
424.2640687	250.8040686	492.8515809	11.9106781	6
494.9747468	258.3047467	558.3201073	2.110678103	7
565.6854249	256.0054248	620.9176898	-7.689321897	8
636.396103	243.9061029	681.5351693	-17.4893219	9
707.1067811	222.006781	741.1389956	-27.2893219	10
777.8174592	190.3074591	800.7602193	-37.0893219	11
848.5281373	148.8081372	861.4777197	-46.8893219	12
919.2388154	97.5088153	924.3960022	-56.6893219	13
989.9494935	36.40949339	990.6188222	-66.48932191	14
1032.3759	-4.954099754	1032.387787	-72.36932191	14.6

TABLE 6.2C.

WHAT IS INITIAL VELOCITY, ANGLE, TIME INCREMENT,
AND PRINT INTERVAL? 100, 45, .01, 100

THEORY: TOTAL TIME = 14.43075064
Y MAX = 255.1020408   TOTAL DIST. = 1020.408163

X VELOCITY = 70.71067812

X DIST.	Y HEIGHT	DISTANCE	Y VELOCITY	TIME
70.71067812	65.85967809	96.63072596	60.91067809	1
141.4213562	121.9193562	186.7199224	51.11067807	2
212.1320344	168.1790342	270.7105235	41.31067805	3
282.8427124	204.6387122	349.1088691	31.51067802	4
353.5533905	231.2983901	422.4913552	21.71067801	5
424.2640685	248.1580681	491.5103525	11.910678	6
494.9747465	255.217746	556.8986421	2.110677999	7
565.6854245	252.477424	619.4714272	-7.689322002	8
636.3961026	239.9371019	680.1248505	-17.48932201	9
707.1067806	217.5967799	739.8299519	-27.28932202	10
777.8174586	185.4564578	799.6212207	-37.08932204	11
848.5281366	143.5161357	860.5793862	-46.88932206	12
919.2388147	91.77581361	923.8088538	-56.68932208	13
989.9494927	30.2354915	990.4111182	-66.48932211	14
1021.769298	-0.654903453	1021.769508	-70.89932212	14.45

TABLE 6.2D.

WHAT IS INITIAL VELOCITY, ANGLE, TIME INCREMENT,
AND PRINT INTERVAL? 100, 45, .001, 1000

THEORY: TOTAL TIME = 14.43075064
Y MAX = 255.1020408   TOTAL DIST. = 1020.408163

X VELOCITY = 70.71067812

X DIST.	Y HEIGHT	DISTANCE	Y VELOCITY	TIME
70.71067812	65.81557797	96.60067445	60.910678	1
141.4213561	121.8311557	186.6623435	51.11067788	2
212.1320338	168.0467331	270.6283508	41.31067777	3
282.8427115	204.4623103	349.0054953	31.51067765	4
353.5533891	231.0778874	422.3706773	21.71067753	5
424.2640668	247.8934645	491.3768086	11.91067744	6
494.9747444	254.9090414	556.7572334	2.110677405	7
565.6854221	252.1246183	619.3277161	-7.689322611	8
636.3960997	239.5401952	679.9849269	-17.48932268	9
707.1067774	217.155772	739.7003609	-27.28932279	10
777.817455	184.9713487	799.508845	-37.08932291	11
848.5281327	142.9869253	860.4912857	-46.88932303	12
919.2388103	91.20250188	923.75207	-56.68932314	13
989.949488	29.61807851	990.3924572	-66.48932326	14
1020.496501	-0.017649964	1020.496501	-70.72292331	14.432

TABLE 6.2E.

APPENDIX

A-6.2

DETAILED DISCUSSION OF THE PROGRAMS 6.2A AND 6.2B

110   PRINT "WHAT IS INITIAL VELOCITY, ANGLE, TIME
        INCREMENT,"
120   PRINT "AND PRINT INTERVAL";
130   INPUT V0, A, T1, C

These statements ask for the input data: V0 (initial velocity), A (initial angle), T1 (time increment, ΔT) and C (number of ΔT iterations desired before printing the result.

140   LET A=A*PI/180, or
140   LET A=A*3.14159205/180

Since the computer deals only in radian angular measure, the degrees are converted to radians. Some computers have the numerical value of π in their memories, others do not.

150   LET V1=V0*COS(A)
160   LET V2=V0*SIN(A)

These statements calculate the initial X and Y component velocities from the initial angle and velocity.

170   LET G=−9.8
180   LET T5=−V2/G
190   LET X9=2*T5*V1
200   LET Y5=V2*T5+G*T5↑2/2
210   PRINT
220   PRINT "THEORY: TOTAL TIME=" 2*T5
230   PRINT "Y MAX=" Y5, "TOTAL DIST. =" X9
240   PRINT
250   PRINT "X VELOCITY =" V1
260   PRINT

These statements calculate and print the theoretical values (NO friction) of total time of flight, maximum value of Y height, total distance traveled (along x-axis) and x-velocity. These values are calculated from the basic motion equations:

$$s = s_0 + v_0 t + 1/2\ at^2$$

$$(A\text{-}6.2\text{-}9)$$

where $a = g = −9.8$ m/s/s in the y direction

or
$$y = y_0 + v_{y0} t + 1/2\ g t^2 \qquad (A\text{-}6.2\text{-}10)$$

$$\text{LET Y} = V2*T + G*T↑2/2 \qquad \text{(Statement 200)}$$

(This is statement 200 after the total time is calculated (2*T5).)

Since there is no friction or acceleration in the x direction

$$x = v_{xo}t \qquad \text{(A-6.2–11)}$$

where

$$v_{yo} = v_o \sin (A) + gt \qquad \text{(A-6.2–12)}$$

and

$$v_{xo} = v_o \cos (A) \qquad \text{(A-6.2–13)}$$

The time of flight is found by solving Equation (6.2–12) for t, when the y velocity, (V2), is zero:

$$v_{yo} = 0 = v_o \sin (A) + gt$$

and

$$t_{max} = -v_o \sin (A)/g$$

or

$$t_{total} = 2\, t_{max}$$

180   LET T5 = −V2/G

Now total x-distance and y-max can be calculated from Equations (6.2–10) and (6.2–11).

$$y_{max} = v_{oy}\, t_{max} + 1/2\, g\, t_{max}^2$$

200   LET Y5 = V2*T5 + G*T5↑2/2

and

$$x_{max} = 2\, t_{max}\, v_{ox}$$

190   LET X9 = 2*T5*V1

The initial and final PRINT statements cause the teletypewriter to skip a line, and make the output easier to read. Note that both printed matter and calculations can be written in the same PRINT statement (220 and 230) by careful use of commas, semicolons, and quotation marks. Some computers will require the semicolon between the printed matter and the variables. The comma assures separation between groups of printed matter. Remember, only 5 fields of 15 columns each are set up by use of commas. If printed matter and number answer take up more than 15 spaces then two fields are used by the computer. In this problem, the X velocity does not change, therefore, it can be listed prior to the numeric solution table (Statement 250). The table of data results, Table 6.2A, needs a tabulation index. This can be done two ways, one by placing the entire line between quotation marks: PRINT "X DIST Y HEIGHT DISTANCE Y VELOC-ITY TIME", or an alternate method is to separate each title of the five fields with a comma which is not under quotation marks: 270 PRINT "X DIST.", "Y HEIGHT", "DISTANCE", "Y VELOCITY", "TIME." This method separates each title automatically and positions it over the proper field. In this case, each descriptive phrase can be no greater than 15 characters.

The most important part of the program is the iterative loop which makes the summations on X, Y, T, V1 and V2. Summations were discussed in detail in Chapters 2 and 4. Statements 300 to 350 do the summation of these values plus one counter (statement 330) and one calculation of total distance, $s = \sqrt{x^2 + y^2}$, (statement 340).

300   LET X=X+X1*T1

$(x_1 = x_0 + v_{ox}\Delta t)$ Incrementing and
$(x_2 = x_1 + v_{ox}\Delta t)$ summing value of x.

. . .
. . .
. . .

310   LET Y=Y+V2*T1

$y_1 = y_0 + v_{oy}\Delta t$ Incrementing and
$y_2 = y_1 + v_{1y}\Delta t$ summing value of y.

. . .
. . .
. . .

320   LET T=T+T1

$t_1 = t_0 + \Delta t$ Incrementing and
$t_2 = t_1 + \Delta t$ summing value of t.

. . .
. . .
. . .

330   LET I=I+1   (Counter)

1=0+1   Summing an integer for
2=1+1   counting numbers of
3=2+1   iterations mode.

. . .
. . .
. . .

350   LET V2=V2+G*T1

$v_{1y} = v_{0y} - 9.8\Delta t$
$v_{2y} = v_{1y} - 9.8\Delta t$ Incrementing and
$v_{3y} = v_{2y} - 9.8\Delta t$ summing value of v_y.

. . .
. . .
. . .

340   LET S=SQR(X*X+Y*Y)

This statement is a calculation for total distance traveled for the present value of X and Y.

Statement 350 ends the loop by finding the initial velocity for the next time increment; the program could now print the values of X, Y, S, V2, and T and then return to statement 300 for the next iteration. However the program would never stop so additional statements are required. (Also a small time increment (T1) would cause an extremely long data list.)

360   IF Y$<=$0 THEN 460

If the projectile hits the ground the loop should surely stop and print the last set of values calculated.

410   IF I$=$C THEN 430

If the counter I has incremented a set number of times equal to C then print the answers. This will allow many iterations and only a few printouts. The counter is set to zero after each printing of the output by statement 440. If the counter has not incremented the proper number of times the loop repeats again.

420   GO TO 300
430   PRINT X, Y, S, V2, T
440   LET I$=$0
450   GO TO 300

Program repeats the iteration loop after printing data.

460   PRINT X, Y, S, V2, T
480   END

Last printing of values after trajectory has hit the ground. This will always be a minus value for Y unless an increment leaves Y equal to zero.

ELIMINATION OF THE ROUND-OFF-ERROR OF TABLE 6.2A

One way to eliminate round-off-error is to periodically integerize the incremental summations (if very small increments are used). In this case, time can be made an integer each one second interval. Before entering the loop, a counter is set, $J=1$. Then after each loop has been calculated check for $T+T1=J$. For example: suppose the loop for $T=1$ second had been completed but it was .999999988 seconds in size according to the computer. If $T1=.01$ seconds was added to it, it would become:

$$T=T+T1=\quad \begin{array}{r} .999999998 \\ +\ .01 \\ \hline 1.009999998 \end{array}$$

which is larger than the desired time of 1 second, by approximately 0.01 seconds. If this number is made an integer, it will be 1.000000000 seconds and it can now be called T, vice $T+\Delta t$. The round-off error is corrected and one has improved the appearance of print-out. This operation should take place after the calculation but before printing the one second intervals:

370   IF T+T1$>=$J THEN 390
380   GO TO 300
390   LET T$=$INT(T+.5)
400   LET J$=$J+1

The following example of two numbers for T which are to be rounded off to the nearest integer value should make the point clear:

$$T = 1.500001, \text{ and } T = 1.999999$$

The INT(T) command, would round both numbers off to a value of one, instead of two. However, the command, INT (T+.5) would round both of these numbers to a value of two.

The modified program is shown as Program 6.2B.

It would be more efficient programming to print the output at the same time the round-off-error was corrected. This would eliminate unnecessary steps in the program: The "I" counter would no longer be needed as well as the print interval "C." All reference to these two variables are deleted in Program 6.2C.

```
100 REM ***************ROCKET TRAJECTORY 1 ***************
110 PRINT"WHAT IS INITIAL VELOCITY, ANGLE, TIME INCREMENT,"
120 PRINT"AND PRINT INTERVAL";
130 INPUT VO , A , T1 , C
140 LET A = A*PI/180
150 LET V1 = VO*COS(A)
160 LET V2 = VO*SIN(A)
170 LET G = -9.8
180 LET T5 = -V2/G
190 LET X9 = 2*T5*V1
200 LET Y5 = V2*T5+G*T5↑2/2
210 PRINT
220 PRINT"THEORY: TOTAL TIME =" 2*T5
230 PRINT"Y MAX ="Y5,"TOTAL DIST. ="X9
240 PRINT
250 PRINT"X VELOCITY ="V1
260 PRINT
270 PRINT"X DIST.","Y HEIGHT","DISTANCE","Y VELOCITY","TIME"
280 PRINT
290 LET J = 1
300 LET X = X+V1*T1
310 LET Y = Y+V2*T1
320 LET T = T+T1
330 LET I = I+1
340 LET S = SQR(X*X+Y*Y)
350 LET V2 = V2+G*T1
360 IF Y<=0 THEN 460
370 IF T+T1>=J THEN 390
380 GOTO 410
390 LET T = INT(T+.5)
400 LET J = J+1
410 IF I = C THEN 430
420 GOTO 300
430 PRINT X , Y , S , V2 , T
440 LET I = 0
450 GOTO 300
460 PRINT X , Y , S , V2 , T
470 PRINT
480 END
```

PROGRAM 6.2B. Simple Euler corrected for round-off error

```
100 REM ***************ROCKET TRAJECTORY 1 ***************
110 PRINT"WHAT IS INITIAL VELOCITY, ANGLE, TIME INCREMENT,"
130 INPUT VO, A, T1
140 LET A = A*PI/180
150 LET V1 = VO*COS(A)
160 LET V2 = VO*SIN(A)
170 LET G = -9.8
180 LET T5 = -V2/G
190 LET X9 = 2*T5*V1
200 LET Y5 = V2*T5+G*T5↑2/2
210 PRINT
220 PRINT"THEORY: TOTAL TIME =" 2*T5
230 PRINT"Y MAX ="Y5,"TOTAL DIST. ="X9
240 PRINT
250 PRINT"X VELOCITY ="V1
260 PRINT
270 PRINT"X DIST.","Y HEIGHT","DISTANCE","Y VELOCITY","TIME"
280 PRINT
290 LET J = 1
300 LET X = X+V1*T1
310 LET Y = Y+V2*T1
320 LET T = T+T1
340 LET S = SQR(X*X+Y*Y)
350 LET V2 = V2+G*T1
360 IF Y<=0 THEN 460
370 IF T+T1>=J THEN 390
380 GOTO 300
390 LET T = INT(T+.5)
400 LET J = J+1
430 PRINT X , Y , S , V2 , T
450 GOTO 300
460 PRINT X , Y , S , V2 , T
470 PRINT
480 END
```

-

PROGRAM 6.2C. Simple Euler controlled printing

6.3   TRAJECTORY II

Lesson Characteristics:

PHYSICS LEVEL   pre-college

MATHEMATICS BACKGROUND REQUIRED   algebra and
  trigonometry

PEDAGOGY   computer learning

PROBLEM APPROACH   numerical method

STUDENT PARTICIPATION   assists in program writing

PROGRAMMING SKILLS   introductory BASIC

TIME OF STUDENT INVOLVEMENT   in class—5 minutes,
out of class—30 minutes

RECOMMENDED READING   same as Lesson 6.2

Lesson Description: The lesson description of Section 6.2 applies to this section. A dramatic improvement to the accuracy of the problem is shown in the sample printed data. The programming effort to realize this improvement is minuscule, and the student will continue to utilize this corrected Euler method for more complex problems. The very similiar modified Euler method is also shown. The comparison of the methods of Section 6.2 at very small integration intervals and Section 6.3 at larger integration intervals demonstrates the danger of error accumulations.

Background and Theory: The general background and theory of Section 6.2 still apply to this section. In order to prepare for difficult problems, methods of greater accuracy than Section 6.2 are required. The student should be expected to adapt to advanced methods as the problems become more difficult. Program 6.3A is an example of the easiest correction which can be made to the simple Euler Method of Section 6.2.

Computer Technique: The technique utilized in Section 6.2 was to find the position at the end of an interval based upon the slope (velocity) at the beginning of the interval. The result is a Y position which is slightly above the true position. (This is evident from the comparison of Y height versus time for the various time increments used in Section 6.2). For cases of constant acceleration, an easy correction that can be made is to pre-compute the velocity at the mid-time-point of the first interval, i.e., for $T = T1/2$. This will allow the predicted value of Y to use the slope at the mid-time-point on each successive iteration instead of the slope at the beginning of each interval. The only difference between this "corrected" Euler Method and the "modified" Euler Method is that the slope at the mid-time-point is calculated inside of the loop instead of prior to entering the loop.

The student should work this particular problem out by hand so as to see the dramatic difference between the accuracies of Section 6.2 and this section (See Figs. 6.3A and 6.3B). In order to get the same approximate accuracy with the simple Euler Method, time increments of .001 seconds had to be used. The methods of this section are approximately 1000 times more accurate for this problem.

Comments About the Computer Program:

To obtain Program 6.3A, one statement has been added to Program 6.2C prior to the iteration loop:

290   LET V2 = V2 + G*T1/2

Now, the initial slope starting the loop for $T1 = 1$ second is: $70.7 - 9.8/2 = 65.8$ m/s vice 70.7 m/s.

The first position in Y will then be: $0 + 65.8*(1) = 65.8$ m.

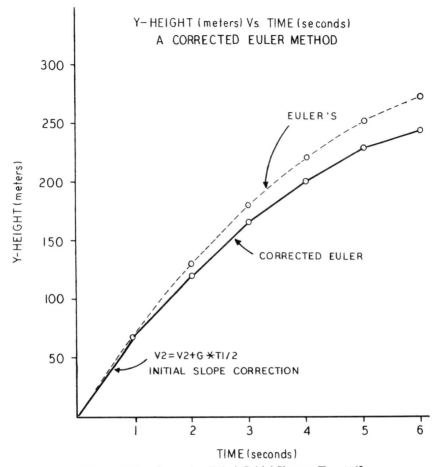

Figure 6.3A.   Correcting Euler's Initial Slope at $T = \Delta t/2$.

From this point on, the method is the same as for Section 6.2. The differences are shown plotted in Fig. 6.3A.

To obtain Program 6.3B, a small change is made to Program 6.3A:

290	LET V3 = V2	(prior to loop)
302	LET V2 = V3 + G*(T + T1/2)	(inside the loop)
310	LET Y = Y + V2*T1	(same as before)

A sample calculation for 2.5 seconds is shown in Fig. 6.3B. The importance of slope determination is of instructive value in addition to emphasizing the numerical method.

Discussion of Computer Results: Two comparisons should be made. First it should be observed that the value of Y in Table 6.3A, where T1 = 1 sec.,

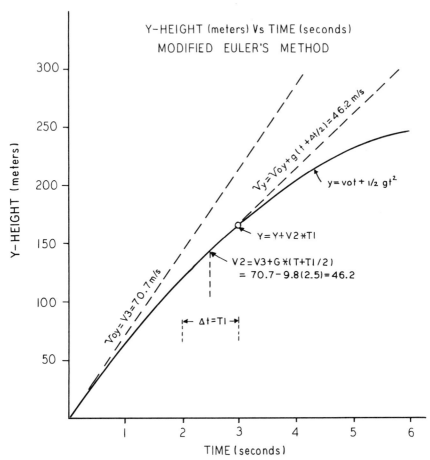

Figure 6.3B. Results of Modifying the slope at time, $T + \Delta t/2$ on every iteration.

is actually more precise than the value of Y in Table 6.2E, where $T1 = .001$ sec.; an improvement of over one thousand to one. Very dramatic indeed. The accuracy of the solution between the smaller time increments of Table 6.3A through 6.3D show very little improvement. In fact the values for $T1 = .01$ and $.001$ seconds indicate a sign of degeneration due to round-off error in the last three or four decimal places.

The Y-height is essentially the same for each time increment. The Y-velocity, however, is not correct for each time since it is the velocity at the mid-time point. If it was desired to have an accurate instantaneous Y-velocity at each time, it would be necessary to add one more statement to calculate it.

The "modified" Euler's results are very similar to those of the "corrected" Euler's Method. Tables 6.3E and 6.3F show the results for one second and .1 second time increments. The slight difference in Y height for the 0.1 second interval in Table 6.3F to that in Table 6.3B is due to placing the correction inside of the loop where round-off errors can occur.

```
100 REM ***************ROCKET TRAJECTORY 2 ***************
110 PRINT"WHAT IS INITIAL VELOCITY, ANGLE, TIME INCREMENT,"
120 INPUT V0, 0, T1
130 LET 0 = 0*PI/180
140 LET V1 = V0*COS(0)
150 LET V2 = V0*SIN(0)
160 LET G = -9.8
170 LET T5 = -V2/G
180 LET X9 = 2*T5*V1
190 LET Y5 = V2*T5+G*T5↑2/2
200 PRINT
210 PRINT"THEORY: TOTAL TIME =" 2*T5
220 PRINT"Y MAX ="Y5,"TOTAL DIST. ="X9
230 PRINT
240 PRINT"X VELOCITY ="V1
250 PRINT
260 PRINT"X DIST.","Y HEIGHT","DISTANCE","Y VELOCITY","TIME"
270 PRINT
280 LET J = 1
290 LET V2 = V2+G*T1/2
300 LET X = X+V1*T1
310 LET Y = Y+V2*T1
320 LET T = T+T1
330 LET S = SQR(X*X+Y*Y)
340 LET V2 = V2+G*T1
350 IF Y<=0 THEN 420
360 IF T+T1>=J THEN 380
370 GOTO 300
380 LET T = INT(T+.5)
390 LET J = J+1
400 PRINT X , Y , S , V2 , T
410 GOTO 300
420 PRINT X , Y , S , V2 , T
430 PRINT

>
```

PROGRAM 6.3A. Corrected Euler

```
100 REM **************ROCKET TRAJECTORY 2C ***************
110 PRINT"WHAT IS INITIAL VELOCITY, ANGLE, TIME INCREMENT,"
120 INPUT VO, A, T1
130 LET A = A*PI/180
140 LET V1 = VO*COS(A)
150 LET V2 = VO*SIN(A)
160 LET G = -9.8
170 LET T5 = -V2/G
180 LET X9 = 2*T5*V1
190 LET Y5 = V2*T5+G*T5↑2/2
200 PRINT
210 PRINT"THEORY: TOTAL TIME =" 2*T5
220 PRINT"Y MAX ="Y5,"TOTAL DIST. ="X9
230 PRINT
240 PRINT"X VELOCITY ="V1
250 PRINT
260 PRINT"X DIST.","Y HEIGHT","DISTANCE","Y VELOCITY","TIME"
270 PRINT
280 LET J = 1
290 LET V3 = V2
300 LET X = X+V1*T1
302 LET V2 = V3 + G*(T+T1/2)
310 LET Y = Y+V2*T1
320 LET T = T+T1
330 LET S = SQR(X*X+Y*Y)
350 IF Y<=0 THEN 420
360 IF T+T1>=J THEN 380
370 GOTO 300
380 LET T = INT(T+.5)
390 LET J = J+1
400 PRINT X , Y , S , V2 , T
410 GOTO 300
420 PRINT X , Y , S , V2 , T
430 PRINT
440 PRINT, "TIME INCREMENT="T1"SECONDS"
```

PROGRAM 6.3B. Modified Euler

WHAT IS INITIAL VELOCITY, ANGLE, TIME INCREMENT,
? 100, 45, 1

THEORY: TOTAL TIME = 14.43075064
Y MAX = 255.1020408   TOTAL DIST. = 1020.408163

X VELOCITY = 70.71067812

X DIST.	Y HEIGHT	DISTANCE	Y VELOCITY	TIME
70.71067812	65.81067812	96.59733616	56.01067811	1
141.4213562	121.8213562	186.6559478	46.21067811	2
212.1320344	168.0320343	270.6192243	36.41067811	3
282.8427125	204.4427125	348.9940152	26.61067811	4
353.5533906	231.0533906	422.3572768	16.81067811	5
424.2640687	247.8640687	491.3619812	7.010678115	6
494.9747468	254.8747468	556.7415348	-2.789321885	7
565.685425	252.0854249	619.3117643	-12.58932189	8
636.3961031	239.496103	679.9693988	-22.38932189	9
707.1067812	217.1067811	739.6859837	-32.18932189	10
777.8174593	184.9174593	799.4963832	-41.98932189	11
848.5281374	142.9281374	860.4815236	-51.78932189	12
919.2388156	91.13881549	923.7457895	-61.58932189	13
989.9494937	29.5494936	990.3904142	-71.38932189	14
1060.660172	-41.83982829	1061.485078	-81.18932189	15

TABLE 6.3A.

WHAT IS INITIAL VELOCITY, ANGLE, TIME INCREMENT,
? 100, 45, .1

THEORY: TOTAL TIME = 14.43075064
Y MAX = 255.1020408   TOTAL DIST. = 1020.408163

X VELOCITY = 70.71067812

X DIST.	Y HEIGHT	DISTANCE	Y VELOCITY	TIME
70.71067812	65.81067811	96.59733616	60.42067811	1
141.4213562	121.8213562	186.6559478	50.62067811	2
212.1320344	168.0320343	270.6192243	40.82067811	3
282.8427125	204.4427124	348.9940152	31.02067811	4
353.5533906	231.0533905	422.3572768	21.2206781	5
424.2640687	247.8640686	491.3619811	11.4206781	6
494.9747468	254.8747467	556.7415348	1.620678103	7
565.6854249	252.0854248	619.3117643	-8.179321897	8
636.396103	239.4961029	679.9693988	-17.9793219	9
707.1067811	217.106781	739.6859836	-27.7793219	10
777.8174592	184.9174591	799.4963831	-37.5793219	11
848.5281373	142.9281372	860.4815235	-47.3793219	12
919.2388154	91.1388153	923.7457894	-57.1793219	13
989.9494935	29.5494934	990.3904141	-66.97932191	14
1025.304833	-4.920167559	1025.316638	-71.87932191	14.5

TABLE 6.3B.

WHAT IS INITIAL VELOCITY, ANGLE, TIME INCREMENT,
? 100, 45, .01

THEORY: TOTAL TIME = 14.43075064
Y MAX = 255.1020408   TOTAL DIST. = 1020.408163

X VELOCITY = 70.71067812

X DIST.	Y HEIGHT	DISTANCE	Y VELOCITY	TIME
70.71067812	65.8106781	96.59733615	60.86167809	1
141.4213562	121.8213562	186.6559477	51.06167807	2
212.1320344	168.0320342	270.6192242	41.26167805	3
282.8427124	204.4427122	348.994015	31.46167802	4
353.5533905	231.0533901	422.3572765	21.66167801	5
424.2640685	247.8640681	491.3619807	11.861678	6
494.9747465	254.874746	556.7415342	2.061677999	7
565.6854245	252.6854245	619.3117636	-7.738322002	8
636.3961026	239.4961019	679.969398	-17.53832201	9
707.1067806	217.1067799	739.6859827	-27.33832202	10
777.8174586	184.9174578	799.4963822	-37.13832204	11
848.5281366	142.9281357	860.4815226	-46.93832206	12
919.2388147	91.1388136	923.7457885	-56.73832208	13
989.9494927	29.54949149	990.3904132	-66.53832211	14
1021.062191	-0.654450239	1021.062401	-70.85032212	14.44

TABLE 6.3C.

WHAT IS INITIAL VELOCITY, ANGLE, TIME INCREMENT,
? 100, 45, .001

THEORY: TOTAL TIME = 14.43075064
Y MAX = 255.1020408   TOTAL DIST. = 1020.408163

X VELOCITY = 70.71067812

X DIST.	Y HEIGHT	DISTANCE	Y VELOCITY	TIME
70.71067812	65.81067798	96.59733607	60.905778	1
141.4213561	121.8213557	186.6559473	51.10577788	2
212.1320338	168.0320331	270.6192231	41.30577777	3
282.8427115	204.4427103	348.9940132	31.50577765	4
353.5533891	231.0533875	422.3572739	21.70577753	5
424.2640668	247.8640645	491.3619774	11.90577744	6
494.9747444	254.8747414	556.7415302	2.105777405	7
565.6854221	252.0854184	619.311759	-7.694222611	8
636.3960997	239.4960953	679.969393	-17.49422268	9
707.1067774	217.1067721	739.6859773	-27.29422279	10
777.817455	184.9174487	799.4963766	-37.09422291	11
848.5281327	142.9281253	860.4815169	-46.89422303	12
919.2388103	91.13880192	923.745783	-56.69422314	13
989.949488	29.54947856	990.3904081	-66.49422326	14
1020.42579	-0.017648694	1020.42579	-70.71802331	14.431

TABLE 6.3D.

WHAT IS INITIAL VELOCITY, ANGLE, TIME INCREMENT,
? 100, 45, 1

THEORY: TOTAL TIME = 14.43075064
Y MAX = 255.1020408   TOTAL DIST. = 1020.408163

X VELOCITY = 70.71067812

X DIST.	Y HEIGHT	DISTANCE	Y VELOCITY	TIME
70.71067812	65.81067812	96.59733616	65.81067812	1
141.4213562	121.8213562	186.6559478	56.01067812	2
212.1320344	168.0320343	270.6192243	46.21067812	3
282.8427125	204.4427125	348.9940153	36.41067812	4
353.5533906	231.0533906	422.3572768	26.61067812	5
424.2640687	247.8640687	491.3619812	16.81067812	6
494.9747468	254.8747468	556.7415348	7.010678115	7
565.685425	252.0854249	619.3117643	-2.789321885	8
636.3961031	239.496103	679.9693989	-12.58932188	9
707.1067812	217.1067812	739.6859837	-22.38932188	10
777.8174593	184.9174593	799.4963832	-32.18932188	11
848.5281374	142.9281374	860.4815236	-41.98932188	12
919.2388156	91.1388155	923.7457895	-51.78932188	13
989.9494937	29.54949361	990.3904142	-61.58932189	14
1060.660172	-41.83982827	1061.485078	-71.38932189	15

TIME INCREMENT= 1 SECONDS

TABLE 6.3E.

WHAT IS INITIAL VELOCITY, ANGLE, TIME INCREMENT,
? 100, 45, .1

THEORY: TOTAL TIME = 14.43075064
Y MAX = 255.1020408   TOTAL DIST. = 1020.408163

X VELOCITY = 70.71067812

X DIST.	Y HEIGHT	DISTANCE	Y VELOCITY	TIME
70.71067812	65.81067811	96.59733616	61.40067812	1
141.4213562	121.8213562	186.6559478	51.60067812	2
212.1320344	168.0320343	270.6192243	41.80067812	3
282.8427125	204.4427124	348.9940152	32.00067812	4
353.5533906	231.0533906	422.3572768	22.20067812	5
424.2640687	247.8640687	491.3619812	12.40067812	6
494.9747468	254.8747468	556.7415348	2.600678117	7
565.6854249	252.0854249	619.3117643	-7.199321882	8
636.396103	239.496103	679.9693988	-16.99932188	9
707.1067811	217.1067811	739.6859836	-26.79932188	10
777.8174592	184.9174592	799.4963831	-36.59932188	11
848.5281373	142.9281373	860.4815235	-46.39932188	12
919.2388154	91.13881546	923.7457894	-56.19932188	13
989.9494935	29.54949357	990.3904141	-65.99932188	14
1025.304833	-4.920167371	1025.316638	-70.89932188	14.5

TIME INCREMENT= 0.1 SECONDS

TABLE 6.3F.

6.4   TRAJECTORY III

Lesson Characteristics:

PHYSICS LEVEL   college, introductory

MATHEMATICS BACKGROUND REQUIRED   analytical geometry

PEDAGOGY   computer learning

PROBLEM APPROACH   numerical method

STUDENT PARTICIPATION   assists in program writing

PROGRAMMING SKILLS   introductory BASIC

TIME OF STUDENT INVOLVEMENT   in class—10 minutes, out of class—30 minutes

(1.5 hours if either of the previous trajectory problems had not been assigned.)

RECOMMENDED READINGS   same as Lesson 6.2

Lesson Description: The basic tenet of Section 6.2 applies to this section. The more advanced student will eventually attack most of the difficult motion problems with one of the Runge-Kutta numerical methods. The improved Euler method demonstrated in this section gives the same results as the corrected or modified Euler of Section 6.3 for problems of constant acceleration. This improved Euler method is identical in performance to the second order Runge-Kutta method, and almost identical in numerical form. It should be studied as a prerequisite to the higher order Runge-Kutta methods.

Background and Theory: The general background and theory of Section 6.2 still applies in this section. It is important to understand the method of Program 6.4 because it represents the type of program required for executing the higher order Runge-Kutta methods. The improved Euler method is equivalent to the second order Runge-Kutta in every way. Mastery of this method will make the higher order Runge-Kutta methods easier to understand. The key to the Runge-Kutta methods is that the slope used to predict the position on the curve, is a weighted average for the interval. The 'order' of the Runge-Kutta methods can be thought of as the number of slope values used in weighting the average slope over the interval. For instance, the fourth order Runge-Kutta uses four slopes; one at the beginning and end of the interval, and two at the mid-time-point of the interval. The improved Euler method uses the beginning and end slope making it a second order Runge-Kutta method. By this definition, the simple Euler method is a first order Runge-Kutta, etc.

In general, the higher the order, the greater the accuracy. For example, the second order method of this section will solve the position of a moving body under constant acceleration precisely at the time increment desired.

If the acceleration were not constant, a higher order method would be required in order to obtain the same precision with the same time increment.

Computer Technique: The improved Euler Method (Second Order Runge-Kutta) can be used without detracting from the basic principles and definitions of the physics problem. New terminology will be introduced for the slope.

$$P0 = \text{Initial slope of the interval}$$
$$P1 = \text{Final slope of the interval}$$

Then the weighted average velocity over the interval will be:

$$V2 = (P0 + P1)/2.$$

Essentially, the remainder of the program will be the same as Program 6.2C. The initial slope of each iteration will equal the final slope of the previous iteration because the slope is independent of Y in this problem. This fact must be accounted for if the slope is dependent upon Y.

Comments About the Computer Program: The initial slope is pre-calculated before entering the iteration loop. Inside of the loop, P0 will equal P1 for each successive loop. The changes in Program 6.2C or 6.3A, to make Program 6.4 are:

```
290   LET  P1=V2                    (initial slope)
300   LET  P0=P1                    (begin loop)
302   LET  P1=P0+G*T1               (end slope)
304   LET  V2=(P0+P1)/2             (average slope)
306   LET  X=X+V1*T1                (X position)
310   LET  Y=Y+V2*T1                (Y position)
  . . .
  . . .
  . . .
  . . . .
```

Discussion of Computer Results: The improved Euler's Method is shown to be completely equivalent to the corrected Euler's Method of Section 6.3. The comparison of Tables 6.3A through 6.3D, shows that the Y positions are identical to the last decimal place, whereas the Y velocity values are different as would be expected.

For this problem the increased accuracy obtained for a time increment of .001 seconds over .01 seconds does not warrant the excessive number of computer calculations for the smaller time increment. By taking the smaller interval, the data shows that, although the slopes at the time involved are still the same, a much better Y-coordinate position can be obtained because the small increment tends to give an instantaneous velocity with which to calculate each change in Y. However, small intervals of time cause round-off errors which are not easily corrected by the program. Time increments should be used as large as possible and still obtain the desired accuracy. The next section will show a correction to the Euler Method which will give a more accurate result for a larger time increment.

```
100 REM **************ROCKET TRAJECTORY 2A ***************
110 PRINT"WHAT IS INITIAL VELOCITY, ANGLE, TIME INCREMENT,"
120 INPUT VO, A, T1
130 LET A = A*PI/180
140 LET V1 = VO*COS(A)
150 LET V2 = VO*SIN(A)
160 LET G = -9.8
170 LET T5 = -V2/G
180 LET X9 = 2*T5*V1
190 LET Y5 = V2*T5+G*T5↑2/2
200 PRINT
210 PRINT"THEORY: TOTAL TIME =" 2*T5
220 PRINT"Y MAX ="Y5,"TOTAL DIST. ="X9
230 PRINT
240 PRINT"X VELOCITY ="V1
250 PRINT
260 PRINT"X DIST.","Y HEIGHT","DISTANCE","Y VELOCITY","TIME"
270 PRINT
280 LET J = 1
290 LET P1 = V2
300 LET P0 = P1
302 LET P1 = P0+G*T1
304 LET V2 = (P0+P1)/2
306 LET X = X+V1*T1
310 LET Y = Y+V2*T1
320 LET T = T+T1
330 LET S = SQR(X*X+Y*Y)
350 IF Y<=0 THEN 420
360 IF T+T1>=J THEN 380
370 GOTO 300
380 LET T = INT(T+.5)
390 LET J = J+1
400 PRINT X , Y , S , V2 , T
410 GOTO 300
420 PRINT X , Y , S , V2 , T
430 PRINT
```

PROGRAM 6.4. Improved Euler or second order Runge Kutta

WHAT IS INITIAL VELOCITY, ANGLE, TIME INCREMENT,
? 100, 45, 1

THEORY: TOTAL TIME = 14.43075064
Y MAX = 255.1020408   TOTAL DIST. = 1020.408163

X VELOCITY = 70.71067812

X DIST.	Y HEIGHT	DISTANCE	Y VELOCITY	TIME
70.71067812	65.81067812	96.59733616	65.81067812	1
141.4213562	121.8213562	186.6559478	56.01067812	2
212.1320344	168.0320343	270.6192243	46.21067812	3
282.8427125	204.4427125	348.9940153	36.41067811	4
353.5533906	231.0533906	422.3572768	26.61067812	5
424.2640687	247.8640687	491.3619812	16.81067811	6
494.9747468	254.8747468	556.7415348	7.010678115	7
565.685425	252.0854249	619.3117643	-2.789321885	8
636.3961031	239.496103	679.9693989	-12.58932189	9
707.1067812	217.1067811	739.6859837	-22.38932189	10
777.8174593	184.9174593	799.4963832	-32.18932189	11
848.5281374	142.9281374	860.4815236	-41.98932189	12
919.2388156	91.13881549	923.7457895	-51.78932189	13
989.9494937	29.5494936	990.3904142	-61.58932189	14
1060.660172	-41.83982828	1061.485078	-71.38932189	15

TABLE 6.4A.

WHAT IS INITIAL VELOCITY, ANGLE, TIME INCREMENT,
? 100, 45, .1

THEORY: TOTAL TIME = 14.43075064
Y MAX = 255.1020408   TOTAL DIST. = 1020.408163

X VELOCITY = 70.71067812

X DIST.	Y HEIGHT	DISTANCE	Y VELOCITY	TIME
70.71067812	65.81067811	96.59733616	61.40067811	1
141.4213562	121.8213562	186.6559478	51.60067811	2
212.1320344	168.0320343	270.6192243	41.80067811	3
282.8427125	204.4427124	348.9940152	32.00067811	4
353.5533906	231.0533905	422.3572768	22.2006781	5
424.2640687	247.8640686	491.3619811	12.4006781	6
494.9747468	254.8747467	556.7415348	2.600678103	7
565.6854249	252.0854248	619.3117643	-7.199321897	8
636.396103	239.4961029	679.9693988	-16.9993219	9
707.1067811	217.106781	739.6859836	-26.7993219	10
777.8174592	184.9174591	799.4963831	-36.5993219	11
848.5281373	142.9281372	860.4815235	-46.3993219	12
919.2388154	91.1388153	923.7457894	-56.1993219	13
989.9494935	29.5494934	990.3904141	-65.99932191	14
1025.304833	-4.920167558	1025.316638	-70.89932191	14.5

TABLE 6.4B.

WHAT IS INITIAL VELOCITY, ANGLE, TIME INCREMENT,
? 100, 45, .01

THEORY: TOTAL TIME = 14.43075064
Y MAX = 255.1020408   TOTAL DIST. = 1020.408163

X VELOCITY = 70.71067812

X DIST.	Y HEIGHT	DISTANCE	Y VELOCITY	TIME
70.71067812	65.8106781	96.59733615	60.95967809	1
141.4213562	121.8213562	186.6559477	51.15967807	2
212.1320344	168.0320342	270.6192242	41.35967805	3
282.8427124	204.4427122	348.994015	31.55967802	4
353.5533905	231.0533901	422.3572765	21.75967801	5
424.2640685	247.8640681	491.3619807	11.959678	6
494.9747465	254.874746	556.7415342	2.159677999	7
565.6854245	252.085424	619.3117636	-7.640322002	8
636.3961026	239.4961019	679.969398	-17.44032201	9
707.1067806	217.1067799	739.6859827	-27.24032202	10
777.8174586	184.9174578	799.4963822	-37.04032204	11
848.5281366	142.9281357	860.4815226	-46.84032206	12
919.2388147	91.1388136	923.7457885	-56.64032208	13
989.9494927	29.54949149	990.3904132	-66.44032211	14
1021.062191	-0.65445024	1021.062401	-70.75232212	14.44

TABLE 6.4C.

WHAT IS INITIAL VELOCITY, ANGLE, TIME INCREMENT,
? 100, 45, .001

THEORY: TOTAL TIME = 14.43075064
Y MAX = 255.1020408   TOTAL DIST. = 1020.408163

X VELOCITY = 70.71067812

X DIST.	Y HEIGHT	DISTANCE	Y VELOCITY	TIME
70.71067812	65.81067798	96.59733607	60.915578	1
141.4213561	121.8213557	186.6559473	51.11557788	2
212.1320338	168.0320331	270.6192231	41.31557777	3
282.8427115	204.4427103	348.9940132	31.51557765	4
353.5533891	231.0533875	422.3572739	21.71557753	5
424.2640668	247.8640645	491.3619774	11.91557744	6
494.9747444	254.8747414	556.7415302	2.115577405	7
565.6854221	252.0854184	619.311759	-7.684422611	8
636.3960997	239.4960953	679.969393	-17.48442268	9
707.1067774	217.1067721	739.6859773	-27.28442279	10
777.817455	184.9174487	799.4963766	-37.08442291	11
848.5281327	142.9281253	860.4815169	-46.88442303	12
919.2388103	91.13880192	923.745783	-56.68442314	13
989.949488	29.54947856	990.3904081	-66.48442326	14
1020.42579	-0.017648694	1020.42579	-70.70822331	14.431

TABLE 6.4D.

6.5   TRAJECTORY IV

Lesson Characteristics:

PHYSICS LEVEL   college, intermediate

MATHEMATICS BACKGROUND REQUIRED   analytical geometry

PEDAGOGY   computer learning

PROBLEM APPROACH   numerical solution

STUDENT PARTICIPATION   assists in program writing

PROGRAMMING SKILLS   introductory BASIC

TIME OF STUDENT INVOLVEMENT   in class—20 minutes, out of class—45 minutes

(2 hours if previous trajectory problems had not been investigated.)

RECOMMENDED READINGS   same as Lesson 6.2

Lesson Description: The basic principles of the previous sections apply to this section. The methods of this section are the second and third order Runge-Kutta methods and are explained in a way which does not require a prerequisite of calculus. These methods will allow the advanced non-calculus student to tackle problems of non-uniform, accelerated motion with an accuracy approaching the analytical calculus solution. The method of applying the Runge-Kutta methods to the analytical differential equation is demonstrated as well as the non-calculus technique. The calculus student should gain a better understanding of the calculus by comparing the two methods.

Background and Theory: The general background and description of Section 6.4 still applies in this section. So far, the differential notation has not been utilized in this chapter, i.e., $a = dv/dt$. Indeed, it is not necessary to use the notation with Runge Kutta methods, including the fourth order methods. However, many problems are presented in differential form, and most numerical analysis books give Runge Kutta examples for the solution of differential equations. In this section the differential form of the equation will be investigated as well as the incremental methods of the previous section. Figures 6.5A and 6.5B demonstrate the fourth order Runge Kutta method for a function whose slope is dependent upon Y (Figure 6.5A), and one whose slope is independent of Y (Figure 6.5B). The trajectory problem with constant acceleration is an example where the slope is independent of Y. There are therefore only three slopes for the fourth order method, making it in fact a third order method.

Computer Technique: In differential form Equation 6.2–6 is:

$$v = dy/dt = v_o + gt$$

$$\text{LET} \quad V2 = V0 + G * T \qquad (6.5\text{–}1)$$

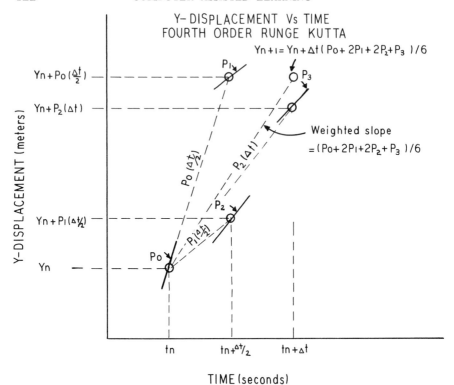

Figure 6.5A. Graphic Description of the Fourth Order Runge Kutta method for $y' = f(y,t)$.

That is, the slope of the displacement Y, dy/dt, is V2. This equation will be applied to the Runge-Kutta methods of this section.

SECOND ORDER RUNGE KUTTA

P0 = initial velocity (slope) at T, the time at the beginning of the interval.

P1 = slope at a position predicted by the value of $y_{n+1} = y_n + P0 \, \Delta t$.

Equation (6.5–1) shows that the slope (velocity) is dependent upon g and t, therefore, the velocity at any time t_{n+1} is:

$$P1 = v_o + g(t + \Delta t)$$

$$\text{LET} \quad P1 = V0 + G*(T + T1)$$

and

$$\text{LET} \quad V2 = (P0 + P1)/2.$$

THIRD ORDER RUNGE KUTTA

P0 is the same as the second order method. P1 = slope at a position

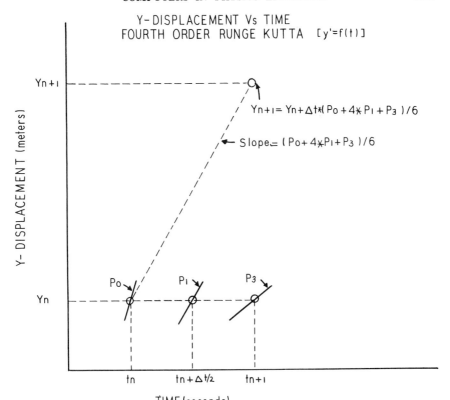

Figure 6.5B.   Graphic Description of the Fourth Order Runge Kutta method for
$$y' = f(t).$$

predicted by the value of $Y_{n+1/2} = Y_n + P0(\Delta t/2)$ or; since the slope is dependent upon g and t:

$$P1 = v_o + g(t + t/2)$$

$$\text{LET } \quad P1 = V0 + G*(T + T1/2)$$

For the fourth order method P2 would be the slope at a position predicted by the value of $Y_{n+1} = Y_n + P1(t + \Delta t/2)$, however P2 = P1 in this case making the method third order. P3 would be the slope at a position predicted by the value of $Y_{n+1} = y_n + P2(t + \Delta t)$ or the slope at the end of the interval.

In this case:

$$P3 = v_o + g(t + \Delta t)$$

$$\text{LET } \quad P3 = V0 + G*(T + T1)$$

The weighted average slope would then be:

$$v_{ave} = (P0 + 4P1 + P3) \div 6$$

$$\text{Let } \quad V2 = (P0 + 4*P1 + P3)/6$$

Comments About the Computer Program: SECOND ORDER RUNGE KUTTA (Program 6.5A)—The average weighted velocity has been designated, V2, as well as the initial velocity in the past method, the initial Y —velocity is required within the loop, and has the designation, V3. P1 is also set equal to the initial velocity prior to entering the loop in order to make the loop itself iterate properly. The changes to the basic program are:

```
290   LET  V3=V2              (Initial velocity before looping)
292   LET  P1=V3
300   LET  P0=P1                          (Start loop)
302   LET  P1=V3+G*(T+T1)                 (End slope)
304   LET  V2=(P0+P1)/2                   (Ave. slope)
306   LET  X=X+V1*T1
310   LET  Y=Y+V2*T1                      (Position)
```

THIRD ORDER RUNGE KUTTA (Program 6.5B)—The initial Y velocity is again used within the loop, requiring a pre-loop designation, V3=V2. The changes to the basic program are:

```
290   LET  V3=V2                (Prior to loop)
300   LET  X=X+V1*T1            (No change
302   LET  P0=V3+G*T            (Initial slope)
304   LET  P1=V3+G*(T+T1/2)     (Mid-slope)
306   LET  P3=V3+G*(T+T1)       (Final slope)
308   LET  V2=(P0+4*P1+P3)/6    (Average slope)
310   LET  Y=Y+V2*T1           (No change)
```

Fig. 6.5B describes this simplification, over the fourth order Runge Kutta.

The same method can more closely resemble the methods of Section 6.4 and remain non-differential. The basic principles are involved to a further extent than for Program 6.5B. The non-differential third order method is completely iterative and does not rely on the differential form of Equation 6.5–2.

The changes to Program 6.5B are:

```
290   LET  P3=V2               (No longer required)
302   LET  P0=P3               (Initial slope)
304   LET  P1=P0+G*T1/2        (Mid-slope)
306   LET  P3=P0+G*T1          (Final slope)
308   LET  V2=(P0+4*P1+P3)/6   (No change)
310   LET  Y=Y+V2*T1           (No change)
```

Discussion of Computer Results: The data of Tables 6.5A and 6.5B are almost completely equivalent to the data in Tables 6.5C and 6.5D. The data of Tables 6.5E and 6.5F are equivalent to within the last one or two decimal places, and also completely equivalent to the data from Tables 6.4A and 6.4B showing that the second order Runge Kutta method approximated by the improved Euler's method is of the same type as the third order Runge Kutta method approximated by Program 6.5C. The very slight difference in the last one or two decimal places is accounted

```
100 REM **************ROCKET TRAJECTORY 2B **************
110 PRINT"WHAT IS INITIAL VELOCITY, ANGLE, TIME INCREMENT,"
120 INPUT VO, A, T1
130 LET A = A*PI/180
140 LET V1 = VO*COS(A)
150 LET V2 = VO*SIN(A)
160 LET G = -9.8
170 LET T5 = -V2/G
180 LET X9 = 2*T5*V1
190 LET Y5 = V2*T5+G*T5†2/2
200 PRINT
210 PRINT"THEORY: TOTAL TIME =" 2*T5
220 PRINT"Y MAX ="Y5,"TOTAL DIST. ="X9
230 PRINT
240 PRINT"X VELOCITY ="V1
250 PRINT
260 PRINT"X DIST.","Y HEIGHT","DISTANCE","Y VELOCITY","TIME"
270 PRINT
280 LET J = 1
290 LET V3 = V2
292 LET P1 = V3
300 LET PO = P1
302 LET P1 = V3 + G*(T+T1)
304 LET V2 = (PO+P1)/2
306 LET X = X + V1*T1
310 LET Y = Y+V2*T1
320 LET T = T+T1
330 LET S = SQR(X*X+Y*Y)
350 IF Y<=0 THEN 420
360 IF T+T1>=J THEN 380
370 GOTO 300
380 LET T = INT(T+.5)
390 LET J = J+1
400 PRINT X , Y , S , V2 , T
410 GOTO 300
420 PRINT X , Y , S , V2 , T
430 PRINT
440 PRINT,"TIME INCREMENT="T1"SECONDS"
```

PROGRAM 6.5A.   Second order Runge Kutta

```
100 REM **************ROCKET TRAJECTORY 2D *****************
110 PRINT"WHAT IS INITIAL VELOCITY, ANGLE, TIME INCREMENT,"
120 INPUT VO, A, T1
130 LET A = A*PI/180
140 LET V1 = VO*COS(A)
150 LET V2 = VO*SIN(A)
160 LET G = -9.8
170 LET T5 = -V2/G
180 LET X9 = 2*T5*V1
190 LET Y5 = V2*T5+G*T5↑2/2
200 PRINT
210 PRINT"THEORY: TOTAL TIME =" 2*T5
220 PRINT"Y MAX ="Y5,"TOTAL DIST. ="X9
230 PRINT
240 PRINT"X VELOCITY ="V1
250 PRINT
260 PRINT"X DIST.","Y HEIGHT","DISTANCE","Y VELOCITY","TIME"
270 PRINT
280 LET J = 1
290 LET V3 = V2
300 LET X = X+V1*T1
302 LET PO = V3 + G*T
304 LET P1 = V3 + G*(T+T1/2)
306 LET P3 = V3 + G*(T+T1)
308 LET V2 = (PO+4*P1+P3)/6
310 LET Y = Y+V2*T1
320 LET T = T+T1
330 LET S = SQR(X*X+Y*Y)
350 IF Y<=0 THEN 420
360 IF T+T1>=J THEN 380
370 GOTO 300
380 LET T = INT(T+.5)
390 LET J = J+1
400 PRINT X , Y , S , V2 , T
410 GOTO 300
420 PRINT X , Y , S , V2 , T
430 PRINT
440 PRINT, "TIME INCREMENT="T1"SECONDS"
```

PROGRAM 6.5B.   Third order Runge Kutta

```
100 REM **************ROCKET TRAJECTORY 2E ****************
110 PRINT"WHAT IS INITIAL VELOCITY, ANGLE, TIME INCREMENT,"
120 INPUT VO, A, T1
130 LET A = A*PI/180
140 LET V1 = VO*COS(A)
150 LET V2 = VO*SIN(A)
160 LET G = -9.8
170 LET T5 = -V2/G
180 LET X9 = 2*T5*V1
190 LET Y5 = V2*T5+G*T5↑2/2
200 PRINT
210 PRINT"THEORY: TOTAL TIME =" 2*T5
220 PRINT"Y MAX ="Y5,"TOTAL DIST. ="X9
230 PRINT
240 PRINT"X VELOCITY ="V1
250 PRINT
260 PRINT"X DIST.","Y HEIGHT","DISTANCE","Y VELOCITY","TIME"
270 PRINT
280 LET J = 1
290 LET P3 = V2
300 LET X = X+V1*T1
302 LET PO = P3
304 LET P1 = PO + G*T1/2
306 LET P3 = PO + G*T1
308 LET V2 = (PO+4*P1+P3)/6
310 LET Y = Y+V2*T1
320 LET T = T+T1
330 LET S = SQR(X*X+Y*Y)
350 IF Y<=0 THEN 420
360 IF T+T1>=J THEN 380
370 GOTO 300
380 LET T = INT(T+.5)
390 LET J = J+1
400 PRINT X , Y , S , V2 , T
410 GOTO 300
420 PRINT X , Y , S , V2 , T
430 PRINT
440 PRINT, "TIME INCREMENT="T1"SECONDS"
```

PROGRAM 6.5C. Third order Runge Kutta (Non calculus)

WHAT IS INITIAL VELOCITY, ANGLE, TIME INCREMENT,
? 100, 45, 1

THEORY: TOTAL TIME = 14.43075064
Y MAX = 255.1020408   TOTAL DIST. = 1020.408163

X VELOCITY = 70.71067812

X DIST.	Y HEIGHT	DISTANCE	Y VELOCITY	TIME
70.71067812	65.81067812	96.59733616	65.81067812	1
141.4213562	121.8213562	186.6559478	56.01067812	2
212.1320344	168.0320343	270.6192243	46.21067812	3
282.8427125	204.4427125	348.9940153	36.41067812	4
353.5533906	231.0533906	422.3572768	26.61067812	5
424.2640687	247.8640687	491.3619812	16.81067812	6
494.9747468	254.8747468	556.7415348	7.010678115	7
565.685425	252.0854249	619.3117643	-2.789321885	8
636.3961031	239.496103	679.9693989	-12.58932188	9
707.1067812	217.1067812	739.6859837	-22.38932188	10
777.8174593	184.9174593	799.4963832	-32.18932188	11
848.5281374	142.9281374	860.4815236	-41.98932188	12
919.2388156	91.1388155	923.7457895	-51.78932188	13
989.9494937	29.54949361	990.3904142	-61.58932188	14
1060.660172	-41.83982827	1061.485078	-71.38932188	15

TIME INCREMENT= 1 SECONDS

TABLE 6.5A

WHAT IS INITIAL VELOCITY, ANGLE, TIME INCREMENT,
? 100, 45, .1

THEORY: TOTAL TIME = 14.43075064
Y MAX = 255.1020408   TOTAL DIST. = 1020.408163

X VELOCITY = 70.71067812

X DIST.	Y HEIGHT	DISTANCE	Y VELOCITY	TIME
70.71067812	65.81067811	96.59733616	61.40067812	1
141.4213562	121.8213562	186.6559478	51.60067812	2
212.1320344	168.0320343	270.6192243	41.80067812	3
282.8427125	204.4427124	348.9940152	32.00067812	4
353.5533906	231.0533906	422.3572768	22.20067812	5
424.2640687	247.8640687	491.3619812	12.40067812	6
494.9747468	254.8747468	556.7415348	2.600678117	7
565.6854249	252.0854249	619.3117643	-7.199321883	8
636.396103	239.496103	679.9693988	-16.99932188	9
707.1067811	217.1067811	739.6859836	-26.79932188	10
777.8174592	184.9174592	799.4963831	-36.59932188	11
848.5281373	142.9281373	860.4815235	-46.39932188	12
919.2388154	91.13881546	923.7457894	-56.19932188	13
989.9494935	29.54949357	990.3904141	-65.99932188	14
1025.304833	-4.920167372	1025.316638	-70.89932188	14.5

TIME INCREMENT= 0.1 SECONDS

TABLE 6.5B

WHAT IS INITIAL VELOCITY, ANGLE, TIME INCREMENT,
? 100, 45, 1

THEORY: TOTAL TIME = 14.43075064
Y MAX = 255.1020408   TOTAL DIST. = 1020.408163

X VELOCITY = 70.71067812

X DIST.	Y HEIGHT	DISTANCE	Y VELOCITY	TIME
70.71067812	65.81067812	96.59733616	65.81067812	1
141.4213562	121.8213562	186.6559478	56.01067811	2
212.1320344	168.0320343	270.6192243	46.21067812	3
282.8427125	204.4427125	348.9940153	36.41067812	4
353.5533906	231.0533906	422.3572768	26.61067812	5
424.2640687	247.8640687	491.3619812	16.81067812	6
494.9747468	254.8747468	556.7415348	7.010678115	7
565.685425	252.0854249	619.3117643	-2.789321885	8
636.3961031	239.496103	679.9693989	-12.58932188	9
707.1067812	217.1067812	739.6859837	-22.38932188	10
777.8174593	184.9174593	799.4963832	-32.18932188	11
848.5281374	142.9281374	860.4815236	-41.98932188	12
919.2388156	91.13881549	923.7457895	-51.78932188	13
989.9494937	29.54949361	990.3904142	-61.58932189	14
1060.660172	-41.83982828	1061.485078	-71.38932189	15

TIME INCREMENT= 1 SECONDS

TABLE 6.5C

WHAT IS INITIAL VELOCITY, ANGLE, TIME INCREMENT,
? 100, 45, .1

THEORY: TOTAL TIME = 14.43075064
Y MAX = 255.1020408   TOTAL DIST. = 1020.408163

X VELOCITY = 70.71067812

X DIST.	Y HEIGHT	DISTANCE	Y VELOCITY	TIME
70.71067812	65.81067811	96.59733616	61.40067812	1
141.4213562	121.8213562	186.6559478	51.60067812	2
212.1320344	168.0320343	270.6192243	41.80067812	3
282.8427125	204.4427124	348.9940152	32.00067812	4
353.5533906	231.0533906	422.3572768	22.20067812	5
424.2640687	247.8640687	491.3619812	12.40067812	6
494.9747468	254.8747468	556.7415348	2.600678117	7
565.6854249	252.0854249	619.3117643	-7.199321882	8
636.396103	239.496103	679.9693988	-16.99932188	9
707.1067811	217.1067811	739.6859836	-26.79932188	10
777.8174592	184.9174592	799.4963831	-36.59932188	11
848.5281373	142.9281373	860.4815235	-46.39932188	12
919.2388154	91.13881545	923.7457894	-56.19932188	13
989.9494935	29.54949357	990.3904141	-65.99932188	14
1025.304833	-4.920167374	1025.316638	-70.89932188	14.5

TIME INCREMENT= 0.1 SECONDS
TABLE 6.5D

```
WHAT IS INITIAL VELOCITY, ANGLE, TIME INCREMENT,
? 100, 45, 1
```

```
THEORY: TOTAL TIME = 14.43075064
Y MAX = 255.1020408              TOTAL DIST. = 1020.408163

X VELOCITY = 70.71067812
```

X DIST.	Y HEIGHT	DISTANCE	Y VELOCITY	TIME
70.71067812	65.81067812	96.59733616	65.81067812	1
141.4213562	121.8213562	186.6559478	56.01067811	2
212.1320344	168.0320343	270.6192243	46.21067811	3
282.8427125	204.4427125	348.9940152	36.41067811	4
353.5533906	231.0533906	422.3572768	26.61067811	5
424.2640687	247.8640687	491.3619812	16.81067811	6
494.9747468	254.8747468	556.7415348	7.010678115	7
565.685425	252.0854249	619.3117643	-2.789321885	8
636.3961031	239.496103	679.9693988	-12.58932189	9
707.1067812	217.1067811	739.6859837	-22.38932189	10
777.8174593	184.9174593	799.4963832	-32.18932189	11
848.5281374	142.9281374	860.4815236	-41.98932189	12
919.2388156	91.13881549	923.7457895	-51.78932189	13
989.9494937	29.5494936	990.3904142	-61.58932189	14
1060.660172	-41.83982828	1061.485078	-71.38932189	15

```
              TIME INCREMENT= 1 SECONDS
```

TABLE 6.5E

```
WHAT IS INITIAL VELOCITY, ANGLE, TIME INCREMENT,
? 100, 45, .1
```

```
THEORY: TOTAL TIME = 14.43075064
Y MAX = 255.1020408              TOTAL DIST. = 1020.408163

X VELOCITY = 70.71067812
```

X DIST.	Y HEIGHT	DISTANCE	Y VELOCITY	TIME
70.71067812	65.81067811	96.59733616	61.40067811	1
141.4213562	121.8213562	186.6559478	51.60067811	2
212.1320344	168.0320343	270.6192243	41.80067811	3
282.8427125	204.4427124	348.9940152	32.00067811	4
353.5533906	231.0533905	422.3572768	22.2006781	5
424.2640687	247.8640686	491.3619811	12.4006781	6
494.9747468	254.8747467	556.7415348	2.600678103	7
565.6854249	252.0854248	619.3117643	-7.199321897	8
636.396103	239.4961029	679.9693988	-16.9993219	9
707.1067811	217.106781	739.6859836	-26.7993219	10
777.8174592	184.9174591	799.4963831	-36.5993219	11
848.5281373	142.9281372	860.4815235	-46.3993219	12
919.2388154	91.1388153	923.7457894	-56.1993219	13
989.9494935	29.5494934	990.3904141	-65.99932191	14
1025.304833	-4.920167559	1025.316638	-70.89932191	14.5

```
              TIME INCREMENT= 0.1 SECONDS
```

TABLE 6.5F

for by the round-off error correction which is always made to $T+T1$ every second, but is not made in summations involving T1 such as: $P1 = P0 + G*T1/2$, where small increments and any errors associated with them may propagate without correction. This slight error is of no consequence in most problems; however, it is mentioned so that those who are familiar with the differential notation can use the method with even more confidence.

6.6 TRAJECTORY WITH FRICTION I

Lesson Characteristics:

PHYSICS LEVEL   college, intermediate

MATHEMATICS BACKGROUND REQUIRED   analytical geometry

PEDAGOGY   computer learning and simulation

PROBLEM APPROACH   numerical method

STUDENT PARTICIPATION   assists in program writing

PROGRAMMING SKILLS   introductory BASIC

TIME OF STUDENT INVOLVEMENT   in class—20 minutes, out of class—45 minutes

RECOMMENDED READINGS   (2) Section 5.4
(3) Ch. 4, Sections 2 and 3
(4) Section 9.7

Lesson Description: Problems of motion are taught at the sophomore levels using constant acceleration. The student is warned that all motion does not have a constant acceleration; however, problems of real life involving changing acceleration are often not studied.

In this section, a problem of motion in a viscous fluid is presented in terms of the basic definition of Newtonian physics. It is an advanced college level physics problem, but can be worked by a non-calculus student using the numerical method studied in Section 6.3, the corrected Euler method. It is therefore listed as an intermediate college level physics problem.

The program studied demonstrates the use of subroutines, and how to have the data either printed or plotted. The student can not only follow the physics of the problem, but can change parameters and conduct a simulated experiment at the same time.

Background and Theory: The drag force of an object traveling through air depends upon the object's size, shape, density of the air, and upon the square of the velocity through the air (or an experimentally derived function dependent upon velocity). For this problem, the magnitude of the drag force will be written as:

$f = kv^2$ (where the force is always in a direction opposite that of the velocity)

LET   F0 = K*V↑2   (6.6–1)

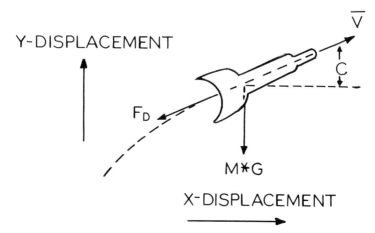

Figure 6.6A   Rocket Force Diagram (Zero Thrust).

Newton's second law states that the sum of all the forces acting upon a body is equal to the mass of the body times the acceleration of the body. By taking the mass (M) to be unity; force will equal acceleration:

$$\frac{\vec{F}}{1} = \vec{A} \qquad\qquad (6.6\text{–}2)$$

The terminology will be that F1 will equal the sum of the forces (acceleration) in the Y-direction. The force vectors are dependent upon friction, (F0) and gravity (G). Figs. 6.6A and 6.6B show the vector components of the friction forces. The total force in the X-direction is dependent only upon the friction force in the X-direction:

$$f_x = kv^2\cos(c)$$

$$\text{LET}\quad F1 = K*V\uparrow2*COS(C) \qquad\qquad (6.6\text{–}3)$$

and the summation of friction forces in the Y-direction is:

$$f_y = kv^2\sin(c)$$

$$\text{LET}\quad F2 = K*V\uparrow2*SIN(C) \qquad\qquad (6.6\text{–}4)$$

where again the direction of the drag force will depend upon the direction

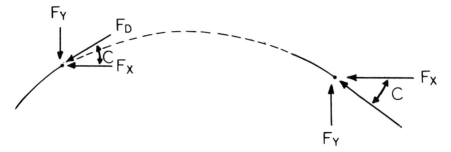

Figure 6.6B   Friction Vector, Rocket going UP and coming DOWN

of the velocity. The total acceleration in the Y-direction is dependent upon friction and gravity:

$$a_y = g - f_y$$

$$\text{LET} \quad A2 = G - F2 \tag{6.6-5}$$

The angle, C, of the trajectory with respect to the horizontal is:

$$c = \arctan (v_y/v_x)$$

$$\text{LET} \quad C = ATN(V2/V1) \tag{6.6-6}$$

The interdependency of relations begins to be complicated, e.g., the calculations required are:

(1) The magnitude of the total velocity in order to find total friction force:

$$v = \sqrt{v_x^2 + v_y^2}$$

$$\text{LET} \quad V = SQR(V1\uparrow2 + V2\uparrow2) \tag{6.6-7}$$

(2) The angle of the trajectory with the horizontal, Equation (6.6-6).
(3) Horizontal and vertical friction force components; Equations (6.6-3) and (6.6-4).
(4) The horizontal and vertical velocity components:

$$v_x = v_{ox} - f_x \Delta t$$

$$\text{LET} \quad V1 = V1 - F1*T1 \tag{6.6-8}$$

$$v_y = v_{oy} + (g - f_y) \Delta t$$

$$\text{LET} \quad V2 = V2 + (G - F2)*T1 \tag{6.6-9}$$

and

(5) The X and Y coordinates of the rocket.

Computer Technique: Program 6.6A is very similar to Program 6.3A, however, there are several changes made by adding friction. The initial X and Y velocities are calculated as before; followed by the initial X and Y friction forces; using Equations 6.6-3 and 6.6-4 with initial velocity:

```
180   LET F1=K*V0↑2*COS(C)          (before loop)
190   LET F2=K*V0↑2*SIN(C)
```

The initial velocity calculation for the slope at the mid-time point is predicted prior to entering the iteration loop.

```
250   LET V2=V2+G*T1/2-F2*T1/2      (before loop)
260   LET V1=V1-F1*T1/2
```

The first thing to calculate inside the loop will then be the position of X and Y followed by the friction, new angle, friction components and the new velocity components based upon the changing values of friction and angle. These iterations are made in a subroutine so that fewer changes will have to be made when changing iterative techniques.

```
100 REM **************ROCKET TRAJECTORY 3P ******************
110 PRINT"WHAT IS INITIAL VELOCITY, ANGLE, TIME INCREMENT,FRICTION"
120 PRINT"COEFFICIENT , 1 = PLOT OR 2 = PRINT."
130 PRINT
140 INPUT V0, C, T1, K, P
150 LET C = C*PI/180
160 LET V1 = V0*COS(C)
170 LET V2 = V0*SIN(C)
180 LET F1 = K*V0↑2*COS(C)
190 LET F2 = K*V0↑2*SIN(C)
200 LET G = -9.8
210 LET T5 = -V2/G
220 LET X5 = 2*T5*V1
230 LET Y5 = V2*T5 + G*T5↑2/2
240 LET J = 1
250 LET V2 = V2 + G*T1/2
260 LET V1 = V1 - F1*T1/2
270 PRINT
280 IF P = 1 THEN 300
290 GOTO 340
300 PRINT"Y=0","TO",,"MAX OF"INT(1000*Y5)/1000
310 PRINT"X=0","TO",,"MAX OF"INT(1000*X5)/1000
320 PRINT"-------------------------------------------------------------"u
330 GOTO 350
340 PRINT"X DIST.","Y HEIGHT","X VELOCITY","Y VELOCITY","TIME"
350 GOSUB 600
360 IF Y<=0 THEN 570
370 IF T+T1>=J THEN 390
380 GOTO 350
390 LET T = INT(T+.5)
400 LET J = J+1
410 IF P = 1 THEN 450
420 PRINT INT(100*X)/100, INT(100*Y)/100, INT(100*V1)/100,
430 PRINT INT(100*V2)/100,T
440 GOTO 350
450 LET E = 70/Y5
460 LET Y9 = INT(E*Y)
470 LET E1 = 70/X5
480 LET X9 = INT(E1*X)
490 IF Y = X THEN 460
500 IF X9<Y9 THEN 550
510 PRINT T; TAB(Y9);"Y"; TAB(X9);"X"
520 GOTO 350
530 PRINT T; TAB(Y9);"*"
540 GOTO 350
550 PRINT T; TAB(X9); "X"; TAB(Y9); "Y"
560 GOTO 350
570 PRINT
580 PRINT"AT"T"SECONDS,Y="INT(1000*Y)/1000,"TIME INCREMENT="T1"SECONDS"
590 STOP
```

PROGRAM 6.6A. Rocket trajectory with drag, print or plot

```
600 LET X = X + V1*T1
610 LET Y = Y + V2*T1
620 LET T = T + T1
630 LET F0 = (V1↑2 + V2↑2)*K
640 LET C = ATN(V2/V1)
650 LET F1 = F0*COS( C )
660 LET F2 = F0*SIN( C )
670 LET V2 = V2 +(G-F2)*T1
680 LET V1 = V1 - F1*T1
690 RETURN
```

PROGRAM 6.6B. Euler subroutine for program 6.6A

EULER METHOD SUBROUTINE

```
600   LET  X=X+V1*T1            (start loop position)
610   LET  Y=Y+V2*T1
620   LET  T=T+T1
630   LET  F0=(V1↑2+V2↑2)*K     (drag force)
640   LET  C=ATN (V2/V1)        (angle)
650   LET  F1=FO*COS(C)         (X-Drag)
660   LET  F2=F0*SIN(C)         (Y-Drag)
670   LET  V2=V2+(G−F2)*T1      (Y-Velocity)
680   LET  V1=V1−F1*T1          (X-Velocity)
690   RETURN                    (end loop)
```

Comments About the Computer Program: Program (6.6A) allows a choice of printing the data, or plotting it. Statements 450 to 550 make up the plotting sequence along with statements 300 to 320 which make the titles for the plot. The IF statements 280 and 410 allow for the decision to plot or print. Both X and Y are plotted versus time (Fig. 6.6C) and the theoretical values for the zero friction case are used to scale the plot. For complicated functions with no known theoretical values, the scaling factors for the plot can then be an input by the user of the program based upon prior knowledge or by trial and error.

The printed values of data have been rounded off after two decimal points by using the INT statement in statements 420 and 430. By successively running the programs, data may be checked, then plotted, or different values of the drag coefficient, initial velocity or, launch angle can be tried in order to study these effects.

Discussion of Computer Results: Table 6.6A and Fig. 6.6C indicate the results of this friction problem with a coefficient of drag of 0.0001. The data

```
WHAT IS INITIAL VELOCITY, ANGLE, TIME INCREMENT,FRICTION
COEFFICIENT , 1 = PLOT OR 2 = PRINT.

? 100, 45, .1, .0001, 1

Y=0              TO                        MAX OF 255.102
X=0              TO                        MAX OF 1020.408
- - - - - - - - - - - - - - - - - - - - - - - - - - - - - - - - - - - - -
 1  X              Y
 2     X        Y                 Y
 3        X                            Y
 4          X                             Y
 5            X                             Y
 6          X                                 Y
 7             X                                Y
 8              X                             Y
 9                 X                        Y
10                  X        Y
11                  Y    X
12              Y            X
13        Y                    X
14 Y                                X

AT 14.2 SECONDS,Y=-4.46       TIME INCREMENT= 0.1 SECONDS
```
Figure 6.6C. Rocket trajectory

```
WHAT IS INITIAL VELOCITY, ANGLE, TIME INCREMENT,FRICTION
COEFFICIENT , 1 = PLOT OR 2 = PRINT.

? 100, 45, .1, .001, 1

Y=0            TO                            MAX OF 255.102
X=0            TO                            MAX OF 1020.408
---------------------------------------------------------------
 1  X            Y
 2      X                     Y
 3          X                           Y
 4              X                             Y
 5                  X                             Y
 6                     X                          Y
 7                        X                      Y
 8                           X              Y
 9                              X    Y
 10                         Y      X
 11             Y                   X
 12 Y                                  X

AT 12.3 SECONDS,Y=-2.284      TIME INCREMENT= 0.1 SECONDS
```

Figure 6.6D. Rocket trajectory

shows a progressive change in X velocity which is barely detectable in the plot. This tendency is more easily seen in Fig. 6.6D when K=.001, simulating a higher drag projectile.

The accuracy of the results are inferred by checking the Y height of Tables 6.6B, C, and D for a particular time, i.e., 12 seconds. Each value is progressively closer to 14 for each smaller increment in T1, i.e., 12.46, 13.59 and 13.76 for a T1 of 1, .1 and .01 seconds. The lower value of total

```
WHAT IS INITIAL VELOCITY, ANGLE, TIME INCREMENT,FRICTION
COEFFICIENT , 1 = PLOT OR 2 = PRINT.

? 100, 45, .1, .0001, 2
```

X DIST.	Y HEIGHT	X VELOCITY	Y VELOCITY	TIME
70.36	65.51	69.99	59.79	1
140.08	120.66	69.37	49.49	2
209.19	165.57	68.8	39.32	3
277.76	200.36	68.28	29.26	4
345.82	225.12	67.78	19.28	5
413.39	239.94	67.32	9.37	6
480.51	244.89	66.86	-0.46	7
547.18	240.03	66.42	-10.23	8
613.4	225.44	65.97	-19.93	9
679.16	201.17	65.51	-29.56	10
744.46	167.32	65.03	-39.11	11
809.27	123.95	64.52	-48.57	12
873.55	71.16	63.99	-57.93	13
937.29	9.06	63.42	-67.18	14

```
AT 14.2 SECONDS,Y=-4.46      TIME INCREMENT= 0.1 SECONDS
```

TABLE 6.6A

WHAT IS INITIAL VELOCITY, ANGLE, TIME INCREMENT,FRICTION
COEFFICIENT , 1 = PLOT OR 2 = PRINT.

? 100, 45, 1, .001, 2

X DIST.	Y HEIGHT	X VELOCITY	Y VELOCITY	TIME
67.17	65.81	60.85	49.82	1
128.03	115.63	56.07	36.1	2
184.1	151.73	52.33	23.89	3
236.43	175.63	49.32	12.72	4
285.75	188.35	46.8	2.27	5
332.56	190.62	44.61	-7.64	6
377.18	182.99	42.59	-17.09	7
419.77	165.9	40.64	-26.11	8
460.42	139.79	38.67	-34.65	9
499.09	105.15	36.66	-42.65	10
535.76	62.51	34.6	-50.05	11
570.37	12.46	32.5	-56.81	12

AT 13 SECONDS,Y=-44.334   TIME INCREMENT= 1 SECONDS

TABLE 6.6B

Y-acceleration is evident from the increased time of flight after Y-maximum
has been reached. Since the velocity in the Y-direction changes direction
after the maximum height is reached, the friction vector of Fig. 6.6B will
oppose the force of gravity for the trip down. Notice that the angle, (C),
of statement 640 will be negative when the y-velocity is negative, therefore
the trigonometry shown in Fig. 6.6B will take care of the changing sign of
the drag force.

WHAT IS INITIAL VELOCITY, ANGLE, TIME INCREMENT,FRICTION
COEFFICIENT , 1 = PLOT OR 2 = PRINT.

? 100, 45, .1, .001, 2

X DIST.	Y HEIGHT	X VELOCITY	Y VELOCITY	TIME
67.42	62.98	64.12	54.58	1
129.26	111.31	59.26	40.97	2
186.71	146.7	55.38	28.77	3
240.62	170.37	52.2	17.57	4
291.58	183.18	49.52	7.09	5
340.02	185.77	47.16	-2.83	6
386.21	178.65	45	-12.3	7
430.27	162.25	42.93	-21.33	8
472.28	137.04	40.87	-29.89	9
512.21	103.49	38.78	-37.94	10
550.05	62.14	36.66	-45.41	11
585.75	13.59	34.51	-52.28	12

AT 12.3 SECONDS,Y=-2.284   TIME INCREMENT= 0.1 SECONDS

TABLE 6.6C

WHAT IS INITIAL VELOCITY, ANGLE, TIME INCREMENT,FRICTION
COEFFICIENT , 1 = PLOT OR 2 = PRINT.

? 100, 45, .01, .001, 2

X DIST.	Y HEIGHT	X VELOCITY	Y VELOCITY	TIME
67.46	62.73	64.45	55.06	1
129.4	110.93	59.58	41.46	2
186.99	146.25	55.68	29.26	3
241.04	169.9	52.49	18.06	4
292.17	182.72	49.79	7.58	5
340.76	185.35	47.42	-2.36	6
387.1	178.27	45.24	-11.82	7
431.31	161.95	43.16	-20.85	8
473.44	136.82	41.09	-29.42	9
513.5	103.38	38.99	-37.47	10
551.45	62.16	36.87	-44.95	11
587.26	13.76	34.71	-51.84	12

AT 12.27 SECONDS,Y=-0.462   TIME INCREMENT= 0.01 SECONDS

Table 6.6D

6.7   TRAJECTORY WITH FRICTION II

Lesson Characteristics:

PHYSICS LEVEL   college, advanced

MATHEMATICS BACKGROUND REQUIRED   analytical
geometry

PEDAGOGY   computer learning and simulation

PROBLEM APPROACH   numerical method

STUDENT PARTICIPATION   assists in program writing

PROGRAMMING SKILLS   intermediate BASIC

TIME OF STUDENT INVOLVEMENT   in class—20 minutes,
out of class—1 hour

RECOMMENDED READINGS   Same as Lesson 6.6

Lesson Description: The problem of Section 6.6 remains the same for this
section. A more advanced Runge-Kutta method is applied to this problem
by essentially changing the subroutine of Program 6.6A. The increased
accuracy of the Runge-Kutta method is demonstrated, and this should
provide the inquiring student with a non-calculus tool for solving problems
which normally require a detailed knowledge of differential equations.

Background and Theory: It was seen in the series of Programs 6.2, 6.3 and
6.4 that the corrected Euler gave surprisingly good results and the other
Runge Kutta methods improved the results very little. However, since the
problem is no longer of second order, it cannot be assumed that the corrected Euler will give an excellent result, (as seen from Tables 6.6B, 6.6C,

6.6D and as discussed in Section 6.6). A Runge Kutta method is required if closer convergence is desired. Program 6.7A is essentially the same program as 6.6A but uses a fourth order Runge Kutta subroutine instead of the Euler subroutine. Program 6.5B and 6.5C are examples of the Runge Kutta method used from the differential equation, and from the basic definitions of the physical phenomena, respectively. A review of Figs. 6.5A and 6.5B is in order, before continuing the Runge Kutta development. Look for the means by which each slope is obtained in this method.

Computer Technique: The first thing to do when solving higher order equations is to list and order all of the variable quantities

(1) Velocity (in X and Y direction)
(2) Angle with respect to the horizon is dependent upon V1 and V2; i.e., $C = ATN(V2/V1)$
(3) The magnitude of the friction force depends upon velocity, i.e.,

$$f = kv^2$$

(where the force is always in a direction opposite that of the velocity)

$$LET \quad F0 = K*(V1\uparrow 2 + V2\uparrow 2)$$

(4) Acceleration in Y direction depends upon friction force in the Y direction, i.e.,

$$a_y = g - f\sin(c)$$
$$LET \quad A = G - F0*SIN(C)$$

(5) Acceleration in X direction depends upon friction force in the X direction, i.e.,

$$a_x = -f\cos(c)$$
$$LET \quad B = -F0*COS(C)$$

That is, find the average acceleration in X and Y, and the average velocity in X and Y over the time interval, in order to calculate the final position of the X and Y coordinates. The cycle is then repeated for each interval until the problem is completed. Since the values are time dependent rather than position and time dependent, the third order method is used. The slope at the mid-time point is weighted by four, and the initial and final slopes are weighted by one:

LET $F = (F0 + 4*F1 + F3)/6$	(Average force of friction over T1)
LET $A = (A0 + 4*A1 + A3)/6$	(Average acceleration in Y over T1)
LET $B = (B0 + 4*B1 + B3)/6$	(Average acceleration in X over T1)
LET $P = (P0 + 4*P1 + P3)/6$	(Average velocity in Y over T1)
LET $S = (S0 + 4*S1 + S3)/6$	(Average velocity in X over T1)

The velocity at the end of the interval is then:

LET V2 = V2 + A*T1   (Instantaneous Y velocity at

                                               $T + T1$)

LET V1 = V1 + B*T1   (Instantaneous X velocity at

                                               $T + T1$)

LET X = X + S*T1   (X position at $T + T1$)

LET Y = Y + P*T1   (Y position at $T + T1$)

This Runge Kutta method is shown as a subroutine beginning with line 600 in Program 6.7A. (See Program 6.7B for subroutine)

Comments About the Computer Program: The other changes to Program 6.6A are:

(1) Calculate initial friction force; replace line 180 with:

$$180 \quad \text{LET } F0 = K*V0\uparrow2$$

```
100 REM **************ROCKET TRAJECTORY 3AP *****************
110 PRINT"WHAT IS INITIAL VELOCITY, ANGLE, TIME INCREMENT,FRICTION"
120 PRINT"COEFFICIENT , 1 = PLOT OR 2 = PRINT."
130 PRINT
140 INPUT V0, C, T1, K, P9
150 LET C = C*PI/180
160 LET V1 = V0*COS(C)
170 LET V2 = V0*SIN(C)
180 LET F0 = K*V0↑2
200 LET G = -9.8
210 LET T5 = -V2/G
220 LET X5 = 2*T5*V1
230 LET Y5 = V2*T5 + G*T5↑2/2
240 LET J = 1
270 PRINT
280 IF P9 = 1 THEN 300
290 GOTO 340
300 PRINT"Y=0","TO",,"MAX OF"INT(1000*Y5)/1000
310 PRINT"X=0","TO",,"MAX OF"INT(1000*X5)/1000
320 PRINT" ---------------------------------------------------------------"
330 GOTO 350
340 PRINT"X DIST.","Y HEIGHT","X VELOCITY","Y VELOCITY","TIME"
350 GOSUB 600
352 LET T = T + T1
360 IF Y<=0 THEN 570
370 IF T+T1>=J THEN 390
380 GOTO 350
390 LET T = INT(T+.5)
400 LET J = J+1
410 IF P9 = 1 THEN 450
420 PRINT INT(100*X)/100, INT(100*Y)/100, INT(100*V1)/100,
430 PRINT INT(100*V2)/100,T
440 GOTO 350
450 LET E = 70/Y5
460 LET Y9 = INT(E*Y)
470 LET E1 = 70/X5
480 LET X9 = INT(E1*X)
490 IF Y = X THEN 460
500 IF X9<Y9 THEN 550
510 PRINT T; TAB(Y9);"Y"; TAB(X9);"X"
520 GOTO 350
530 PRINT T; TAB(Y9);"*"
540 GOTO 350
550 PRINT T; TAB(X9); "X"; TAB(Y9); "Y"
560 GOTO 350
570 PRINT
580 PRINT"AT"T"SECONDS,Y="INT(1000*Y)/1000,"TIME INCREMENT="T1"SECONDS"
590 STOP
```

PROGRAM 6.7A

```
600 LET PO = V2
610 LET SO = V1
620 LET C  = ATN(PO/SO)
630 LET FO = K*(V2†2 + V1†2)
640 LET AO = G - FO*SIN(C )
650 LET BO = -FO*COS(C )
660 LET P1 = PO + AO*T1/2
670 LET S1 = SO + BO*T1/2
680 LET C  = ATN(P1/S1)
690 LET F1 = K*(P1†2 + S1†2)
700 LET A1 = G - F1*SIN(C )
710 LET B1 = -F1*COS(C )
720 LET P3 = PO + A1*T1
730 LET S3 = SO + B1*T1
740 LET C  = ATN(P3/S3)
750 LET F3 = K*(P3†2 + S3†2)
760 LET A3 = G - F3*SIN(C )
770 LET B3 = -F3*COS(C )
780 LET F = (FO + 4*F1 +F3)/6
790 LET A = (AO + 4*A1 + A3)/6
800 LET B = (BO + 4*B1 + B3)/6
810 LET P = (PO + 4*P1 + P3)/6
820 LET S = (SO + 4*S1 + S3)/6
830 LET V2 = V2 + A*T1
840 LET V1 = V1 + B*T1
850 LET X = X + S*T1
860 LET Y = Y + P*T1
870 RETURN
```

PROGRAM 6.7B

(2) Delete lines 190, 250 and 260.

Care is taken in obtaining initial values for each iteration, i.e.,

830	LET V2=V2+A*T1	(Near end of loop
840	LET V1=V1+B*T1	for final
		velocities)

```
WHAT IS INITIAL VELOCITY, ANGLE, TIME INCREMENT,FRICTION
COEFFICIENT , 1 = PLOT OR 2 = PRINT.

? 100,45,1,.001,1
```

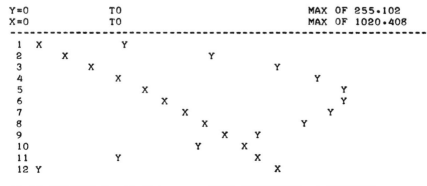

Figure 6.7

600	LET P0 = V2	(Initial slope is best
610	LET S0 = V1	known value for
		that time)
620	LET C1 = ATN(P0/0)	(Best known values
630	LET F0 = K*(V2↑2 + V2↑2)	for angle, drag,
640	LET A0 = G − F0*SIN(C1)	Y and X
650	LET B0 = − F0*COS(C1)	acceleration)

WHAT IS INITIAL VELOCITY, ANGLE, TIME INCREMENT, FRICTION
COEFFICIENT , 1 = PLOT OR 2 = PRINT.

? 100,45,1,.001,2

X DIST.	Y HEIGHT	X VELOCITY	Y VELOCITY	TIME
67.32	62.5	64.51	55.14	1
129.21	110.56	59.65	41.56	2
186.78	145.83	55.76	29.37	3
240.84	169.45	52.57	18.17	4
291.99	182.27	49.87	7.69	5
340.63	184.91	47.49	-2.25	6
387.01	177.86	45.31	-11.72	7
431.27	161.56	43.22	-20.74	8
473.46	136.46	41.15	-29.31	9
513.57	103.04	39.05	-37.36	10
551.57	61.85	36.92	-44.85	11
587.43	13.46	34.76	-51.73	12

AT 13 SECONDS, Y= -41.494 　　　　TIME INCREMENT= 1 SECONDS

TABLE 6.7A

```
600 LET PO = V2
610 LET SO = V1
620 LET C  = ATN(PO/SO)
630 LET FO = K*(V2↑2 + V1↑2)
640 LET AO = G - FO*SIN(C )
650 LET BO = -FO*COS(C )
660 LET P1 = PO + AO*T1/2
670 LET S1 = SO + BO*T1/2
680 LET C  = ATN(P1/S1)
690 LET F1 = K*(P1↑2 + S1↑2)
700 LET A1 = G - F1*SIN(C )
710 LET B1 = -F1*COS(C )
720 LET P3 = PO + A1*T1
730 LET S3 = SO + B1*T1
740 LET C  = ATN(P3/S3)
750 LET F3 = K*(P3↑2 + S3↑2)
760 LET A3 = G - F3*SIN(C )
770 LET B3 = -F3*COS(C )
780 LET F = (FO + 4*F1 +F3)/6
790 LET A = (AO + 4*A1 + A3)/6
800 LET B = (BO + 4*B1 + B3)/6
810 LET P = (PO + 4*P1 + P3)/6
820 LET S = (SO + 4*S1 + S3)/6
830 LET V2 = V2 + A*T1
840 LET V1 = V1 + B*T1
850 LET X = X + S*T1
860 LET Y = Y + P*T1
870 RETURN
```

PROGRAM 6.7B.   Runge Kutta subroutine

The same six steps are repeated for each value at the mid-time point and the end point. This subroutine has three times as many statements as does the program of Section 6.6.

Discussion of Computer Results: The print-out of Program 6.7A shown in Tables 6.7A, B, and C show rapid convergence for all values as compared to Program 6.6A. The values for a time increment of 1 second, Table 6.7A are almost as good as the values for a time increment of 0.01 seconds from Table 6.6C, or approximately 100 times more accurate. The values have definitely converged for a time increment of 0.1 seconds.

The data is plotted in Fig. 6.7A to show the effect of wind resistance on the body.

```
WHAT IS INITIAL VELOCITY, ANGLE, TIME INCREMENT,FRICTION
COEFFICIENT , 1 = PLOT OR 2 = PRINT.

?  100,45,.1,.001,2
```

X DIST.	Y HEIGHT	X VELOCITY	Y VELOCITY	TIME
67.46	62.71	64.48	55.11	1
129.42	110.88	59.61	41.51	2
187.02	146.2	55.72	29.31	3
241.09	169.85	52.52	18.11	4
292.23	182.67	49.82	7.63	5
340.84	185.3	47.45	-2.3	6
387.19	178.23	45.27	-11.77	7
431.42	161.91	43.18	-20.8	8
473.57	136.8	41.11	-29.36	9
513.65	103.37	39.02	-37.41	10
551.61	62.16	36.89	-44.9	11
587.43	13.77	34.73	-51.79	12

```
AT 12.3 SECONDS,Y=-2.05          TIME INCREMENT= 0.1 SECONDS
```
TABLE 6.7B

WHAT IS INITIAL VELOCITY, ANGLE, TIME INCREMENT,FRICTION
COEFFICIENT , 1 = PLOT OR 2 = PRINT.

? 100,45,.01,.001,2

X DIST.	Y HEIGHT	X VELOCITY	Y VELOCITY	TIME
67.46	62.71	64.48	55.11	1
129.42	110.88	59.61	41.51	2
187.02	146.2	55.71	29.31	3
241.09	169.85	52.52	18.11	4
292.23	182.67	49.82	7.63	5
340.85	185.3	47.45	-2.3	6
387.2	178.23	45.27	-11.77	7
431.42	161.92	43.18	-20.8	8
473.57	136.8	41.11	-29.36	9
513.65	103.37	39.02	-37.42	10
551.61	62.17	36.89	-44.9	11
587.43	13.78	34.73	-51.79	12

AT 12.27 SECONDS,Y=-0.438   TIME INCREMENT= 0.01 SECONDS

TABLE 6.7C

6.8   THE SIMPLE HARMONIC OSCILLATOR

Lesson Characteristics:

PHYSICS LEVEL   college, introductory

MATHEMATICS BACKGROUND REQUIRED   analytic
geometry

PEDAGOGY   computer learning and simulation

PROBLEM APPROACH   numerical solution

STUDENT PARTICIPATION   assists in program writing

PROGRAMMING SKILLS   introductory BASIC

TIME OF STUDENT INVOLVEMENT   in class—1 hour,
out of class—5 hours

SUGGESTED READINGS   (2) Chapter 15, (5) Chapter II

Lesson Description: The introduction of periodic motion normally begins
with the solution of a second-order differential equation. This lesson demonstrates a computer approach to the equation of motion of a spring-mass
system which requires only a knowledge of the basic physics involved and
an understanding of the slope of a line. After a brief explanation of the
spring force acting on a block, the lesson is developed in BASIC with the
computer solution plotted by the simple TAB function.

The student should be required to draw a free-body diagram of all the
forces influencing the motion of the mass. From this diagram, a computer
program can be developed in a manner parallel to the discussion of this
lesson.

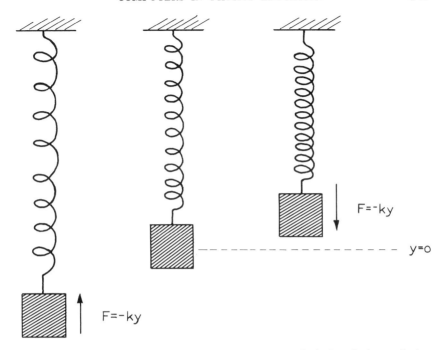

Figure 6.8A   Simple Harmonic Motion: Diagram of a Block Attached to a Spring

The lesson is intended to encourage the student to measure quantitatively the effect of changes in amplitude, mass, or spring constant on the resulting period of motion. A functional relationship for the period in terms of the above parameters can easily be obtained from the computer-generated results.

Background and Theory: Any motion that repeats itself in equal intervals of time is called periodic, or harmonic. If a body moves about an equilibrium position due to a force that is proportional to the distance from the equilibrium position to the body, then the body is said to undergo simple harmonic motion. An ideal example of such a system is a block suspended from the spring as shown in Fig. 6.8A. The force on the block due to the spring is always such as to pull the block back to its equilibrium position $(y = 0)$ and is properly called the restoring force. At equilibrium, of course, the upward force of the spring on the block is equal to the downward force of gravity. At any particular instant, the force of the spring on the block is by Hooke's law,

$$f = -ky \qquad (6.8-1)$$

The minus sign indicates that the force will always be in a direction opposite to the direction of the displacement in the Y-direction thereby always opposing the motion of the block.

If Newton's second law, $f = ma$, is applied to the motion of the block of mass, m, and if the force F is replaced by the expression $-ky$, the following relationship results:

$$-ky = ma \qquad (6.8\text{--}2)$$

In review, the following definitions will be helpful (See also Section 6.2):

$$a = \text{acceleration} \cong \Delta v / \Delta t$$

$$v = \text{velocity} \cong \Delta y / \Delta t \qquad (6.8\text{--}3)$$

Therefore, Equation 6.8–2 becomes,

$$-ky = m(\Delta v / \Delta t) \qquad (6.8\text{--}4)$$

The problem is to calculate the position, y, of the block at any instant of time after it starts to move from an initial displacement of 30 meters (this is a big spring). Before beginning one must realize and understand what is known. In this case, at time $t = 0$,

$$v = 0 \text{ m/s}$$

$$y = 30 \text{ m,}$$

and after a small change in time, Δt

$$y = 30 + \Delta y$$

$$v = 0 + \Delta v.$$

y and v change during each time increment as described by re-writing Equations 6.8–3 and 6.8–4.

$$\Delta y / \Delta t = v \qquad (6.8\text{--}5)$$

$$\Delta v / \Delta t = -k \, y/m \qquad (6.8\text{--}6)$$

Computer Techniques: This interesting problem can be solved if the incremental changes in velocity (Δv) and displacement (Δy) which occur during small changes in time (Δt) can be accurately approximated. In other words, after a small change in time, (Δt in BASIC will be call D and $\Delta y = D1$ and $\Delta v = D2$). The new displacement and velocity can be found by:

$$\text{LET} \quad Y = Y + D1$$

$$\text{LET} \quad V = V + D2$$

$$\text{LET} \quad A = -K*Y/M \quad \text{(from Equation 6.8–2)}$$

Notice that the equations are in computer form, that is for example, the algorithm, $Y = Y + D1$, directs the computer to calculate a new value of Y by taking the existing value and adding the quantity ΔY. The values of ΔY and ΔV can be calculated by,

$$\text{LET} \quad D1 = V*D$$

(Change in Displacement) = *(velocity)* * *(change in time)*

$$\text{LET} \quad D2 = A*D$$

(Change in Velocity) − *(acceleration)* * *(change in time)*

where V and A represent the best estimate of the velocity and acceleration respectively during the time interval, D. Therefore, after each increment of time, the new values of Y, V, and A become,

$$\text{LET } Y = Y + V*D \qquad (6.8-7)$$

$$\text{LET } V = V + A*D \qquad (6.8-8)$$

$$\text{LET } A = -K*Y/M \qquad (6.8-9)$$

(Watch for these recursion equations in Program 6.8)

An excellent estimate of the values of V and A during the time interval, D, can be made using the fourth order Runge-Kutta (See Section 6.3) as explained below.

Comments About the Computer Program: In Program 6.8, the initial slopes of the Runge-Kutta method are calculated by (refer to Fig. 5.2),

$$390 \quad \text{LET } Y1 = Y$$

$$400 \quad \text{LET } V1 = V$$

$$410 \quad \text{LET } A1 = -K*Y1/M.$$

These slopes are used to determine the slopes, V2 and A2, at the midpoint of the time interval, D/2,

$$420 \quad \text{LET } Y2 = Y1 + V1*D/2$$

$$430 \quad \text{LET } V2 = V1 + A1*D/2$$

$$440 \quad \text{LET } A2 = -K*Y2/M.$$

Then the values of V2 and A2 are used to make a second prediction of the midpoint values of the slopes, V3 and A3 (refer to Fig. 5.2),

$$450 \quad \text{LET } Y3 = Y1 + V2*D/2$$

$$460 \quad \text{LET } V3 = V1 + A2*D/2$$

$$470 \quad \text{LET } A3 = -K*Y3/M,$$

and finally, this set of slopes is used to predict V4 and A4, the slopes at the end of the time interval, D,

$$480 \quad \text{LET } Y4 = Y1 + V3*D$$

$$490 \quad \text{LET } V4 = V1 + A3*D$$

$$500 \quad \text{LET } A4 = -K*Y4/M.$$

The weighted average of these slopes is found by,

$$\text{LET } V = (V1 + 2*V2 + 2*V3 + V4)/6$$

where

$$V = \textit{weighted average during the time interval } D,$$

```
100 REM ************* SIMPLE HARMONIC MOTION *************
110 REM
120 REM
130 REM
140 READ K, D, T0, Y0, V0, M
150 DATA 11.2, 0.1, 0, 25, 0, 1
160 PRINT "SPRING CONSTANT = "K"NEWTONS/METER"
170 REM
180 REM
190 REM
200 LET T = T0
210 LET Y = Y0
220 LET V = V0
230 LET N = 0
240 REM
250 REM
260 REM
270 PRINT "                         Y - DISPLACEMENT IN METERS"
280 PRINT
290 PRINT TAB(33); "0"
300 PRINT "SECONDS ----------------------------------------";
310 PRINT "----------------"
320 LET Y1 = INT(Y + .5) + 36
330 PRINT T; TAB(Y1); "*"
340 LET N = N + 1
350 IF N = 40 THEN 570
360 REM
370 REM
380 LET Y1 = Y
390 LET V1 = V
400 LET A1 = -K*Y1/M
410 LET Y2 = Y1 + V1*D/2
420 LET V2 = V1 + A1*D/2
430 LET A2 = -K*Y2/M
440 LET Y3 = Y1 + V2*D/2
450 LET V3 = V1 + A2*D/2
460 LET A3 = -K*Y3/M
470 LET Y4 = Y1 + V3*D
480 LET V4 = V1 + A3*D
490 LET A4 = -K*Y4/M
500 REM
510 LET Y = Y + (V1 + 2*V2 + 2*V3 + V4)*D/6
520 LET V = V + (A1 + 2*A2 + 2*A3 + A4)*D/6
530 LET A = -K*Y/M
540 LET T = T + D
550 SETDIGITS(3)
560 GO TO 320
570 END
```

PROGRAM 6.8 Simple Harmonic Motion.

and

$$\text{LET } A = (A1 + 2*A2 + 2*A3 + A4)/6$$

where

$A =$ *weighted average during the time interval D.*

The new values of displacement and velocity are found by using the weighted averages as follows:

$$\text{LET } Y = Y + V*D \qquad\qquad (6.8\text{--}7)$$

thus

$$520 \quad \text{LET } Y = Y + (V1 + 2*V2 + 2*V3 + V4)*D/6$$

and

$$\text{LET } V = V + A*D \qquad\qquad (6.8\text{--}8)$$

thus

$$530 \quad \text{LET } V = V + (A1 + 2*A2 + 2*A3 + A4)*D/6,$$

TIME	Y-DISPLACEMENT	VELOCITY
0	10	10
1.	17.335	4.03839
2	18.0589	-2.87258
3.	12.4283	-8.24933
4.	2.89662	-10.3347
5.	·6.9112	-8.65489
6.	-13.5531	-4.08575
7.	-14.9563	1.55651
8.	-11.0349	6.22131
9.	-3.56671	8.35691
10.	4.57025	7.41326
11.	10.4865	3.95666
12.	12.2895	-.613726
13.	9.66723	-4.61804
14.	3.87517	-6.70323
15.	-2.82237	-6.28983
16.	-8.01965	-3.71447
17.	-10.0195	-4.19235E-2
18.	-8.37066	3.36238
19.	-3.92926	5.33173
20.	1.54052	5.28977
21.	6.05169	3.40605
22.	8.10467	.479439
23.	7.17274	-2.38898
24.	3.81084	-4.20322
25.	-.621279	-4.41171
26.	-4.49533	-3.0654
27.	-6.5031	-.753625
28.	-6.08804	1.64295
29.	-3.58153	3.2819
30.	-1.88955E-2	3.64993

TABLE 6.8A   Simple Harmonic Motion: Numerical Output for a Spring Constant of 11.2 Newtons/Meter.

SPRING CONSTANT   =   2.8 NEWTONS/METER

TIME (SECS.)	Y-DISPLACEMENT (METERS)	Y-VELOCITY (METERS/SECOND)	Y-ACCELERATION (METERS/SECOND↑2)
0	30	C	0
.5	20.1	-37.1	-74.2
1	-2.9	-49.7	-25.3
1.5	-23.9	-29.8	40.
2	-29.2	9.62	78.8
2.5	-15.3	42.5	65.8
3	8.52	47.5	9.83
3.5	26.7	21.3	-52.4
4	27.3	-18.7	-80.
4.5	10.	-46.3	-55.1
5	-13.7	-43.4	5.73
5.5	-28.4	-12.1	62.6
6	-24.4	27.	78.2
6.5	-4.44	48.2	42.5
7	18.3	37.8	-20.8
7.5	29.	2.7	-70.3
8	20.6	-34.	-73.5
8.5	-1.21	-48.3	-28.6
9	-22.2	-30.9	34.8
9.5	-28.5	6.68	75.2

TABLE 6.8B   Simple Harmonic Motion: Numerical Output for a Spring Constant of 2.8 Newtons/Meter.

and finally,

540   LET A= −K*Y/M.

Therefore, at every instant of time, T+D, the computer calculates new values of the Y-displacement, velocity, and acceleration.

Program 6.8 is a clear example of how the use of simple recursion Equations (6.8–7, 6.8–8, and 6.8–9) leads to the solution of motion of a spring-mass system. Students should be encouraged to write a program involving harmonic motion and explore the effect of changing the mass of the block, M, or the spring constant, K, on the period of motion.

The accuracy of each approximation of the calculated slopes is dependent upon the choice of the time interval, D. It is interesting for the student to change the time interval in statements 150 and 160 and observed the change in accuracy of the final calculation.

Discussion of Computer Results: In the tabular output of Program 6.8 (Table 6.8A), the values of displacement, velocity, and acceleration are shown. Use of the SETDIGITS (3) function in statement 560 causes the results to be limited to 3 significant figures.

The graphical output in Figs. 6.8B, 6.8C and 6.8D can be used by the student to explore the effect of changes in the mass, spring constant, or amplitude on the period of the oscillation. In the three figures, the spring constant is changed by a factor of two, i.e., 2.8, 5.6, and 11.2 newtons/meter. How does this affect the period? What would be the relationship of spring constant to period? Try changing the mass hanging from the spring.

SPRING CONSTANT = 2.8 NEWTONS/METER

TIME (SECS.)	Y-DISPLACEMENT (METERS)	Y-VELOCITY (METERS/SECOND)	Y-ACCELERATION (METERS/SECOND↑2)
0	30	0	0
.05	29.9	-4.2	-83.9
.1	29.6	-8.36	-83.3
.15	29.1	-12.5	-82.1
.2	28.3	-16.5	-80.4
.25	27.4	-20.4	-78.1
.3	26.3	-24.2	-75.2
.35	25.	-27.7	-71.9
.4	23.5	-31.1	-68.
.45	21.9	-34.3	-63.6
.5	20.1	-37.3	-58.8
.55	18.2	-39.9	-53.6
.6	16.1	-42.3	-48.
.65	13.9	-44.5	-42.1
.7	11.7	-46.2	-35.9
.75	9.32	-47.7	-29.4
.8	6.9	-48.9	-22.7
.85	4.44	-49.6	-15.9
.9	1.94	-50.1	-8.94
.95	-.566	-50.2	-1.93
1.	-3.07	-49.9	5.09
1.05	-5.55	-49.3	12.1
1.1	-8.	-48.4	19.
1.15	-10.4	-47.1	25.8
1.2	-12.7	-45.5	32.3
1.25	-14.9	-43.5	38.7
1.3	-17.1	-41.3	44.8
1.35	-19.1	-38.8	50.6
1.4	-20.9	-36.	56.
1.45	-22.6	-32.9	61.

TABLE 6.8C. Simple Harmonic Motion: Numerical output for a spring constant of 2.8 newtons/meter and a printing time of 0.05 seconds.

SPRING CONSTANT   =   11.2 NEWTONS/METER

Y - DISPLACEMENT IN METERS

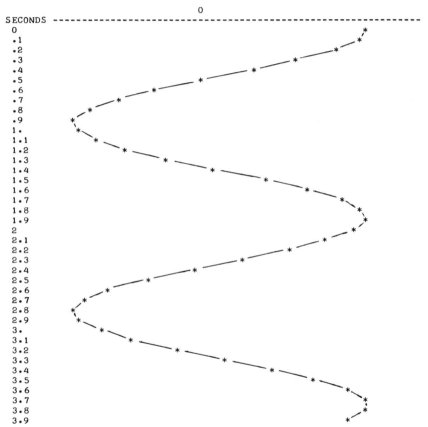

Figure 6.8B   Simple Harmonic Motion: Graphical Output of Y-Displacement for Spring Constant = 11.2 Newtons/Meter.

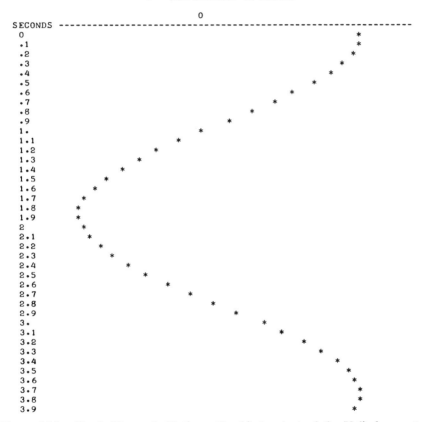

Figure 6.8C.   Simple Harmonic Motion: Graphical output of the Y-displacement
for a spring constant of 2.8 newtons/meter.

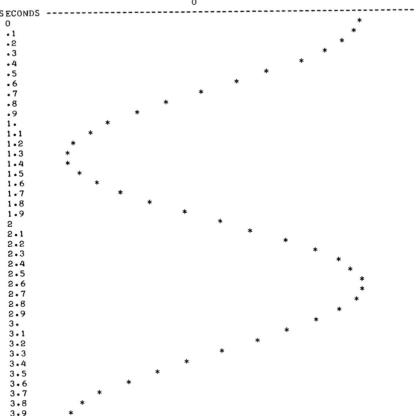

SPRING CONSTANT = 5.6 NEWTONS/METER

Y - DISPLACEMENT IN METERS

Figure 6.8D   Simple Harmonic Motion: Graphical output of the Y-displacement for a spring constant of 5.6 newtons/meter.

6.9   DAMPED HARMONIC MOTION

Lesson Characteristics:

PHYSICS LEVEL   college, intermediate

MATHEMATICS BACKGROUND REQUIRED   analytic geometry

PEDAGOGY   computer learning and simulation

PROBLEM APPROACH   numerical solution

STUDENT PARTICIPATION   assists in program writing

PROGRAMMING SKILLS   intermediate BASIC

TIME OF STUDENT INVOLVEMENT   in class—1 hour, out of class—5 hours

SUGGESTED READINGS   (2) Chapter 15, (3) Chapter 12.

Lesson Description: Before starting this lesson, Section 6.8 must be read and understood. This lesson describes a computer approach to the solution of the equation of motion of a spring-mass system under the influence of friction. The consideration of friction makes the problem more real and normally makes it very difficult. If the computer is instructed to make accurate approximations of displacement and velocity during small time increments, only simple physical relationships are required. The student can write his own program after reading this lesson. The student program may be directed to determine the effect of the damping coefficient on the resulting period of motion.

Background and Theory: In a real spring, such as may be studied in the laboratory, the amplitude of oscillation gradually decreases to zero. This is, of course, due to friction and can be accounted for in the equations of motion of the spring-mass system. The oscillations that result are called 'damped harmonic motion.' In Fig. 6.9A friction has been simulated by immersing a disk attached to the spring-mass system in a fluid. As a first approximation one could assume that the faster the disk moves the greater will be the force of friction, or in equation form,

Friction Force $= (constant) * (velocity\ in\ y\text{-}direction)$

or

$$f = -b(\Delta y/\Delta t) \qquad (6.9\text{–}1)$$

where

$\Delta y/\Delta t = velocity\ (change\ of\ distance\ over\ change\ in\ time)$

The minus sign indicates that the friction force will be in a direction opposite to the direction of motion at any instant of time.

In a free-body diagram, it would be clear that both the spring force $(-ky)$ and the friction force $(-b(\Delta y/\Delta t))$ act upon the mass, m, at all times to produce the resulting motion which is to be determined. If one begins with Newton's second law,

$$\Sigma f = m\ a$$

and if one adds the two forces acting on the block,

$$-ky - b(\Delta y/\Delta t) = m\ a, \qquad (6.9\text{–}2)$$

but

$$a = \Delta v/\Delta t \qquad (\text{see } 6.8\text{–}3)$$

and

$$v = \Delta y/\Delta t$$

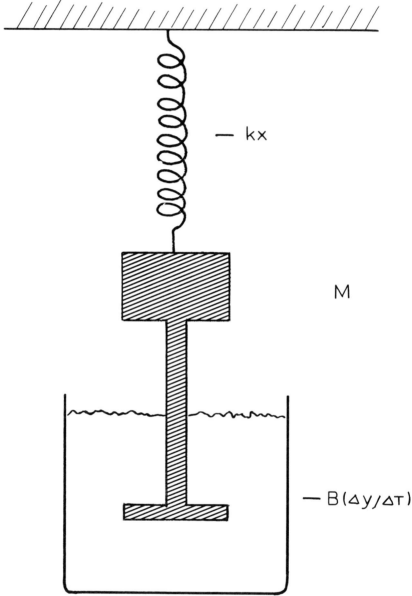

Figure 6.9A   Damped Harmonic Motion: Diagram of a block attached to a spring
with a damping surface.

thus,

$$-ky - bv = m(\Delta v / \Delta t) \qquad (6.9\text{--}3)$$

Dividing through this equation by m and re-arranging terms yields,

$$\Delta v / \Delta t = ky/m - bv/m. \qquad (6.9\text{--}4)$$

The problem is to calculate the position, y, of the block at any instant of time after it starts to move from an initial displacement of 30 meters (a big spring). The initial conditions are, in this case, at time $t=0$,

$$y = 30 \text{ m}$$

$$v = 0 \text{ m/s}$$

and after a small change in time, Δt

$$y = 30 + \Delta y$$

$$v = 0 + \Delta v$$

y and v change during each time increment as described by Equation 6.9–3 and 6.9–4,

$$\Delta y / \Delta t = v \qquad\qquad (6.9\text{–}5)$$

$$\Delta v / \Delta t = -ky/m - bv/m \qquad\qquad (6.9\text{–}6)$$

These two equations could be called rate equations because they indicate the rate at which the parameters y and v are changing with time. How can these relationships (which are taken directly from the physics of the problem) be used to give an accurate approximation of y and v at any instant of time, t?

Computer Techniques: From Equations 6.9–5 and 6.9–6 the rate at which y and v are changing with time, and the new value of y and v after a small change in time, Δt, would be,

$$y_1 = y_0 + \Delta y$$

$$v_1 = v_0 + \Delta y$$

and

$$a = -ky/m - bv/m \qquad \text{(from Equation 6.9–6)}$$

The values of Δy and Δv can be calculated by,

$$\Delta y = v(\Delta t)$$

$(change\ in\ displacement) = (velocity) * (change\ in\ time)$

$$\Delta v = a(\Delta t)$$

$(change\ in\ velocity) = (acceleration) * (change\ in\ time)$

where v and a represent the best estimates of the velocity and acceleration respectively during the time interval, Δt, (Δt is very small). Therefore, after each increment of time, the new values of y, v, and a become (for the program let $D = \Delta t$)

$$y_1 = y_0 + v(\Delta t)$$

$$\text{LET } Y = Y + V*D \qquad\qquad (6.9\text{–}7)$$

$$v_1 = v_0 + a(\Delta t)$$

$$\text{LET } V = V + A*D \qquad\qquad (6.9\text{–}8)$$

$$\text{LET } A = -K*Y/M - B*V/M \qquad\qquad (6.9\text{–}9)$$

One method of approximating the values of V and A during the time interval, D, can be made with the fourth order Runge-Kutta (See Section 5.3) as explained below.

Comments About the Computer Program: In Program 6.9, the initial slopes of the Runge-Kutta method are calculated by (refer to Fig. 5.2),

$$360 \quad \text{LET } Y1 = Y$$

$$370 \quad \text{LET } V1 = V$$

$$380 \quad \text{LET } A1 = C1*V1 + C2*Y$$

Notice that C1 and C2 are defined in lines 230 and 240 respectively. These slopes are used to determine the new values of Y2, V2, and A2 at the midpoint of the time interval, D/2,

$$390 \quad \text{LET } Y2 = Y1 + V1*D/2$$

$$400 \quad \text{LET } V2 = V1 + A1*D/2$$

$$410 \quad \text{LET } A2 = C1*V2 + C2*Y2$$

Then the values of V2 and A2 are used to make a second prediction of the midpoint values of the slopes, V3 and A3 (See Fig. 5.2 again if necessary),

$$420 \quad \text{LET } Y3 = Y1 + V2*D/2$$

$$430 \quad \text{LET } V3 = V1 + A2*D/2$$

$$440 \quad \text{LET } A3 = C1*V3 + C2*Y3,$$

and finally, this set of slopes is used to predict V4 and A4, the slopes at the end of the time interval, D,

$$450 \quad \text{LET } Y4 = Y1 + V3*D$$

$$460 \quad \text{LET } V4 = V1 + A3*D$$

$$470 \quad \text{LET } A4 = C1*V4 + C2*Y4.$$

The new values of Y, V, and A are then found by using the weighted average (See Section 6.8 for explanation). These new values are calculated in statements numbered 510, 520, and 530. Time is incremented in 540. Notice in statement 550 that a counter, M, is checked for size. Only when $M = 10$ does the program go to statement 320 for printing.

Discussion of Computer Results: Program 6.9 appears to be written only for numerical output and not for plotting. However, the plot routine of Program 6.8 (statements 280 through 340) can easily be added to allow plotting. In fact, this was done to obtain the results in Figs. 6.9B, 6.9C, and 6.9D. From these graphs one can determine the effect of a change in the spring constant, K, or the damping coefficient, B, on the period of motion. Does the damping coefficient affect the period?

```
100 REM ************* DAMPED HARMONIC MOTION *************
110 REM
120 REM
130 REM
140 READ K, B, M, D, V0, T0, Y0
150 DATA 2.8, 0.4, 5, 0.10, 0, 0, 30
160 PRINT
170 PRINT "SPRING CONSTANT = "K"NEWTONS/METER"
180 PRINT
190 PRINT "DAMPING COEFFICIENT = "B"NEWTONS/METER/SEC"
200 REM
210 REM
220 REM
230 LET C1 = -B/M
240 LET C2 = -K/M
250 LET Y = Y0
260 LET V = V0
270 LET T = T0
280 REM
290 PRINT
300 PRINT "TIME", "Y-DISPLACEMENT",   , "VELOCITY"
310 LET M = 0
320 PRINT T, Y, , V
330 IF (T - 30) > = 0 THEN 570
340 REM
350 LET M = M + 1
360 LET Y1 = Y
370 LET V1 = V
380 LET A1 = C1*V1 + C2*Y1
390 LET Y2 = Y1 + V1*D/2
400 LET V2 = V1 + A1*D/2
410 LET A2 = C1*V2 + C2*Y2
420 LET Y3 = Y1 + V2*D/2
430 LET V3 = V1 + A2*D/2
440 LET A3 = C1*V3 + C2*Y3
450 LET Y4 = Y1 + V3*D
460 LET V4 = V1 + A3*D
470 LET A4 = C1*V4 + C2*Y4
480 REM
490 REM
500 REM
510 LET Y = Y + (V1 + 2*V2 + 2*V3 + V4)*D/6
520 LET V = V + (A1 + 2*A2 + 2*A3 + A4)*D/6
530 LET A = C1*V + C2*Y
540 LET T = T + D
550 IF M = 10 THEN 310
560 GO TO 330
570 END
```

PROGRAM 6.9 Damped Harmonic Motion.

```
SPRING CONSTANT = 5.6 NEWTONS/METER

DAMPING COEFFICIENT = .8 NEWTONS/METER/SEC

                Y - DISPLACEMENT IN METERS

                           0
```

Figure 6.9B. Damped Harmonic Motion: Graphical output of the Y-displacement for a spring constant of 5.6 newtons/meter and a damping coefficient of 5.6 newtons/meter/seconds.

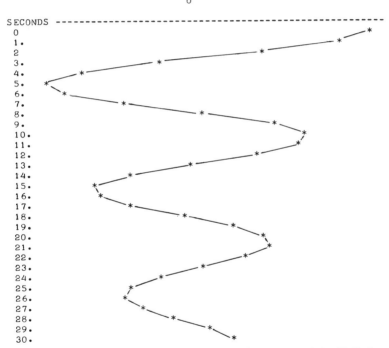

SPRING CONSTANT = 2.8 NEWTONS/METER

DAMPING COEFFICIENT = .4 NEWTONS/METER/SEC

Y - DISPLACEMENT IN METERS

Figure 6.9C   Damped Harmonic Motion: Graphical output of the Y-displacement for a spring constant of 2.8 newtons/meter and a damping coefficient of .4 newtons/meter/second.

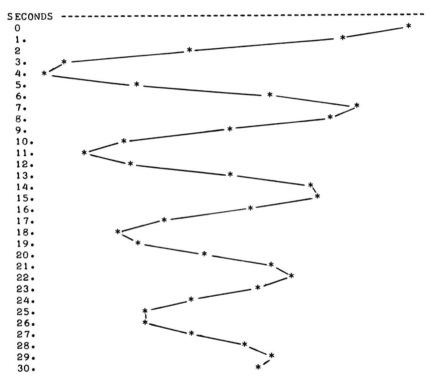

Figure 6.9D. Damped Harmonic Motion: Graphical output of the Y-displacement for a spring constant of 5.6 newtons/meter and a damping coefficient of 0.4 newtons/meter/second.

SPRING CONSTANT = 2.8 NEWTONS/METER

DAMPING COEFFICIENT = .4 NEWTONS/METER/SEC

TIME	Y-DISPLACEMENT	VELOCITY
0	30	0
1.	24.9499	-10.1607
2	11.5866	-15.9949
3.	-4.7886	-15.801
4.	-18.2324	-10.1108
5.	-24.2815	-1.33245
6.	-21.3957	7.23454
7.	-11.2697	12.6184
8.	2.00713	13.1865
9.	13.5613	9.11154
10.	19.4955	2.17251
11.	18.173	-4.9898
12.	10.6138	-9.86009
13.	-6.50444E-2	-10.9162
14.	-9.89872	-8.08357
15.	-15.5225	-2.64969
16.	-15.2991	3.28984
17.	-9.75677	7.62444
18.	-1.23836	8.9659
19.	7.05587	7.07686
20.	12.2503	2.86502
21.	12.7719	-2.02169
22.	8.79869	-5.82688
23.	2.06266	-7.30666
24.	-4.87397	-6.12401
25.	-9.57636	-2.89649
26.	-10.5765	1.09269
27.	-7.81064	4.39351
28.	-2.5336	5.9077
29.	3.22067	5.24474
30.	7.40841	2.80357

TABLE 6.9A. Damped Harmonic Motion: The displacement and velocity of the block are shown at intervals of 1.0 second. The damping coefficient is equal to 0.4 newtons/meter/second.

SPRING CONSTANT = 2.8 NEWTONS/METER

DAMPING COEFFICIENT = .8 NEWTONS/METER/SEC

TIME	Y-DISPLACEMENT	VELOCITY
0	10	10
1.	17.0222	3.5276
2	17.278	-3.17074
3.	11.6854	-7.8089
4.	2.99294	-9.13278
5.	-5.41627	-7.18894
6.	-10.7563	-3.11595
7.	-11.6867	1.40057
8.	-8.54893	4.77593
9.	-3.00179	6.04436
10.	2.73175	5.0919
11.	6.69589	2.56841
12.	7.82006	-.444389
13.	6.14761	-2.86071
14.	2.65592	-3.95646
15.	-1.21084	-3.55911
16.	-4.09666	-2.02381
17.	-5.17662	-3.57255E-2
18.	-4.35547	1.66938
19.	-2.19146	2.56009
20.	.388435	2.4577
21.	2.4549	1.54399
22.	3.38918	.246631
23.	3.04508	-.94117
24.	1.728	-1.63622
25.	2.52356E-2	-1.67789
26.	-1.43336	-1.14912
27.	-2.19351	-.312364
28.	-2.1032	.505279
29.	-1.31901	1.03168
30.	-.2076	1.13303

TABLE 6.9B. Damped Harmonic Motion: The displacement and velocity of the block are shown at intervals of 1.0 second. The damping coefficient is 0.8 newtons/meter/second.

SPRING CONSTANT = 2.8 NEWTONS/METER

DAMPING COEFFICIENT = .8 NEWTONS/METER/SEC

TIME	Y-DISPLACEMENT	VELOCITY
0	10	0
1.	8.35392	-3.27178
2	4.14272	-4.95782
3.	-.836784	-4.72642
4.	-4.79604	-2.93989
5.	-6.55495	-.429786
6.	-5.8485	1.85241
7.	-3.28007	3.17302
8.	1.03209E-2	3.23062
9.	2.80902	2.19325
10.	4.2478	.572221
11.	4.0446	-1.00071
12.	2.51138	-2.00372
13.	.361099	-2.18407
14.	-1.59156	-1.60318
15.	-2.71925	-.569338
16.	-2.76516	.502566
17.	-1.87435	1.24641
18.	-.485395	1.46073
19.	.860708	1.15202
20.	1.71763	.501694
21.	1.86978	-.220849
22.	1.37056	-.761913
23.	.484504	-.966469
24.	-.433012	-.815658
25.	-1.06877	-.412924
26.	-1.25078	6.89153E-2
27.	-.985151	.456085
28.	-.42764	.632429
29.	.19096	.569926
30.	.653555	.325036

TABLE 6.9C. Damped Harmonic Motion: The displacement and velocity of the block are shown at intervals of 1.0 second. The increment of time between successive calculations has been decreased by a factor of ten.

6.10   FORCED HARMONIC MOTION

Lesson Characteristics:

PHYSICS LEVEL   college, intermediate

MATHEMATICS BACKGROUND REQUIRED   analytic geometry

PEDAGOGY   computer learning and simulation

PROBLEM APPROACH   numerical solution

STUDENT PARTICIPATION   assists in program writing

PROGRAMMING SKILLS   intermediate BASIC

TIME OF STUDENT INVOLVEMENT   in class—2 hours, out of class—5 hours

RECOMMENDED READINGS   (2) Chapter 15, (6) Chapter 12

Lesson Description: The study of a spring-mass system under the influence of a variable but oscillatory force is an extension of the discussion in Section 6.8. Two examples are (1) a bridge that vibrates under the influence of marching soldiers and (2) a tuning fork that vibrates when exposed to the periodic force of a sound wave. The computer treatment of this type of problem is unique in that only the simplest and most basic physics is necessary for solution. By using the fourth-order Runge-Kutta and a small time increment, accurate results are found. The student should be encouraged to study resonance conditions of this system, that is, those conditions when the amplitude of oscillation of the spring-mass system is a maximum.

Background and Theory: Often a spring-mass system is under the influence, not of a friction force as discussed in Section 6.9, but instead an oscillatory external force. The wheel of a car may vibrate due to periodic impulses from an unbalanced weight on the hub of the tire. These oscillations produce 'forced harmonic motion.' The forced harmonic motion has the frequency of the external force and not the natural frequency of the spring-mass system. However, the response of the spring-mass system depends upon a combination of the forced frequency and the natural frequency. Obviously, if the external forces are properly timed the resulting motion can have larger and larger amplitudes. These amplitudes can often be larger than amplitudes produced by a steady force of the same magnitude as the oscillating external force. Everyone that has been on a outdoor swing will realize that a small periodic force (properly timed) will produce large amplitudes after many successive pulses.

As shown in Fig. 6.10A, a rotating unbalanced bicycle wheel fastened to a spring-mass system will serve as an example of forced oscillation. As the wheel spins, the y-component of the radial force of the unbalanced mass varies between a maximum and minimum

$$f = \pm m_2 w^2 r. \qquad (6.10\text{--}1)$$

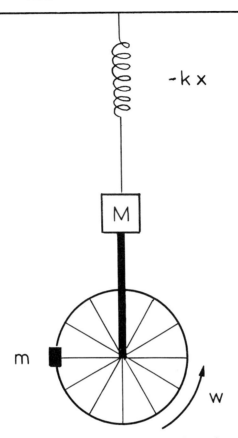

Figure 6.10A.   Forced Harmonic Motion.

Where m_2 is the unbalanced mass, w is the angular velocity of the wheel and r is the radius of the wheel. The equation of motion of the block results from Newton's second law (Equation 6.8–1) and Hook's law (Equation 6.8–2),

$$-k\,y + m_2\,w^2\,r\cos(w\,t) = m_1\,a \qquad (6.10\text{–}2)$$

where a is the acceleration of the block. Notice that the force due to the rotating wheel varies sinusoidally with time and has a maximum amplitude of $m_2\,w^2\,r$. The problem is to describe the motion of the block by calculating the y-displacement at any time, t, after the wheel begins to spin.

Computer Techniques: Dividing Equation 6.10–2 by m_1 and re-arranging the terms yields,

$$\text{LET } A = -K*Y/M1 + M2/M1*W{\uparrow}2*R*COS(W*T) \qquad (6.10\text{–}3)$$

and recalling from previous sections,

$$\Delta v/\Delta t = a \qquad (6.10\text{–}4)$$

$$\Delta y/\Delta t = v \qquad (6.10\text{–}5)$$

The equations are approximate (small Δt) values and define the slopes of the v versus t, and the y versus t curve. The initial conditions in this problem are: at time t=0,

$$y = 0 \text{ m}$$

$$v = 0 \text{ m/s}.$$

After a small change in time, Δt (Δt will be labelled D in BASIC),

LET Y = Y + V*D   (6.10–6)

LET V = V + A*D   (6.10–7)

LET A = $-$K*Y/M1 + M2/M1*W↑2*R*COS(W*T) (6.10–8)

where

$$T = T + D.$$

Notice once more in the above equations that a computer equality replaces the information that was in that location (for example the value of Y) by the old value, Y, plus V*D.

In Equations 6.10–6 and 6.10–7 above, the values of V and A represent the best estimate of the velocity and acceleration during the time increment D. Although there are several computer methods to estimate the values of V and A, the fourth-order Runge-Kutta will be used in this case (See Section 5.2).

Comments About the Computer Program: In Program 6.10 the Runge-Kutta slopes are determined as follows:

(a) *initial values,*

```
390    LET  Y1 = Y
400    LET  V1 = V
410    LET  A1 = --K*Y1/M1 + M2/M1*W↑2*R*COS(W*T)
```

(b) *first midpoint estimate,*

```
420    LET  Y2 = Y1 + V1*D/2
430    LET  V2 = V1 + A1*D/2
440    LET  A2 = -K*Y2/M1 + M2/M1*W↑2*R*COS(W*(T+D/2))
```

(c) *second midpoint estimate,*

```
450    LET  Y3 = Y1 + V2*D/2
460    LET  V3 = V1 + A2*D/2
470    LET  A3 = -K*Y3/M1 + M2/M1*W↑2*R*COS(W*(T+D/2))
```

(d) *estimate at the end of time interval,*

```
480    LET  Y4 = Y1 + V3*D
490    LET  V4 = V1 + A3*D
500    LET  A4 = -K*Y4/M1 + M2/M1*W↑2*R*COS(W*(T+D))
```

```
100 REM*************** FORCED HARMONIC MOTION ***************
110 READ K, M, D, V0, T0, Y0
120 DATA 2.8, .5, .1, 0, 0, 0
130 READ R, W, M2, M3
140 DATA .5, 30, .01, .1
150 PRINT "SPRING CONSTANT ="K"NEWTONS/METER"
160 LET M1 = M + M2 + M3
170 PRINT "MASS OF BLOCK PLUS WHEEL ="M1"KILOGRAMS"
180 PRINT "ANGULAR VELOCITY OF THE WHEEL ="W"RADIANS/SEC"
190 PRINT "ECCENTRIC MASS ON WHEEL ="M2"KILOGRAMS"
200 LET C1=M2/M1*W*W*R
210 LET C2=-K/M1
220 LET Y=Y0
230 LET T=T0
240 LET V=V0
250 LET Z = 0
260 SETDIGITS(3)
270 PRINT
280 PRINT "                        Y - DISPLACEMENT IN METERS"
290 PRINT "SECONDS -------------------------- 0 --------------";
300 PRINT "------------------"
310 LET Y1 = INT(Y + .5)*2 + 36
320 PRINT T; TAB(Y1); "*"
330 IF Z = 40 THEN 470
340 LET Z = Z + 1
350 LET M0 = V
360 LET K0 = C1*COS(W*T) + C2*Y
370 LET M1 = V + K0*D/2
380 LET K1 = C1*COS(W*T) + C2*(Y + M0*D/2)
390 LET M2 = V + K1*D/2
400 LET K2 = C1*COS(W*T) + C2*(Y + M1*D/2)
410 LET M3 = V + K2*D
420 LET K3 = C1*COS(W*T) + C2*(Y + M2*D)
430 LET Y = Y + (M0 + 2*M1 + 2*M2 + M3)*D/6
440 LET V = V + (K0 + 2*K1 + 2*K2 + K3)*D/6
450 LET T = T + D
460 GO TO 310
470 END
```

PROGRAM 6.10. Forced Harmonic Motion.

The new values of displacement, Y, and velocity, V, can be found using Equations 6.10–6 and 6.10–7,

(a) *displacement,*

$$\text{LET } Y = Y + V*D$$

thus

$$520 \quad \text{LET } Y = Y + (V1 + 2*V2 + 2*V3 + V4)*D/6$$

(b) *velocity,*

$$\text{LET } V = V + A*D$$

thus

$$530 \quad \text{LET } V = V + (A1 + 2*A2 + 2*A3 + A4)*D/6$$

Time is incremented by

$$540 \quad \text{LET } T = T + D$$

```
PRING CONSTANT = 2.8 NEWTONS/METER
MASS OF BLOCK PLUS WHEEL = .61 KILOGRAMS
ANGULAR VELOCITY OF THE WHEEL = 240 RADIANS/SEC
ECCENTRIC MASS ON WHEEL = .01 KILOGRAMS
```

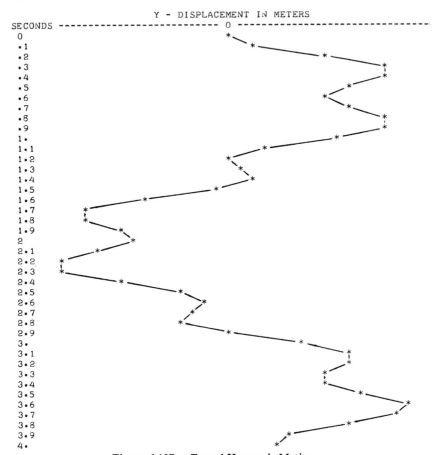

Figure 6.10B.   Forced Harmonic Motion.

and the new acceleration is,

$$550 \quad \text{LET} \quad A = -K + Y/M1 + M2/M1*W \uparrow 2*R*COS(W*T)$$

These recursions equations (statements 390 through 550) are the bulk of the Program 6.10. The other statements are basically for "housekeeping," that is, input data, initial conditions, and output instructions. In this program, a single variable TAB function has been used for plotting (see statements 260 through 290).

Discussion of Computer Results: The effect of an oscillatory force on a spring-mass system is normally a very complicated problem. The computer solution which can be seen graphically in Figure 6.10B, results from Newton's second law and careful approximations of the velocity and

SPRING CONSTANT = 2.8 NEWTONS/METER
MASS OF BLOCK PLUS WHEEL = .61 KILOGRAMS
ANGULAR VELOCITY OF THE WHEEL = 120 RADIANS/SEC
ECCENTRIC MASS ON WHEEL = .01 KILOGRAMS

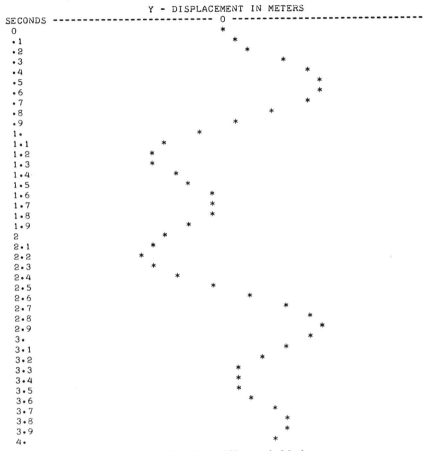

Figure 6.10C.   Forced Harmonic Motion.

acceleration during each time interval. In this program, the computer makes 10 calculations between each plotted point in Figure 6.10B. Numerical output of the computer solution is shown in Table 6.10A. Notice the effect of the SETDIGITS function on the size of each value of displacement and velocity.

Program 6.10 is a good example of the computer used to expand the students' intuitive process while learning science. Here in one lesson, the student can discover that the frequency of the resulting motion depends upon the forcing function, and at what frequency resonance occurs. The student should be encouraged to vary the mass of the block, M1, or the eccentric weight, M2, or the angular velocity of the rotating wheel.

```
SPRING CONSTANT = 2.8 NEWTONS/METER
MASS OF BLOCK PLUS WHEEL = .61 KILOGRAMS
ANGULAR VELOCITY OF THE WHEEL = 60 RADIANS/SEC
ECCENTRIC MASS ON WHEEL = .01 KILOGRAMS

                      Y - DISPLACEMENT IN METERS
SECONDS --------------------------- 0 ------------------------------
   0                                 *
   .1                                *
   .2                                  *
   .3                                  *
   .4                                    *
   .5                                     *
   .6                                      *
   .7                                      *
   .8                                        *
   .9                                        *
  1.                                     *
  1.1                                    *
  1.2                                  *
  1.3                                 *
  1.4                             *
  1.5                          *
  1.6                      *
  1.7                    *
  1.8                 *
  1.9             *
  2              *
  2.1            *
  2.2              *
  2.3                *
  2.4                   *
  2.5                      *
  2.6                        *
  2.7                           *
  2.8                             *
  2.9                               *
  3.                                  *
  3.1                                    *
  3.2                                      *
  3.3                                     *
  3.4                                    *
  3.5                                   *
  3.6                                *
  3.7                            *
  3.8                        *
  3.9                     *
  4.                  *
```

Figure 6.10D. Forced Harmonic Motion: Graphical output of the Y-displacement for an angular velocity of 60 radian/second.

```
SPRING CONSTANT = 2.8 NEWTONS/METER
MASS OF BLOCK PLUS WHEEL = 1.11 KILOGRAMS
ANGULAR VELOCITY OF THE WHEEL = 60 RADIANS/SEC
ECCENTRIC MASS ON WHEEL = .01 KILOGRAMS

                       Y - DISPLACEMENT IN METERS
SECONDS ----------------------- 0 -------------------------------
  0                               *
   .1                             *
   .2                             *
   .3                              *
   .4                              *
   .5                                *
   .6                                *
   .7                                 *
   .8                                 *
   .9                                 *
  1.                                  *
  1.1                                 *
  1.2                                 *
  1.3                                *
  1.4                               *
  1.5                              *
  1.6                             *
  1.7                            *
  1.8                           *
  1.9                          *
  2                           *
  2.1                     *
  2.2                     *
  2.3                     *
  2.4                      *
  2.5                      *
  2.6                       *
  2.7                        *
  2.8                         *
  2.9                           *
  3.                            *
  3.1                            *
  3.2                             *
  3.3                              *
  3.4                              *
  3.5                              *
  3.6                              *
  3.7                              *
  3.8                              *
  3.9                             *
  4.                            *
```

Figure 6.10E.   Forced Harmonic Motion: Graphical output of the Y-displacement
for an angular velocity of 60 radians/second with a mass of 1.11 kilograms.

```
SPRING CONSTANT = 2.8 NEWTONS/METER
MASS OF BLOCK PLUS WHEEL = 1.11 KILOGRAMS
ANGULAR VELOCITY OF THE WHEEL = 240 RADIANS/SEC
ECCENTRIC MASS ON WHEEL = .01 KILOGRAMS

                        Y - DISPLACEMENT IN METERS
SECONDS -----------------------  0  ---------------------------------
  0                                 *
 .1                                   *
 .2                                      *
 .3                                         *
 .4                                          *
 .5                                       *
 .6                                       *
 .7                                        *
 .8                                            *
 .9                                            *
 1.                                         *
 1.1                                      *
 1.2                                      *
 1.3                                        *
 1.4                                        *
 1.5                                      *
 1.6                                  *
 1.7                              *
 1.8                              *
 1.9                              *
 2                               *
 2.1                         *
 2.2                      *
 2.3                    *
 2.4                    *
 2.5                     *
 2.6                     *
 2.7                  *
 2.8               *
 2.9               *
 3.                    *
 3.1                     *
 3.2                     *
 3.3                 *
 3.4                  *
 3.5                    *
 3.6                       *
 3.7                          *
 3.8                        *
 3.9                        *
 4.                           *
```

Figure 6.10F. Forced Harmonic Motion: Graphical output of the Y-displacement for an angular velocity of 240 radians/second with a mass of 1.11 kilograms.

SPRING CONSTANT = 2.8 NEWTONS/METER
MASS OF BLOCK PLUS WHEEL = 1.11 KILOGRAMS
ANGULAR VELOCITY OF THE WHEEL = 120 RADIANS/SEC
ECCENTRIC MASS ON WHEEL = .01 KILOGRAMS

TIME (SECS.)	Y-DISPLACEMENT (METERS)	VELOCITY (METERS/SEC.)
0	0	0
.1	.324	6.46
.2	1.24	11.7
.3	2.53	14.
.4	3.85	12.4
.5	4.83	7.13
.6	5.17	-.322
.7	4.76	-7.86
.8	3.7	-13.4
.9	2.26	-15.3
1.	.834	-13.2
1.1	-.23	-8.01
1.2	-.702	-1.41
1.3	-.552	4.42
1.4	4.78E-2	7.54
1.5	.774	6.95
1.6	1.26	2.81
1.7	1.22	-3.59
1.8	.534	-10.2
1.9	-.718	-14.8
2	-2.26	-16.
2.1	-3.71	-13.1
2.2	-4.72	-6.93
2.3	-5.03	.765
2.4	-4.6	7.81
2.5	-3.59	12.2
2.6	-2.34	12.8
2.7	-1.21	9.65
2.8	-.534	3.93
2.9	-.456	-2.37
3.	-.93	-7.1
3.1	-1.72	-8.61
3.2	-2.46	-6.29
3.3	-2.82	-.761
3.4	-2.54	6.33
3.5	-1.58	12.8
3.6	-9.94E-2	16.7
3.7	1.57	16.7
3.8	3.05	12.8
3.9	4.	6.12
4.	4.24	-1.39

TABLE 6.10A. Forced Harmonic Motion: The y-displacement and velocity of the block are shown at intervals of 0.1 second. The angular velocity of the wheel is 120 radians/second.

```
SPRING CONSTANT = 2.8 NEWTONS/METER
MASS OF BLOCK PLUS WHEEL = 70.01 KILOGRAMS
ANGULAR VELOCITY OF THE WHEEL = 120 RADIANS/SEC
ECCENTRIC MASS ON WHEEL = .01 KILOGRAMS
```

TIME (SECS.)	Y-DISPLACEMENT (METERS)	VELOCITY (METERS/SEC.)
0	0	0
.1	5.14E-3	.103
.2	1.98E-2	.19
.3	4.09E-2	.233
.4	6.35E-2	.22
.5	8.22E-2	.154
.6	9.26E-2	5.53E-2
.7	9.32E-2	-4.46E-2
.8	8.52E-2	-.115
.9	7.28E-2	-.134
1.	6.13E-2	-9.54E-2
1.1	.056	-1.19E-2
1.2	5.99E-2	9.06E-2
1.3	7.34E-2	.18
1.4	9.38E-2	.228
1.5	.116	.22
1.6	.135	.158
1.7	.146	6.12E-2
1.8	.147	-4.01E-2
1.9	.139	-.115
2	.127	-.139
2.1	.114	-.106
2.2	.108	-.026
2.3	.11	7.59E-2
2.4	.123	.168
2.5	.142	.22
2.6	.164	.217
2.7	.183	.16
2.8	.194	6.48E-2
2.9	.195	-3.77E-2
3.	.188	-.116
3.1	.174	-.146
3.2	.161	-.118
3.3	.153	-.042
3.4	.154	.059
3.5	.165	.153
3.6	.183	.21
3.7	.204	.212
3.8	.222	.159
3.9	.234	6.64E-2
4.	.235	-3.69E-2

TABLE 6.10B. Forced Harmonic Motion: The y-displacement and velocity of the block are shown at intervals of 0.1 seconds. The mass of the block is equal to 70.01 kilograms.

6.11   YOUNG'S INTERFERENCE EXPERIMENT

Lesson Characteristics:

PHYSICS LEVEL   college, intermediate

MATHEMATICS BACKGROUND REQUIRED   algebra and trigonometry

PEDAGOGY   computer simulation

PROBLEM APPROACH   analytic solution

STUDENT PARTICIPATION   uses prepared program

PROGRAMMING SKILLS   none

TIME OF STUDENT INVOLVEMENT   in class—1 hour, out of class—1 hour

RECOMMENDED READINGS   (2) Chapter 43, (7) Chapter 8

Lesson Description: The discussion of optics has particular challenge to the teacher and student. Certainly the optical phenomenon of interference can be easily viewed by experiment, however, the physical and mathematical concepts required for its description are not always clear. This lesson is intended for those physics courses which treat interference of light without recourse to higher mathematics. The computer's ability to treat finite parts of the interference pattern in small angular increments accounts for this straightforward approach.

This lesson is an example of the power of the computer to demonstrate a rather difficult functional relationship (superposition of two traveling waves) by using simple addition. Students should be required to understand the geometry involved in this problem by tracing light rays through the slits. The students should be encouraged to change the wavelength to slit separation ratio and follow the computer generated interference patterns.

Background and Theory: It is an experimental fact that two or more waves can traverse the same space independently of one another. The fact that waves act independently of one another means that the displacement of any particle at a given time is simply the sum of the displacements that the individual waves alone would give to that particle. This process of vector addition of the displacement of a particle is called superposition. When the two waves act at the same point in space and produce no displacement, they are said to destructively interfere. On the other hand, constructive interference would mean that at another point in space the two waves add to produce a displacement larger than either of the waves acting alone.

In Figure 6.11A incident light is allowed to pass first through slit S_0 and then through slit S_1 and S_2. The slit width is made much smaller than the wavelength of the incident light. Thomas Young first experimentally

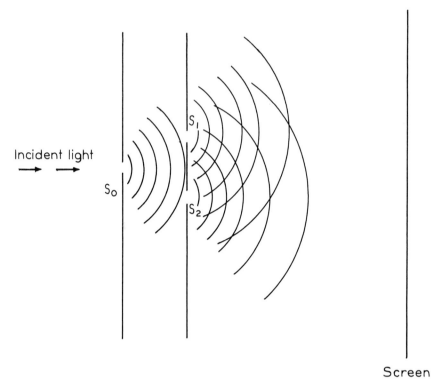

Incident light

S_o

S_1

S_2

Screen

Figure 6.11A.   Monochromatic Light is incident upon slit S_o.

established the wave theory of light in 1801 by showing that the light from slits S_2 and S_1 interferred, that is, when the light from S_2 was added to the light from S_1 there appeared at some points bright bands (constructive interference) and at some points dark bands (destructive interference). Light must then be wave-like since it obeys the principle of superposition.

Let us analyze the results of Young's experiment in an attempt to simulate the process (called interference) on the computer. From Figure 6.11B it is clear that a wave traveling from S_1 must travel a shorter optical distance to reach point P than a wave traveling from S_2. The added distance is equal to D*SIN(B) where D is the distance between slits and where B is the angle that the rays make with the horizontal. One can be certain that the electric field components (E) of the two waves (E_1 and E_2) vary with time and with angle at any point P. The two waves are of equal intensity and in phase at S1 and S2, thus

$$\text{LET } E_1 = E_0 * \text{COS}(W*T) \qquad (6.11-1)$$

$$\text{LET } E_2 = E_0 * \text{COS}(W*T+A) \qquad (6.11-2)$$

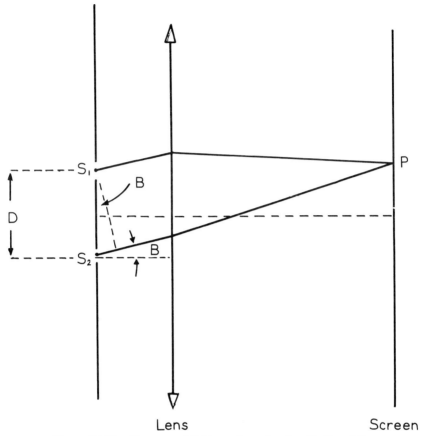

Figure 6.11B.   Two rays of light are shown leaving slits S_1 and S_2.

where A is the added distance in radians that wave 2 must travel as compared to wave 1 to reach point P. The angular displacement A is determined by:

$$A/2\pi = D*SIN(B)/L \qquad (6.11-3)$$

where L is the wavelength of incident light and B is the angle with reference to the horizontal being considered (See Fig. 6.11B).

The total wave disturbance at the screen for each angle B is the sum

$$LET \ E = E1 + E2$$

The purpose of the computer program is to add the two vectors for many specific angles with the horizontal to study where maxima and minima of intensity might occur on the screen.

```
100 REM*************** YOUNG'S EXPERIMENT ****************
110 READ D, L, EO
120 DATA 2.5 E-4, 5500, 4
130 LET P = 3.14159265
140 PRINT "SLITS ARE"D*1E3"MILLIMETERS APART"
150 PRINT "THE WAVELENGTH OF INCIDENT LIGHT IS"L"ANGSTROMS"
160 PRINT
170 PRINT "                    LIGHT INTENSITY"
180 PRINT
190 PRINT "              0                              I(MAX)"
200 PRINT "ANGLE -------------------------------------------------U
210 FOR J = 0 TO 45
220 LET B = J/57.3/100
230 LET A = 2*P*D*SIN(B)/L*1E10
240 LET E = EO + EO*COS(A)
250 LET I = E*E
260 LET I = INT(I)
270 PRINT J/100, TAB(I); "*"
280 NEXT J
290 END
```

PROGRAM 6.11A.   Young's Interference Experiment.

Computer Techniques: In this problem, only trigonometric functions have been used. The computer becomes important mainly because the operations must be repeated many times in order to construct the interference pattern.

Comments About the Computer Program: Program 6.11 is short and relates directly to the theory developed above. A TAB plot routine has been used, and the magnitude of the electric field vector, E_0, has been arbitrarily chosen to keep the intensity scale on the page. In statement 250, the intensity is assumed to be directly proportional to the amplitude of the electric field strength.

In statement 230, the linear distance which causes the two waves to be out of phase, is converted to radians by Equation 6.11–3. The angle B (with the horizontal) is changed from degrees to radians in statement 220. These changes are made because the trigonometric functions in BASIC use the angle in radians.

Discussion of Computer Results: In Figure 6.11C the interference pattern of coherent light (wavelength 5500 angstroms) is shown. The peaks would appear as bright spots on the screen of Figure 6.11B and the dark bands would occur where the intensity is zero. Figure 6.11D shows that, by reducing the distance between the slits S_1 and S_2, the bright bands (peaks) move apart. In Figure 6.11E, the bright bands (peaks) have moved yet further apart as the slit separation is reduced.

The student should study the effect of slit separation on interference patterns and compare the computer-generated results with those observed in a laboratory situation.

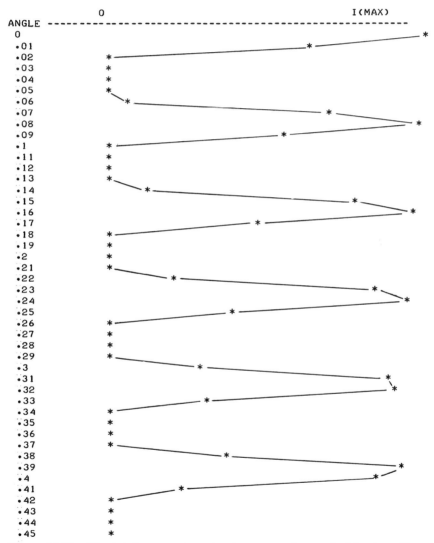

Figure 6.11C.   The interference pattern has been computer graphed for two slits a
distance 0.4 millimeters apart.

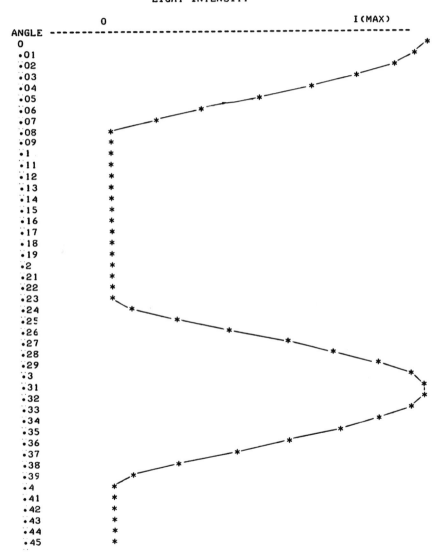

SLITS ARE •1 MILLIMETERS APART
THE WAVELENGTH ØF INCIDENT LIGHT IS 5500 ANGSTRØMS

LIGHT INTENSITY

Figure 6.11D. The interference pattern has been computer graphed for two slits
0.1 millimeters apart.

SLITS ARE .25 MILLIMETERS APART
THE WAVELENGTH ØF INCIDENT LIGHT IS 5500 ANGSTRØMS

LIGHT INTENSITY

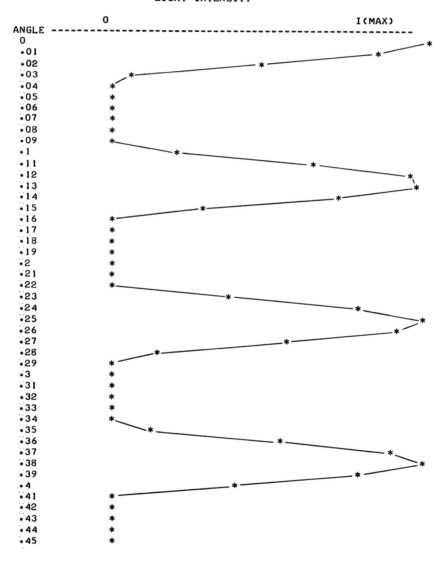

Figure 6.11E.   The interference pattern has been computer graphed for two slits .25 millimeters apart.

6.12   Single Slit Diffraction

Lesson Characteristics:

PHYSICS LEVEL   college, intermediate

MATHEMATICS BACKGROUND REQUIRED   algebra and trigonometry

PEDAGOGY   computer learning and simulation

PROBLEM APPROACH   analytical solution, iteration

STUDENT PARTICIPATION   used prepared program

PROGRAMMING SKILLS   none

TIME OF STUDENT INVOLVEMENT   in class—1 hour, in laboratory—½ hour

RECOMMENDED READING   (2) Chapter 44, (7) Chapter 9

Lesson Description: Diffraction is the bending of light around an obstacle such as the edge of a slit. Although diffraction effects are small, they are quite easily observed in a properly designed laboratory apparatus. The quantitative description of diffraction is however difficult. In this lesson, the computer has been instructed to treat a light wave as a continuous set of small generators of light energy (sources called Huggen's wavelets). The effect of these small light sources on a distant screen are analyzed by the computer. Students should be required to understand the trigonometry used to describe the light from one of the small light sources. The diffraction patterns generated by the computer can be studied so that the effect of slit width on the location of maxima and minima of light intensity can be understood.

Background and Theory: Figure 6.12A shows the crests of parallel light waves falling on a narrow slit of width, W. The light, coming from a distant source, must pass through the slit. The problem is to determine the effect of the slit on the light pattern at the screen. The slit in Figure 6.12A has been divided into N parallel strips of width W/N. If N is large, one can imagine that each strip acts as a small source of light from which wavelets of lights immerge in all directions. In Figure 6.12A, light rays emanating from each of these small sources are shown drawn parallel and falling on the screen at point P. Since none of the small light sources are the same optical distance from point P or from the screen, all the wavelets arriving at point P are slightly out of phase (See Figure 6.12A).

The wave disturbances from adjacent strips have optical paths (x) that differ (Δx) by:

$$\Delta x = w/n \sin(I/57.3). \qquad (6.12\text{–}1)$$

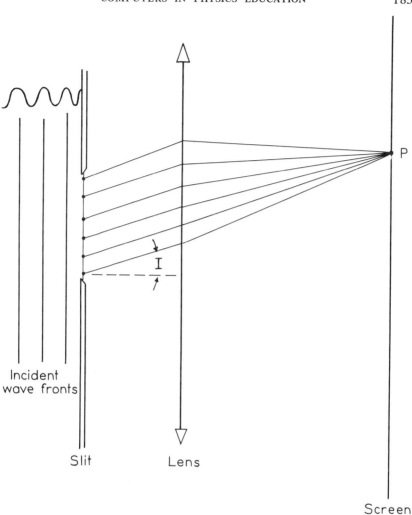

Figure 6.12A.   Single Slit Diffraction.

The phase difference ($\Delta\phi$) in radians can be found by,

$$\frac{\text{phase difference}}{2\pi} = \frac{\text{path difference}}{\lambda}$$

therefore,

$$\Delta\phi = (2\,\pi/\lambda)\,\text{w/n}\,\sin(\text{I}/57.3) \qquad (6.12\text{--}2)$$

The equations for the electric field components of the wavelets from the small light sources at point P would be,

$$e_1 = e_0 \cos(w\,t)$$
$$e_2 = e_0 \cos(w\,t + \Delta\phi)$$
$$e_3 = e_0 \cos(w\,t + 2\,\Delta\phi)$$
$$\cdot$$
$$\cdot$$
$$e_n = e_0 \cos(w\,t + n\,\Delta\phi) \qquad\qquad (6.12\text{--}3)$$

where N is the total number of small strips into which the slit was divided. The problem then is reduced to adding all the electric field components to determine the light intensity at point P.

Comments About the Computer Program: Program 6.12 must direct the computer to do the following:

    (a) divide the slit into N strips
    (b) for each angle (I) with the horizontal, the computer must calculate the phase difference $(\Delta\phi)$ for each small source of light.
    (c) with the phase difference, the computer must calculate the electric field vector for each wavelet at point P.
    (d) and finally, the computer must add all the electric field components at point P.

These steps are carried out by two loops, one inside the other. The first loop,

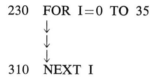

```
100 REM************** SINGLE SLIT DIFFRACTION **************
110 READ L,W,N
120 DATA 5500, 55000, 1000
130 PRINT "WAVELENGTH OF INCIDENT LIGHT ="L"ANGSTROMS"
140 PRINT "WIDTH OF DIFFRACTION SLIT ="W*1E-7"MILLIMETERS"
150 PRINT "RATIO OF SLIT WIDTH TO WAVELENGHT ="W/L
160 PRINT
170 PRINT "                          LIGHT INTENSITY"
180 PRINT "        0 --------------------------------------------";
190 PRINT "------------------"
200 PRINT "ANGLE IN"
210 PRINT "DEGREES"
220 LET P = 3.14159265
230 FOR I = 0 TO 35
240 LET A1 = 2*P*W/N/L*SIN(I/57.3)
250 LET E = 0
260 FOR J=1 TO N
270 LET E = E + .05*COS(J*A1)
280 NEXT J
290 LET E = INT(E + .5) + 20
300 PRINT I; TAB(E); "*"
310 NEXT I
320 END
```

PROGRAM 6.12. Single Slit Diffraction Patterns.

increments the angle (I) which the rays make with the horizontal. In this case, from 0 to 35 degrees. At each angle (I), the computer calculates the phase difference ($\Delta\phi$ is replaced by A1 in BASIC) from Equation 6.12–2,

240   LET A1=2*P*W/N/L*SIN(I/57.3).

Notice that W/N is equal to the strip width, and that π has been replaced by P.

The second loop begins by,

260   FOR J=1 to N

and ends by,

280   NEXT J.

```
WAVELENGTH OF INCIDENT LIGHT = 5500 ANGSTROMS
WIDTH OF DIFFRACTION SLIT = .00055 MILLIMETERS
RATIO OF SLIT WIDTH TO WAVELENGHT = 1

                       LIGHT INTENSITY
            0 --------------------------------------------------------- -
ANGLE IN
DEGREES
   0                                                                  *
   1                                                                  *
   2                                                                  *
   3                                                                 *
   4                                                                *
   5                                                                *
   6                                                              *
   7                                                             *
   8                                                            *
   9                                                          *
  10                                                         *
  11                                                        *
  12                                                      *
  13                                                     *
  14                                                   *
  15                                                 *
  16                                               *
  17                                             *
  18                                           *
  19                                         *
  20                                       *
  21                                     *
  22                                   *
  23                                 *
  24                               *
  25                             *
  26                           *
  27                         *
  28                       *
  29                      *
  30                    *
  31                  *
  32                *
  33               *
  34             *
  35           *
```

Figure 6.12B.   Single Slit Diffraction Pattern.

In this loop, the electric field components of each wavelet is calculated and added to the total electric field at point P.

270   LET E=E+EO*COS(J*A1)

After the total electric field at point P has been determined, the result is plotted by,

300   PRINT I; TAB (E); "*"

Discussion of Computer Results: Program 6.12 can be of considerable instructive value when used to study the effects of slit width and wavelength on diffraction patterns. Figure 6.12B shows the resulting diffraction pattern for a slit width of .00055 millimeters and a wavelength of 5500 angstroms. The effect of increasing the slit width can be seen in Figures 6.12C through 6.12F. Similar plots can be produced by changing the wavelength of the incident light.

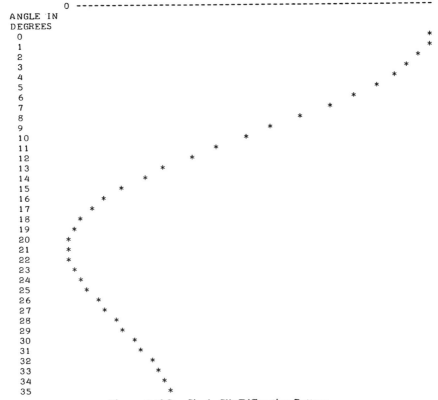

```
AVELENGTH OF INCIDENT LIGHT = 5500 ANGSTROMS
WIDTH OF DIFFRACTION SLIT = .0011 MILLIMETERS
RATIO OF SLIT WIDTH TO WAVELENGHT = 2
```

Figure 6.12C.   Single Slit Diffraction Pattern.

WAVELENGTH OF INCIDENT LIGHT = 5500 ANGSTROMS
WIDTH OF DIFFRACTION SLIT = .00165 MILLIMETERS
RATIO OF SLIT WIDTH TO WAVELENGHT = 3

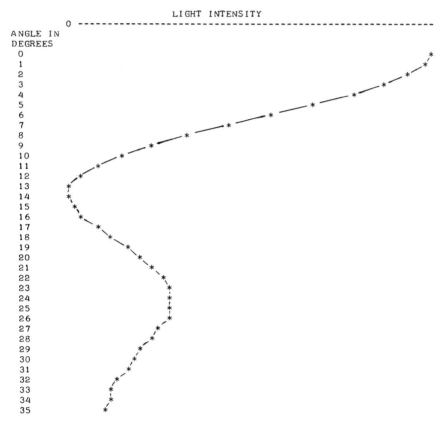

Figure 6.12D.   Single Slit Diffraction Pattern.

WAVELENGTH OF INCIDENT LIGHT = 5500 ANGSTROMS
WIDTH OF DIFFRACTION SLIT = .00275 MILLIMETERS
RATIO OF SLIT WIDTH TO WAVELENGHT = 5

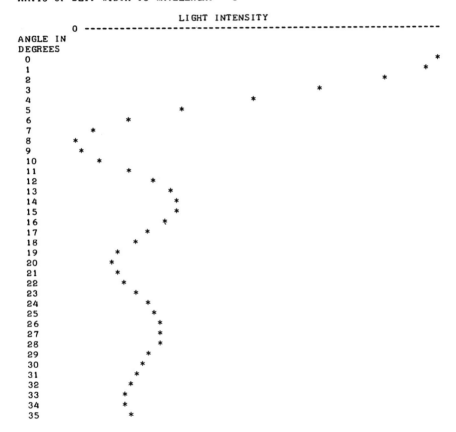

Figure 6.12E.   Single Slit Diffraction Pattern.

```
WAVELENGTH OF INCIDENT LIGHT = 5500 ANGSTROMS
WIDTH OF DIFFRACTION SLIT = .0055 MILLIMETERS
RATIO OF SLIT WIDTH TO WAVELENGHT = 10

                              LIGHT INTENSITY
          0  ----------------------------------------------------
ANGLE IN
DEGREES
    0                                                                          *
    1                                                              *
    2                                             *
    3                *
    4        *
    5          *
    6                   *
    7                      *
    8                     *
    9              *
   10           *
   11             *
   12                *
   13                 *
   14                 *
   15             *
   16            *
   17             *
   18               *
   19                *
   20                *
   21             *
   22            *
   23            *
   24              *
   25              *
   26              *
   27             *
   28           *
   29           *
   30             *
   31              *
   32              *
   33             *
   34            *
   35            *
```

Figure 6.12F.   Single Slit Diffraction Pattern.

CHAPTER 7

COMPUTERS IN CHEMICAL EDUCATION

7.1   INTRODUCTION

The subject matter of chemistry lends itself readily to the use of computer-assisted learning. The teacher must lead a group of students, whose backgrounds may vary widely, to an understanding of the basic concepts of chemistry. The student, moreover, is required to use this knowledge to solve problems in the laboratory and on paper, and to explain physical phenomenon in the light of theory. In chemistry, each unit must be understood before proceeding to the next, and the individual must be able to correlate the separate units. These requirements demand a thorough yet complete mastery of all aspects of the subject. Furthermore, there is often little time, in the rush to cover the course syllabus, for individual student-teacher interaction. The slow learners may be left by the wayside while the faster learners may find the pace boring.

Computer-assisted learning may supply the answers to these problems. The computer can be a powerful companion who guides each student through mastery of the basic concepts with computer *drills, tutorials,* and *quizzes.* Furthermore, each student may proceed at his own pace under the guidance of this faithful tutor. And one need not stop here. The computer can free the student from the drugery of *data reduction* as well as expand his horizons through the use of *simulation* programs and *numerical methods* of analysis. The ingredients have been developed—what is required now are students and teachers who will incorporate these tools into a course designed to encourage each individual to achieve his full potential.

The remainder of this chapter will discuss the use of a time-sharing computer system in the teaching of chemistry. Some of the lessons, particularly those involving numerical methods and data reduction, can also be used in conventional batch-processing systems. In general, however, the real-time interaction available in time-sharing is an invaluable, if not essential, asset.

Each lesson discusses one *type* of computer program while the entire chapter encompasses a wide range of topics at several levels of student achievement. The types of programs discussed include a quiz, a tutorial, a drill, a simulation, a demonstration, computer learning, and data reduction. (The program classifications are explained in the introduction to part II). While the first three programs in this chapter are written for the elementary college level, the last five are classified as college intermediate. These programs were chosen as representative examples of the type of material which teachers can write for student use (7.2–7.5), or the type of programs which both students and teachers can write (7.6–7.9).

The use of a computer *quiz* (Section 7.2—Atomic Weights and Formula Weights) to assess student retention of subject matter is shown. This type of quiz can be used to provide feedback to the teacher on the effectiveness of teaching methods and to guide the student to the appropriate tutorials where necessary. For example, a quiz can be prepared by the instructor to examine students on a particular area covered in class. A student could take the quiz during his free time, at his own pace. The printed output of the computer console provides the student with a permanent record of the quiz. The student's scores (which could be recorded as discussed below) provide the teacher with an indication of the effectiveness of the teaching method employed. Furthermore, the student can be referred to tutorials as indicated by his performance.

The recording of student scores and responses on a separate program which can be accessed and manipulated is also discussed. As each student takes the quiz, his scores are recorded on another program file. This frees the teacher from the drudgery of grading quizzes and the student receives his grade as soon as all students have taken the quiz.

Computers are also useful for the *drill* and *tutorial* necessary to ensure that students have mastered the current topic as well as to expand concepts presented in class. An example of a program used to reiterate lecture material in an interactive manner (Section 7.3—The Mole) is included. The progression of a tutorial program must depend on the answers given by the student. The program is constructed so that when a student gives the correct answer, program control is directed (branches) to the next question. When a student gives the wrong answer, however, the program must branch to a section which gives the student additional help. The basic branching sequence for such a program is illustrated as well as the use of "multiple-choice" questions, "hidden response" questions, and "verbal response" questions. (These questions are discussed in detail in lesson 7.3). Furthermore, when a student's performance on a quiz indicates that he has not understood a concept (such as the mole), he can be directed to use the tutorial program. Most students will find the computer tutorial sufficient and the instructor can spend his time with those students who require more specialized attention.

A lesson on *problem drill* (Section 7.4—Ideal Gases) illustrates how the computer may be used to provide students with a means of mastering the types of problems important in chemistry. Each drill provides the student with a chemistry problem (in this example, one involving ideal gases). The student works the problem and types his answer into the computer. If his answer is correct, he is immediately told so and given the opportunity to work another similar problem. If his answer is not correct, he is first shown how to do the problem, and then given another problem. The student can thus work problems, aided by his patient tutor (the computer), until he is confident of his ability to solve problems of the type being studied.

The value of computer *simulation* is demonstrated (Section 7.5—Consecutive First-Order Reactions) by using an experiment which takes 70 hours to run in the laboratory and only seconds using computer simulation. The student is allowed to enter values of the specific rate constants for the reaction. The computer then tabulates the amounts of reactants and products which are present, in 5 hour increments, from 0 to 70 hours after the reaction is started. This information is also presented in graphical form to promote rapid student comprehension. In this manner, the laboratory reaction is "simulated" on the computer. The student may conduct the experiment over and over again, using different rate constants, to observe their effect on the reaction. The computer is thus used as an interactive partner to reinforce and expand the chemists knowledge of kinetics.

The first four lessons involve student use of prepared programs. These programs may be lifted bodily from the text and used as is, provided small changes are made to conform to the language rules of the time-sharing system to be employed. The last four lessons, however, are designed to allow varying degrees of student involvement in the writing of programs.

The power of *numerical methods* (as explained in Section 5.3) is suggested by showing the use of the Runge-Kutta Method in chemical kinetics. The Runge-Kutta Method can be used to solve ordinary differential equations with initial conditions. This is a well developed method suitable for use on a digital computer. It is applied in several lessons to the rate equation of a chemical kinetics reaction, the rate equation being an ordinary differential equation. The initial conditions are those present at the start of the reaction.

The student can gain insight into this method by comparing the values obtained using the analytical (closed-form) solutions of a second-order reaction to those obtained using the Runge-Kutta Method (Lesson 7.6—Chemical Kinetics—Second-Order Reaction). This allows the student to observe the ease of using a numerical method as well as to observe the operational limitations which must be met for the proper use of the numerical method. The method may then be applied to a third-order reaction (Lesson 7.7) or to many of those rate equations for which there are no known closed-form solutions. This application points out the real importance of numerical methods which is their use in the solution of equations which cannot be solved in any other manner. It is also shown that numerical methods can be used to teach kinetics to students with no background in calculus (Lesson 7.8—Radioactive Decay).

Finally, the use of the computer for *data reduction* (Lesson 7.9—The Hydrolysis of Methyl Acetate) is illustrated. Data reduction refers to the mathematical treatment of the experimentally obtained data. This program uses the method of least squares to determine the slope of a line, and from this slope, the rate constant. This is a tedious, time-consuming process when done by hand while the computer can accomplish the task in seconds.

7.2 ATOMIC WEIGHTS AND FORMULA WEIGHTS

Lesson Characteristics:

CHEMISTRY LEVEL   college, introductory

MATHEMATICS BACKGROUND REQUIRED   algebra

PEDAGOGY   computer quiz

PROBLEM APPROACH   analytical solution

STUDENT PARTICIPATION   uses prepared program

PROGRAMMING SKILLS   none

TIME OF STUDENT INVOLVEMENT   in class—maximum of 50 minutes

RECOMMENDED READING   (8)   Chapters 2, 3
                                       (9)   Chapter 7
                                     (10)   Chapters 2, 3

Lesson Description: This lesson is intended for use at the freshman college level. It is an example of the general class of quizzes which can easily be written in time-sharing BASIC. Three types of questions are illustrated: (1) multiple choice, (2) verbal response, and (3) hidden response. In a *multiple-choice* question, the student is presented with a question followed by three possible answers, labeled 1, 2, and 3. The student is then asked to type the number of the correct response. The *verbal* response is most often used for definitions. The student is given a sentence and asked to type the missing word or alternatively, he is given a definition and asked to state what word is being defined. (It is important that the choice of word be unambiguous.) The *hidden-response* is just what the name implies: the student is not shown any list of possible answers. For example, the student may be asked to calculate a quantity and type the answer. The relative merits of different types of questions will not be considered here. The three types of questions presented are discussed so that the teacher may be provided with examples of the mechanics of programming. Each teacher must tailor the questions used in a quiz to suit his own opinions as well as the needs of the students.

The subject matter was chosen as being representative of the material which chemistry students must master. Such a quiz may be used to evaluate student progress and/or to provide feedback on the efficiency of previous lectures. The student uses a prepared program; the length of time required to take the quiz depends on the student. For example, the quiz may be taken in 15 minutes by the brightest students while slow students may take as long as 50 minutes. The output may be retained by the student as a permanent record of his performance. It can further serve as an outline of the topic covered.

As each question is answered, the response of the student is stored on an external program file. In most time-sharing systems, the external program file (or simply, another program in the system) is saved in advance. When the student takes the quiz, special commands are used to write his responses on another program file. For example, let us call the external program SCOR. After all the students have taken the quiz, the teacher can list SCOR to obtain a record of the performance of each student. In fact, the teacher can use the computer to calculate individual grades, class averages, or any of the other parameters commonly tabulated. The instructor is thus freed from the tedium of record keeping.

Computer Techniques: This lesson is written for those who have to write programs; in the case of quizzes, the discussion is intended primarily for teachers. The programming methods used to handle the various types of quiz questions will be discussed in the next section. The discussion will first explain how to program (a) multiple-choice, (b) verbal response, and (c) hidden response questions. Attention will then be directed towards the techniques of recording the student responses on an external program file.

As written here, one student takes the quiz at a time. It is, however, possible to treat external file output in such a manner that many students, using separate consoles, may take the quiz at the same time. In this case, only one item should be printed on a line and the lines should be given a line number (for data manipulation) followed by the student's number, name, and the response.

It is also possible to extend the capabilities for alphabetic response using several string variables. While the constraints of the system are evident, these constraints are not nearly so rigid as those often employed by over-burdened teachers who are attempting to keep the time necessary for exam correction and record keeping to a minimum.

Comments About the Computer Program: The first type of question which will be discussed is the *multiple-choice* question. The Program (7.2) includes 15 questions. Question numbers 1, 3, 8 and 13 are multiple-choice; question 8 will be used to illustrate the technique.

The question and answer choices are presented using PRINT statements (lines 1190–1250). The student is then told the desired response:

1260   PRINT "TYPE THE CORRECT NUMBER."

The answer will be assigned to X using

1270   INPUT X

Execution of the above statement causes the computer to generate a question mark, at which time the student types in his answer.

Remember that there are three statements which can be used to assign numeric values to variables in BASIC:

100   READ X

110   LET X=4

120   INPUT X

The first two statements are used when the value of X is assigned prior to program execution. The third statement, INPUT X, is used to assign values during the running of a program. It is therefore used in a program to request a response from the program user during program execution. It is usually used in connection with a PRINT statement (see line 1260 above) so the user knows what value to type. It should be noted that X can be used for the answers to *all* the questions, unless an alphabetic response is required (see for example, question 9.)

```
100 PRINT"* * QUIZ: ATOMIC WEIGHTS AND FORMULA WEIGHTS * *"
110 PRINT
120 PRINT"WHAT IS YOUR LAST NAME?(TYPE A MAXIMUM OF 15 LETTERS)."
130 INPUT Z$
140 PRINT"WHAT IS YOUR STUDENT NUMBER ?"
150 INPUT N
160 PRINT:SCOR:Z$,N
170 LET A$ = "FORMULA"
180 LET D$ = "MOLE"
190LET R = 0
200LET W = 0
210 PRINT
220PRINT"GIVE ALL NUMERICAL ANSWERS TO 3 SIGNIFICANT FIGURES."
230PRINT
240PRINT"1.   THE ATOMIC MASS (WEIGHT) OF AN ELEMENT IS A NUMBER"
250PRINT"    WHICH RELATES THE MASS OF AN AVERAGE ATOM OF THE"
260PRINT"    GIVEN ELEMENT TO AN ATOM OF:"
270PRINT"            (1) HYDROGEN"
280PRINT"            (2) CARBON"
290PRINT"            (3) OXYGEN"
300PRINT
310PRINT"TYPE THE CORRECT NUMBER"
320 INPUT X
330IF X <> 2 THEN 370
340LET R = R+1
350 PRINT:SCOR:LNM(N);"1R,";
360 GO TO 390
370LET W = W+1
380 PRINT:SCOR:LNM(N);"1W,";
390 PRINT
400PRINT"2.   THE ATOMIC MASS OF CARBON-12 IS          ATOMIC"
410PRINT"    MASS UNITS."
420PRINT
430PRINT"TYPE THE MISSING NUMBER"
440 INPUT X
450IF X <> 12 THEN 490
460LET R = R+1
470 PRINT:SCOR:"2R,";
480 GO TO 510
490LET W = W+1
500 PRINT:SCOR:"2W,";
510 PRINT
520PRINT"3.   THE ATOMIC MASS OF MAGNESIUM IS 24.   THIS NUMBER"
530PRINT"    INDICATES THAT THE AVERAGE MAGNESIUM ATOM HAS A"
540PRINT"    MASS:"
```

PROGRAM 7.2   Atomic Weights and Formula Weights.

The scoring sequence:

```
1280   IF X<>2 THEN 1320

1290   LET R=R+1

1300   PRINT: SCOR: "8R,";

1310   GO TO 1340

1320   LET W=W+1

1330   PRINT: SCOR: "8W,";

1340   PRINT
```

```
550PRINT"              (1) TWICE THAT OF THE STANDARD CARBON ATOM"
560PRINT"              (2) THE SAME AS THE STANDARD CARBON ATOM"
570PRINT"              (3) OF 2 ATOMIC MASS UNITS"
580PRINT
590PRINT"TYPE THE CORRECT NUMBER."
600 INPUT X
610IF X <> 1 THEN 650
620LET R = R+1
630 PRINT:SCOR:"3R,";
640 GO TO 670
650LET W = W+1
660 PRINT:SCOR:"3W,";
670 PRINT
680PRINT"4.  THE SUM OF THE ATOMIC WEIGHTS OF ALL THE ATOMS IN A"
690PRINT"    FORMULA IS CALLED THE        WEIGHT."
700PRINT
710PRINT"TYPE THE MISSING WORD"
720INPUT B$
730IF B$ <> A$ THEN 770
740LET R = R+1
750 PRINT:SCOR:"4R,";
760 GO TO 790
770LET W = W+1
780 PRINT:SCOR:"4W,";
790 PRINT
800PRINT"5.  CALCULATE THE FORMULA WEIGHT OF NACL."
810PRINT"    (ATOMIC WEIGHTS:  NA = 23.0, CL = 35.5)"
820 PRINT
830PRINT"TYPE THE FORMULA WEIGHT OF NACL."
840 INPUT X
850IF X <> 58.5 THEN 890
860LET R = R+1
870 PRINT:SCOR:"5R,";
880 GO TO 910
890LET W = W+1
900 PRINT:SCOR:"5W,";
910 PRINT
920PRINT"6.  WHAT IS THE % BY WEIGHT OF OXYGEN IN H(2)O (WATER)?"
930PRINT"    (A.W.H  =  1.01,  O  =  16.00)"
940 PRINT
950PRINT"TYPE THE % OXYGEN."
960INPUT X
970 IF X < 88.0 THEN 1020
980 IF X > 89.5 THEN 1020
990LET R = R+1
1000 PRINT:SCOR:"6R,";
1010 GO TO 1040
1020LET W = W+1
1030 PRINT:SCOR:"6W,";
```

PROGRAM 7.2—Continued

is simple. The correct answer to this question is 2. If the student response is *not* equal to 2 (line 1280), the program adds 1 to the count of wrong answers (W, line 1320), prints the response on the external file called SCOR (line 1330), and the next question is presented (line 1350). If the student response is 2, the program adds one to the number of right answers (R, line 1290), prints the response on an external file (line 1300), and branches to the next question (line 1310).

```
1040 PRINT
1050PRINT"7.  THERE ARE 208 GRAMS OF BACL(2) (BARIUM CHLORIDE)"
1060PRINT"    IN A BEAKER.  CALCULATE THE NUMBER OF GRAMS OF"
1070PRINT"    CHLORIDE PRESENT (AW: BA = 137.3, CL = 35.5)."
1080 PRINT
1090 PRINT"TYPE THE GRAMS OF CHLORIDE PRESENT."
1100 INPUT X
1110 IF X < 70.0 THEN 1160
1120 IF X > 71.0 THEN 1160
1130LET R = R+1
1140 PRINT:SCOR:"7R,";
1150 GO TO 1180
1160LET W = W+1
1170 PRINT:SCOR:"7W,";
1180 PRINT
1190PRINT"8.  THE WEIGHT OF AN ELEMENT WHICH CONTAINS THE SAME"
1200PRINT"    NUMBER OF ATOMS AS 12 GRAMS OF CARBON IS CALLED"
1210PRINT"    THE:"
1220PRINT"           (1) ATOMIC WEIGHT"
1230PRINT"           (2) GRAM ATOMIC WEIGHT"
1240PRINT"           (3) FORMULA WEIGHT"
1250 PRINT
1260PRINT"TYPE THE CORRECT NUMBER."
1270INPUT X
1280IF X <> 2 THEN 1320
1290LET R = R+1
1300 PRINT:SCOR:"8R,";
1310 GO TO 1340
1320LET W = W+1
1330 PRINT:SCOR:"8W,";
1340 PRINT
1350PRINT"9.  ONE GRAM FORMULA WEIGHT OF A SUBSTANCE IS COMMONLY"
1360PRINT"    REFERRED TO AS A            ."
1370 PRINT
1380PRINT"TYPE THE MISSING WORD."
1390INPUT C$
1400IF C$ <> D$ THEN 1440
1410LET R = R+1
1420 PRINT:SCOR:"9R,";
1430 GO TO 1460
1440LET W = W+1
1450 PRINT:SCOR:"9W,";
1460 PRINT
1470PRINT"10.  CALCULATE THE GRAM FORMULA WEIGHT OF C(6)H(6)."
1480PRINT"     (ATOMIC WEIGHTS:  C = 12.01,  H = 1.01)"
1490 PRINT
1500PRINT" TYPE THE GRAM FORMULA WEIGHT."
1510INPUT X
1520IF X <> 78.1 THEN 1560
```

PROGRAM 7.2—Continued

In the scoring sequence (lines 1280–1340 above), a new type of PRINT statement was introduced. For example,

1300   PRINT: SCOR: "8R,";

This statement is used when, during the execution of a program, data is to be printed on another program file. The exact format varies from one time-sharing system to another. In the system used here, the external program file name (SCOR) is enclosed in colons following the PRINT state-

```
1530LET R = R+1
1540 PRINT:SCOR:"10R,";
1550 GO TO 1580
1560LET W = W+1
1570 PRINT:SCOR:"10W,";
1580 PRINT
1590PRINT"11.   CALCULATE THE NUMBER OF GRAMS IN 2.50 MOLES OF"
1600PRINT"     WATER (H(2)O).  (AW:  H = 1.01,  O = 16.00)."
1610 PRINT
1620PRINT"TYPE THE NUMBER OF GRAMS."
1630 INPUT X
1640IF X < 44.5 THEN 1690
1650IF X > 45.5 THEN 1690
1660LET R = R+1
1670 PRINT:SCOR:"11R,";
1680 GO TO 1710
1690LET W = W+1
1700 PRINT:SCOR:"11W,";
1710 PRINT
1720PRINT"12.   CALCULATE THE NUMBER OF MOLES IN 22.3 GRAMS OF SODIUM"
1730PRINT"     NITRATE (NANO(3)).  (AW:  NA = 23.0,  N = 14.0,  O = 16.0)"
1740 PRINT
1750PRINT"TYPE THE NUMBER OF MOLES."
1760 INPUT X
1770IF X < 2.60 THEN 1820
1780IF X > 2.65 THEN 1820
1790LET R = R+1
1800 PRINT:SCOR:"12R,";
1810 GO TO 1840
1820LET W = W+1
1830 PRINT:SCOR:"12W,";
1840 PRINT
1850PRINT"13.   THERE ARE 6.02E23 ATOMS IN:"
1860PRINT"          (1) ONE GRAM MOLECULAR WEIGHT OF WATER"
1870PRINT"          (2) ONE GRAM ATOMIC WEIGHT OF CARBON"
1880PRINT"          (3) ONE FORMULA WEIGHT OF SODIUM CHLORIDE"
1890 PRINT
1900PRINT"TYPE THE CORRECT NUMBER"
1910 INPUT X
1920IF X <> 2 THEN 1960
1930LET R = R+1
1940 PRINT:SCOR:"13R,";
1950 GO TO 1980
1960LET W = W+1
1970 PRINT:SCOR:"13W,";
1980 PRINT
1990PRINT"14.   CALCULATE THE NUMBER OF MOLECULES IN 8.0 GRAMS OF"
2000PRINT"     OXYGEN (O(2)).  (AW:  O = 16.00)"
2010 PRINT
```

PROGRAM 7.2—Continued

ment. In all systems, the external file (that is, external to the program being executed) must be saved in advance. Similar to the usual PRINT statement, material enclosed in quotation marks (8R,) will be printed on the SCOR program verbatim, and the semi-colon is used for spacing. In fact, the semi-colon causes the response to each question to be printed on a single line (see Table 7.2B, line 13207).

The next question, number 9 (line 1350) requires a *verbal* response, that is, the student is required to verbalize an answer. The question is

```
2020PRINT"TYPE THE NUMBER OF GRAMS"
2030 INPUT X
2040IF X < 1.45E23 THEN 2090
2050IF X > 1.55E23 THEN 2090
2060LET R = R+1
2070 PRINT:SCOR:"14R,";
2080 GO TO 2110
2090LET W = W+1
2100 PRINT:SCOR:"14W,";
2110 PRINT
2120PRINT"15.  CALCULATE THE WEIGHT IN GRAMS OF ONE MOLECULE OF"
2130PRINT"    METHANE (CH(4)).  (AW:  C - 12.01,  H = 1.01)"
2140 PRINT
2150PRINT"TYPE THE NUMBER OF GRAMS"
2160 INPUT X
2170IF X < 2.6E-23 THEN 2220
2180IF X > 2.7E-23 THEN 2220
2190LET R = R+1
2200 PRINT:SCOR:"15R"
2210 GO TO 2240
2220LET W = W+1
2230 PRINT:SCOR:"15W"
2240 PRINT:SCOR:LNM(N);Z$,"R =";R,"W =";W
2250 PRINT"YOU HAVE FINISHED THE QUIZ ON ATOMIC AND FORMULA WEIGHTS."
2260 END
```

PROGRAM 7.2—Concluded

presented as usual (lines 1350,1370), and the student is directed to make the required response (line 1380). This time, however, a string variable must be used since the desired input is alphabetic (the answer consists of alphabetic symbols). A string variable is denoted by a letter followed by a "$" (for example, C$) where a string is any sequence of alphanumeric (alphabetic and numeric) characters. The string size is limited to 15 characters. The correct answer to this question is "mole." The correct response is defined with the statement.

180   LET D$=MOLE

The student answer is then requested

1390   INPUT C$

and compared to the correct answer

1400   IF C$=D$ THEN 1440

The program branching from this point on (lines 1410–1460) is exactly the same as in the previous question.

The final question to be discussed, question 10 (line 1470) is a *hidden response*. The student is required to calculate the gram formula weight of a molecule (lines 1470–1490) and no choices are given from which to choose. The format is the same as in previous questions. Question 11 (line 1590) is also a hidden response question requiring a calculation. In this problem, it was felt that use of the slide rule could lead to a small variance in the accepted answer. This variance can be accomodated by using two logical IF statements:

1640   IF X<44.5 THEN 1690

1650   IF X>45.5 THEN 1690

where the accepted answer lies in the range 44.5 to 45.5.

```
* * QUIZ: ATOMIC WEIGHTS AND FORMULA WEIGHTS * *

WHAT IS YOUR LAST NAME?(TYPE A MAXIMUM OF 15 LETTERS).
 ? VIERLING
WHAT IS YOUR STUDENT NUMBER ?
 ? 13207

GIVE ALL NUMERICAL ANSWERS TO 3 SIGNIFICANT FIGURES.

1.   THE ATOMIC MASS (WEIGHT) OF AN ELEMENT IS A NUMBER
     WHICH RELATES THE MASS OF AN AVERAGE ATOM OF THE
     GIVEN ELEMENT TO AN ATOM OF:
               (1) HYDROGEN
               (2) CARBON
               (3) OXYGEN

TYPE THE CORRECT NUMBER
  ? 2

2.   THE ATOMIC MASS OF CARBON-12 IS          ATOMIC
     MASS UNITS.

TYPE THE MISSING NUMBER
  ? 12

3.   THE ATOMIC MASS OF MAGNESIUM IS 24.  THIS NUMBER
     INDICATES THAT THE AVERAGE MAGNESIUM ATOM HAS A
     MASS:
               (1) TWICE THAT OF THE STANDARD CARBON ATOM
               (2) THE SAME AS THE STANDARD CARBON ATOM
               (3) OF 2 ATOMIC MASS UNITS

TYPE THE CORRECT NUMBER.
  ? 1

4.   THE SUM OF THE ATOMIC WEIGHTS OF ALL THE ATOMS IN A
     FORMULA IS CALLED THE          WEIGHT.

TYPE THE MISSING WORD
 ? FORMULA

5.   CALCULATE THE FORMULA WEIGHT OF NACL.
     (ATOMIC WEIGHTS:  NA = 23.0, CL = 35.5)

TYPE THE FORMULA WEIGHT OF NACL.
 ? 58/5
```

TABLE 7.2A   A Sample Run of a Quiz.

Now that the three types of quiz questions have been discussed, some record-keeping is in order. The use of an external file for purposes of keeping a record of individual student responses has been briefly discussed in the section on verbal response questions. The basic points will be reiterated. The external file capabilities and formats vary from system to system. The examples discussed here are only representative of a small

INCORRECT FORMAT --RETYPE
? 58.5

6. WHAT IS THE % BY WEIGHT OF OXYGEN IN H(2)O (WATER)?
   (A.W.H = 1.01, O = 16.00)

TYPE THE % OXYGEN.
? 88.9

7. THERE ARE 208 GRAMS OF BACL(2) (BARIUM CHLORIDE)
   IN A BEAKER. CALCULATE THE NUMBER OF GRAMS OF
   CHLORIDE PRESENT (AW: BA = 137.3, CL = 35.5)

TYPE THE GRAMS OF CHLORIDE PRESENT.
? 70.9

8. THE WEIGHT OF AN ELEMENT WHICH CONTAINS THE SAME
   NUMBER OF ATOMS AS 12 GRAMS OF CARBON IS CALLED
   THE:
           (1) ATOMIC WEIGHT
           (2) GRAM ATOMIC WEIGHT
           (3) FORMULA WEIGHT

TYPE THE CORRECT NUMBER.
? 2

9. ONE GRAM FORMULA WEIGHT OF A SUBSTANCE IS COMMONLY
   REFERRED TO AS A

TYPE THE MISSING WORD.
? MOLE

10. CALCULATE THE GRAM FORMULA WEIGHT OF C(6)H(6).
    (ATOMIC WEIGHTS: C = 12.01, H = 1.01)

 TYPE THE GRAM FORMULA WEIGHT.
 ? 78.1

11. CALCULATE THE NUMBER OF GRAMS IN 2.50 MOLES OF
    WATER (H(2)O). (AW: H = 1.01, O = 16.00).

TYPE THE NUMBER OF GRAMS.
? 45.0

TABLE 7.2A—Continued

number of items which can be treated. At the beginning of the program, the student is asked to give his name (lines 120, 130), and student number (lines 140, 150). This information is then printed on another program file which has previously been saved with the statement

160 PRINT: SCOR: Z$,N

The external file name, SCOR, is simply enclosed in colons after PRINT

```
12.   CALCULATE THE NUMBER OF MOLES IN 22.3 GRAMS OF SODIUM
      NITRATE (NANO(3)).    (AW:   NA = 23.0, N = 14.0, O = 16.0)

TYPE THE NUMBER OF MOLES.
 ? 2.60

13.   THERE ARE 6.02E23 ATOMS IN:
                  (1) ONE GRAM MOLECULAR WEIGHT OF WATER
                  (2) ONE GRAM ATOMIC WEIGHT OF CARBON
                  (3) ONE FORMULA WEIGHT OF SODIUM CHLORIDE

TYPE THE CORRECT NUMBER
 ? 2

14.   CALCULATE THE NUMBER OF MOLECULES IN 8.0 GRAMS OF
      OXYGEN (O(2)).    (AW:   O = 16.00)

TYPE THE NUMBER OF GRAMS
 ? 1.50E-23

15.   CALCULATE THE WEIGHT IN GRAMS OF ONE MOLECULE OF
      METHANE (CH(4)).    (AW:   C = 12.01,   H = 1.01)

TYPE THE NUMBER OF GRAMS
 ? 2.60E-23
YOU HAVE FINISHED THE QUIZ ON ATOMIC AND FORMULA WEIGHTS.
```

TABLE 7.2A—Concluded

when it is desired to write on the file. This format is variable depending on the particular system used. The number of correct responses (R) and wrong responses (W) are initialized to zero (line 190, 200). After the student answers a question, if he is correct, the following typical statements are executed

$$340 \quad \text{LET } R = R + 1$$

$$350 \quad \text{PRINT: SCOR: LNM(N); "1R,";}$$

the function LNM(X) gives the external file line a number. Anything enclosed in quotation marks is printed verbatim on the file. At the end of the quiz (line 2240), the students name, the number of right responses (R) and the number of wrong responses (W) are printed on the file. The program SCOR has been listed (Table 7.2B) after a typical student run of the quiz (Table 7.2A)

Discussion of Computer Generated Results: The output which is presented to the student is shown in Table 7.2A. The format is easy to follow and the responses appear directly after the question marks. If the external file SCOR is listed after this student has finished taking the quiz, the listing

```
VIERLING         13207
13207 1R,2R,3R,4R,5R,6R,7R,8R,9R,10R,11R,12R,13R,14W,15R
13208 VIERLING R = 14          W = 1
```

TABLE 7.2B The output from SCOR after one student has taken the quiz.

```
OLD

PROBLEM NAME: SCOR

READY
LISTNH
VIERLING           13207
13207  1R,2R,3R,4R,5R,6R,7R,8R,9R,10R,11R,12R,13R,14W,15R
13208  VIERLING  R = 14          W = 1
KROPF              63471
63471  1R,2W,3W,4W,5R,6W,7R,8R,9R,10W,11R,12R,13R,14W,15R
63472  KROPF     R = 9           W = 6
```

TABLE 7.2C A listing of SCOR after two students have taken the quiz.

(Table 7.2B) will include the total number of right and wrong answers (line 13208) as well as the response to each question (line 13207). For example, this student gave the right answer to all questions except number 14. If another student takes the quiz, his responses will be added to the file SCOR (Table 7.2C). This file (SCOR) can be accessed by another program which makes possible almost unlimited record keeping and evaluation.

7.3 THE MOLE

Lesson Characteristics:

CHEMISTRY LEVEL   college, introductory

MATHEMATICS BACKGROUND REQUIRED   algebra

PEDAGOGY   computer tutorial

PROBLEM APPROACH   analytical solution

STUDENT PARTICIPATION   uses prepared program

PROGRAMMING SKILLS   none

TIME OF STUDENT INVOLVEMENT   in class—maximum of 50 minutes

RECOMMENDED READING   (8) Chapters 2, 3
(9) Chapter 7
(10) Chapter 3

Lesson Description: This tutorial covers the concept of the mole which is normally presented in freshman chemistry courses. After the term mole is defined, the student is required to perform calculations using this quantity. A knowledge of simple algebra is necessary to solve the problems given in the program. In using this prepared program, the student requires no programming skills. The time of student involvement varies depending on the ability of the student. For example, if a student gives the correct answer to a question, he is immediately referred to the next question. When a student gives the wrong answer, however, he is given a hint and then asked to solve the problem step by step. In some cases, if he cannot solve the question, he is shown how to work the problem in detail. Thus a slow student may take twice as long to use the tutorial as a bright student. This type of program is beneficial to the student in several ways. To begin with, it is not unusual for students to fail exams because they had no concept of the important points to study—this kind of sophistication requires cultivation. The tutorial therefore helps the student since the questions asked indicate the relative importance of the material covered by the program. Furthermore, correct student responses are immediately recognized while incorrect responses cause the program to branch to statements which lead the student to the answer. If the student cannot solve the problem with the additional hints and comments provided by the program, he is shown how to work the problem step by step. Thus a tutorial tells a student what is important and it insures that he knows how to work the appropriate problems. The teacher, moreover, is freed to devote his talents to the slowest students who require personal attention.

Background and Theory: In MOLE1 (Program 7.3A), the gram formula weight is defined as *"the sum of the gram atomic weights of all the atoms in a formula."* This operational definition is simple to grasp and therefore often used in freshman chemistry. The student can use this definition to calculate the gram formula weight, given a formula, by looking up the atomic weights on a chart and taking their sum. A distinction is made between gram formula weight and gram molecular weight; the term gram molecular weight being used in the special case where the formula represents a molecular substance.

A mole is defined as one gram formula weight of a substance. Some texts restrict the definition to one gram molecular weight. The definition used here, however, is more common and will be further discussed in connection with MOLE2.

In working the problems for the students, the following techniques are employed. Consider, for example, the calculation of the weight of a mole of methane, CH_4. The student must be told prior to using the program that BASIC allows only capital letters and that subscripts are put in parentheses. Thus CH_4 becomes CH(4) and KCl becomes KCL. If these points are carefully explained, no confusion should result. The weight of a mole of methane may be calculated as follows:

$$1 \times C = 1 \times 12.00 = 12.00 \text{ GRAMS}$$

$$\text{Plus } 4 \times H = 4 \times 1.01 = 4.04$$

$$\text{Equals} \qquad CH(4) = 16.04 \text{ GRAMS}$$

This mechanistic approach, in which the student tabulates the number and kind of each atom, is used because experience has shown it to be successful. Whatever approach is used, it should be the same as that used in classroom lectures.

Another technique is involved in the calculation, for example, of the number of moles in 54.4 grams of methane. Two approaches can be used: (a) the ratio or (b) the factor technique.

In the ratio technique, the problem solution is set up as follows:

$$\frac{1 \text{ mole}}{16.0 \text{ grams } CH_4} = \frac{X \text{ moles}}{54.4 \text{ grams}}$$

One of the difficulties with the ratio technique is that the student can use this method without understanding what he is doing. In order to avoid this, a factor technique is often employed. Thus, the problem solution becomes:

$$X \text{ moles } CH_4 = 54.4 \text{ grams} \times \frac{1 \text{ mole } CH_4}{16.0 \text{ grams}}$$

$$X = 3.40 \text{ moles}$$

The factor method is employed in both tutorials.

In MOLE2 (Program 7.3B), it is stated that when a mole refers to a molecular substance, one mole contains 6.02×10^{23} molecules. Several types of problems involving moles, grams, and molecules can now be considered. For example, what is the weight of one molecule of water? Using the factor method:

$$weight \text{ of } 1 \text{ molecule } H_2O = 1 \text{ molecule } \times \frac{18.0 \text{ grams}}{6.02 \times 10^{23} \text{ molecules}}$$

$$weight \text{ of } 1 \text{ molecule} = 2.90 \times 10^{-23} \text{ grams}$$

It may be noted that the use of the term mole in regard to a non-molecular substance, such as KCl, has not been amplified. Such discussion is usually reserved to a later date when solutions are studied. At this point, it becomes obvious why it is useful to define the mole as one gram formula weight. In discussing the addition of KCl to water, it may be stated that

$$KCl \rightarrow K^+ + Cl^-$$

means

one mole $KCl \rightarrow$ one mole K^+ ions and one mole Cl^- ions.

Computer Techniques: Since tutorials are usually written by teachers for student use, the comments in this lesson are intended primarily for teachers. Computer tutorials should be written in such a manner that the computer is used as a *"teaching assistant."* In effect then, each teacher programs his own method of teaching into a computer tutorial. The general approach to tutorial program writing is as follows. First, define the area to be covered. Second, list the important points which the student must know at the end of the lesson. Third, determine how you will make these points (i.e., give a definition, ask for a verbal response, give a problem to be worked, etc.). Fourth, determine how you will measure the students understanding of the points you have chosen to cover. MOLE1 and MOLE2 will be discussed in the above context.

```
100 PRINT "THIS PROGRAM EXPLORES THE CHEMICAL CONCEPT OF THE"
110 PRINT "MOLE."
120 PRINT
130 PRINT "IN NUMERICAL PROBLEMS, THE UNITS ARE STATED IN THE"
140 PRINT "QUESTION.  YOU ARE EXPECTED TO GIVE THE NUMERICAL"
150 PRINT "ANSWER TO 3 SIGNIFICANT FIGURES."
160 PRINT
170 PRINT
180 PRINT "THE SUM OF THE GRAM ATOMIC WEIGHTS OF ALL THE ATOMS"
190 PRINT "IN A FORMULA IS EQUAL TO THE GRAM FORMULA WEIGHT."
200 PRINT "WHAT IS THE GRAM FORMULA WEIGHT OF POTASSIUM CHLORIDE, KCL?"
210 INPUT X
220 IF X = 74.6 THEN 550
230 IF X = 74.5 THEN 550
240 PRINT
250 PRINT "YOU SEEM TO BE HAVING DIFFICULTY.  LET US WORK THE PROBLEM"
260 PRINT "IN STEPS."
270 PRINT "WHAT IS THE GRAM ATOMIC WEIGHT OF POTASSIUM IN GRAMS?"
280 INPUT X
290 IF X = 39.1 THEN 340
300 PRINT "WRONG.  CONSULT THE TABLE OF ATOMIC WEIGHTS AND YOU"
310 PRINT "WILL FIND THAT THE ATOMIC WEIGHT OF POTASSIUM IS LISTED"
320 PRINT "AS 39.102.  THE GRAM ATOMIC WEIGHT OF POTASSIUM IS THUS 39.1"
330 PRINT "GRAMS USING 3 SIGNIFICANT FIGURES."
340 PRINT "WHAT IS THE GRAM ATOMIC WEIGHT OF CHLORINE IN GRAMS?"
350 INPUT X
360 IF X = 35.5 THEN 410
370 PRINT "WRONG.  THE TABLE OF ATOMIC WEIGHTS LISTS THE ATOMIC WEIGHT"
380 PRINT "OF CHLORINE AS 35.453.  THE GRAM ATOMIC WEIGHT OF CHLORINE"
390 PRINT "IS THUS 35.5 GRAMS (3 SIGNIFICANT FIGURES)."
400 PRINT
410 PRINT "NOW, WHAT IS THE GRAM FORMULA WEIGHT OF KCL, POTASSIUM"
420 PRINT "CHLORIDE, IN GRAMS?"
430 INPUT X
440 IF X = 74.6 THEN 550
450 IF N = 1 THEN 500
460 LET N = 1
470 PRINT "WRONG.  REMEMBER, THE GRAM FORMULA WEIGHT IS THE SUM"
480 PRINT "OF THE GRAM ATOMIC WEIGHTS OF ALL THE ATOMS IN THE FORMULA"
490 GO TO 410
500 PRINT"WRONG. THE GRAM ATOMIC WEIGHT OF POTASSIUM (K) IS 39.1"
510 PRINT"AND THE GRAM ATOMIC WEIGHT OF CHLORINE (CL) IS 35.5."
520 PRINT"THE GRAM FORMULA WEIGHT OF KCL IS THUS :"
530 PRINT"        39.1 + 35.5 = 74.6"
540 GO TO 560
550 PRINT "CORRECT.  THE GRAM FORMULA WEIGHT OF KCL IS 74.6 GRAMS."
560 PRINT
570 PRINT "IN THE SPECIAL CASE WHERE THE FORMULA REPRESENTS"
580 PRINT "A MOLECULAR SUBSTANCE, THE GRAM FORMULA WEIGHT IS"
590 PRINT "CALLED THE GRAM MOLECULAR WEIGHT."
600 PRINT
```

PROGRAM 7.3A   MOLE1: Weight Relations in Formulas.

In MOLE1 (Program 7.3A) and MOLE2 (Program 7.3B), for example, the area covered is the concept of the mole as it applies to weight relations in formulas. The use of this concept as it applies to equations is not covered. The important points in MOLE1 are the definitions of (a) gram formula weight, (b) gram molecular weight, and (c) the mole. In MOLE2, the important point covered is that one gram molecular weight of any substance contains 6.02×10^{23} molecules. These points are made by printing the definitions on the computer console (see lines 180–190, lines 570–590, and lines 730–740 in MOLE1 and lines 420–440 in MOLE2). These tutorials were written to be taken by students after the mole had been discussed in

```
610 PRINT "OXYGEN IS A DIATOMIC MOLECULE (IT CONTAINS 2 ATOMS OF OXYGEN"
620 PRINT "PER MOLECULE). WHAT IS THE GRAM MOLECULAR WEIGHTS OF O(2),"
630 PRINT "OXYGEN IN GRAMS?"
640 INPUT X
650 IF X = 32.0 THEN 700
660 PRINT "WRONG.  THE GRAM ATOMIC WEIGHT OF OXYGEN IS 16.0 GRAMS."
670 PRINT "THE GRAM MOLECULAR WEIGHT IS THE SUM OF THE GRAM"
680 PRINT "ATOMIC WEIGHTS OF THE ATOMS IN THE MOLECULE."
690 GO TO 610
700 PRINT "CORRECT.  THE GRAM MOLECULAR WEIGHT OF O(2), OXYGEN,"
710 PRINT "IS 32.0 GRAMS."
720 PRINT
730 PRINT "ONE GRAM FORMULA WEIGHT OF A SUBSTANCE IS COMMONLY"
740 PRINT "REFERRED TO AS A MOLE."
750 PRINT "WHAT IS THE WEIGHT IN GRAMS OF ONE MOLE OF O(2), OXYGEN?"
760 INPUT X
770 IF X = 32.0 THEN 830
780 PRINT "WRONG.  YOU HAVE JUST CALCULATED THE GRAM MOLECULAR"
790 PRINT "WEIGHT OF OXYGEN, O(2), TO BE 32.0 GRAMS.  THIS IS"
800 PRINT "ALSO THE GRAM FORMULA WEIGHT OF OXYGEN.  THUS,"
810 PRINT "ONE MOLE OF OXYGEN WEIGHS 32.0 GRAMS."
820 GO TO 850
830 PRINT "CORRECT."
850 PRINT "WHAT IS THE WEIGHT OF ONE MOLE OF ETHANE, C(2) H(5),"
860 PRINT "IN GRAMS?"
870 INPUT X
880 IF X = 29.0 THEN 1100
890 IF X = 29.1 THEN 1100
900 PRINT "WRONG.  ONE MOLE OF A SUBSTANCE IS ONE GRAM FORMULA WEIGHT."
910 PRINT "THE GRAM ATOMIC WEIGHT OF C IS 12.0 GRAMS."
920 PRINT "THE GRAM ATOMIC WEIGHT OF H IS 1.01 GRAMS."
930 PRINT "WHAT IS THE WEIGHT OF ONE MOLE OF ETHANE, C(2)H(5) IN GRAMS?"
940 INPUT X
950 IF X = 29.0 THEN 1100
960 IF X = 29.1 THEN 1100
970 PRINT "WRONG."
980 PRINT "THE GRAM FORMULA WEIGHT, OR ONE MOLE, OF C(2)H(5) IS"
990 PRINT "EQUAL TO:"
1000 PRINT "              2 X C = 2 X 12.00 = 24.00 GRAMS"
1010 PRINT "  PLUS:       5 X H = 5 X  1.01 =  5.05 GRAMS"
1020 PRINT "EQUALS:              C(2)H(5)   = 29.1   GRAMS"
1030 PRINT
1040 PRINT "TRY ANOTHER COMPOUND.  WHAT IS THE WEIGHT OF ONE MOLE OF"
1050 PRINT "METHANE, CH(4)?"
1060 INPUT X
1070 IF X = 16.0 THEN 1100
1080 PRINT "WRONG.  STUDY THE EXAMPLE AGAIN."
1090 GO TO 980
```

PROGRAM 7.3A—Continued

classroom lectures and briefly covered in reading assignments and homework problems. Student comprehension of the important points is thus
determined by requiring him to work problems. At the end of MOLE1 or
MOLE2, most students should be able to judge for themselves whether or
not they understand the topic. However, two approaches are possible.
First, the teacher can make available additional tutorials, covering the area
in greater detail, for the students to take at their own option. Secondly, the
teacher can write the program so that the students responses during the
program are tabulated. Then at the end of the program, based on his score,
a list of recommended tutorials which can be taken may be printed. In
either case, the fact that the scores on the tutorials do not count against his
grade will usually motivate the students to give them a try.

```
1100 PRINT "CORRECT."
1110 PRINT
1120 PRINT "HOW MANY MOLES ARE THEIR IN 54.4 GRAMS OF METHANE, CH(4)?"
1130 INPUT X
1140 IF X = 3.40 THEN 1350
1150 PRINT "WRONG.  THE FIRST THING TO DO TO CALCULATE THE WEIGHT"
1160 PRINT "OF 1 MOLE OF CH(4).  WHAT IS THE WEIGHT"
1170 PRINT "OF A MOLE OF CH(4) IN GRAMS?"
1180 INPUT X
1190 IF X = 16.0 THEN 1250
1200 PRINT "WRONG.  REMEMBER THAT A MOLE EQUALS ONE GRAM FORMULA"
1210 PRINT "WEIGHT.  A MOLE OF METHANE, CH(4) EQUALS:"
1220 PRINT "           1 X C = 1 X 12.00 = 12.00 GRAMS"
1230 PRINT "   PLUS:   4 X H = 4 X  1.01 =  4.04 GRAMS"
1240 PRINT "EQUALS:              CH(4) = 16.00 GRAMS"
1250 PRINT "HOW MANY MOLES ARE THEIR IN 54.4 GRAMS OF METHANE, CH(4)?"
1260 INPUT X
1270 IF X = 3.40 THEN 1350
1280 PRINT "ONE MOLE OF CH(4) WEIGHS 16.0 GRAMS."
1290 PRINT "TO FIND THE NUMBER OF MOLES IN 54.4 GRAMS OF CH(4) SET"
1300 PRINT "UP THE FOLLOWING EQUATION:"
1310 PRINT "# MOLES CH(4) = 54.4 GRAMS X (1 MOLE)/(16.0 GRAMS)"
1320 PRINT "# MOLES CH(4) = 54.4/16.0 GRAMS."
1330 PRINT "THEN, 54.4 GRAMS OF CH(4) EQUALS 3.40 MOLES."
1340 GO TO 1360
1350 PRINT "CORRECT.  54.4 GRAMS OF CH(4) EQUALS 3.40 MOLES."
1360 PRINT
1370 PRINT "YOU HAVE FINISHED THE FIRST HALF OF THE TUTORIAL"
1380 PRINT "ON THE CONCEPT OF THE MOLE.  CALL 'MOLE 2'"
1390 PRINT "TO FINISH THE PROGRAM."
1400 END
```

PROGRAM 7.3A—Concluded

Comments About the Computer Program: This tutorial on the concept of the mole was divided into two parts (MOLE1 and MOLE2) because the original program was too large for the time-sharing system being used. In general, the length of tutorial programs should be such that the student is able to concentrate' and retain information during the time it takes to run the program. For this reason, system limitations often provide a convenient breaking point for programs which are too long.

There are several techniques which can be illustrated for use in tutorial programs. Two will be discussed here.

The first type of question is utilized in MOLE1 (Program 7.3A) (lines 180–480); this general type of formulation can be called *question segmentation*. The term gram formula weight is defined (lines 180–190) and the question is posed

200 PRINT "WHAT IS THE GRAM FORMULA WEIGHT OF POTASSIUM CHLORIDE, KCL?"

If the response is correct (lines 220, 230) the correct response is reinforced (line 550) and the next question is stated. However, if the response is incorrect, the problem is broken into smaller segments. In this case, the gram atomic weight of potassium is requested (line 270). If the response is again wrong, the student is told how to find the correct answer (lines 300–330). A similar problem is then presented (lines 340–390). Finally, the entire response is again requested (lines 410, 420). An incorrect response causes a hint to be given (lines 470, 480) and the same question

```
100 PRINT "THIS PROGRAM IS THE SECOND HALF OF A TUTORIAL"
110 PRINT "ON THE CONCEPT OF THE MOLE.  YOU ARE EXPECTED"
120 PRINT "TO KNOW THE CONCEPTS PRESENTED IN 'MOLE 1'."
130 PRINT "GIVE ALL NUMERICAL ANSWERS TO 3 SIGNIFICANT FIGURES."
140 PRINT
150 PRINT "HOW MANY GRAMS OF NITROGEN ARE THERE IN"
160 PRINT "4.60 MOLES OF NITROGEN, N(2)?"
170 INPUT X
180 IF X = 129 THEN 380
190 PRINT
200 PRINT "WRONG.  FIRST CALCULATE THE WEIGHT OF ONE MOLE OF N(2)."
210 PRINT "WHAT IS THE WEIGHT OF ONE MOLE OF N(2) IN GRAMS?"
220 INPUT X
230 IF X = 28.0 THEN 280
240 PRINT"WRONG. CALCULATE THE GRAM FORMULA WEIGHT, OR THE WEIGHT"
250 PRINT"OF ONE MOLE, OF N(2) AS FOLLOWS:"
260 PRINT "ONE MOLE N(2) = 2 X N = 2 X 14.0 = 28.0 GRAMS."
270 GO TO 300
280 PRINT "CORRECT."
290 PRINT
300 PRINT "HOW MANY GRAMS OF NITROGEN ARE THEIR IN 4.60 MOLES"
310 PRINT "OF NITROGEN, N(2)?"
320 INPUT X
330 IF X = 129 THEN 380
340 PRINT "WRONG.  SET UP THE ANSWER AS FOLLOWS:"
350 PRINT "# GRAMS N(2) = 4.60 MOLES X 28.0 GRAMS/1 MOLE"
360 PRINT "# GRAMS N(2) = 4.60 X 28.0 = 129 GRAMS."
370 GO TO 390
380 PRINT "CORRECT."
390 PRINT "4.60 MOLES N(2) EQUALS 129 GRAMS OF NITROGEN."
400 PRINT
410 PRINT
420 PRINT "WHEN A MOLE REFERS TO A MOLECULAR SUBSTANCE,"
430 PRINT"REFERRED TO AS ONE GRAM MOLECULAR WEIGHT, IT HAS BEEN"
440 PRINT "FOUND THAT ONE MOLE CONTAINS 6.02E23 MOLECULES."
450 PRINT
460 PRINT "HOW MANY MOLECULES ARE THERE IN 32.0 GRAMS OF OXYGEN, O(2)?"
470 INPUT X
480 IF X = 6.02E23 THEN 530
490 PRINT "WRONG.  ONE MOLE OF OXYGEN, O(2), WEIGHS 32.0 GRAMS."
500 PRINT "SINCE EACH MOLE OF OXYGEN CONTAINS 6.02E23 MOLECULES,"
510 PRINT "32.0 GRAMS OXYGEN CONTAINS 6.02E23 MOLECULES OXYGEN."
520 GO TO 550
530 PRINT "CORRECT."
540 PRINT
550 PRINT "HOW MANY MOLECULES ARE THERE IN 57.6 GRAMS O(2), OXYGEN?"
560 INPUT X
570 IF X < 10.8E23 THEN 590
580 IF X < 11.0E23 THEN 690
590 PRINT "WRONG.  REMEMBER THAT 32.0 GRAMS OXYGEN CONTAINS 6.02E23"
600 PRINT "MOLECULES."
610 PRINT "HOW MANY MOLECULES ARE THERE IN 57.6 GRAMS OXYGEN, O(2)?"
620 INPUT X
```

PROGRAM 7.3B   MOLE2: Relationships between moles, molecules, and grams.

is again asked. In this case, the loop is broken only when the correct response is given or when the loop has been encountered twice. Finally, if the student cannot give the correct answer, he is told how to formulate the response (lines 500–530).

The second type of formulation which can be used in tutorials employs *hints*. The question is posed (lines 850, 860). If the response is not correct a hint is given (lines 910–930) and the question is again asked (line 930). Depending on the complexity of the question, a single hint or several hints may be given before the correct response is printed (lines 980–1020). In

```
630 IF X < 10.8E23 THEN 650
640 IF X < 11.0E23 THEN 690
650 PRINT "WRONG.  THE CORRECT ANSWER IS FORMULATED AS FOLLOWS:"
660 PRINT "# MOLECULES O(2) = 57.6 GRAMS X 6.02E23 MOLECULES/32.0 GRAMS"
670 PRINT "# MOLECULES O(2) = 57.6 X (6.02E23/32) = 10.85E23"
680 GO TO 700
690 PRINT "CORRECT"
700 PRINT "57.6 GRAMS OXYGEN CONTAINS 10.8E23 MOLECULES OXYGEN."
710 PRINT
720 PRINT "WHAT IS THE WEIGHT OF ONE MOLECULE OF WATER, H(2)O?"
730 INPUT X
740 IF X < 2.80E-23 THEN 760
750 IF X < 3.01E-23 THEN 980
760 PRINT"WRONG.  REMEMBER THAT ONE GRAM FORMULA WEIGHT, OR 1 MOLE,"
770 PRINT "OF A MOLECULAR SUBSTANCE CONTAINS 6.02E23 MOLECULES."
780 PRINT"WHAT IS THE WEIGHT OF 1 MOLECULE OF WATER, H(2)O?"
790 INPUT X
800 IF X < 2.80E-23 THEN 820
810 IF X < 3.01E-23 THEN 980
820 PRINT "WRONG.  THE GRAM FORMULA WEIGHT OF H(2)O EQUALS:"
830 PRINT "                    2 X H = 2 X 1.01 = 2.02 GRAMS"
840 PRINT "    PLUS:           1 X O = 1 X 16.0 = 16.0 GRAMS"
850 PRINT "EQUALS:                     H(2)O = 18.0 GRAMS"
860 PRINT "ONE MOLE OF WATER, 18.0 GRAMS, CONTAINS 6.02E23 MOLECULES."
870 PRINT
880 PRINT "WHAT IS THE WEIGHT OF 1 MOLECULE OF WATER?"
890 INPUT X
900 IF X < 2.80E-23 THEN 920
910 IF X < 3.01E-23 THEN 980
920 PRINT "WRONG.  THE ANSWER IS FORMULATED AS FOLLOWS:"
930 PRINT "WEIGHT 1 MOLECULE H(2)O = 1 MOLECULE X 18.0 GRAMS/";
940 PRINT "6.02E23 MOLECULES"
960 PRINT"WEIGHT 1 MOLECULE H(2)O = 18.0/6.02E23 GRAMS"
970 GO TO 990
980 PRINT "CORRECT."
990 PRINT "ONE MOLECULE OF WATER WEIGHS 2.90E-23 GRAMS."
1000 PRINT
1010 PRINT
1020 PRINT "THE IMPORTANT CONCEPTS COVERED IN MOLE 1 AND MOLE 2"
1030 PRINT "MAY BE SUMMARIZED:"
1035 PRINT
1040 PRINT "1. THE SUM OF THE GRAM ATOMIC WEIGHTS OF ALL THE"
1050 PRINT "ATOMS IN A FORMULA IS THE GRAM FORMULA WEIGHT."
1060 PRINT
1070 PRINT "2. ONE MOLE EQUALS ONE GRAM FORMULA WEIGHT."
1080 PRINT
1090 PRINT "3. IN THE SPECIAL CASE WHERE THE FORMULA REPRESENTS A"
1100 PRINT "MOLECULAR SUBSTANCE, ONE GRAM FORMULA WEIGHT IS"
1110 PRINT "CALLED ONE GRAM MOLECULAR WEIGHT."
1120 PRINT
1130 PRINT "4.  ONE GRAM MOLECULAR WEIGHT, OR ONE MOLE OF A"
1140 PRINT "MOLECULAR SUBSTANCE, CONTAINS 6.02E23 MOLECULES."
1150 PRINT
1160 END
```

PROGRAM 7.3B—Concluded

this manner, the student is given several opportunities to answer the question. If the correct response is never given, another similar example should be tried (lines 1040–1050) in an effort to promote understanding of the concept involved.

These formulations are but two examples of the various ways in which tutorials can be written. Some of the important points to remember in writing tutorials are:

1. Reinforce the correct response.

THIS PROGRAM EXPLORES THE CHEMICAL CONCEPT OF THE
MOLE.

IN NUMERICAL PROBLEMS, THE UNITS ARE STATED IN THE
QUESTION. YOU ARE EXPECTED TO GIVE THE NUMERICAL
ANSWER TO 3 SIGNIFICANT FIGURES.

THE SUM OF THE GRAM ATOMIC WEIGHTS OF ALL THE ATOMS
IN A FORMULA IS EQUAL TO THE GRAM FORMULA WEIGHT.
WHAT IS THE GRAM FORMULA WEIGHT OF POTASSIUM CHLORIDE, KCL?
 ? 77.7

YOU SEEM TO BE HAVING DIFFICULTY. LET US WORK THE PROBLEM
IN STEPS.
WHAT IS THE GRAM ATOMIC WEIGHT OF POTASSIUM IN GRAMS?
 ? 39.0
WRONG. CONSULT THE TABLE OF ATOMIC WEIGHTS AND YOU
WILL FIND THAT THE ATOMIC WEIGHT OF POTASSIUM IS LISTED
AS 39.102. THE GRAM ATOMIC WEIGHT OF POTASSIUM IS THUS 39.1
GRAMS USING 3 SIGNIFICANT FIGURES.
WHAT IS THE GRAM ATOMIC WEIGHT OF CHLORINE IN GRAMS?
 ? 35.6
WRONG. THE TABLE OF ATOMIC WEIGHTS LISTS THE ATOMIC WEIGHT
OF CHLORINE AS 35.453. THE GRAM ATOMIC WEIGHT OF CHLORINE
IS THUS 35.5 GRAMS (3 SIGNIFICANT FIGURES).

NOW, WHAT IS THE GRAM FORMULA WEIGHT OF KCL, POTASSIUM
CHLORIDE, IN GRAMS?
 ? 74.5
WRONG. REMEMBER, THE GRAM FORMULA WEIGHT IS THE SUM
OF THE GRAM ATOMIC WEIGHTS OF ALL THE ATOMS IN THE FORMULA
NOW, WHAT IS THE GRAM FORMULA WEIGHT OF KCL, POTASSIUM
CHLORIDE, IN GRAMS?
 ? 74.7
WRONG. THE GRAM ATOMIC WEIGHT OF POTASSIUM (K) IS 39.1
AND THE GRAM ATOMIC WEIGHT OF CHLORINE (CL) IS 35.5.
THE GRAM FORMULA WEIGHT OF KCL IS THUS :
     39.1 + 35.5 = 74.6

IN THE SPECIAL CASE WHERE THE FORMULA REPRESENTS
A MOLECULAR SUBSTANCE, THE GRAM FORMULA WEIGHT IS
CALLED THE GRAM MOLECULAR WEIGHT.

OXYGEN IS A DIATOMIC MOLECULE (IT CONTAINS 2 ATOMS OF OXYGEN
PER MOLECULE). WHAT IS THE GRAM MOLECULAR WEIGHTS OF O(2),
OXYGEN IN GRAMS?
 ? 32.06
WRONG.   THE GRAM ATOMIC WEIGHT OF OXYGEN IS 16.0 GRAMS.

TABLE 7.3A   The output obtained from a typical student run of MOLE1.

2. Make every effort to *draw* the correct response from the student.
3. If the correct response is never given, show the correct response and
    then pose another similar question.

Computer Generated Results: Sample runs of MOLE1 and MOLE2 are
shown (Table 7.3A, Table 7.3B and Table 7.3C). The student retains a

THE GRAM MOLECULAR WEIGHT IS THE SUM OF THE GRAM
ATOMIC WEIGHTS OF THE ATOMS IN THE MOLECULE.
OXYGEN IS A DIATOMIC MOLECULE (IT CONTAINS 2 ATOMS OF OXYGEN
PER MOLECULE).   WHAT IS THE GRAM MOLECULAR WEIGHTS OF O(2),
OXYGEN IN GRAMS?
 ? 32.0
CORRECT.   THE GRAM MOLECULAR WEIGHT OF O(2), OXYGEN,
IS 32.0 GRAMS.

ONE GRAM FORMULA WEIGHT OF A SUBSTANCE IS COMMONLY
REFERRED TO AS A MOLE.
WHAT IS THE WEIGHT IN GRAMS OF ONE MOLE OF O(2), OXYGEN?
 ? 16
WRONG.   YOU HAVE JUST CALCULATED THE GRAM MOLECULAR
WEIGHT OF OXYGEN, O(2), TO BE 32.0 GRAMS.   THIS IS
ALSO THE GRAM FORMULA WEIGHT OF OXYGEN.   THUS,
ONE MOLE OF OXYGEN WEIGHS 32.0 GRAMS.
WHAT IS THE WEIGHT OF ONE MOLE OF ETHANE, C(2) H(5),
IN GRAMS?
 ? 28
WRONG.   ONE MOLE OF A SUBSTANCE IS ONE GRAM FORMULA WEIGHT.
THE GRAM ATOMIC WEIGHT OF C IS 12.0 GRAMS.
THE GRAM ATOMIC WEIGHT OF H IS 1.01 GRAMS.
WHAT IS THE WEIGHT OF ONE MOLE OF ETHANE, C(2)H(5) IN GRAMS?
 ? 30
WRONG.
THE GRAM FORMULA WEIGHT, OR ONE MOLE, OF C(2)H(5) IS
EQUAL TO:
                    2 X C = 2 X 12.00 = 24.00 GRAMS
   PLUS: 5 X H = 5 X 1.01 = 5.05 GRAMS
EQUALS: C(2)H(5) = 29.1   GRAMS

TRY ANOTHER COMPOUND.   WHAT IS THE WEIGHT OF ONE MOLE OF
METHANE, CH(4)?
 ? 15
WRONG.   STUDY THE EXAMPLE AGAIN.
THE GRAM FORMULA WEIGHT, OR ONE MOLE, OF C(2)H(5) IS
EQUAL TO:
                    2 X C = 2 X 12.00 = 24.00 GRAMS
   PLUS: 5 X H = 5 X 1.01 = 5.05 GRAMS
EQUALS: C(2)H(5) = 29.1   GRAMS

TRY ANOTHER COMPOUND.   WHAT IS THE WEIGHT OF ONE MOLE OF
METHANE, CH(4)?
 ? 16.0
CORRECT.

HOW MANY MOLES ARE THEIR IN 54.4 GRAMS OF METHANE, CH(4)?
 ? 3.6

TABLE 7.3A—Continued

WRONG.   THE FIRST THING TO DO TO CALCULATE THE WEIGHT
OF 1 MOLE OF CH(4).   WHAT IS THE WEIGHT
OF A MOLE OF CH(4) IN GRAMS?
 ? 15.9
WRONG.   REMEMBER THAT A MOLE EQUALS ONE GRAM FORMULA
WEIGHT.   A MOLE OF METHANE, CH(4) EQUALS:
                  1 X C = 1 X 12.00 = 12.00 GRAMS
   PLUS: 4 X H = 4 X 1.01 = 4.04 GRAMS
EQUALS: CH(4) = 16.00 GRAMS
HOW MANY MOLES ARE THEIR IN 54.4 GRAMS OF METHANE, CH(4)?
 ? 3.7
ONE MOLE OF CH(4) WEIGHS 16.0 GRAMS.
TO FIND THE NUMBER OF MOLES IN 54.4 GRAMS OF CH(4) SET
UP THE FOLLOWING EQUATION:
MOLES CH(4) = 54.4 GRAMS X (1 MOLE)/(16.0 GRAMS)
MOLES CH(4) = 54.4/16.0 GRAMS.
THEN, 54.4 GRAMS OF CH(4) EQUALS 3.40 MOLES.

YOU HAVE FINISHED THE FIRST HALF OF THE TUTORIAL
ON THE CONCEPT OF THE MOLE.   CALL 'MOLE 2'
TO FINISH THE PROGRAM.

TABLE 7.3A—Concluded

THIS PROGRAM IS THE SECOND HALF OF A TUTORIAL
ON THE CONCEPT OF THE MOLE. YOU ARE EXPECTED
TO KNOW THE CONCEPTS PRESENTED IN 'MOLE 1'.
GIVE ALL NUMERICAL ANSWERS TO 3 SIGNIFICANT FIGURES.

HOW MANY GRAMS OF NITROGEN ARE THERE IN
4.60 MOLES OF NITROGEN, N(2)?
 ? 129
CORRECT.
4.60 MOLES N(2) EQUALS 129 GRAMS OF NITROGEN.

WHEN A MOLE REFERS TO A MOLECULAR SUBSTANCE,
REFERRED TO AS ONE GRAM MOLECULAR WEIGHT, IT HAS BEEN
FOUND THAT ONE MOLE CONTAINS 6.02E23 MOLECULES.

HOW MANY MOLECULES ARE THERE IN 32.0 GRAMS OF OXYGEN, O(2)?
 ? 6.02E23
CORRECT.

HOW MANY MOLECULES ARE THERE IN 57.6 GRAMS O(2), OXYGEN?
 ? 10.9E23
CORRECT
57.6 GRAMS OXYGEN CONTAINS 10.8E23 MOLECULES OXYGEN.

WHAT IS THE WEIGHT OF ONE MOLECULE OF WATER, H(2)O?
 ? 3.00E-23
CORRECT.
ONE MOLECULE OF WATER WEIGHS 2.90E-23 GRAMS.

THE IMPORTANT CONCEPTS COVERED IN MOLE 1 AND MOLE 2
MAY BE SUMMARIZED:

1. THE SUM OF THE GRAM ATOMIC WEIGHTS OF ALL THE
ATOMS IN A FORMULA IS THE GRAM FORMULA WEIGHT.

2. ONE MOLE EQUALS ONE GRAM FORMULA WEIGHT.

3. IN THE SPECIAL CASE WHERE THE FORMULA REPRESENTS A
MOLECULAR SUBSTANCE, ONE GRAM FORMULA WEIGHT IS
CALLED ONE GRAM MOLECULAR WEIGHT.

4. ONE GRAM MOLECULAR WEIGHT, OR ONE MOLE OF A
MOLECULAR SUBSTANCE, CONTAINS 6.02E23 MOLECULES.

TABLE 7.3B The output obtained from MOLE2 when a student answers all questions correctly.

THIS PROGRAM IS THE SECOND HALF OF A TUTORIAL
ON THE CONCEPT OF THE MOLE. YOU ARE EXPECTED
TO KNOW THE CONCEPTS PRESENTED IN 'MOLE 1'.
GIVE ALL NUMERICAL ANSWERS TO 3 SIGNIFICANT FIGURES.

HOW MANY GRAMS OF NITROGEN ARE THERE IN
4.60 MOLES OF NITROGEN, N(2)?
  ? 132.4

WRONG. FIRST CALCULATE THE WEIGHT OF ONE MOLE OF N(2).
WHAT IS THE WEIGHT OF ONE MOLE OF N(2) IN GRAMS?
  ? 14.0
WRONG. CALCULATE THE GRAM FORMULA WEIGHT, OR THE WEIGHT
OF ONE MOLE, OF N(2) AS FOLLOWS:
ONE MOLE N(2) = 2 X N = 2 X 14.0 = 28.0 GRAMS.
HOW MANY GRAMS OF NITROGEN ARE THEIR IN 4.60 MOLES
OF NITROGEN, N(2)?
  ? 128
WRONG. SET UP THE ANSWER AS FOLLOWS:
GRAMS N(2) = 4.60 MOLES X 28.0 GRAMS/1 MOLE
GRAMS N(2) = 4.60 X 28.0 = 129 GRAMS.
4.60 MOLES N(2) EQUALS 129 GRAMS OF NITROGEN.

WHEN A MOLE REFERS TO A MOLECULAR SUBSTANCE,
REFERRED TO AS ONE GRAM MOLECULAR WEIGHT, IT HAS BEEN
FOUND THAT ONE MOLE CONTAINS 6.02E23 MOLECULES.

HOW MANY MOLECULES ARE THERE IN 32.0 GRAMS OF OXYGEN, O(2)?
  ? 6,02

INCORRECT FORMAT --RETYPE
  ? 6.02
WRONG. ONE MOLE OF OXYGEN, O(2), WEIGHS 32.0 GRAMS.
SINCE EACH MOLE OF OXYGEN CONTAINS 6.02E23 MOLECULES,
32.0 GRAMS OXYGEN CONTAINS 6.02E23 MOLECULES OXYGEN.
HOW MANY MOLECULES ARE THERE IN 57.6 GRAMS O(2), OXYGEN?
  ? 10
WRONG. REMEMBER THAT 32.0 GRAMS OXYGEN CONTAINS 6.02E23
MOLECULES.
HOW MANY MOLECULES ARE THERE IN 57.6 GRAMS OXYGEN, O(2)?
  ? 10E23
WRONG. THE CORRECT ANSWER IS FORMULATED AS FOLLOWS:
MOLECULES O(2) = 57.6 GRAMS X 6.02E23 MOLECULES/32.0 GRAMS
MOLECULES O(2) = 57.6 X (6.02E23/32) = 10.85E23
57.6 GRAMS OXYGEN CONTAINS 10.8E23 MOLECULES OXYGEN.

TABLE 7.3C   A typical student run of MOLE2.

```
WHAT IS THE WEIGHT OF ONE MOLECULE OF WATER, H(2)O?
 ? E-23
WRONG.   REMEMBER THAT ONE GRAM FORMULA WEIGHT, OR 1 MOLE,
OF A MOLECULAR SUBSTANCE CONTAINS 6.02E23 MOLECULES.
WHAT IS THE WEIGHT OF 1 MOLECULE OF WATER, H(2)O?
 ? 2E-23
WRONG.   THE GRAM FORMULA WEIGHT OF H(2)O EQUALS:
             2 X H = 2 X 1.01 = 2.02 GRAMS
   PLUS:     1 X O = 1 X 16.0 = 16.0 GRAMS
EQUALS:               H(2)O = 18.0 GRAMS
ONE MOLE OF WATER, 18.0 GRAMS, CONTAINS 6.02E23 MOLECULES.

WHAT IS THE WEIGHT OF 1 MOLECULE OF WATER?
 ? 2.60E-23
WRONG.   THE ANSWER IS FORMULATED AS FOLLOWS:
WT. 1 MOLECULE H(2)O = 1 MOLECULE X 18.0 GRAMS/6.02E23MOLECULES.

WEIGHT 1 MOLECULE H(2)O = 18.0/6.02E23 GRAMS
ONE MOLECULE OF WATER WEIGHS 2.90E-23 GRAMS.


THE IMPORTANT CONCEPTS COVERED IN MOLE 1 AND MOLE 2
MAY BE SUMMARIZED:

1. THE SUM OF THE GRAM ATOMIC WEIGHTS OF ALL THE
ATOMS IN A FORMULA IS THE GRAM FORMULA WEIGHT.

2. ONE MOLE EQUALS ONE GRAM FORMULA WEIGHT.

3. IN THE SPECIAL CASE WHERE THE FORMULA REPRESENTS A
MOLECULAR SUBSTANCE, ONE GRAM FORMULA WEIGHT IS
CALLED ONE GRAM MOLECULAR WEIGHT.

4. ONE GRAM MOLECULAR WEIGHT, OR ONE MOLE OF A
MOLECULAR SUBSTANCE, CONTAINS 6.02E23 MOLECULES.
```

TABLE 7.3C—Concluded

printed copy of his performance. This printed copy contains important definitions (see for example paragraph 3, p. 214) as well as solutions to the problems he was unable to solve (last paragraph, p. 216). The computer results can thus be saved as a guide in studying for exams.

7.4   IDEAL GASES

Lesson Characteristics:

CHEMISTRY LEVEL   college, introductory

MATHEMATICS BACKGROUND REQUIRED   algebra

PEDAGOGY   problem drill

PROBLEM APPROACH   analytical solution

STUDENT PARTICIPATION   uses prepared program

PROGRAMMING SKILLS   none

TIME OF STUDENT INVOLVEMENT   out of class—
unlimited

RECOMMENDED READING   (8) Chapter 6
                      (9) Chapters 9, 10
                      (10) Chapter 6

Lesson Description: This lesson is designed to show how the computer may be used to drill students in problem solving. Since the program is written by teachers for use by students, the discussion which follows is directed toward those in a teaching capacity. (In other words, it applies both to teachers and to upperclassmen who assist in the teaching of fellow students.)

The subject presented is freshman college level and the only math requirement is algebra. The basic rationale is as follows: In chemistry, there are many types of problems which students must be able to solve. These types include, for example, problems involving moles, grams, and molecules and problems involving ideal gases where the amount, the pressure, the volume, and the temperature are the important variables. The problem drill program sets up a specific kind of problem with varying parameters so that the student can work the problem over and over until he understands it. In this program, attention is focused on an ideal gas problem. One gram molecular weight of an ideal gas occupies 22.4 liters at STP (0° centigrade and 760 mm. of mercury). Given the amount of gas present in a certain volume under specific conditions of temperature and pressure, a student can calculate the molecular weight of the gas by calculating the amount present in 22.4 liters at 0°C and 760 mm. Hg. This program uses a random number generator to generate the temperature, pressure, and volume, and then uses the molecular weight of a gas to calculate the amount present under those conditions. The student is given the pressure, temperature, volume, and amount and asked to calculate the molecular weight. Each time he works the problem, he is given different values of these variables. Furthermore, if the student requests help, he is shown how to work the problem. Since the student uses a prepared program, no programming skills are required. The student works the type problem until he feels confident he understands the concept involved. Thus the time of student involvement is as long as is required by the student. In each area covered in class, there can be problem drill programs to cover all of the important type problems.

Background and Theory: The type question covered in this *problem drill* program is: given the amount of a gas (g) present in a specific volume (V), and at a specified temperature (T) and pressure (p), and assuming ideal behavior, what is the molecular weight (M) of the gas?

This problem can be solved in two ways. If the student has memorized the ideal gas law:

$$pV = \frac{g}{M}RT \qquad (7.4\text{–}1)$$

where R=ideal gas constant=.082 liter atm. deg.$^{-1}$ mole^{-1} (the other variables are defined in the first paragraph—the units are p atm., V liters, T °K) he may solve for the molecular weight

$$M = \frac{gRT}{pV} \qquad (7.4\text{--}2)$$

Thus the answer may be obtained simply by substituting the values given into the ideal gas law.

The second method of solving this problem is the factor method. This method is often used in elementary chemistry courses because it emphasizes understanding. (Once the student understands the relationships between p, V, T, and amount, it is probably easiest to use the ideal gas law in solving subsequent problems.) The student knows that one mole (one gram molecular weight) of an ideal gas occupies 22.4 liters at STP (0° centigrade or 273° Kelvin and 760 mm. of mercury.) The problem then is to convert the amount given to the amount present in 22.4 liters at STP. This is done by using factors for the pressure, temperature, and volume change involved. The problem shown in the sample run (Table 7.4) can be used as an example. The initial and final conditions are listed in the following table:

	p	V	T	amount
initial	774 mm Hg	19.980 liters	50.0°C	21.5 grams
final	760	22.400	0°C	M

The factors are divided as follows: the amount present at STP is proportional to the pressure and volume changes and inversely proportional to the temperature change. Each factor is then set up:

decrease in p= decrease in amount

$$p \text{ factor} = 760/774 = 0.981$$

increase in V= increase in amount

$$V \text{ factor} = 22.40/19.98 = 1.12$$

decrease in T= increase in amount

$$T \text{ factor} = (50.0+273)/(0+273) = 1.18$$

(note that °C+273=°K)

The molecular weight then is given by

$$M = \text{amount} \times p \text{ factor} \times V \text{ factor} \times T \text{ factor} \qquad (7.4\text{--}3)$$

$$M = 21.5 \text{ grams} \times 0.982 \times 1.12 \times 1.18$$

$$M = 28 \text{ which is the molecular weight of nitrogen}$$

This second method is used in the program (7.4).

Computer Techniques: This type of program, problem drill, is written to provide students with an effective means of learning to solve problems. In

```
100 PRINT"******** PROBLEM DRILL IN MOLECULAR WEIGHT CALCULATION ******"
110 LET Y$ = "YES"
120 FOR I = 1 TO 8
130 READ A(I)
140 DATA 2.02, 32.0, 71.0, 28.0, 30.0, 4.0, 39.9, 28.0
150 LET N = 1
160 NEXT I
170 LET A$(1) = "HYDROGEN"
180 LET A$(2) = "OXYGEN"
190 LET A$(3) = "CHLORINE"
200 LET A$(4) = "NITROGEN"
210 LET A$(5) = "NITROGEN OXIDE"
220 LET A$(6) = "HELIUM"
230 LET A$(7) = "ARGON"
240 LET A$(8) = "CARBON MONOXIDE"
250 PRINT
260 LET X = RND(X)
270 IF X = 0 THEN 260
280 LET I = INT(X*8 +.5)
290 IF N = 1 THEN 330
300 LET T = -100*X
310 LET N = -1*N
320 GO TO 350
330 LET T = 100*X
340 LET N = -1*N
350 LET P = 1550*X
360 LET V = 40000*X
370 LET G = A(I)*P/760*V/(82.05*(T + 273))
380 SETDIGITS(4)
390 PRINT"GIVEN:   "G"GRAMS OF A GAS AT "T"DEGREES CENTIGRADE AND"
400 PRINT"A PRESSURE OF"P"MM. OF MERCURY OCCUPIES"V"MILLILITERS."
410 PRINT
420 PRINT"CALCULATE: THE MOLECULAR WEIGHT, OR THAT WEIGHT WHICH OCCUPIES
430 PRINT"22.4 LITERS AT STANDARD TEMPERATURE AND PRESSURE (0 DEGREES"
440 PRINT"CENTIGRADE AND 760 MM. OF HG)."
450 PRINT
460 PRINT"TYPE IN A ZERO FOR ASSISTANCE."
470 PRINT
480 PRINT"TYPE A MINUS ONE (-1) IF YOU WISH TO STOP THE PROGRAM."
490 PRINT
500 PRINT"WHEN YOU HAVE THE CORRECT ANSWER, TYPE IT IN USING"
510 PRINT"3 SIGNIFICANT FIGURES."
520 INPUT Z
530 PRINT
540 IF Z = 0 THEN 820
550 IF Z = -1 THEN 1410
560 IF Z = A(I) THEN 760
570 PRINT"I DON'T AGREE WITH YOU.  WOULD YOU LIKE TO TRY THE "
580 PRINT"CALCULATION AGAIN ?"
```

PROGRAM 7.4   Ideal Gases.

this context, the computer is used as a tutor. The student is given a problem to solve—if he types in the correct answer he is immediately told so. If his answer is not correct, he is again told immediately and is shown how to work the problem if he so desires. This would appear to be an improvement over the normal procedure. Usually, students are given a problem assignment, and in some cases, the answers are in the back of the book. If the student cannot work the problem, he has to wait for his discussion class to find out how it is done. And all too often, particularly if he is a slow learner, he doesn't find out until the next exam that he really didn't understand the problem. The computer, in contrast, provides an immediate response tailored to individual student needs.

```
590 PRINT"(TYPE YES OR NO)."
600 INPUT T$
610 PRINT
620 IF T$ = Y$ THEN 500
630 PRINT"WOULD YOU LIKE ASSISTANCE ?"
640 PRINT"(TYPE YES OR NO)."
650 INPUT T$
660 PRINT
670 IF T$ = Y$ THEN 820
680 PRINT"MY ANSWER TO THIS PROBLEM IS,"
690 PRINT
700 PRINT"      MOLECULAR WEIGHT ="A(I)
710 PRINT
720 PRINT"      WHICH IS THE MOLECULAR WEIGHT OF "A$(I)" GAS."
730 PRINT
740 PRINT"WHY DON'T YOU TRY ANOTHER PROBLEM."
750 GO TO 250
760 PRINT"YOU ARE CORRECT. "A(I)" IS THE MOLECULAR WEIGHT OF "A$(I)"."
770 PRINT"DO YOU WANT TO TRY ANOTHER PROBLEM ?"
780 PRINT"(TYPE YES OR NO)."
790 INPUT T$
800 IF T$ = Y$ THEN 250
810 STOP
820 PRINT"LET'S SET THIS ONE UP TOGETHER:"
830 PRINT
840 PRINT"        P              V              T          AMOUNT"
850 PRINT
860 PRINT"INITIAL"
870 PRINTP"MM OF HG,    "V"ML,    "T"DEGREES C,   "G"GRAMS"
880 PRINT
890 PRINT"FINAL"
900 PRINT"760 MM. OF HG,        22400 ML,        0 DEGREES C,        ?????"
910 PRINT
920 PRINT"    WE KNOW THAT AT STANDARD PRESSURE AND TEMPERATURE"
930 PRINT"ONE MOLE OF AN IDEAL GAS OCCUPIES 22.4 LITERS, THAT IS,"
940 PRINT"THE AMOUNT OF THE GAS IN GRAMS WHICH OCCUPIES 22.4 "
950 PRINT"LITERS AT STP IS THE GRAM MOLECULAR WEIGHT."
960 PRINT
970 PRINT"    THE PROBLEM WOULD BE SOLVED IF YOU KNEW HOW MUCH"
980 PRINT"(IN GRAMS) OF THE GAS WOULD BE PRESENT AT STANDARD TEMPERATURE
990 PRINT"AND PRESSURE (STP)."
1000 PRINT
1010 PRINT"THE GENERAL EXPRESSION NEEDED TO SOLVE FOR THE AMOUNT OF THE"
1020 PRINT"UNKNOWN GAS AT STANDARD TEMPERATURE AND PRESSURE IS:"
1030 PRINT
1040 PRINT"AMOUNT(STP) = AMOUNT(INITIAL)*FACTOR(V)*FACTOR(T)*FACTOR(P)"
```

PROGRAM 7.4—Continued

Comments About the Computer Program

This program (Program 7.4) can be discussed in three segments:

1. input of data (lines 110–370)
2. communication with the student about the problem (lines 390–810)
3. showing the student how to work the problem (lines 820–1390)

Initially, the problem parameters must be read and/or generated. The first line (110) defines a string variable for use later in the program. A string variable is a letter followed by a dollar sign (A$, B$, V$, etc.) and it must be used when alphabetic or alphanumeric data is used. In some systems, string variables can be assigned values using the READ statement; in other systems (such as the one used here), the LET statement must be used. Next, the molecular weights of 8 molecules are read (lines 120–160), and the names of these elements and compounds are also stored (lines

```
1050 PRINT
1060 PRINT"FOR INSTANCE, IN THIS PROBLEM:"
1070 PRINT
1080 PRINT"        AMOUNT(INITIAL) ="G"GRAMS"
1090 PRINT
1100 IF V < 22400 THEN 1150
1110 PRINT"        DECREASE IN V = DECREASE IN AMOUNT"
1120 PRINT"        FACTOR(V) = 22400/"V"="22400/V
1130 PRINT
1140 GO TO 1180
1150 PRINT"        INCREASE IN V = INCREASE IN AMOUNT"
1160 PRINT"        FACTOR(V) = 22400/"V"="22400/V
1170 PRINT
1180 IF T < 0 THEN 1230
1190 PRINT"        DECREASE IN T = INCREASE IN AMOUNT"
1200 PRINT"        FACTOR(T) = ("T" + 273)/(0 + 273) ="(T + 273)/273
1210 PRINT
1220 GO TO 1260
1230 PRINT"        INCREASE IN T = DECREASE IN AMOUNT"
1240 PRINT"        FACTOR(T) = (0 + 273)/("T" + 273) ="273/(T + 273)
1250 PRINT
1260 IF P < 760 THEN 1310
1270 PRINT"        DECREASE IN P = DECREASE IN AMOUNT"
1280 PRINT"        FACTOR(P) = 760/"P"="760/P
1290 PRINT
1300 GO TO 1340
1310 PRINT"        INCREASE IN P = INCREASE IN AMOUNT"
1320 PRINT"        FACTOR(P) = 760/"P"="760/P
1330 PRINT
1340 PRINT
1350 PRINT"WHEN THESE QUANTITIES ARE MULTIPLIED, THE RESULT YIELDS:"
1360 PRINT
1370 PRINT"        MOLECULAR WEIGHT = "A(I)
1380 PRINT"        WHICH IS THE MOLECULAR WEIGHT OF "A$(I)" GAS."
1390 PRINT"NOW YOU SHOULD TRY A SIMILAR PROBLEM."
1400 GO TO 250
1410 END
```

PROGRAM 7.4—Concluded

170–240). The next series of statements (lines 260–370) generate the values of the parameters which will be given the student in the problem. The statement

$$270 \ \text{LET} \ X = RND(X)$$

uses a random number generator available in most time-sharing BASIC systems. Thus, X will be assigned the value of a random number ranging from 0 to .9 (i.e., .1, .2, .3, etc.). Values of $X=0$ are rejected (line 270). Another variable, N, is used to make the temperature alternately negative and positive. The first time through the program, $N=1$ (line 150). Each time the student works a problem, the sign of N is changed (line 340) and the sign of N is used to select $+T$ or $-T$ (line 290). It can be seen from the appropriate statements (lines 300, 330, 350, & 360) that since X can have values from .1 up to .9, the ranges in the parameters used in the problem are: $T=-100°C$ to $T=90°C$, $p=155$ to $p=1395$ mm. mercury, and $V=4,000$ to $V=36,000$ ml. Finally, a molecule is chosen from the list (lines 170–240) using the random number X.
The statement

$$280 \ \text{LET} \ I = INT(X*8 + .5)$$

```
******** PROBLEM DRILL IN MOLECULAR WEIGHT CALCULATION **********

GIVEN:    21.51 GRAMS OF A GAS AT   49.96 DEGREES CENTIGRADE AND
A PRESSURE OF 774.4 MM. OF MERCURY OCCUPIES 1.998E 4 MILLILITERS.

CALCULATE: THE MOLECULAR WEIGHT, OR THAT WEIGHT WHICH OCCUPIES
22.4 LITERS AT STANDARD TEMPERATURE AND PRESSURE (0 DEGREES
CENTIGRADE AND 760 MM. OF HG).

TYPE IN A ZERO FOR ASSISTANCE.

TYPE A MINUS ONE (-1) IF YOU WISH TO STOP THE PROGRAM.

WHEN YOU HAVE THE CORRECT ANSWER, TYPE IT IN USING
3 SIGNIFICANT FIGURES.
 ? 35.5

I DON'T AGREE WITH YOU.  WOULD YOU LIKE TO TRY THE
CALCULATION AGAIN ?
(TYPE YES OR NO).
 ? NO

WOULD YOU LIKE ASSISTANCE ?
(TYPE YES OR NO).
 ? YES

LET'S SET THIS ONE UP TOGETHER:

        P                 V              T            AMOUNT

INITIAL
 774.4 MM OF HG,   1.998E 4 ML,   49.96 DEGREES C,   21.51 GRAMS

FINAL
760 MM. OF HG,     22400 ML,      0 DEGREES C,       ??????

    WE KNOW THAT AT STANDARD PRESSURE AND TEMPERATURE
ONE MOLE OF AN IDEAL GAS OCCUPIES 22.4 LITERS, THAT IS,
THE AMOUNT OF THE GAS IN GRAMS WHICH OCCUPIES 22.4
LITERS AT STP IS THE GRAM MOLECULAR WEIGHT.

    THE PROBLEM WOULD BE SOLVED IF YOU KNEW HOW MUCH
(IN GRAMS) OF THE GAS WOULD BE PRESENT AT STANDARD TEMPERATURE
AND PRESSURE (STP).
```

TABLE 7.4   The sample output from a drill in molecular weight calculations.

defines I as an integer, using the statement INT(X), which can take on values of 1 to 8. All these parameters are then used to calculate the amount present (line 370) using the values of p, T, and V which were generated.

The next section (lines 390–810) involves communication with the student. First the problem is presented to the student (lines 390–440). He is then given the options of requesting assistance (line 460) or stopping the program (line 480); in these two cases he indicates his response by typing a number when shown a question mark. If he elects to type the answer to the problem (line 500–520), his answer is checked immediately (line 560). If his answer is correct, he is told so and given the option of trying another problem (lines 760–800). This time, however, his response is to type either "yes" or "no." This response is more conversational and is preferable to the numerical response shown earlier in the program. If

THE GENERAL EXPRESSION NEEDED TO SOLVE FOR THE AMOUNT OF THE
UNKNOWN GAS AT STANDARD TEMPERATURE AND PRESSURE IS:

AMOUNT(STP) = AMOUNT(INITIAL)*FACTOR(V)*FACTOR(T)*FACTOR(P)

FOR INSTANCE, IN THIS PROBLEM:

      AMOUNT(INITIAL) = 21.51 GRAMS

      INCREASE IN V = INCREASE IN AMOUNT
      FACTOR(V) = 22400/ 1.998E 4 = 1.121

      DECREASE IN T = INCREASE IN AMOUNT
      FACTOR(T) = (49.96 + 273)/(0 + 273) = 1.183

      DECREASE IN P = DECREASE IN AMOUNT
      FACTOR(P) = 760/ 774.4 = .9814

WHEN THESE QUANTITIES ARE MULTIPLIED, THE RESULT YIELDS:

        MOLECULAR WEIGHT = 28
        WHICH IS THE MOLECULAR WEIGHT OF NITROGEN GAS.
NOW YOU SHOULD TRY A SIMILAR PROBLEM.

GIVEN: .1157 GRAMS OF A GAS AT -12.25 DEGREES CENTIGRADE AND
A PRESSURE OF 189.9 MM. OF MERCURY OCCUPIES 4901. MILLILITERS.

CALCULATE: THE MOLECULAR WEIGHT, OR THAT WEIGHT WHICH OCCUPIES
22.4 LITERS AT STANDARD TEMPERATURE AND PRESSURE (0 DEGREES
CENTIGRADE AND 760 MM. OF HG).

TYPE IN A ZERO FOR ASSISTANCE.

TYPE A MINUS ONE (-1) IF YOU WISH TO STOP THE PROGRAM.

WHEN YOU HAVE THE CORRECT ANSWER, TYPE IT IN USING
3 SIGNIFICANT FIGURES.
 ? 2.20

I DON'T AGREE WITH YOU. WOULD YOU LIKE TO TRY THE
CALCULATION AGAIN ?
(TYPE YES OR NO).
 ? YES

TABLE 7.4—Continued

the student gives the wrong answer, he is told so (line 570) and given the
options of trying the calculation again (lines 570–600) or of requesting
assistance (lines 630–670).

The third segment of the program (lines 820–1390) gives the student
assistance when he requests it. First, a table of the initial and final values
of the problem parameters is printed on the teletypewriter console (lines
820–900). Then the student is told in words how to solve the problem
(lines 920–990). The problem solution is then expressed as an equation
(line 1040) and the three factors for the problem being worked are printed

WHEN YOU HAVE THE CORRECT ANSWER, TYPE IT IN USING
3 SIGNIFICANT FIGURES.
  ? 2.02

YOU ARE CORRECT. 2.02 IS THE MOLECULAR WEIGHT OF HYDROGEN.
DO YOU WANT TO TRY ANOTHER PROBLEM ?
(TYPE YES OR NO).
  ? YES

GIVEN: 67.12 GRAMS OF A GAS AT 94.07 DEGREES CENTIGRADE AND
A PRESSURE OF 1458. MM. OF MERCURY OCCUPIES 3.763E 4 MILLILITERS.

CALCULATE: THE MOLECULAR WEIGHT, OR THAT WEIGHT WHICH OCCUPIES
22.4 LITERS AT STANDARD TEMPERATURE AND PRESSURE (0 DEGREES
CENTIGRADE AND 760 MM. OF HG).

TYPE IN A ZERO FOR ASSISTANCE.

TYPE A MINUS ONE (-1) IF YOU WISH TO STOP THE PROGRAM.

WHEN YOU HAVE THE CORRECT ANSWER, TYPE IT IN USING
3 SIGNIFICANT FIGURES.
  ? 29.1

I DON'T AGREE WITH YOU. WOULD YOU LIKE TO TRY THE
CALCULATION AGAIN ?
(TYPE YES OR NO).
  ? NO

WOULD YOU LIKE ASSISTANCE ?
(TYPE YES OR NO).
  ? NO

MY ANSWER TO THIS PROBLEM IS,

        MOLECULAR WEIGHT = 28

        WHICH IS THE MOLECULAR WEIGHT OF CARBON MONOXIDE GAS.

WHY DON'T YOU TRY ANOTHER PROBLEM.

TABLE 7.4—Continued

(lines 1080–1320). The student is finally given the correct answer (lines 1350–1380) and directed to try another problem (line 1390). This general program format can be used to program a whole range of "type" problems for students to practice.

Discussion of Computer Generated Results:

A sample student run is shown (Table 7.4). The copy is suitable for the student to file in his notebook to use when studying for exams. The student in this example requested assistance on the first problem and was shown how to work the problem. He then worked several additional problems and was given different values of the parameters for each problem. In this context, the computor assumes the role of a tutor; the student benefits since the problem session is tailored to meet his own needs.

```
GIVEN:    140.4 GRAMS OF A GAS AT -82.18 DEGREES CENTIGRADE AND
A PRESSURE OF 1274. MM. OF MERCURY OCCUPIES 3.287E 4 MILLILITERS.

CALCULATE: THE MOLECULAR WEIGHT, OR THAT WEIGHT WHICH OCCUPIES
22.4 LITERS AT STANDARD TEMPERATURE AND PRESSURE (O DEGREES
CENTIGRADE AND 760 MM. OF HG).

TYPE IN A ZERO FOR ASSISTANCE.

TYPE A MINUS ONE (-1) IF YOU WISH TO STOP THE PROGRAM.

WHEN YOU HAVE THE CORRECT ANSWER, TYPE IT IN USING
3 SIGNIFICANT FIGURES.
 ? 39.9

YOU ARE CORRECT.  39.9  IS THE MOLECULAR WEIGHT OF ARGON.
DO YOU WANT TO TRY ANOTHER PROBLEM ?
(TYPE YES OR NO).
 ? NO
```

TABLE 7.4—Concluded

7.5 CONSECUTIVE FIRST-ORDER REACTIONS

Lesson Characteristics:

CHEMISTRY LEVEL   college, intermediate

MATHEMATICS BACKGROUND REQUIRED   none

PEDAGOGY   simulation and demonstration

PROBLEM APPROACH   analytical solution

STUDENT PARTICIPATION   uses prepared program

PROGRAMMING SKILLS   none

TIME OF STUDENT INVOLVEMENT   in laboratory—30 minutes

RECOMMENDED READING   (11) Chapter 13

(12) Chapter 16

Lesson Description: This program is written by teachers and is intended for presentation to college level students who need not have a calculus background. The student uses a prepared program; therefore, he requires no programming skills. The analytical (closed-form) solutions of the rate equations are used in the program. These solutions can be derived in class or as a homework assignment when the course prerequisites include calculus. Alternately, attention can be focussed on a qualitative understanding of the kinetics leaving the derivations for a more advanced course.

The computer is used to explore consecutive first-order reactions. Initially, the program runs with values of the rate constant supplied with the program. The program tabulates the amounts of reactants and products, as a function of time, from the start of the reaction until 70 hours have

* * CHEMICAL KINETICS: CONSECUTIVE REACTIONS * *

THE FIRST-ORDER CONSECUTIVE REACTION USED IS:
         A --> B --> C
WHERE THE REACTION RATE CONSTANT FOR A --> B IS K1
AND THE CONSTANT FOR B --> C IS K2. THE INITIAL
CONCENTRATION OF A IS ONE MOLE WHILE B = C = 0.
THE PROGRAM WILL RUN INITIALLY USING K1 = .1, AND
K2 = .05. A TABULATION AND A PLOT OF THE AMOUNTS OF A,
B, AND C AT INTERVALS OF FIVE HOURS WILL BE LISTED. YOU WILL
THEN BE GIVEN THE OPPORTUNITY TO CHANGE THE VALUES OF K1
AND K2 AND OBSERVE THEIR EFFECT ON THE REACTION. TRY AT
LEAST ONE RUN WHERE K1 >> K2 AND ANOTHER RUN WHERE
K2 >> K1. TO END THE PROGRAM, LET K1 = 0.

THE REACTION-RATE CONSTANTS USED FOR THIS RUN ARE:
         K1 = .1   K2 = .05

TIME(HOURS)	QUANTITY A	QUANTITY B	QUANTITY C
0	1	0	0
5	.606531	.34454	4.89291E-2
10	.367879	.477302	.154818
15	.22313	.498473	.278397
20	.135335	.465088	.399576
25	.082085	.40884	.509075
30	4.97871E-2	.346686	.603527
35	3.01974E-2	.287153	.682649
40	1.83156E-2	.234039	.747645
45	.011109	.18858	.800311
50	6.73795E-3	.150694	.842568
55	4.08677E-3	.119682	.876231
60	2.47875E-3	9.46166E-2	.902905
65	1.50344E-3	7.45415E-2	.923955
70	9.11882E-4	.058571	.940517

TABLE 7.5   The output obtained from a program simulating consecutive reactions when K1 = 0.1 and K2 = 0.05.

elapsed (Table 7.5). A plot of these variables versus time is also output on the teletypewriter terminal (Figure 7.5A) to facilitate rapid comprehension of the progress of the reaction. In this manner, the computer *"simulates,"* in a matter of seconds, a reaction which takes 70 hours to conduct in the laboratory.

The student is then required to actively participate in the *"simulation"* by entering new values of the specific rate constants. The effect of the values of the rate constants on the kinetics of the reaction can be observed from the tabular and graphical output which the program produces. The graphical output is particularly effective for a qualitative understanding of the kinetics. This lesson is envisioned as a means of using the computer as an interactive partner to reinforce and expand one's knowledge of kinetics.

```
* * CHEMICAL KINETICS: CONSECUTIVE REACTIONS * *


THE REACTION-RATE CONSTANTS USED FOR THIS RUN ARE:
            K1 = .1          K2 = .05


TIME(HOURS)     QUANTITY A       QUANTITY B       QUANTITY C

0               1                0                0
5               .606531          .34454           4.89291E-2
10              .367879          .477302          .154818
15              .22313           .498473          .278397
20              .135335          .465088          .399576
25              .082085          .40884           .509075
30              4.97871E-2       .346686          .603527
35              3.01974E-2       .287153          .682649
40              1.83156E-2       .234039          .747645
45              .011109          .18858           .800311
50              6.73795E-3       .150694          .842568
55              4.08677E-3       .119682          .876231
60              2.47875E-3       9.46166E-2       .902905
65              1.50344E-3       7.45415E-2       .923955
70              9.11882E-4       .058571          .940517
```

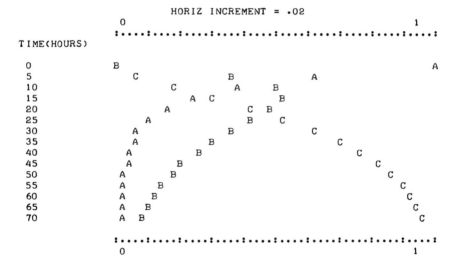

Figure 7.5A.   Consecutive First Order Reactions: Output when K1 = 2*K2.

Background and Theory: The reactions considered are

$$A \rightarrow B \rightarrow C$$

where the specific reaction rate constant for $A \rightarrow B$ is k_1, and the constant for $B \rightarrow C$ is k_2 (this discussion follows closely the treatment of Daniels and Alberty[11] on pages 337 and 338).

The initial amount of A is one mole; the initial amounts B and C are zero. If x is the amount of A which has decomposed in time t, then there are (1-x) moles of A at time t. If y moles of C have been produced, the amount of $B = x - y$.

Summarizing:

	$\overline{A}$	$\overline{B}$	$\overline{C}$
Initial Concentration	1	0	0
Concentration at time T	$(1-x)$	$(x-y)$	y

The general rate equation for the decomposition of A is:

$$\frac{-dA}{dt} = k_1 A$$

substituting from the table for the amounts of C and B:

$$\frac{-d(1-x)}{dt} = k_1(1-x) \qquad (7.5\text{--}1)$$

then

$$\frac{-d(1-x)}{(1-x)} = k_1(dt)$$

integrating

$$-\ln(1-x) = k_1 t$$

and

$$(1-x) = e^{-k_1 t}$$

or

$$A = e^{-k_1 t} \qquad (7.5\text{--}2)$$

The rate of formation of C is given by:

$$\frac{dC}{dt} = k_2(B)$$

substituting from the table for the amounts of C and B:

$$\frac{dy}{dt} = k_2(x-y) \qquad (7.5\text{--}3)$$

rearranging

$$\frac{dy}{dt} + k_2 y = k_2 x \qquad (7.5\text{--}4)$$

since

$$(1-x) = e^{-k_1 t}$$
$$x = 1 - e^{-k_1 t}$$

substituting into 7.5–4 gives

$$\frac{dy}{dt} + k_2 y = k_2(1 - e^{-k_1 t})$$

which upon integration yields:

$$C = y = \frac{k_2(1-e^{-k_1 t}) - k_1(1-e^{-k_2 t})}{k_2 - k_1} \qquad (7.5\text{--}5)$$

Finally, since $B = x - y$

$$\text{and } x = (1-A)$$

$$y = C$$

$$B = (1-A) - C \qquad (7.5\text{--}6)$$

The equations which will be used in the program are therefore

$$A = e^{-k_1 t} \qquad (7.5\text{--}2)$$

$$C = \frac{k_2(1-e^{-k_1 t}) - k_1(1-e^{-k_2 t})}{k_2 - k_1} \qquad (7.5\text{--}5)$$

$$B = (1-A) - C \qquad (7.5\text{--}6)$$

These equations must be rewritten in the BASIC format. Since BASIC allows only capital letters, the following changes will be made:

substitute T for t

K1 for k_1

K2 for k_2

In addition, exponentional notation in BASIC is EXP(X) not e^x, an asterisk indicates multiplication as in K1*T (not $k_1 t$), and division is indicated by a slash as in X/Y (not $\frac{x}{y}$). When these changes are made, the BASIC equations are:

A = EXP (−K1*T) $\qquad (7.5\text{--}2)$

C = (K2*(1−EXP(−K1*T))−K1*(1−EXP(−K2*T)))/
(K2−K1) $\qquad (7.5\text{--}5)$

B = (1−A)−C $\qquad (7.5\text{--}6)$

It should be noted that equation (2) cannot be used when K1=K2.

Computer Techniques: The rationale for this program is computer simulation of a chemical reaction. When a student conducts an experiment in the laboratory, he first conducts the experiment and collects the data, then he sits down and analyzes the data. In this simulation program, however, the student defines the experimental limitations (for example, the values of the rate constants). Then, without entering the laboratory, he can collect and analyze the data. Thus the emphasis is on an understanding of the effects of various parameters (in this case the rate constants) on chemical reactions. The student still must spend time in the laboratory in order to develop the facility to conduct experiments. His total breadth of comprehension is increased when he has access to both lab experiments and simulation programs.

This program (7.5) was written by teachers for student use. It is entirely possible that both students and teachers can write such programs for their own edification.

Comments About the Computer Program: The basic format used in this program (see Program 7.5) can be applied to many types of kinetics reactions normally presented in class. The program starts with a paragraph which will be printed on the teletypewriter (lines 130–250). This informs the student of the reaction being studied, the initial conditions of the problem, the output to be expected, the values which must be entered during execution, the limitations of the program, and the manner in which the program is ended. The values of the following variables are then assigned with a READ statement: (lines 270–280)

```
100 PRINT" * * CHEMICAL KINETICS: CONSECUTIVE REACTIONS * *"
110 PRINT
120 PRINT
130 PRINT "THE FIRST-ORDER CONSECUTIVE REACTION USED IS:"
140 PRINT"        A --> B --> C"
150 PRINT "WHERE THE REACTION RATE CONSTANT FOR A --> B IS K1"
160 PRINT "AND THE CONSTANT FOR B --> C IS K2. THE INITIAL "
170 PRINT "CONCENTRATION OF A IS ONE MOLE WHILE B = C = 0."
180 PRINT "THE PROGRAM WILL RUN INITIALLY USING K1 = .1, AND"
190 PRINT "K2 = .05. A TABULATION AND A PLOT OF THE AMOUNTS OF A,"
200 PRINT "B, AND C AT INTERVALS OF FIVE HOURS WILL BE LISTED. YOU WILL"
210 PRINT "THEN BE GIVEN THE OPPORTUNITY TO CHANGE THE VALUES OF K1"
220 PRINT "AND K2 AND OBSERVE THEIR EFFECT ON THE REACTION. TRY AT"
230 PRINT "LEAST ONE RUN WHERE K1 >> K2 AND ANOTHER RUN WHERE"
240 PRINT "K2 >> K1. THE PROGRAM WILL NOT RUN FOR THE SPECIAL CASE"
250 PRINT "WHERE K1 = K2. TO END THE PROGRAM, LET K1 = 0."
260 DIM A(25), B(25), C(25)
270 READ A, B, C, K1, K2, T1
280 DATA 1,0,0,.1,.05,0
290 IF K1 = K2 THEN 1100
300 PRINT
310 PRINT "THE REACTION-RATE CONSTANTS USED FOR THIS RUN ARE:"
320 PRINT , "K1 ="; K1, "K2 ="; K2
330 PRINT
340 PRINT
350 PRINT "TIME(HOURS)", "QUANTITY A", "QUANTITY B", "QUANTITY C"
360 PRINT
370 PRINT T1, A, B, C
380 FOR T = 5 TO 70 STEP 5
390 LET A = EXP(-K1*T)
400 LET C = (K2*(1-A)-K1*(1-EXP(-K2*T)))/(K2-K1)
410 LET B = (1-A) - C
420 PRINT T, A, B, C
430 NEXT T
440 GOSUB 570
450 PRINT
460 PRINT" . . . . . . . . . . . . . . . . . . . . . . . . . ."
470 PRINT
480 PRINT
490 PRINT "WHAT VALUE DO YOU WANT TO USE FOR K1";
500 INPUT K1
510 IF K1 = 0 THEN 1120
520 PRINT "WHAT VALUE DO YOU WANT TO USE FOR K2";
530 INPUT K2
540 RESTORE
550 READ A,B,C
560 GO TO 290
```

PROGRAM 7.5   Consecutive First Order Kinetics Reactions.

```
570 DATA 3, 5,70,5,0,1
580 READ A1, H, I, J, E1, F1
590 LET G = (F1-E1)/50
600 LET G1 = G/2
610 PRINT
620 PRINT
630 PRINT
640 PRINT " ", "          HORIZ INCREMENT ="; G
650 GOSUB 1060
660 GOSUB 1080
670 PRINT "TIME(HOURS)"
680 LET X = H-J
690 PRINT
700 PRINT T1," B
710 GO TO 730
720 PRINT
730 LET L1 = 0
740 LET X = X+J
750 IF X>I THEN 1020
760 PRINT X,
770 LET A = EXP(-K1*X)
780 LET C = (K2*(1-A)-K1*(1-EXP(-K2*X)))/(K2-K1)
790 LET B = (1-A)-C
800 LET Y = E1-G
810 PRINT " ";
820 LET Y = Y+G
830 IF Y>F1 THEN 720
840 IF ABS(A-Y)<G1 THEN 900
850 IF A1<2 THEN 810
860 IF ABS(B-Y)<G1 THEN 940
870 IF A1<3 THEN 810
880 IF ABS(C-Y)<G1 THEN 980
890 GO TO 810
900 PRINT "A";
910 LET L1 = L1 + 1
920 IF L1 = A1 THEN 720
930 GO TO 820
940 PRINT "B";
950 LET L1 = L1 + 1
960 IF L1 = A1 THEN 720
970 GO TO 820
980 PRINT "C";
990 LET L1 = L1 + 1
1000 IF L1 = A1 THEN 720
1010 GO TO 820
1020 PRINT
1030 GOSUB 1080
1040 GOSUB 1060
1050 RETURN
1060 PRINT ,E1;TAB(61);F1
1070 RETURN
1080 PRINT ,":....:....:....:....:....:....:....:....:....:"
1090 RETURN
1100 PRINT "THIS PROGRAM WILL NOT WORK IF K1 = K2. TRY AGAIN."
1110 GO TO 490
1120 END
```

PROGRAM 7.5—Continued

$A = 1 =$ initial amount of A

$B = 0 =$ initial amount of B

$C = 0 =$ initial amount of C

$K1 = .1 =$ rate constant for reaction $A \rightarrow B$

$K2 = .05 =$ rate constant for reaction $B \rightarrow C$

$T1 = 0 =$ time at start of reaction

The program next prints the rate constants being used for the particular run (lines 310, 320). The statement

320   PRINT, "K1="; K1, "K2="; K2

creates the following output:

$$K1 = .1 \qquad K2 = .05$$

The comma directly after PRINT causes the typewriter to space 15 spaces; a semi-colon is used for close packing and a comma is used for wider separation. It is important that computer output be suitably labeled (Table 7.5) for the student will retain the pages of output as a permanent copy of the lesson.

The program then tabulates the amount of A, B, and C present at 5 hour intervals from 5 to 70 hours. The tabulation is accomplished with a loop (lines 370–430), using the equations derived previously (Background and Theory). This is an experiment which is not well suited for the laboratory because the reaction rate is relatively slow. However, a 70 hour experiment can be simulated on the computer in a matter of seconds. It was noted earlier that the program cannot run when $K1 = K2$ since this would amount to division by zero in one of the equations (line 400). This limitation is noted in the instructions. It is further necessary to check for the possibility of $K1 = K2$ (line 290) during program execution in the event the student forgets the instructions (a not uncommon event). When it is found that $K1 = K2$, the program prints an error message (line 1100), and then branches to the portion of the program requesting new values of K1 and K2 (line 490). Program limitations must always be noted and it is wise to provide checks which ensure proper use of program variables.

The computer also plots the amount of A, B, and C versus time because of the instructive value of graphical output (Figure 7.5A). The plotting statements are listed as a subroutine at the end of the program (lines 570–1090) and this routine is accessed with a GOSUB statement (line 440).* (A description of other plot routines is given in Section 6.8.)

The program is run once using values of K1 and K2 supplied in the program (lines 270, 280) so that the user can see the computer output to be expected (Figure 7.5A). A dotted line (line 460) separates successive runs for clarity. The user is then required to input values of the rate constants. Note the use of RESTORE

        540 RESTORE

to reread the initial values of A, B, and C. At the start of each program, all DATA statements are stored in a data block and the values are assigned as each READ statement is encountered. For example, after execution of

        100 DATA 10, 9, 8, 7

        110 READ A, B

the data pointer would point to the number 8 in the data block and this value will be assigned the next time a READ statement is encountered. Use of RESTORE simply returns the pointer to the first number in the data block. If 540 RESTORE is left out of the program, execution of:

        550 READ A, B, C

---

* This plot routine is a slightly modified version of the program "PLOTTO***" taken from the General Electric Program Library of time-sharing programs.

would generate the error message

OUT OF DATA

since all the data has already been read.

Discussion of Computer Generated Results: The initial run (Figure 7.5A) uses the values of the rate constants supplied by the program. For this run, K1=2*K2 and the qualitative results are readily apparent in the graphical output. Note that the amount of B present reaches a peak of 0.5 moles after 15 hours, the amount of C present reaches 0.5 moles after 25 hours and continues rising, and the amount of A present is negligible at 50 hours. In the tabulation of data (Table 7.5) some numbers are printed in decimal form (.011109) and some are printed in exponential form (4.89291E–2). The particular time-sharing system used for this program run employs the following convention: when a number is less than .1, the exponential (E) notation is used unless the entire significant part of the number can be printed as a six decimal number. In other words, .011109 was exactly .011109000 while 4.89291E–2 was rounded off to 6 figures. The different values of the specific constants can now be explored.

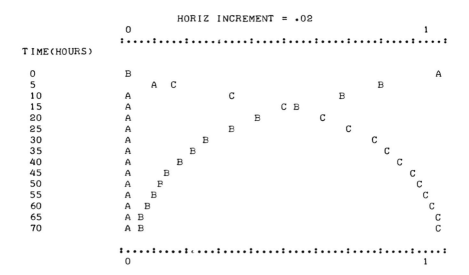

```
WHAT VALUE DO YOU WANT TO USE FOR K1 ? .5
WHAT VALUE DO YOU WANT TO USE FOR K2 ? .05


THE REACTION-RATE CONSTANTS USED FOR THIS RUN ARE:
          K1 = .5          K2 = .05




                    HORIZ INCREMENT = .02
               0                                          1
               :....:....:....:....:....:....:....:....:....:
TIME(HOURS)

    0          B                                          A
    5              A  C                             B
   10          A              C               B
   15          A                   C B        C
   20          A              B        C
   25          A          B              C
   30          A      B                     C
   35          A   B                         C
   40          A  B                           C
   45          A  B                            C
   50          A  P                            C
   55          A  B                             C
   60          A B                               C
   65          A B                               C
   70          A B                               C

               :....:....:....:....:....:....:....:....:....:
               0                                          1
```

Figure 7.5B   Consecutive First Order Reactions: Graphical output when
K1 = 10*K2.

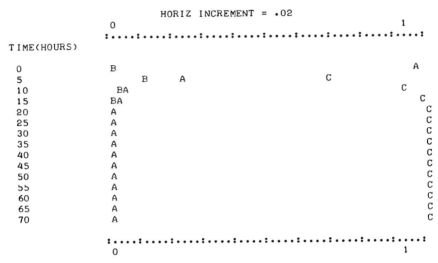

```
WHAT VALUE DO YOU WANT TO USE FOR K1 ? .3
WHAT VALUE DO YOU WANT TO USE FOR K2 ? 1


THE REACTION-RATE CONSTANTS USED FOR THIS RUN ARE:
            K1 = .3        K2 = 1



                    HORIZ INCREMENT = .02
            0                                                    1
            :....:....:....:....:....:....:....:....:....:....:
TIME(HOURS)

   0        B                                                  A
   5          B     A                          C
  10        BA                                                C
  15        BA                                              C
  20        A                                               C
  25        A                                               C
  30        A                                               C
  35        A                                               C
  40        A                                               C
  45        A                                               C
  50        A                                               C
  55        A                                               C
  60        A                                               C
  65        A                                               C
  70        A                                               C

            :....:....:....:....:....:....:....:....:....:....:
            0                                                  1
```

Figure 7.5C Consecutive First Order Reactions: Graphical Output when
K2 = 3*K1.

Consider, for example, the case where K1 = 10*K2 (Figure 7.5B). [Only the graphs are shown in this figure and in succeeding figures for simplicity. The program (7.5), however, generates both a graphical output and a tabulation of the data as shown in Figure 7.5A]. It is easily seen that (Figure 7.5B) the amount of B present reaches a peak of 0.8 moles after only 5 hours and that the amount of A falls to zero in 10 hours in contrast to the results obtained previously (Figure 7.5A). Furthermore, the effects of increasing K2 relative to K1 are observed in successive runs using K2 = 3*K1 (Figure 7.5C), K2 = 10*K1 (Figure 7.5D), and K2 = 100*K1 (Figure 7.5E). The qualitative and quantitative effects on the reactions are apparent from the tabular and graphical output; the most obvious result being that the amount of B present at any time is negligibly small. Finally, note the effect on the quantities of A, B, and C present as the reaction proceeds when K1 and K2 are small and where K2 = 2*K1 (Figure 7.5F) as opposed to the original run (Figure 7.5A). In this final run, the amount of B present reaches a peak of 0.3 moles after 20 hours and A is still present after 70 hours. In this manner, it is possible to study in a period of perhaps a half hour reactions that are prohibitively long for laboratory use.

```
WHAT VALUE DO YOU WANT TO USE FOR K1 ? .1
WHAT VALUE DO YOU WANT TO USE FOR K2 ? 1


THE REACTION-RATE CONSTANTS USED FOR THIS RUN ARE:
                 K1 = .1        K2 = 1
```

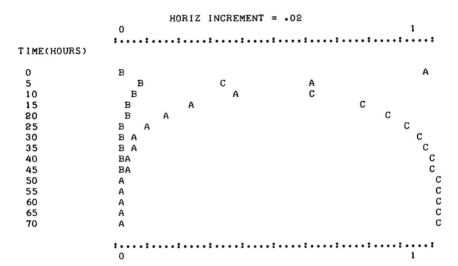

```
                        HORIZ INCREMENT = .02
                  0                                           1
                  :....:....:....:....:....:....:....:....:....:
T IME(HOURS)

   0              B                                           A
   5                B             C             A
  10                B                  A        C
  15              B          A                       C
  20              B      A                               C
  25             B    A                                    C
  30             B A                                         C
  35             B A                                          C
  40             BA                                            C
  45             BA                                            C
  50             A                                             C
  55             A                                             C
  60             A                                             C
  65             A                                             C
  70             A                                             C

                  :....:....:....:....:....:....:....:....:....:
                  0                                           1
```

Figure 7.5D Consecutive First Order Reactions: Graphical output when
K2 = 10*K1.

WHAT VALUE DO YOU WANT TO USE FOR K1 ? .05
WHAT VALUE DO YOU WANT TO USE FOR K2 ? 5

THE REACTION-RATE CONSTANTS USED FOR THIS RUN ARE:
                K1 = .05   K2 = 5

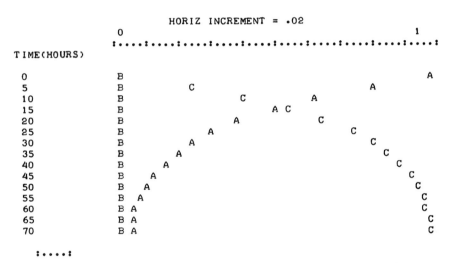

Figure 7.5E Consecutive First Order Reactions: Graphical output when
K2 = 100*K1.

```
WHAT VALUE DO YOU WANT TO USE FOR K1 ? .03
WHAT VALUE DO YOU WANT TO USE FOR K2 ? .05


THE REACTION-RATE CONSTANTS USED FOR THIS RUN ARE:
              K1 = .03        K2 = .05
```

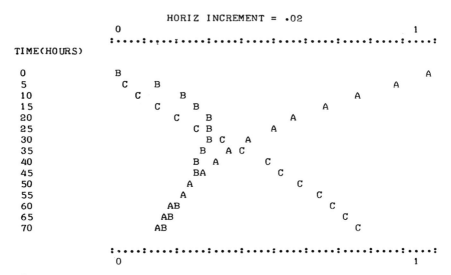

Figure 7.5F   Consecutive First Order Reactions: Graphical output when rate constants are small and K2 > K1.

7.6 CHEMICAL KINETICS: SECOND-ORDER REACTION

Lesson Characteristics:

CHEMISTRY LEVEL   college, intermediate

MATHEMATICS BACKGROUND REQUIRED   calculus

PEDAGOGY   demonstration

PROBLEM APPROACH   analytical solution and numerical method (Runge-Kutta)

STUDENT PARTICIPATION   uses prepared program

PROGRAMMING SKILLS   introductory BASIC

TIME OF STUDENT INVOLVEMENT   in class—30 minutes

RECOMMENDED READING   (11) chapter 13
                       (12) chapter 16
                       (13) chapter 7

Lesson Description: Chemical kinetics is usually presented to college chemistry students in the physical chemistry course. While chemical kinetics is often mentioned in freshman chemistry, a detailed treatment of the integration of the rate equation must await the completion of required calculus courses. However, even when chemical kinetics is presented at the intermediate college level, the material covered is limited to rate equations for which there is a closed-form solution, and perhaps further, to rate equations which are easily integrated. When kinetics is presented in this manner, there is often a tendency to lose sight of the goal of understanding how to formulate the rate equation. Instead, attention is all-too-often focussed on the memorization of the derived closed-form solutions of a handful of typical rate equations. The use of computers in chemical education can lead to the liberation of both student and teacher from the confines discussed above. It is possible, using numerical methods of analysis, to teach chemical kinetics to those who have no calculus background (See Lesson 7.8). Moreover, numerical methods can be presented along with chemical kinetics to students with a calculus background in order that the formulation of the rate equation may be emphasized. Alternately, using numerical methods, the treatment of chemical kinetics may be extended to include those rate equations difficult to integrate as well as those for which there is no closed-form solution.

This lesson is intended for students with a calculus background. The subject treated is a second-order reaction and it is expected that the derivation of the closed-form solution of the rate equation is covered in class. The Runge-Kutta method is the numerical method employed and it should be presented in a lecture or as a homework assignment prior to the use of this lesson. The objective of this lesson is to allow the student to compare the results generated using the Runge-Kutta method, with those results obtained from the analytical solution. Different time increments are employed in order to become familiar with the application of this numerical method to chemical kinetics. The amount of student participation can vary. At one extreme, the student is merely expected to run the program and verify the Runge-Kutta method as a useful approach to the solution of rate equations, and at the other extreme, the student is assigned the task of setting up the Runge-Kutta coefficients and writing the program. In this lesson, the program is written by the instructor and used by the students. Student formulation of the Runge-Kutta coefficients is reserved for the next lesson (7.7). The computer output is presented in tabular form.

Background and Theory:

Consider the second-order reaction

$$A + B \rightarrow AB$$

If x denotes the number of moles per liter which react in time t, the rate equation may be formulated as follows:

$$\frac{dx}{dt} = k(A0 - x)(B0 - x) \qquad (7.6-1)$$

where

$$k = \text{specific rate constant}$$
$$A0 = \text{initial concentration of A}$$
$$B0 = \text{initial concentration of B}$$
$$(A0 - x) = \text{concentration of A at time t}$$
$$(B0 - x) = \text{concentration of B at time t}$$

For the special case where $A0 = B0$, equation 7.6–1 becomes—

$$\frac{dx}{dt} = k(A0 - x)^2 \qquad (7.6\text{--}2)$$

or, on rearranging,

$$\frac{dx}{(A0 - x)^2} = kdt$$

which on integrating gives—

$$\frac{1}{(A0 - x)} = kt + C \qquad (7.6\text{--}3)$$

where C is the constant of integration.

At $t = 0$, $x = 0$, and from 7.6–3,

$$C = \frac{1}{A0}$$

Substituting this value of C into 7.6–3 and rearranging gives:

$$A1 = \frac{A0}{1 + A0 \cdot k \cdot t} \qquad (7.6\text{--}4)$$

where $A1 = (A0 - x) = \text{concentration of A0 at time t}$

From the definition of x,

$$AB = x$$

but $A1 = (A0 - x)$, or $x = (A0 - A1)$, thus

$$AB = (A0 - A1) \qquad (7.6\text{--}5)$$

Finally, the analytical solutions of the rate equations (7.6–4, 7.6–5) may be written in BASIC:

$$A1 = A0/(1 + A0*K*T) \qquad (7.6\text{--}4)$$
$$C1 = A0 - A1 \qquad (7.6\text{--}5)$$

where C1 has been substituted for AB.

Computer Techniques: The Runge-Kutta method with Runge's coefficients is generally stated[13] in terms of the variable x:

$$x_{n+1} = x_n + \Delta x_n \qquad (7.6\text{--}6)$$

where

$$\Delta x_n = \frac{\Delta t}{6}(k_0 + 2k_1 + 2k_2 + k_3) \qquad (7.6\text{–}7)$$

and

$$k_0 = f(x_n) \qquad (7.6\text{–}8)$$
$$k_1 = f(x_n + (k_0/2)\,\Delta t) \qquad (7.6\text{–}9)$$
$$k_2 = f(x_n + (k_1/2)\,\Delta t) \qquad (7.6\text{–}10)$$
$$k_3 = f(x_n + k_2\,\Delta t) \qquad (7.6\text{–}11)$$

Using this notation, $k_0 = f(x_n)$ is interpreted as: "k_0 is a function of x_n."

This method is well suited for ordinary differential equations with initial conditions when the equations are difficult to integrate or when they do not possess closed-form solutions. In this lesson, it is applied to a second-order rate equation, whose closed-form solution has previously been derived in class, for the purpose of introducing the numerical method.

The Runge-Kutta coefficients are simple to formulate. Observe from the rate Equation 7.6–2 that:

$$f(x_n) = k(A0 - x_n)^2 \qquad (7.6\text{–}12)$$

Since $k_0 = f(x_n)$ (Equation 7.6–8), $k_0 = k(A0 - x_n)^2$. It was also stated that $k_1 = f(x_n + (k_0/2)\,\Delta t)$ (Equation 7.6–9); k_1 is thus obtained by substituting $(x_n + (k_0/2)\,\Delta t)$ for (x_n) in Equation (7.6–12) or

$$k_1 = k[A0 - (x_n + k_0/2\,\Delta t)]^2$$

The other coefficients are similarly formulated by making the appropriate substitutions (Equations 7.6–10, 7.6–11 into 7.6–12). When this is done, the following equations are obtained:

$$k_0 = k(A0 - x_n)^2 \qquad (7.6\text{–}13)$$

$$k_1 = k[A0 - (x_n + \frac{k_0}{2}\,\Delta t)]^2 \qquad (7.6\text{–}14)$$

$$k_2 = k[A0 - (x_n + \frac{k_1}{2}\,\Delta t)]^2 \qquad (7.6\text{–}15)$$

$$k_3 = k[A0 - (x_n + k_2\,\Delta t)]^2 \qquad (7.6\text{–}16)$$

and

$$x_{n+1} = x_n + \frac{\Delta t}{6}(k_0 + 2k_1 + 2k_2 + k_3) \qquad (7.6\text{–}17)$$

(It should be noted in the above equations that k is the specific rate constant, while all the subscripted k's result from the Runge-Kutta method.)

These equations can be written in BASIC with only slight modifications:

```
K0 = K*(A0 − X)↑2                    (7.6–13)
K1 = K*(A0 − (X + .5*K0*D))↑2        (7.6–14)
K2 = K*(A0 − (X + .5*K1*D))↑2)       (7.6–15)
K3 = K*(A0 − (X + K2*D))↑2           (7.6–16)
```

where

$$D = \text{\textit{time increment,}} \ \Delta T$$

$$K = \text{\textit{specific rate constant of the second-order reaction}}$$

$$\text{K0, K1, K2, K3} = \text{\textit{Runge-Kutta Coefficients}}$$

$$X = x_n$$

and finally,

$$X1 = D/6*(K0+2*K1+2*K2+K3) \qquad (7.6-17)$$

$$\text{LET } X = X + X1 \qquad (7.6-18)$$

where, in 7.6–17,

$$X1 = \Delta x_n$$

When 7.6–18 is executed as an instruction during the running of a BASIC program:

$$X = X_{n+1} \ \text{\textit{on left side of equal sign in}} \ (7.6-18)$$

$$X = X_n \ \text{\textit{on right side of equal sign in}} \ (7.6-18)$$

Comments About the Computer Program: The reaction being investigated in Program 7.6 is:

$$A + B \xrightarrow{\text{K}} AB$$

where the initial concentrations of A and B are equal. The following variables are assigned values using a read statement (line 190):

$$A0 = \text{\textit{initial concentration of}} \ A$$

$$K = \text{\textit{specific rate constant}}$$

$$D = \Delta T = \text{\textit{time increment used in Runge-Kutta Method}}$$

$$T = \text{\textit{value of time (sec) at start of tabulation}}$$

$$T2 = \text{\textit{value of time (sec) at end of tabulation}}$$

$$X = \text{\textit{number of moles per liter which react in time}} \ T = \text{\textit{conc.}} \ AB$$

The computer output sheet is suitably labeled (lines 220–270); this is an important step since these pages will be retained as a permanent record of the run. The label should include the name of the program, a list of the variables which can be changed from one run to another and the headings for the tabular output. The statement

$$230 \ \text{PRINT "DELTA } T=\text{"; } D; \text{ "SEC"}$$

illustrates how alphanumeric and alphabetic information can be printed using a single statement; note that a semi-colon is used for close-packing of the output. The print statements used to produce the table headings (lines 260, 270) and those used to output the results (lines 290, 400)

```
100 PRINT "* * * * SECOND ORDER REACTION * * * *"
110 REM THE FOLLOWING REACTION  IS BEING STUDIED:
120 REM          A + B --> AB
130 REM THE REACTION IS FIRST ORDER A AND FIRST ORDER B;
140 REM AND THE INITIAL CONCENTRATIONS OF A AND B ARE EQUAL.
150 REM THE PROGRAM TABULATES THE CONCENTRATION OF A AND AB AS A
160 REM FUNCTION OF TIME USING:
170 REM          1) THE ANALYTICAL SOLUTION OF THE RATE EQUATION
180 REM          2) THE RUNGE-KUTTA METHOD WITH RUNGE'S COEFFICIENTS.
190 READ AO,K,D,T,T2,X
200 DATA .05,.107,100,0,2400,0
210 PRINT
220 PRINT "THE RATE CONSTANT =";K;"LITER/MOLE-SEC"
230 PRINT "DELTA T =";D;"SEC"
240 PRINT
250 PRINT
260 PRINT "TIME(SEC)", "CONC. A",, "CONC. AB"
270 PRINT, "ANALYTICAL", "RUNGE-KUTTA", "ANALYTICAL", "RUNGE-KUTTA"
280 PRINT
290 PRINT T, AO, AO, X, X
300 FOR T = (T+D) TO T2 STEP D
310 LET A1 = AO/(1 + AO*K*T)
320 LET C1 = AO - A1
330 LET KO = K*(AO-X)↑2
340 LET K1 = K*(AO-(X+.5*KO*D))↑2
350 LET K2 = K*(AO-(X+.5*K1*D))↑2
360 LET K3 = K*(AO-(X+K2*D))↑2
370 LET X1= D/6*(KO+2*K1+2*K2+K3)
380 LET X = X + X1
390 LET A2 = AO - X
400 PRINT T, A1, A2, C1, X
410 NEXT T
420 END
```

PROGRAM 7.6   Chemical Kinetics: Second Order Reaction.

must employ identical spacing. In this instance, a comma is used to generate the output in five columns. The variables not previously identified are:

$A1 = $ *concentration of* A *calculated from closed-form solution*

$A2 = $ *concentration of* A *calculated using Runge-Kutta Method*

$C1 = $ *concentration of* AB *calculated from closed-form solution*

$X = $ *concentration of* AB *calculated using Runge-Kutta Method*

After the initial values of A1, A2, C1, and X are printed (line 290), the numerical output is generated using a loop (lines 300–410). The equations used in the body of the loop have already been discussed. The flexibility of the FOR statement is evident in

$$300 \text{ FOR } T = (T+D) \text{ TO } T2 \text{ STEP } D$$

which causes the computer to execute lines 310 to 400 starting with $T = T+D$ (100 sec) and ending with $T = T2$ (2400 sec), proceeding in increments of D (100 seconds). It should be remembered that

$$380 \text{ LET } X = X + X1$$

is interpreted as: take the current value of X, add X1, and store this new value of X in the cell labeled X.

```
* * * * SECOND ORDER REACTION * * * *

THE RATE CONSTANT = .107 LITER/MOLE-SEC
DELTA T = 100 SEC
```

TIME(SEC)	CONC. A ANALYTICAL	RUNGE-KUTTA	CONC. AB ANALYTICAL	RUNGE-KUTTA
0	.05	.05	0	0
100	3.25733E-2	3.25709E-2	1.74267E-2	1.74291E-2
200	2.41546E-2	2.41546E-2	2.58454E-2	2.58454E-2
300	1.91939E-2	1.91942E-2	3.08061E-2	3.08058E-2
400	1.59236E-2	1.59239E-2	3.40764E-2	3.40761E-2
500	1.36054E-2	1.36058E-2	3.63946E-2	3.63942E-2
600	1.18765E-2	1.18767E-2	3.81235E-2	3.81233E-2
700	1.05374E-2	1.05376E-2	3.94626E-2	3.94624E-2
800	9.4697E-3	9.46988E-3	4.05303E-2	4.05301E-2
900	8.59845E-3	8.5986E-3	4.14015E-2	4.14014E-2
1000	7.87402E-3	7.87414E-3	.042126	4.21259E-2
1100	7.26216E-3	7.26227E-3	4.27378E-2	4.27377E-2
1200	6.73854E-3	6.73864E-3	4.32615E-2	4.32614E-2
1300	6.28536E-3	6.28544E-3	4.37146E-2	4.37146E-2
1400	5.88928E-3	5.88935E-3	4.41107E-2	4.41106E-2
1500	5.54017E-3	5.54023E-3	4.44598E-2	4.44598E-2
1600	5.23013E-3	5.23018E-3	4.47699E-2	4.47698E-2
1700	4.95295E-3	.004953	4.50471E-2	.045047
1800	4.70367E-3	4.70372E-3	4.52963E-2	4.52963E-2
1900	4.47828E-3	4.47832E-3	4.55217E-2	4.55217E-2
2000	4.2735E-3	4.27354E-3	4.57265E-2	4.57265E-2
2100	4.08664E-3	4.08667E-3	4.59134E-2	4.59133E-2
2200	3.91543E-3	3.91546E-3	4.60846E-2	4.60845E-2
2300	3.75799E-3	3.75802E-3	.046242	.046242
2400	3.61272E-3	3.61274E-3	4.63873E-2	4.63873E-2

TABLE 7.6A   Chemical Kinetics: Second Order Reaction—comparison of analytical and numerical solutions using time increment of 100 seconds.

Discussion of Computer Generated Results: The results generated using $\Delta T = 100$ seconds are shown in Table 7.6A. The results obtained using the Runge-Kutta method agree very well with those calculated from the closed-form solution; in most cases the agreement is good to five significant figures. The variable format of the numerical output (See for example the line printed when $T = 1000$ seconds) is due to the conventions of the particular

```
THE RATE CONSTANT = .107 LITER/MOLE-SEC
DELTA T = 300 SEC
```

TIME(SEC)	CONC. A ANALYTICAL	RUNGE-KUTTA	CONC. AB ANALYTICAL	RUNGE-KUTTA
0	.05	.05	0	0
300	1.91939E-2	7.05434E-3	3.08061E-2	4.29457E-2
600	1.18765E-2	5.75193E-3	3.81235E-2	4.42481E-2
900	8.59845E-3	4.85546E-3	4.14015E-2	4.51445E-2
1200	6.73854E-3	4.20074E-3	4.32615E-2	4.57993E-2
1500	5.54017E-3	3.70161E-3	4.44598E-2	4.62984E-2
1800	4.70367E-3	3.30849E-3	4.52963E-2	4.66915E-2
2100	4.08664E-3	2.99085E-3	4.59134E-2	4.70091E-2
2400	3.61272E-3	2.72887E-3	4.63873E-2	4.72711E-2

TABLE 7.6B   Chemical Kinetics: Second Order Reaction—comparison of analytical and numerical solutions using time increment of 300 seconds.

time-sharing system. One convention is that trailing zeros after the decimal point are not printed. Another is that for a number less than 0.1, the E notation is used unless the entire significant part of the number can be printed as a 6 decimal number. Thus .042126 means that the number is exactly .0421260000 while the number 4.21259E–2 has been rounded off to .0421259.

It can be seen that increasing ΔT to 300 seconds (Table 7.6B) results in a decreased accuracy of the Runge-Kutta Method. The accuracy of the numerical method is thus shown to depend on the magnitude of the time increment, ΔT.

7.7 CHEMICAL KINETICS: THIRD-ORDER REACTION

Lesson Characteristics:

CHEMISTRY LEVEL   college, intermediate

MATHEMATICS BACKGROUND REQUIRED   algebra

PEDAGOGY   computer learning

PROBLEM APPROACH   numerical method: Runge-Kutta

STUDENT PARTICIPATION   assists in program writing

PROGRAMMING SKILLS   introductory BASIC

TIME OF STUDENT INVOLVEMENT   in class—1 hour to debug and run program; out of class—1 hour to write program

RECOMMENDED READING   (11) chapter 13
　　　　　　　　　　　　　　　(12) chapter 16
　　　　　　　　　　　　　　　(13) chapter 7

Lesson Description: After the application of the Runge-Kutta method to ordinary differential equations with initial conditions has been explained and demonstrated (see previous lesson), the student should be able to set up the Runge-Kutta coefficients. Furthermore, only an introductory knowledge of BASIC is required to incorporate this numerical method into a computer program which tabulates the concentrations of reactants and products in a chemical kinetics reaction. Since the closed-form solution of the rate equation need not be derived, a knowledge of college algebra is the only math pre-requisite. This lesson applies the numerical method learned in the previous lesson to a third-order kinetics reaction. The student is expected to formulate the Runge-Kutta coefficients and to take an active part in the program writing. This type of problem is suitable as a homework assignment where the student writes, debugs, and runs the program in the computer lab and hands in the computer output at the completion of the run. The computer output in this lesson is in tabular form.

Background and Theory: The reaction between nitrogen monoxide, NO, and hydrogen, H_2, is a third order reaction. If the concentration of NO is held constant, doubling the concentration of H_2 doubles the reaction rate; if the concentration of H_2 is held constant, doubling the concentration of NO quadruples the reaction rate. The reaction is thus first order with respect to hydrogen, second order with respect to nitrogen monoxide, and third order overall.

The rate equation may be formulated:

$$\frac{dx}{dt} = C(P1 - 2x)^2(P2 - x) \qquad (7.7\text{--}1)$$

where

$$x = \text{partial pressure of the product}$$

$$P1 = \text{partial pressure of NO before reaction}$$

$$(P1 - 2x) = \text{partial pressure of NO at time t}$$

$$P2 = \text{partial pressure of } H_2 \text{ before reaction}$$

$$(P2 - x) = \text{partial pressure of } H_2 \text{ at time t}$$

$$C = \text{specific rate constant}$$

Computer Techniques: The Runge-Kutta method with Runge's coefficients will be used to determine the concentrations of the reactants and products as a function of time. In terms of the variable x, the general equations have been previously given (lesson 7.6). Observe from equation 7.7–1 that, in this case,

$$f(x_n) = C(P1 - 2x_n)^2(P2 - x_n) \qquad (7.7\text{--}2)$$

The Runge-Kutta coefficients are formulated by substituting the expressions given in Lesson 7.6 for x_n into equation 7.7–2.

The appropriate Runge-Kutta equations are as follows: (given here directly in BASIC)

$$K0 = C(P1 - 2*X)\uparrow2*(P2 - X) \qquad (7.7\text{--}3)$$

$$K1 = C(P1 - 2*(X + .5*D*K0))\uparrow2*(P2 - (X + .5*D*K0)) \ (7.7\text{--}4)$$

$$K2 = C(P1 - 2*(X + .5*D*K1))\uparrow2*(P2 - (X + .5*D*K1)) \ (7.7\text{--}5)$$

$$K3 = C(P1 - 2*(X + K2*D))\uparrow2*(P2 - (X + K2*D)) \qquad (7.7\text{--}6)$$

and

$$X1 = D*(K0 + 2*K1 + 2*K2 + K3)/6 \qquad (7.7\text{--}7)$$

$$\text{LET } X = X + X1 \qquad (7.7\text{--}8)$$

where

$$X1 = \Delta X_n$$

$$D = \Delta T$$

and when

7.7–8 is executed as a BASIC statement:

$X = X_n$ *on right side of equal sign in 7.7–8*

$X = X_{n+1}$ *on left side of equal sign in 7.7–8*

The method will be utilized in the range $0 < T < 3$ min., using $\Delta T = .125$.

Comments About the Computer Program: The initial conditions of Program 7.7 are that at $T = 0$, the partial pressure (pp.) of $NO = 359$ mm, pp. $H_2 = 400$ mm, and pp. product is zero[13]. The following variables are assigned values using a read statement (line 130):

P1 = *pp.* NO *before reaction*

P2 = *pp.* H_2 *before reaction*

C = *specific rate constant in* mm^{-2} sec^{-1}

D = *time increment*

X = *pp. of product before reaction*

T = *time at beginning of tabulation*

T2 = *time at end of tabulation*

The columns to be used for output are then given headings (line 150) since the pages of output will be retained and therefore should be properly identified. Note that a comma is used (line 170) to divide the page into 5 columns.

```
100 PRINT"    * * * * THIRD-ORDER REACTION * * * *"
110 PRINT
120 REM RUNGE-KUTTA METHOD WITH RUNGE'S COEFFICIENTS
130 READ P1,P2,C,D,X,T,T2
140 DATA 359,400,1.12E-7,.125,0,0,2
150 PRINT"TIME(SEC)","PP. NO","PP. H2","PP. PRODUCT"
160 PRINT
170 PRINT T, P1, P2, X
180 FOR T = (T + D) TO T2 STEP D
190 LET K0 = C*(P1-2*X)†2*(P2-X)
200 LET K1 = C*(P1-2*(X+.5*D*K0))†2*(P2-(X+.5*D*K0))
210 LET K2 = C*(P1-2*(X+.5*D*K1))†2*(P2-(X+.5*D*K1))
220 LET K3 = C*(P1-2*(X+K2*D))†2*(P2-(X+K2*D))
230 LET X1 = (D*(K0+2*K1+2*K2+K3))/6
240 LET X = X+X1
250 LET N = P1-2*X
260 LET H = P2-X
270 PRINT T, N, H, X
280 NEXT T
290 END
```

PROGRAM 7.7 Chemical Kinetics: Third Order Reaction.

* * * * THIRD-ORDER REACTION * * * *

TIME(SEC)	PP. NO	PP. H2	PP. PRODUCT
0	359	400	0
.125	357.564	399.282	.718199
.25	356.141	398.571	1.42941
.375	354.733	397.866	2.13373
.5	353.337	397.169	2.83128
.625	351.956	396.478	3.52216
.75	350.587	395.794	4.20647
.875	349.231	395.116	4.88432
1	347.888	394.444	5.5558
1.125	346.558	393.779	6.22102
1.25	345.24	393.12	6.88006
1.375	343.934	392.467	7.53302
1.5	342.64	391.82	8.18
1.625	341.358	391.179	8.82107
1.75	340.087	390.544	9.45633
1.875	338.828	389.914	10.0859
2	337.581	389.29	10.7097

TABLE 7.7 Chemical Kinetics—Numerical analysis of third order reaction.

After the initial values are printed (line 170), the pp. of NO, H_2, and the product are tabulated in a loop using the Runge-Kutta method. The loop (lines 180–280) begins at $T = T + D$ (.125) and ends at T2 (2.00), proceeding in increments of D (.125). The variables not previously defined are:

$$N = P1 - 2*X = pp. \text{ of } NO \text{ at time } T$$
$$H = P2 - X = pp. \text{ of } H_2 \text{ at time } T$$

It can be seen that the Program (7.7) is short and straight-forward.

Discussion of Computer Generated Results: The results (Table 7.7) are generated in a neat tabular form. It can thus be seen that a third-order kinetics reaction may be studied without reference to integral calculus.

7.8 RADIOACTIVE DECAY EQUILIBRIUM

CHEMISTRY LEVEL college, introductory

MATHEMATICS BACKGROUND REQUIRED algebra

PEDAGOGY computer learning

PROBLEM APPROACH numerical method: Runge Kutta

STUDENT PARTICIPATION assists in program writing

PROGRAMMING SKILLS introductory BASIC

TIME OF STUDENT INVOLVEMENT in class—1 hour, out of class—3 hours

RECOMMENDED READING (14) chapter 5, part B

Lesson Description: The study of radioactive elements is of great interest to both teachers and students. This lesson demonstrates how a teacher might guide his students to a thorough understanding of the nature of radioisotopes and their decay into other elements without an involved mathematical approach. This lesson should enable a student to study radioactive elements of large half-life and also appreciate the effect of the relative size of the half-life on the amount of the element present.

The student is expected to write a program which calculates the variation in the amount of a radioactive substance present as a function of time using the Runge-Kutta Method. However, the student is not required to understand the numerical method. The numerical method is to be used essentially as a subroutine. The lesson therefore encourages the student to explore the radioactive element with the minimum of involvement in equations or functional relationships.

Background and Theory: For a given radioactive species, every nucleus has a definite probability of decaying in unit time; this decay probability has a constant value, characteristic of the particular radioisotope. Experiments have shown that the value of this decay constant remains the same irrespective of the chemical or physical state of the element at all readily accessible temperatures and pressures. What typifies this reaction is that the rate of decay, for a given specimen at any instant, is always directly proportional to the number of radioactive atoms of the isotope under consideration present at that instant. In a 'word' equation this could be written as follows:

$$\begin{pmatrix} rate\ of\ decay \\ of\ the\ element \end{pmatrix} = -(constant)\ \text{times} \begin{pmatrix} amount\ of\ the \\ element\ present \end{pmatrix}$$

or,

$$\text{rate of decay} = -(L) \times (N), \tag{7.8-1}$$

where L, called the decay constant of the radioactive species, is a measure of its decay probability. N represents the total number of atoms of the radioactive species and the minus sign indicates that after a small increment of time there will be fewer atoms left.

In a series of decay stages, such as those which follow nonfission neutron capture by thorium-232 or uranium-238, or as represented by the members of a natural radioactive series, or as exhibited by many fission products, each radioactive member of the series decays in accordance with the above equation with its own specific value for the decay constant. Such a series can be represented by

$$A \rightarrow B \rightarrow C \rightarrow D \rightarrow X$$

where A may be the parent of a natural radioactive series, or the species formed when a neutron is captured, for instance, thorium-233 or uranium-239, or it may be a radioactive fission product; the stable end-product of the series is represented by X. Referring to the previous equation (7.8–1) it can be seen that for element A:

$$\text{rate of decay of } A = -L_1 \times A \qquad (7.8\text{–}2)$$

where

$$L_1 = \text{decay constant of element A}$$

$$A = \text{total number of atoms of A present}$$

While the rate of decay of A is given above, it must be remembered that, at the same time, B is being formed by the decay of A. Hence at any specified time, the net rate of change of B with time is given by

$$\text{rate of decay of } B = L_1 \times A - L_2 \times B \qquad (7.8\text{–}3)$$

where L_1 and L_2 are the decay constants for elements A and B respectively. Equations 7.8–2 and 7.8–3 will be solved by the computer using the numerical method described in Section 5.3.

Computer Techniques: In this lesson for the radioactive decay series being considered

$$A \rightarrow B \rightarrow X$$

it has been shown that the appropriate rate equations are:

$$\text{rate of decay of element } A = -L_1 \times A$$
$$\text{from } (7.8\text{–}2)$$

$$\text{rate of decay of element } B = L_1 \times A - L_2 \times B$$
$$\text{from } (7.8\text{–}3)$$

These equations may be presented without recourse to calculus. The student can also be taught to use the Runge-Kutta Method. This method can be explained in depth or presented briefly, depending on the background of the students and the goals of the course. The Runge-Kutta Method has already been discussed (Chapter 5, and lesson 7.6 of this chapter). The Runge-Kutta coefficients for element A can be derived from Equation 7.8–2 and written in BASIC as follows:

$$M0 = -L1*A \qquad (7.8\text{–}4)$$

$$M1 = -L1*(A+M0*D/2) \qquad (7.8\text{–}5)$$

$$M2 = -L1*(A+M1*D/2) \qquad (7.8\text{–}6)$$

$$M3 = -L1*(A+M2*D) \qquad (7.8\text{–}7)$$

and the change in A is given by:

$$\text{change in } A = (M0+2*M1+2*M2+M3)*D/6 \qquad (7.8\text{–}8)$$

where

$$L1 = \text{the decay constant for element A}$$

$$D = \text{increment of time}$$

Similarly, for element B, the Runga-Kutta coefficients are written in BASIC:

$$K0 = L1*A - L2*B \qquad (7.8-9)$$

$$K1 = L1*(A + M0*D/2) - L2*(B + K0*D/2) \qquad (7.8-10)$$

$$K2 = L1*(A + M1*D/2) - L2*(B + K1*D/2) \qquad (7.8-11)$$

$$K3 = L1*(A + M2*D) - L2*(B + K2*D) \qquad (7.8-12)$$

where

$$L2 = \text{decay constant for element B}$$

$$D = \text{increment of time}$$

and, the change in B is given by:

$$\text{change in } B = (K0 + 2*K1 + 2*K2 + K3)*D/6 \qquad (7.8-13)$$

These coefficients can be used by the student in a program which calculates the amounts of element A and B present at time T. At time T, it should be noted that:

$$\text{new estimate of } A = \text{previous estimate of } A + \text{change in } A$$
$$(7.8-14)$$

$$\text{new estimate of } B = \text{previous estimate of } B + \text{change in B}$$
$$(7.8-15)$$

Since the Runge-Kutta method is suitable for differential equations with initial conditions, the initial conditions (i.e., when $T = 0$) provide the first estimates of A and B.

Comments About the Computer Program: The first time the student writes a program using the Runge-Kutta Method, he can be given the exact solutions of the rate equations (Program 7.8, lines 310, 320, and 330) so that he can compare the answers from the analytical solution and the numerical method. In this program, the following variables are assigned values with a READ statement (line 120):

$$T0 = 0 = \text{initial value of time}$$

$$A0 = 100 = \text{initial value of A}$$

$$B0 = 0 = \text{initial value of B}$$

$$T1 = 10 = \text{half-life of element A}$$

$$T2 = 112 = \text{half-life of element B}$$

$$D = .1 = \text{increment}$$

The following variables are then initialized (lines 140–180)

$$T = \text{time}$$

$$A1 = \text{amount of element A from analytical solution}$$

$$B1 = \text{amount of element B from analytical solution}$$

```
100 PRINT"* * * * RADIOACTIVE DECAY EQUILIBRIUM * * * *"
110 PRINT
120 READ T0, A0, B0, T1, T2, D
130 DATA 0, 100, 0, 10, 112, .1
140 LET T = T0
150 LET A = A0
160 LET B = B0
170 LET A1 = A0
180 LET B1 = B0
190 LET L1 = .693/T1
200 LET L2 = .693/T2
210 PRINT
220 PRINT"THE HALF LIVES USED FOR THIS RUN ARE:"
230 PRINT , "T1 ="T1, "T2 ="T2
240 PRINT
250 PRINT
260 PRINT, "AMOUNT OF ELEMENT A", "AMOUNT OF ELEMENT B"
270 PRINT
280 PRINT "MINUTES","EXACT","APPROXIMATE","EXACT","APPROXIMATE"
290 PRINT
300 LET M = 0
310 LET A1 = A0*EXP(-L1*T)
320 LET B1 = L1*A0/(L2-L1)*(EXP(-L1*T)-EXP(-L2*T))
330 LET B1 = B1 + B0*EXP(-L2*T)
340 PRINT T, A1, A, B1, B
350 IF (T -240) >= 0 THEN 500
360 LET M = M + 1
370 LET M0 = -L1*A
380 LET K0 = L1*A - L2*B
390 LET M1 = -L1*(A + M0*D/2)
400 LET K1 = L1*(A + M0*D/2) - L2*(B + K0*D/2)
410 LET M2 = -L1*(A + M1*D/2)
420 LET K2 = L1*(A + M1*D/2) -L2*(B + K1*D/2)
430 LET M3 = -L1*(A + M2*D)
440 LET K3 = L1*(A + M2*D) - L2*(B + K2*D)
450 LET A = A + (M0 + 2*M1 + 2*M2 + M3)*D/6
460 LET B = B + (K0 + 2*K1 + 2*K2 + K3)*D/6
470 LET T = T + D
480 IF M = 100 THEN 300
490 GO TO 350
500 END
```

PROGRAM 7.8   Radioactive Decay Equilibrium.

A = amount of element A from Runge-Kutta Method

B = amount of element B from Runge-Kutta Method

The decay constants of the two elements (L1 for element A, and L2 for element B) can be calculated from the half-lives (lines 190, 200). After the headings for the data output are printed (lines 220–280), the variable M is set to zero. This variable keeps track of the number iterations. Each time through the loop (lines 350–490) M is incremented by 1 (line 360). When M = 100 (line 480), the values of T, A1, A, B1, and B are printed. The loop is executed from T = 0 to T = 240 (line 350) in increments of 0.1 minute (line 470); since the values of the parameters are printed every 100 iterations, the output is tabulated in (100 minutes) (.1) = 10 minute

* * * * RADIOACTIVE DECAY EQUILIBRIUM * * * *

THE HALF LIVES USED FOR THIS RUN ARE:
          T1 = 10   T2 = 112

| | AMOUNT OF ELEMENT A | | AMOUNT OF ELEMENT B | |
MINUTES	EXACT	APPROXIMATE	EXACT	APPROXIMATI
0	100	100	0	0
10.	50.0074	50.0074	48.3057	48.3057
20.	25.0074	25.0074	69.5638	69.5638
30.	12.5055	12.5055	77.4699	77.4699
40.	6.25368	6.25368	78.8626	78.8626
50.	3.1273	3.1273	77.1518	77.1518
60.	1.56388	1.56388	74.0334	74.0334
70.	.782055	.782055	70.3469	70.3469
80.	.391085	.391085	66.5038	66.5038
90.	.195571	.195571	62.7026	62.7026
100.	9.78001E-2	9.78001E-2	59.0349	59.0349
110.	4.89072E-2	4.89072E-2	55.5401	55.5401
120.	2.44572E-2	2.44572E-2	52.2313	52.2313
130.	1.22304E-2	1.22304E-2	49.1093	49.1093
140.	6.11611E-3	6.11611E-3	46.1686	46.1686
150.	3.0585E-3	3.0585E-3	43.4015	43.4015
160.	1.52948E-3	1.52948E-3	40.7989	40.7989
170.	7.64851E-4	7.64851E-4	38.3517	38.3517
180.	3.82482E-4	3.82482E-4	36.051	36.051
190.	1.91269E-4	1.91269E-4	33.8881	33.8881
200.	9.56486E-5	9.56486E-5	31.855	31.855
210.	4.78313E-5	4.78313E-5	29.9437	29.9437
220.	2.39192E-5	2.39192E-5	28.1471	28.1471
230.	1.19614E-5	1.19614E-5	26.4583	26.4583
240.	5.98156E-6	5.98156E-6	24.8708	24.8708

TABLE 7.8A   Radioactive Decay: Comparison of analytical and numerical solutions when T1 = 10 and T2 = 112.

intervals. This is one way of ensuring the accuracy of the Runge-Kutta method, which depends on a small increment of time (D), without producing reams of data.

Discussion of the Computer Generated Output: This Program (7.8) generates the output in tabular form (Table 7.8A). The results of using a small time increment (D = .1) can be seen since the "exact" results from the analytical solution and the "approximate" results from the numerical method are identical. The student should feel free to explore the effects of different values of the decay constants on the rates of the reactions. Two additional runs (Table 7.8B, 7.8C) are shown for comparison. It should be noted from the computer output (Table 7.8C) that the analytical solution cannot be used for the special case where T1 = T2. In this case, L1 = L2 and the expression for B1 (Program 7.8, line 320) contains the quantity L2 − L1 in the denomenator. Each time line 320 is executed, the computer will note DIVISION BY ZERO, give the line number, set B1 equal to zero, and continue with the program.

* * * * RADIOACTIVE DECAY EQUILIBRIUM * * * *

THE HALF LIVES USED FOR THIS RUN ARE:
                T1 = 40   T2 = 60

	AMOUNT OF ELEMENT A		AMOUNT OF ELEMENT B	
MINUTES	EXACT	APPROXIMATE	EXACT	APPROXIMATE
0	100	100	0	0
10.	84.0927	84.0927	14.998	14.998
20.	70.7159	70.7159	25.9742	25.9742
30.	59.4669	59.4669	33.7469	33.7469
40.	50.0074	50.0074	38.9846	38.9846
50.	42.0526	42.0526	42.2323	42.2323
60.	35.3631	35.3631	43.9326	43.9326
70.	29.7378	29.7378	44.4442	44.4442
80.	25.0074	25.0074	44.0564	44.0564
90.	21.0294	21.0294	43.0013	43.0013
100.	17.6842	17.6842	41.4647	41.4647
110.	14.8711	14.8711	39.5941	39.5941
120.	12.5055	12.5055	37.5055	37.5055
130.	10.5162	10.5162	35.29	35.29
140.	8.84339	8.84339	33.0178	33.0178
150.	7.43665	7.43665	30.7426	30.7426
160.	6.25368	6.25368	28.5045	28.5045
170.	5.25889	5.25889	26.3332	26.3332
180.	4.42235	4.42235	24.2495	24.2495
190.	3.71887	3.71887	22.2677	22.2677
200.	3.1273	3.1273	20.3965	20.3965
210.	2.62983	2.62983	18.6407	18.6407
220.	2.2115	2.2115	17.0018	17.0018
230.	1.85971	1.85971	15.4789	15.4789
240.	1.56388	1.56388	14.0694	14.0694

TABLE 7.8B   Radioactive Decay: Comparison of analytical and numerical solutions when T1 = 40 and T2 = 60.

* * * * RADIOACTIVE DECAY EQUILIBRIUM * * * *

THE HALF LIVES USED FOR THIS RUN ARE:
                T1 = 60   T2 = 60

	AMOUNT OF ELEMENT A		AMOUNT OF ELEMENT B	
MINUTES	EXACT	APPROXIMATE	EXACT	APPROXIMATE

DIVISION BY ZERO LINE # 320
0   100   100   0   0

DIVISION BY ZERO LINE # 320
10.   89.0921   89.0921   0   10.2901

DIVISION BY ZERO LINE # 320
20.   79.3739   79.3739   0   18.3354

TABLE 7.8C   Radioactive Decay—error noted by computer when T1 = T2.

7.9 THE HYDROLYSIS OF METHYL ACETATE

Lesson Characteristics:

CHEMISTRY LEVEL   college, intermediate

MATHEMATICS BACKGROUND REQUIRED   algebra

PEDAGOGY   data reduction

PROBLEM APPROACH   analytical

STUDENT PARTICIPATION   assists in program writing

PROGRAMMING SKILLS   introductory BASIC

TIME OF STUDENT INVOLVEMENT   out of class—1 hour, in class—½ hour

RECOMMENDED READING   (15) chapter 7 (experiment 22), chapter 18
(11) chapter 13

Lesson Description: In this lesson, the computer is used to accomplish the data reduction of a laboratory experiment which studies the hydrolysis of methyl acetate. In dilute solutions, and in the early stages of hydrolysis, the reaction is first order. The goal of the experiment is to determine the specific rate constant of this first-order reaction. Although chemical kinetics is usually presented to students with a calculus background, it is possible to present this material with only algebra as a prerequisite.

In the conventional laboratory, the logarithm of the equivalents of methyl acetate remaining at time T is plotted as a function of T, the best straight line is drawn through the points, and the specific rate constant is determined from the slope of the line. With a computer available, however, the raw data may be fed directly into the computer during the laboratory session. The method of least-squares is then used to determine the slope of the best straight line, and the rate constant is obtained from the slope.

In more advanced classes, the student can be expected to write the entire program. At an intermediate level, the method of least-squares can be given to the student as a subroutine. In freshman labs, the entire program may be written by the instructor. The computer output is in tabular form and it includes the raw data, intermediate results, and the rate constant.

Background and Theory: [(64) EXPERIMENT 22] The hydrolysis of methyl acetate is catalyzed by hydrogen ion:

$$CH_3COOCH_3 + H_2O + H^+ \rightleftharpoons CH_3COOH + CH_3OH + H^+ \quad (7.9\text{--}1)$$

and the reaction is reversible. If k_1 is the rate constant for the forward reaction, and k_2 is the rate constant for the reverse reaction, the net rate of hydrolysis at any time is

$$-dC(CH_3COOCH_3)/dT = k_1 \times C(H_2O) \times C(CH_3COOCH_3)$$
$$- k_2 \times C(CH_3COOH) \times C(CH_3OH) \quad (7.9\text{--}2)$$

where

$$C(CH_3COOCH_3) = \text{concentration of methyl acetate}$$
$$C(H_2O) = \text{concentration of water}$$
$$C(CH_3COOH) = \text{concentration of acetic acid}$$
$$C(CH_3OH) = \text{concentration of methanol}$$

In dilute solutions, the concentration of water remains essentially constant, and one could define a new constant

$$K1 = k_1 \times C(H_2O) \qquad (7.9\text{--}3)$$

Furthermore, the concentrations of acetic acid and methanol remain negligible during the early stages of the reaction and the term involving them may be neglected. The reaction thus appears to be first order and the rate equation can be written:

$$-dC(CH_3COOCH_3)/dT = K1 \times C(CH_3COOCH_3) \qquad (7.9\text{--}4)$$

In the laboratory, the reaction is initiated by adding a known amount of methyl acetate (5 ml) to a known amount of standard acid (100 ml). At various time intervals, a 5 ml sample of the reaction mixture is removed and run into cold water to arrest the reaction. This aliquot is then titrated with standard base.

The reaction (Equation 7.9–1) shows that one mole of acetic acid is produced for every mole of methyl acetate hydrolyzed. Let VT represent the titrant volume per aliquot if hydrolysis is complete and V represent the titrant volume per aliquot at time T. Then (VT-V) measures the number of equivalents of methyl acetate per aliquot remaining at time T. VT must be calculated since unhydrolyzed methyl acetate remains when the reaction reaches equilibrium. The formula used to calculate VT is:

$$VT = \frac{100 \, V1}{V2} + \frac{25 \cdot D \cdot 10^3}{V2 \cdot M \cdot B} \qquad (7.9\text{--}5)$$

or in BASIC,

$$VT = 100*V1/V2 + (25*D*1E3)/(V2*M*B)$$

where the original reaction mixture contained 100 ml of standard acid and 5 ml of methyl acetate. In the above equation:

V1 = volume of NaOH required to titrate a 5 ml aliquot of the standard acid (about 1N)

V2 = initial volume of the acid – methyl acetate solution (this volume is 104.6 ml because of a volume change on mixing)

D = density of methyl acetate = 0.9141 g/ml at 35 °C

M = molecular weight of methyl acetate = 74.08

B = normality of sodium hydroxide (about 0.2N)

A plot of log (VT-V) versus T has the same slope as a plot of the log [C(CH₃COOCH₃)] versus T. It is therefore not necessary to determine the actual concentrations of methyl acetate. If the natural logarithm (base e) of (VT-V) is plotted versus T, then, the rate constant is obtained from the equation

$$K = -S \qquad (7.9\text{–}6)$$

where

$K =$ the specific rate constant

$S =$ the slope of the line

Computer Techniques: This lesson uses the method of least-squares to determine the slope of the line obtained when log (VT-V) is plotted versus T. The equation for a straight line is

$$y = mx + b \qquad (7.9\text{–}7)$$

where

$m =$ the slope of the line

$b =$ the y intercept

The differences between the values of y calculated from the empirical equation and the experimentally determined values, y_i, are called the residuals. The method of least-squares obtains the best representative curve by finding that curve for which the sum of the squares of the residuals (D) are a minimum. Then

$$D_i = y - y_i = (mx_i + b - y_i) \qquad (7.9\text{–}8)$$

and, or rearranging,

$$D_i^2 = \sum_{i=1}^{N} (y_i - mx_i - b)^2 \qquad (7.9\text{–}9)$$

One has already defined the sum of the squares of the residuals, D_i^2, as D. To obtain a minimum value, take the first derivate of D (7.9–9) and set it equal to zero:

$$\delta D/\delta b = -2 \sum_{i=1}^{N} (y_i - mx_i - b) = 0 \qquad (7.9\text{–}10)$$

$$\delta D/\delta m = -2 \sum_{i=1}^{N} x_i (y_i - mx_i - b) = 0 \qquad (7.9\text{–}11)$$

where the sum is taken for $i=1$ to $i=N$ for N measurements. The resulting equations (7.9–10, 7.9–11) are solved simultaneously to yield an expression for the slope of the line:

$$m = (N\Sigma y_i x_i - \Sigma x_i \Sigma y_i)/N\Sigma x_i^2 - (\Sigma x_i)^2 \qquad (7.9\text{–}12)$$

where the sums are taken from $i=1$ to $i=N$.

In terms of this lesson, one defines the following BASIC variables:

$$S = m = \text{slope of the line}$$

$$X = \Sigma x_i$$

$$Y = \Sigma y_i$$

$$X1 = \Sigma x_i y_i$$

$$X2 = \Sigma x_i^2$$

In terms of the above BASIC variables, the slope of the line (7.9–12) is given by:

$$S = (N*X1 - X*Y)/(N*X2 - X*X) \qquad (7.9–13)$$

Comments About the Computer Program: The program (7.9) is similar to what can be written by an intermediate level college student. The program can be divided into three sections:

1.   remarks, data and dimension statements (lines 100–250),
2.   body of the program (lines 260–530), and
3.   the least-squares subroutine (lines 540–660).

REM statements are used at the beginning of the program (line 100–130) to identify the program. The data is listed in a block (lines 160–230). Alternately, the data can be stored in an external data file and input during the program. The end of data is indicated by

240 DATA 0

which is used to stop the program. The four subscripted variables $X(J)$, $B(J)$, $C(J)$, and $Y(J)$ are next dimensioned (line 250). This paves the way for the body of the program.
    The following variables are read:

$$A = \text{normality of standard acid}$$

$$B = \text{normality of standard base}$$

$$V2 = \text{initial volume of reaction mixture}$$

$$D = \text{density of methyl acetate at } 35°C$$

$$M = \text{molecular weight of methyl acetate}$$

The volume of standard base required to titrate a 5 ml sample of standard acid is calculated with

270 LET V1 = 5*A/B

for use in the calculation of VT (equation 7.9–5). The titrant volume per aliquot if hydrolysis were complete (VT) is called V in the program to conform to BASIC rules. Thus (VT) is calculated in line 280. The variables which change with each experiment are printed (line 290). Then the pro-

```
100 REM * * * * LABORATORY DATA REDUCTION * * * *
110 REM CALCULATION OF THE SPECIFIC RATE CONSTANT FOR THE HYDROLYSIS
120 REM OF METHYL ACETATE USING THE LEAST-SQUARES METHOD TO
130 REM DETERMINE THE SLOPE OF THE LINE.
140 PRINT
150 PRINT
160 DATA 1.149,.187,104.6,.9141,74.08
170 DATA 9,1,27.10,7,27.12,13,29.23,19,29.42,26,30.49,36,31.70,
180 DATA 46,33.00,66,35.72,86,35.90
190 DATA 7,1,25.55,5,26.60,11,28.05,18,29.30,23,29.83,33,31.36,
200 DATA 47,32.80
210 DATA 16,1,27.10,7,27.12,13,29.23,19,29.42,26,30.49,36,31.70,
220 DATA 46,33.00,66,35.72,86,35.90,1,25.55,5,26.60,11,28.05,
230 DATA 18,29.30,23,29.83,33,31.36,47,32.80
240 DATA 0
250 DIM X(50),B(50),C(50),Y(50)
260 READ A,B,V2,D,M
270 LET V1 = 5*A/B
280 LET V = 100*V1/V2 +(25*D*1E3)/(V2*M*B)
290 PRINT "N-HCL=";A,"N-NAOH=";B,"VT=";V
300 PRINT
310 PRINT
320 READ N
330 IF N=0 THEN 530
340 PRINT "N=";N
350 PRINT
360 PRINT "TIME","NAOH","VT-V","LOG(VT-V)"
370 PRINT "(MIN)","(ML)"
380 PRINT
390 FOR J = 1 TO N
400 READ X(J),B(J)
410 LET C(J) = V - B(J)
420 LET Y(J) = LOG(C(J))
430 PRINT X(J),B(J),C(J),Y(J)
440 NEXT J
450 GOSUB 540
460 LET K = -S
470 PRINT
480 PRINT "THE RATE CONSTANT FOR THE HYDROLYSIS OF METHYL ACETATE"
490 PRINT "IS";K;"PER MIN."
500 PRINT
510 PRINT
520 GO TO 320
530 STOP
540 LET X = 0
550 LET Y = 0
560 LET X1 = 0
570 LET X2 = 0
580 FOR J = 1 TO N
590 LET X = X + X(J)
600 LET Y = Y + Y(J)
610 LET X1 = X1 + X(J)*Y(J)
620 LET X2 = X2 + X(J)*X(J)
630 NEXT J
640 LET D = N*X2 - X*X
650 LET S = (N*X1-X*Y)/D
660 RETURN
670 END
```

PROGRAM 7.9   The Hydrolysis of Methyl Acetate.

gram reads N, the number of data points in a run (line 320). Since the end of data is signaled by $N=0$, the statement

$$330 \text{ IF } N=0 \text{ THEN } 530$$

causes the program to branch to

$$530 \text{ STOP}$$

which terminates the run. If $N \langle \rangle 0$, the program prints N:

$$340 \text{ PRINT "N="; N}$$

Note how the PRINT statement is used to print both alphabetic ($N=$) and numeric (the value of N) data.

The program is now at the point of reading data and performing the calculations. Before executing the loop which reads and prints the intermediate data (lines 390–440), the headings for the output are printed. Note the use of the comma to provide four columns, 15 spaces wide, for the data.

The loop (lines 390–440) is controlled by (J) which is also used as the subscript for the subscripted variables. (J) is incremented from 1 to N in steps of one with the line:

$$390 \text{ FOR } J=1 \text{ TO N}$$

Since N is the number of data points in a run, the loop will be executed once for each data point. The loop reads the amount of base required to titrate an aliquot of the reaction mixture, $B(J)$, at each time the aliquot was taken, $X(J)$. Then $VT-V$ (line 410), and log VT-V (line 420) are calculated. In BASIC the log function is the log to base e. At this point, the data taken in the lab, and the calculated values of $(VT-V)$ and log $(VT-V)$ are printed (line 430), and the program loops back (line 440) to the start of the loop. It is important to observe how the loop index (J) is also used to label the data by using subscripted variables. The program is now ready to calculate the slope of the line which would be obtained if log (VT-V) were plotted against T.

The least-squares subroutine is placed at the end of the program (lines 540–660) and accessed with the statement

$$450 \text{ GOSUB } 540$$

The last line of a subroutine must be a RETURN statement (line 660) which returns the program control to the line following the GOSUB statement (line 460). The subroutine itself is straight forward since the appropriate equation (7.9–13) has been discussed.

The equations for the slope of line are:

$$640 \text{ LET } D=N*X2-X*X$$

$$650 \text{ LET } S = (N*X1-X*Y)/D$$

These sums will be calculated by means of a loop (lines 580–630). Before

N-HCL= 1.149   N-NAOH= .187   VT= 45.1419

N= 9

TIME (MIN)	NAOH (ML)	VT-V	LOG(VT-V)
1	27.1	18.0419	2.8927
7	27.12	18.0219	2.89159
13	29.23	15.9119	2.76707
19	29.42	15.7219	2.75505
26	30.49	14.6519	2.68457
36	31.7	13.4419	2.59837
46	33	12.1419	2.49666
66	35.72	9.42187	2.24303
86	35.9	9.24187	2.22374

THE RATE CONSTANT FOR THE HYDROLYSIS OF METHYL ACETATE
IS 8.74956E-3 PER MIN.

N= 7

TIME (MIN)	NAOH (ML)	VT-V	LOG(VT-V)
1	25.55	19.5919	2.97511
5	26.6	18.5419	2.92003
11	28.05	17.0919	2.8386
18	29.3	15.8419	2.76266
23	29.83	15.3119	2.72863
33	31.36	13.7819	2.62335
47	32.8	12.3419	2.513

THE RATE CONSTANT FOR THE HYDROLYSIS OF METHYL ACETATE
IS 9.97075E-3 PER MIN.

TABLE 7.9A   The Hydrolysis of Methyl Acetate: Data reduction for two experimental runs.

entering the loop, the variables are initialized (set equal to zero) (lines 540–570) as for example

540 LET X=0

Some BASIC time-sharing systems automatically initialize all variables, in which case, the appropriate lines (540–570) may be deleted.

As was noted (7.9–10, 7.9–11, 7.9–12) the sums are taken from $i=1$ to $i=N$ (line 580). In this problem, the plot involves log (VT-V) versus T, and $X=T$, $Y=\log$ (VT-V). When the loop has been executed N times, the slope of the line is calculated (lines 640–650), and "660 RETURN" returns program control to line 460.

N= 16

TIME (MIN)	NAOH (ML)	VT-V	LOG(VT-V)
1	27.1	18.0419	2.8927
7	27.12	18.0219	2.89159
13	29.23	15.9119	2.76707
19	29.42	15.7219	2.75505
26	30.49	14.6519	2.68457
36	31.7	13.4419	2.59837
46	33	12.1419	2.49666
66	35.72	9.42187	2.24303
86	35.9	9.24187	2.22374
1	25.55	19.5919	2.97511
5	26.6	18.5419	2.92003
11	28.05	17.0919	2.8386
18	29.3	15.8419	2.7626L
23	29.83	15.3119	2.72863
33	31.36	13.7819	2.62335
47	32.8	12.3419	2.513

THE RATE CONSTANT FOR THE HYDROLYSIS OF METHYL ACETATE IS 9.15322E-3 PER MIN.

TABLE 7.9B   The Hydrolysis of Methyl Acetate: Two sets of experimental data are combined in this run.

At this point, the rate constant is calculated (line 460), and printed (line 480, 490). The line

520 GO TO 320

causes a new set of data to be read. As long as N ⟨ ⟩ 0, the program will run. When N=0, the program is terminated. It should be noted that

530 STOP

is equivalent to

530 GO TO 670

where 670 is the end of the program.

Discussion of Computer Generated Results: The results of an experiment in which two separate runs were conducted by the student are shown in Table 7.9A. The average rate constant for the two runs (Table 7.9B) is also shown. It took about 5 minutes to punch the data onto paper tape, and less than 3 seconds to run the program. It is thus possible to analyze the data during the lab if time-sharing is available. Even if the student has written the program himself, the total time spent is *less* than would be required to calculate VT and (VT-V) for *each* data point, plot log (VT-V) versus T, draw the best straight line, determine the slope of the line, and calculate K. Furthermore, telling the computer what to do requires an understanding of what must be done. Invariably, the writing of computer programs is a learning process in itself.

CHAPTER 8

COMPUTERS IN ENGINEERING EDUCATION

8.1 INTRODUCTION

Theories generated by physicists and mathematicians are often translated into new and useful products by the engineer. Engineering, or applied science is responsible for the practical development and implementation of theory. The basic scientific principles which must be applied to engineering problems invariably become mathematically complicated resulting in equations which challenge human ingenuity for their solution. These complicated relationships have forced the engineer to find more efficient ways to produce realistic answers. The analog computer was developed as a device to design complicated machinery by simulating the anticipated machine with electrical analogs. This allowed the engineer to design changes on paper before spending the time and effort required to build the final product. Because the precision of the analog computer was not sufficient for all types of problems, the digital computer was developed by the engineer to increase his problem solving ability.

The rapid growth of the digital computer has required the engineer to continually refresh his knowledge about the computer, and how it can help him. Consequently, engineering colleges and universities are requiring their students to take courses in computers. Some graduate schools even allow proficiency in a computer language to satisfy the language requirement of a post-graduate degree. The discovery of how to time-share computers has made input terminals (See Fig. 2.3) available to people at prices of less than $10 per hour for rental, and as low as $.50 per hour per terminal for "in-house" computer systems. To integrate the methods of computer-learning into the engineering curriculum is essential. Engineering students and, above all, the engineering teacher will find that this chapter contains a number of useful computer-learning techniques.

How can the engineering student learn about using computers in his already over-crowded schedule? Normally students spend most of their first two years in acquiring the basic concepts such as physics, chemistry and mathematics. Training in computer use has been restricted to courses in computer languages, mostly FORTRAN and ALGOL, which are taught at many engineering colleges. Some schools require computer programming courses in their first year, while others use it as a higher level course. Unfortunately many of these programming courses emphasize only the particular computer language, (FORTRAN, ALGOL, etc.), instead of a computer problem solving method. The student should be introduced to computer methods early in his education so that applications of these methods might be integrated with other course work when feasible. A better understanding of mathematical principles combined with the computer applications of real-life problems, that is, problems without idealized assumptions is required. For instance, the finite length wire should be studied versus the infinite wire, the finite capacitor versus the infinite parallel plates, the trajectory of a body in air versus a frictionless fluid, and so on. This chapter will give examples of some of these real-life problems, and indicate methods of solution without recourse to calculus while retaining the fundamental scientific principles of the problem.

Next, how can the engineering teacher integrate the computer into his course to the advantage of the learning situation? The examples of this chapter are chosen to help the engineering teacher to:

(a) Gain experience in programming.
(b) Gain a knowledge of how to use numerical methods in learning situations.
(c) Help his students gain a better understanding of basic principles.
(d) Introduce new methods of problem solution.
(e) Extend the special case, analytical solution problems, to real-life examples of the basic principles.
(f) Use the computer to help the student better understand the use of the analytical methods.

The examples are intended to follow an orderly increase in the complexity of problem types and computer methods. Lesson 8.2 and 8.3 treat a simple torsion problem which involves the solution of a transcendental equation in easy to learn steps. Lesson 8.4 uses a Fourier series to make a mathematical simulation of an acoustical pressure pulse.

In Lesson 8.5 through 8.9, the reader will find a computer solution to the exponential process. Several levels of numerical solution are presented giving the reader sufficient background to understand the harmonic oscillator of Lesson 8.11 which uses the Runge-Kutta numerical method for a foundation in simulation and design. An example of numerical integration using Simpson's rule is used to solve the work in a thermodynamic cycle in Lesson 8.10. Lessons 8.12 and 8.13 respectively solve a one-dimensional heat transfer problem and a two-dimensional temperature distribution problem using the relaxation method of solving partial differential equations. The laboratory data analysis of the "charge to mass ratio of an electron" experiment (Lesson 8.14) is last not because of level of difficulty but because it represents the type of program which requires the dovetailing of several mathematical methods, i.e., statistical routine, least square fit of a straight line routine and the algebraic manipulation of several sets of data points, and as such does not always lead to computer learning in a direct manner.

8.2 TORSION ANALYSIS I

Lesson Characteristics:

ENGINEERING LEVEL   college, introductory

MATHEMATICS BACKGROUND REQUIRED   algebra and
    trigonometry

PEDAGOGY   computer learning and simulation

PROBLEM APPROACH   numerical method

STUDENT PARTICIPATION   assists in program writing

PROGRAMMING SKILLS   none

TIME OF STUDENT INVOLVEMENT   in class—20 minutes,
    out of class—45 minutes

RECOMMENDED READING   (2) Ch. 12, Sec. 15.5
                                                (3) Ch. 11, Sec. 1 and 4

Lesson Description: Many worthwhile engineering problems are neglected because they are not easily solved by analytical means. The transcendental equation is one of these types of problems. This section demonstrates an iterative process which will solve the drop angle of a torsion bar under an angular strain. (See Figure 8.2). An iterative computing technique to solve for the real roots of a transcendental equation is demonstrated. In addition, the input parameters can be varied in order to conduct an experiment in design.

Background and Theory: A transcendental equation results from the analysis of the torsion problem of Figure 8.2. The object is to find the angular displacement, T, for the mass, M, acting on the lever arm at a radius, R, from the end attached to a torsion spring with a spring constant, K.

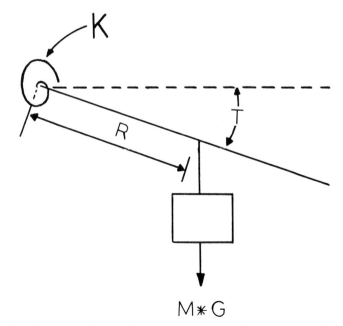

Figure 8.2 Torsion Spring Problem, depressed angle, T, due to mass, M, and spring constant, k.

The torque applied by an external force is equal to the force times the lever arm.

$$Q = mgr \cos(T)$$

$$\text{LET } Q = M*G*R*COS(T) \qquad (8.2\text{--}1)$$

The reactive torque due to the spring is:

$$Q = kT$$

$$\text{LET } Q = K*T \qquad (8.2\text{--}2)$$

Equations (8.2–1) and (8.2–2) in terms of the variable desired, T, is:

$$T = \frac{mgr}{K} \cos(T)$$

$$\text{LET } T = M*G*R*COS(T)/K \qquad (8.2\text{--}3)$$

Typically, undergraduate textbooks lack a rigorous treatment of many interesting problems because of the non-analytical solution required, or the time required to develop another method. Transcendental equation problems are included in this category. Without a computer, transcendental equations are solved by first graphing the function, and then determining the roots from the graph. For a more accurate solution, the value of the root obtained from the graph is substituted into the function to check the accuracy of the result. If the accuracy is unsatisfactory, a guess is made to additional significant figures and checked for accuracy. This procedure is repeated until the desired accuracy is obtained. This technique could be duplicated by the computer.

Computer Technique: The constants of equation 8.2–3 should be pre-calculated for efficiency:

$$\text{LET } C = M*G*R/K \qquad (8.2\text{--}4)$$

The iteration technique of Program 8.2A uses an angle increment of 0.1 radians (T1), to build the total angle, T.

(1) Try first value of T (.1 radian).
(2) Check the value of the dummy variable, A:

$$\text{LET } A = C*COS(T) \qquad (8.2\text{--}5)$$

(3) If the value of A-T is within the desired accuracy the solution is known.
(4) If not add T1 to T and try the new value of T in Equation (8.2–5).

Another iteration technique would be to refine Program 8.2A by making the interval, T1, very small, or as small as the intended accuracy of the results. The disadvantage of this method would be the thousands, and perhaps millions of calculations which may have to be made in order to obtain the desired accuracy.

The method of Program 8.2B refines the solution by consecutively choos-

```
100 REM ********************TORSION 1 *************************
110 REM DATA M=MASS, R=RADIUS, K = SPRING CONSTANT, T1 = DELTA T
120 DATA 2,.5,20,.1
130 READ M, R, K, T1
140 LET C = 9.8*M*R/K
150 FOR 1 = T1 TO PI/2 STEP T1
160 LET A = C*COS(T)
170 IF A - T <= T1 THEN 210
180 PRINT T, A-T
190 IF T >= PI/2 THEN 230
200 NEXT T
210 PRINT"THETA = "T"+-"T1/2
220 STOP
230 PRINT
240 PRINT"MASS, RADIUS, OR DELTA T TOO LARGE OR K TOO SMALL."
250 END
```

PROGRAM 8.2A   Torsion analysis I

ing a smaller angle increment, T1, i.e., after a solution is obtained by the method of Program 8.2A, the angle increment, T1 is made equal to T1/10, 1/10 of its original value. This value is added to the first solution until a solution with an accuracy of T1/10 is obtained. The increment is divided by 10 again making the angle increment 1/100 of its original value, etc., until the desired accuracy is found.

Comments About the Computer Program: Program 8.2 computes this simple iteration using a FOR statement to increment the angle, T. Statements 160 and 170 do the calculating while statements 150 and 200 increment the angle. Statement 180 allows the value of T and the error to be printed. It is known, from the problem, that the weight cannot cause the arm to go

```
100 REM *******************:TORSION 2 ***********************:
110 REM DATA SAME AS FOR TOR1 PLUS E9 = ERROR
120 DATA 2, .5, 20, .1, .0001
130 READ M, R, K, T1, E9
140 LET C = 9.8*M*R/K
150 LET T = T + T1
160 LET A = C*COS(T)
170 IF A-T <= T1 THEN 200
180 IF T >= PI/2 THEN 300
190 GOTO 150
200 LET T1 = T1/10
210 LET T = T + T1
220 LET A = C*COS(T)
230 IF ABS(A-T) <= T1 THEN 250
240 GOTO 210
250 IF ABS(A-T) <= E9 THEN 270
260 GOTO 200
270 PRINT
280 PRINT"THETA = "T"+-"ABS(A-T)/2
290 STOP
300 PRINT
310 PRINT"MASS, RADIUS, OR DELTA T TOO LARGE OR K TOO SMALL."

>
```

PROGRAM 8.2B.   Torsion analysis II

```
        0.1                0.387552041
        0.2                0.280232623
        0.3                0.16811488
   THETA =   0.4 +-  0.05

>              TABLE 8.2A.
```

beyond a 90° arc. A safeguard, statement 190, stops the program and causes a suggested error message to be printed.

Program 8.2B does not use the FOR- NEXT combination for incrementing the angle. Instead, an IF-GOTO sequence performs the operation of deciding when to reduce the increment size. Statement 250 determines that the final iteration is made when the solution is as accurate as desired (within .0001 radian).

Discussion of Computer Results: Table 8.2A shows values for the problem with an angle increment of 0.1 radians. Decreasing the angle increment would give more accurate results. By removing statement 180, a practical limit for T1 would be .01 radians. Intervals less than .01 radians would (1) be ineffcient use of computer time, and (2) begin to cause round-off error. Program 8.2B employs this method to obtain a rough solution, and then refines the solution to the desired accuracy with progressively smaller increments. The results of Program 8.2B are much superior to those of Program 8.2A. The results of each iteration were suppressed, as there would have been 17 data points before printing the final result.

Either of these methods could be utilized as an assignment in a class of students with little or no experience in computer programming. The instructions in preparing the student should require no more than twenty minutes.

```
    THETA =   0.4427 +-  3.15909156E-05

>              TABLE 8.2B.
```

APPENDIX

A-8.2

PROGRAM 8.2B   (STEP BY STEP SOLUTION)

120, 130
DATA for mass, radius, torsion constant, initial angle increment and acceptable error is read in by statement 130.

140   LET C=9.8*M*R/K
Calculates all of the constants of the equations to save computer time and programming effort and neatness.

150   LET T=T+T1
Calculates initial value of angular displacement Trial, T.

160 LET A=C*COS(T)

Calculates value of angular displacement using trail T. A perfect solution would make A=C COS (T).

170 IF A−T<T1 THEN 200

Check to see if the solution is as close as allowed by present value of T. If it is jump out of loop.

180 IF T>PI/2 THEN 300

Check to see if a solution is possible due to physical limitations.

190 GOTO 150

Continue to search for a solution by adding another angle increment to angular displacement, T.

200 LET T1=T1/10

Reduce the old value of T1 by a factor of 10. Start of new loop.

210 Let T=T+T1

Repeat calculation of time.

220 LET A=C*COS(T)

First loop, (150 and 160).

230 IF ABS(A−T)<=T1 THEN 250

240 GOTO 210

Does the same thing as statement 170, if solution is not as close as allowed by the present T1 continue the loop by going to 210 and increasing the displacement again. If solution is as close as possible check to see if it is close enough by statement 250.

250 IF ABS(A−T)<=E9 THEN 270

260 GOTO 200

If solution is not close enough go to 200 and try a smaller T1 by replacing the old value of T1 by T1/10. If the solution is close enough go to 270 and print the answer.

270 PRINT

280 PRINT

290 STOP

For neatness, print the answer with limits of accuracy, then STOP.

300 PRINT

310 PRINT

Give hint as to what the trouble is if an impossible solution is tried but tested for by statement 180.

8.3   TORSION ANALYSIS II

Lesson Characteristics:

ENGINEERING LEVEL   pre-college

MATHEMATICS BACKGROUND REQUIRED   algebra and trigonometry

PEDAGOGY   computer learning and simulation

PROBLEM APPROACH   numerical method

STUDENT PARTICIPATION   assists in program writing

PROGRAMMING SKILLS   introductory BASIC

TIME OF STUDENT INVOLVEMENT   in class—20 minutes, out of class—1 hour

RECOMMENDED READING   Same as Section 8.2

Lesson Description: The torsion problem of Section 8.2 remains the same for this section. A more advanced and efficient method of solution demonstration is to observe the solution convergence on the computer printout. The half-interval method of transcendental equation solution is particularly easy to use when the boundary conditions of the problem are clear, and there are no multiple roots in close approximation to each other.

Background and Theory: The real roots of transcendental or polynomial equations can be searched for by using large increments. However, the increment size is limited by the interval between adjacent roots, e.g., in the problem of Figure 8.2, the interval must be less than 90°.

The example of Figure 8.2 can be rewritten in function notation:

$$f(t) = t - c \cos(t) = 0$$

$$\text{LET } T = T - C*COS(T) = 0 \qquad (8.3\text{--}1)$$

If the value of adjacent iterations of Equation 8.3–1 are the same sign, the two values are on the same side of the root. If the value of adjacent iterations are of opposite sign, the two values are on opposite sides of the root. See Figures 8.3A and 8.3B.

Computer Technique: If the sign of the function value is known, then the computer can keep track of the position of each consecutive function value with respect to the true value of the root. The sign can be checked by:

$$\text{IF } F*F1 < 0 \text{ THEN (values opposite)}$$

$$\text{IF } F*F1 = 0 \text{ THEN (true root)}$$

The computer technique of Program 8.3 is an iterative procedure of checking consecutive function values for sign and selecting a new test value for the

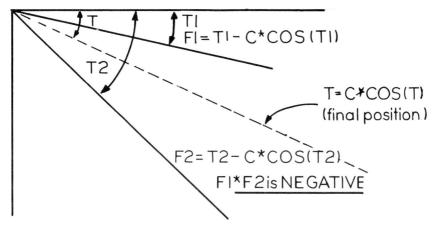

Figure 8.3A   Two Function values of the Consecutive half-interval and their relation to final position.

function variable as shown in Figures 8.3A and 8.3B. A new trial value based upon the two closest previous values of the function variable is then made and the iteration repeated. The method is called the method of consecutive half-intervals.

Comments About the Computer Program: Two values of T are selected to start the program, T1 and T2. As an example, the two extremes of zero and $\pi/2$ were chosen. Two function values are calculated, F1 from T1, and F from $(T1+T2)/2$. The product of $F*F1$ is checked for positive or negative. If negative, T2 is made equal to T and a new value of T and F is calculated, retaining the old value of F1. If $F*F1$ is positive, then T1 is made equal to T and F1 becomes F, throwing away the old value of F1.

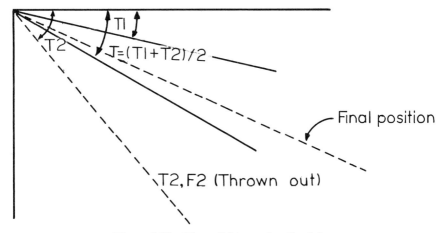

Figure 8.3B   Figure 8.3A one iteration later.

```
1 REM M=MASS,R=RADIUS,K=SPRING CONSTANT,E9=ERROR
10 DATA 2,.5,20,.0001
20 READ M,R,K,E9
30 LET C=9.8*M*R/K
40 IF C>.5*3.141592 THEN 300
50 LET T1=0
60 LET T2=.5*3.141592
70 LET F1=T1-C*COS(T1)
80 LET T=.5*(T1+T2)
90 LETF=T-C*COS(T)
100 IF ABS(F)<E9 THEN 200
110 IF F*F1<0 THEN 160
120 IF F*F1=0 THEN 250
130 LET T1=T
140 LET F1=F
150 GOTO 80
160 LET T2=T
180 GOTO 80
200 PRINT
210 LET E8=.5*ABS(C*COS(T)-T)
220 PRINT"THETA=",T;"+-";E8
230 STOP
250 PRINT
260 PRINT"TRUE VALUE=",T
280 STOP
300 PRINT
310 PRINT"MASS,RADIUS,OR DELTA T TOO LARGE OR K TOO SMALL."
999 END
```

PROGRAM 8.3.   Torsion Analysis III

The loop starts in each case by calculating a new value of $T = (T1 + T2)/2$, as demonstrated in Figures 8.3A and 8.3B.

Discussion of Computer Results: The method of consecutive half-intervals can best be traced by studying Table 8.3. The first column is the variable, and the second column is the function value using the variable. The value of the sign in the second column allows the reader to reconstruct the progressive solution followed by the computer. In the first row, T and $\pi/2$ are both greater than their respective calculated value, $C \cos(T)$, and the two corresponding functional values are both positive. The $\pi/2$ angle was thrown away and the angle 0.785398 was averaged with the initial angle, zero, for the second value of T, 0.392699. This value of T gives an opposite sign to its functional value and causes the initial angle, zero, to be thrown away, as shown by Figure 8.3B. The final result is more accurate, with fewer iterations, than for Program 8.2B.

This method could be used as a first assignment for students who have had some previous experience with programming. With simple modifications, only one precalculation would have to be made prior to entering the iteration loop.

The reader should have no difficulty in proceeding to more advanced methods found in numerical analysis books, such as the method of interpolation.

.785398	.438916	
.392699	-.060002	
.589049	.181628	
.490874	5.87323	E-2
.441786	-1.16840	E-3
.46633	2.86501	E-2
.454058	1.37077	E-2
.447922	6.26134	E-3
.444854	2.54439	E-3
.44332	6.87474	E-4
.442553	-2.40592	E-4
.442937	2.23408	E-4
.442745	-8.60076	E-6

THETA=   .442745 +- 4.30038 E-6

TABLE 8.3.

8.4 PRODUCTION OF SQUARE WAVES

Lesson Characteristics:

ENGINEERING LEVEL   college, introductory

MATHEMATICS BACKGROUND REQUIRED   analytical geometry

PEDAGOGY   computer learning and simulation

PROBLEM APPROACH   qualitative and analytical

STUDENT PARTICIPATION   uses prepared programs, or assists in program writing

PROGRAMMING SKILLS   none (for prepared programs), introductory BASIC (for writing programs)

TIME OF STUDENT INVOLVEMENT   in class—1 hour, out of class—1 hour (2 hours if writing programs)

RECOMMENDED READING   (17) Chapter 17

Lesson Description: The engineering student is introduced to Fourier series problems early in his career. A knowledge of calculus is necessary for him to evaluate the coefficients, and the problems often become very mathematical and mysterious. This lesson will prepare the student to accept the underlying principles of the Fourier series without actually requiring the calculus. Once the student has experimented with several wave forms, he is ready to learn about numerical analysis of any wave form, or the rigor of the analytical Fourier series and integrals. The square wave expanded as an odd function is demonstrated as possible acoustical pressure pulses, or an electronic square wave generator.

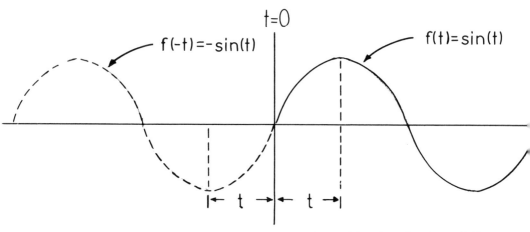

Figure 8.4A   The SINE function as an example of an odd function, $[f(-t) = -f(t)]$.

Background and Theory: In essence, any function, $f(t)$ can be described by a series of sine and cosine terms, each with particular amplitudes, phase, and frequency. The example under discussion is an odd function (defined odd by $f(-t) = -f(t)$). The sine function is odd, as shown in Figure 8.4A, i.e., $\sin(-t) = -\sin(t)$. Consequently, a very rough approximation to a square wave could be a sine wave as shown in Figure 8.4B. It can be seen that a sine wave of three times the fundamental frequency, but of lower amplitude could fit into the square wave very nicely (Figure 8.4C), knocking down the central peak, and raising up the value on each side of the central peak. Indeed the odd harmonics of the fundamental frequency

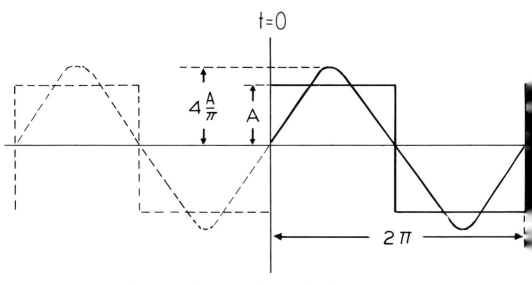

Figure 8.4B   Sin (ωt) as a first approximation to a square-wave.

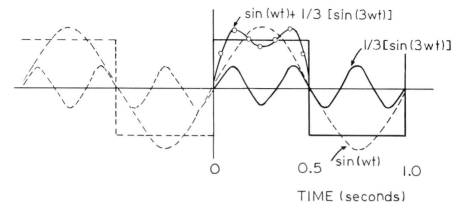

Figure 8.4C   Sin $(\omega t) + \frac{1}{3}[\sin (3\omega t)]$ as a second approximation to a square-wave.

summed together will describe the square wave as accurately as necessary. The summing is special in the following manner:

(a) Initial amplitude of the fundamental frequency is: $4\left(\dfrac{A}{\pi}\right)$.

(b) Remaining amplitudes are: $\dfrac{4A}{(2N-1)\pi}$ or initial amplitude divided

by the harmonic number. Thus:

$$F(t) = \frac{4A}{\pi}\left[\; \sin (\omega t) + \frac{\sin 3 \;\omega t}{3} + \frac{\sin 5 \;\omega t}{5} \cdots \right.$$
$$\left. \cdots \frac{\sin [(2n-1)\omega T]}{2n-1} \right] \qquad (8.4\text{--}1)$$

for as many iterations as is desired for the required accuracy. The usual introduction to Fourier series requires the student to laboriously compute and plot several iterations of Equation (8.4–1). It would be more instructive if he were taught to program these simple steps, and then manipulate the program for several types of wave forms. Even the use of a prepared Fourier program in a computer experiment would be of a more lasting experience. Several assignments could be expanded based upon the technique used in Program 8.4, e.g., several even functions, odd functions, combined functions, and finally the analysis by numerical integration of the outline of a beach or the face of a pretty girl.

Computer Techniques: Equation (8.4–1) combined with a TAB plot will make a very simple program with which to begin the study of waveforms. Equation (8.4–1) is summed by calculating the sin (θ) at a particular angle and adding to it the sin $(3\theta)/3$, sin $(5\theta)/5$ . . . etc. at the same angle. Once the value of the function at the particular angle is summed, it is plotted. The angle is then incremented and the summing and plotting operation is repeated. The problem is finished when one cycle has been plotted. An angle increment of $10°$ has been chosen giving 36 calculations for one cycle of the fundamental frequency.

Comments About the Computer Program: The main working portion of Program 8.4, is the summing operation:

$$160 \quad \text{FOR } I = 1 \text{ TO } 2*N-1 \text{ STEP } 2$$

$$170 \quad \text{LET } F = F + \text{SIN}(I*K)/I \qquad \text{(Summing Loop)}$$

$$180 \quad \text{NEXT } I$$

which is in fact Equation (8.4–1) with unity magnitude; for a particular angle, K. The secondary operation is the plotting routine:

$$190 \quad \text{LET } F = 4*F/P \qquad \text{(Amplitude Factor}$$

$$200 \quad \text{LET } F = \text{INT}(20*F+.5)+36 \qquad \text{(Scaling Factor)}$$

$$210 \quad \text{PRINT J; TAB(F); ``*''} \qquad \text{(Plot)}$$

These operations are both enclosed within the large angle incrementing loop, 140 to 220. The function initial value *must* be reset to zero (statement 150) prior to each summing loop regardless of the kind of computer used. Statements 110 and 120 could be changed to an INPUT statement if the program were to be used for demonstration.

Discussion of Computer Results: Figure 8.4D shows the fundamental sine wave for when the value of N, (the number of terms of Equation 8.4–1), is equal to one. The partial plot of Figure 8.4C is completed, by the computer in Figure 8.4E when $N=2$ and the third harmonic frequency is added to the fundamental. Figures 8.4F and 8.4G show the increased square wave approximations as the number of terms, N, is increased. Many additional examples can be assigned as homework after the particular theory has been investigated.

```
100   REM *******************FOURIER ANALYSIS*******************
110   INPUT N
130   PRINT "                    PRESSURE IN NEWTONS/METER??"
135   PRINT "DEGREES -------------------------------0---------------"
140   FOR J = 0 TO 360 STEP 10
150   LET F = 0
155   LET K = J/57.3
160   FOR I = 1 TO 2*N-1 STEP 2
170   LET F = F + SIN(I*K)/I
180   NEXT I
190   LET F = INT(20*F + .5) + 36
210   PRINT J; TAB(F); "*"
220   NEXT J
230   PRINT
240   PRINT " NUMBER OF TERMS = ";N
250   END
```

PROGRAM 8.4.   Fourier Analysis: Production of square-waves

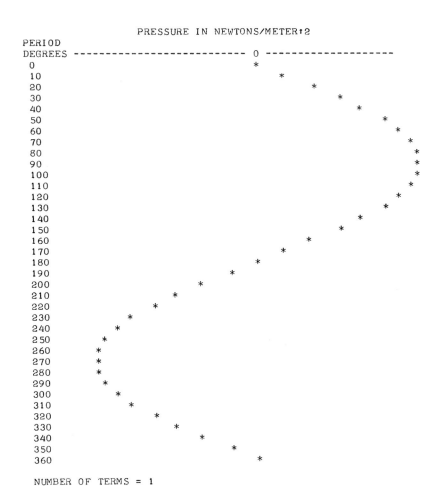

Figure 8.4D.   Pressure Pulse: Graphical results of first approximation to a square-wave.

2

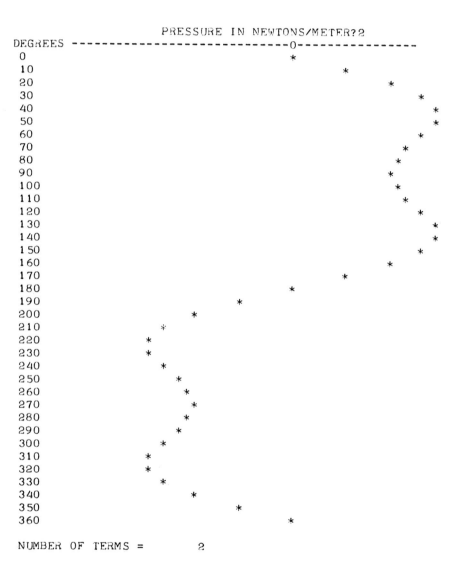

Figure 8.4E. Pressure Pulse: Graphical results of second approximation to a square-wave.

PRESSURE IN NEWTONS/METER↑2

```
PERIOD
DEGREES --------------------------- 0 --------------------
  0                                   *
 10                                           *
 20                                                  *
 30                                                     *
 40                                                  *
 50                                           *
 60                                        *
 70                                           *
 80                                           *
 90                                              *
100                                              *
110                                        *
120                                     *
130                                        *
140                                           *
150                                              *
160                                           *
170                                     *
180                     *
190               *
200          *
210        *
220         *
230            *
240             *
250            *
260          *
270         *
280          *
290           *
300            *
310           *
320          *
330        *
340          *
350              *
360                     *
```

NUMBER OF TERMS = 3

Figure 8.4F. Pressure Pulse: Graphical results´ of third approximation to a square-wave.

PRESSURE IN NEWTONS/METER↑2

```
PERIOD
DEGREES -------------------------- 0 --------------------
   0                                      *
  10                                                  *
  20                                                       *
  30                                                *
  40                                             *
  50                                                  *
  60                                                  *
  70                                              *
  80                                                *
  90                                                 *
 100                                                *
 110                                              *
 120                                                 *
 130                                                 *
 140                                             ⸜
 150                                              *
 160                                                   *
 170                                              *
 180                                  *
 190              *
 200         *
 210              *
 220               *
 230            *
 240            *
 250             *
 260            *
 270           *
 280            *
 290             *
 300           *
 310           *
 320              *
 330            *
 340         *
 350            *
 360                               *
```

NUMBER OF TERMS = 5

Figure 8.4G.   Pressure Pulse: Graphical results of fifth approximation to a square-wave.

8.5   DISCHARGING CAPACITOR I (RC1)

Lesson Characteristics:

ENGINEERING LEVEL   college, introductory

MATHEMATICS BACKGROUND REQUIRED   analytical geometry

PEDAGOGY   computer learning

PROBLEM APPROACH   numerical method

STUDENT PARTICIPATION   assists in program writing

PROGRAMMING SKILLS   introductory BASIC

TIME OF STUDENT INVOLVEMENT   in class—30 minutes, out of class—1.5 hours

RECOMMENDED READING   (18) Section 7.1–7.5, (19) Chapter 13, Section 10 and 11, (3) Chapter 30, Sec. 1, Chapter 32, Sec. 5

Lesson Description: In this section, a problem involving the exponential process of a discharging capacitor will be analyzed with basic definitions of charge, current and potential, in incremental rather than the differential form. This non-calculus approach to a familiar engineering process is: (1) easily understood, (2) meaningful, (3) allows numerical methods to be successfully applied by the non-calculus student, and (4) gives the calculus student a clearer understanding of the final results obtained from the analytical solution (if one can be found).

The method used is the simple Euler's method in a student written program, the output of which will show the student: (1) the step by step relationship between charge and current in an example problem; (2) the comparison of the simple Euler method to the analytical solution, and (3) the value of the initial slope in order to relate the time-constant to problem parameters.

Background and Theory: The discharging of a capacitor, or the emptying of a tank of water both require the solution to a simple differential equation. The student learns the mechanics of solving these types of problems from the mathematics department. He often cannot relate this process to the varied basic principles required in the many engineering fields, or he works with the basic principles in the engineering department before he has had the mathematical background to make the analytical solutions.

If the student were required to write simple steps using the basic principles in a manner similar to this program, he would obtain meaningful results prior to being able to compute the analytical solution. The circuit of Figure 8.5A showing a capacitor being discharged from a charged condi-

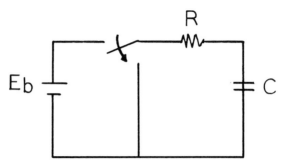

Figure 8.5A   Initially charged RC circuit at the instant the switch is thrown for discharge. $Q_0 = EC$.

tion will be the first example. The basic definitions the student (engineer) has to work with are:

(1) Current $(I) = \dfrac{\text{change of charge}}{\text{change of time}}$, i.e., the instantaneous current is approximately

$$I = \Delta Q / \Delta T \qquad (8.5\text{--}1)$$

(2) The potential across a capacitor is

$$V_c = Q / C \qquad (8.5\text{--}2)$$

(3) Ohms Law

$$V_R = RI \qquad (8.5\text{--}3)$$

The problem statement could be to calculate the amount of:

(a) Charge left on the capacitor at any time after discharge.
(b) Current flowing through the system with respect to time.

Using Kirchoff's voltage law, the voltage equation for the circuit is:

$$V_R + V_C = 0 = R\Delta Q / \Delta T + Q / C$$

from Equations (8.5–1, 2, and 3):

$$I = \Delta Q / \Delta T = -Q / (RC) \qquad (8.5\text{--}4)$$

The value, I for current, can be thought of as the slope of the curve of Q versus T at a certain time, T. From the relations just presented, this would mean that if there was a curve Q versus T, that $\Delta Q / \Delta T$ would be the slope of curve Q at a specified time, T, (Figure 8.5B).

Computer Technique: By using small increments of time, the student may see a microscopic view of how the problem behaves when the governing equations are applied in small increments.
From Equation (8.5–4),

$$\Delta Q = -Q\Delta T / (RC) \qquad (8.5\text{--}5)$$

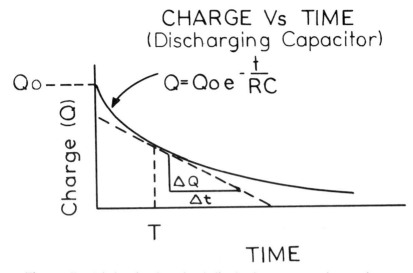

CHARGE Vs TIME
(Discharging Capacitor)

Figure 8.5B Discharging Capacitor indicating instantaneous slope at time, T.

If the charge on a capacitor at an instant of time, T is Q and a small time, Δt, later the charge has changed by ΔQ, then the total charge at time $t+\Delta t$ will be:

$$Q_{T+\Delta T}=Q_T+\Delta Q \qquad (8.5\text{–}6)$$

where ΔQ is defined by Equation (8.5–5). The initial charge of circuit 8.5A is from Equation (8.4–2), $Q_0=E_bC$. Equations (8.5–5) and (8.5–6) can be iterated, using the initial charge as a starting value, with very few steps:

Therefore

$$Q=E_bC \qquad \text{(Initial Condition)}$$

$$\text{LET } Q9=-Q*T1/(R*C) \qquad \text{(Equation 8.5–5)}$$

$$\text{LET } Q\ =Q+Q9 \qquad \text{(Equation 8.5–6)}$$

$$\text{LET } T\ =T+T1 \qquad \text{(Summation of Time)}$$

$$\text{PRINT } Q,\ T \qquad \text{(Print answers)}$$

It was observed by Equation (8.5–4), that the current (I) at any time could be solved in terms of the charge at that time, i.e.,

$$I=-Q/RC$$

$$\text{LET } I=-Q/(R*C) \qquad (8.5\text{–}7)$$

where Equation (8.5–7) is the slope of Equation (8.5–5). Equation (8.5–6) can now be written:

$$Q_{T+\Delta T}=Q_T+I\Delta T \qquad (8.5\text{–}8)$$

According to this equation, the charge at the end of an interval is equal to the charge at the beginning of an interval plus the slope over the interval times the time increment of the interval. In computer summations this statement is written:

$$\text{LET} \quad Q = Q + I*T1 \qquad (8.5\text{--}9)$$

Equations (8.5–7) and (8.5–9) can now be iterated to produce both charge and current; i.e.,

```
130   LET Q=E*C              (initial condition)
140   LET I=-Q/(R*C)  (Equation 8.5-7, begin loop)
160   LET Q=Q+I*T1            (Equation 8.5-9)
180   LET T=T+T1
190   PRINT T, Q, I
```

The smaller the time increment, T1, the more accurate the solution.

The student can be introduced to this method by having him calculate and plot a series of these steps. If this plot is saved, it can be compared to other numerical methods which will be considered.

The calculations will be demonstrated for a problem with $E_b = 10$ volts, $R = 10$ ohms, $c = 0.01$ farads, and $\Delta T = .01$ sec.: (ΔT must be less than .1 seconds since the value of RC is .1 seconds and the first value of Q would be zero for $\Delta T = .1$ seconds.) $Q_0 = E_b C = 10 \times 0.01 = 0.1$ coulombs. $1/RC = 1/(10 \times 0.01) = 10$.

$$I_0 = -(Q/(RC))$$
$$= -(.1 \times 10) = -1 \qquad \text{initial slope}$$
$$Q_1 = Q_0 + I_0 T \qquad (\Delta t < RC)$$
$$= E_b C - Q_0/(RC)\Delta T$$
$$= .1 - 1 \times .01 = .09$$
$$I_1 = -.09 \times 10 = -.9$$
$$Q_2 = .09 - .9 \times .01 = .081,$$

etc.

The values are tabulated in Table 8.5A and plotted on Figure 8.5C. This numerical method is called Euler's Method.

TIME	CHARGE	CURRENT
0	.1	−1
.01	.09	−.9
.02	.081	−.81
.03	.0729	−.729
.04	.06461	−.6461
. .	. .	. .
. .	. .	. .
. .	. .	. .

TABLE 8.5A. Hand Calculated Data for Demonstrating the Euler Method of Differential Equation Solution.

```
100 REM *********************************RC1****************************
110 INPUT E,R,C,T1
120 PRINT"TIME","CHARGE","CURRENT"
130 LET Q = E*C
140 LET I = -Q/(R*C)
150 PRINT T,Q,I
160 LET Q = Q + I*T1
170 LET I = -Q/(R*C)
180 LET T = T + T1
190 PRINT T, Q, I
200 IF T>=10*T1 THEN 220
210 GOTO 160
220 STOP
```

PROGRAM 8.5A.   Simple Euler (Discharging Capacitor).

Comments About the Computer Program: Program 8.5A does this same work under program control. The iterations and summations of Q, T, and the calculations of I are produced by the loop of statements 160 to 210. The program is stopped arbitrarily by statement 200 after 10 loops. The accuracy of this method can be checked by comparing it to the analytic solution:

$$Q = Q_o e^{-t/RC} \qquad (8.5\text{–}10)$$

The program can be changed to include this theoretical value by adding a new statement, 182, following the time summation, and changing the print statements 120, 150, and 190. These changes are shown in Program 8.5B.

Discussion of Computer Results: The data of Table 8.5C is plotted in Figure 8.5C, showing the differences between the simple Euler method and the analytical solution. Considerable information is expressed to the student by studying Table 8.5C and Figure 8.5C, i.e.,

(1) Initial slope intersects the time axis when the value of time is equal to RC, the time-constant of the circuit.
(2) Current is proportional to charge.
(3) The approximate percentage change in initial conditions, with respect to time, especially at that point where time is equal to RC, or one time-constant.

```
100 REM *********************************RC1****************************
110 INPUT E,R,C,T1
120 PRINT"TIME","CHARGE","EULERS","CURRENT"
130 LET Q = E*C
140 LET I = -Q/(R*C)
150 PRINT T, Q, Q, I
160 LET Q = Q + I*T1
170 LET I = -Q/(R*C)
180 LET T = T + T1
182 LET Q1 = E*C*EXP(-T/(R*C))
190 PRINT T, Q1, Q, I
200 IF T>=10*T1 THEN 220
210 GOTO 160
220 STOP
```

PROGRAM 8.5B.   Program 8.5A with theoretical values added.

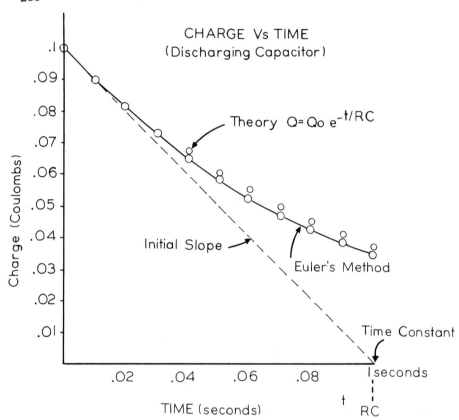

Figure 8.5C   Discharging Capacitor Plot, comparing Theory to the Euler method.

? 10,? 10,? .01,? .01

TIME	CHARGE	CURRENT
0	0.1	-1
0.01	0.09	-0.9
0.02	0.081	-0.81
0.03	0.0729	-0.729
0.04	0.06561	-0.6561
0.05	0.059049	-0.59049
0.06	0.0531441	-0.531441
0.07	0.04782969	-0.4782969
0.08	0.043046721	-0.43046721
0.09	0.038742049	-0.387420489
0.1	0.034867844	-0.34867844
0.11	0.03138106	-0.313810596

TABLE 8.5B.

```
? 10,? 10,? .01,? .01
TIME              CHARGE              EULERS              CURRENT
0                 0.1                 0.1                 -1
0.01              0.090483742         0.09                -0.9
0.02              0.081873075         0.081               -0.81
0.03              0.074081822         0.0729              -0.729
0.04              0.067032005         0.06561             -0.6561
0.05              0.060653066         0.059049            -0.59049
0.06              0.054881164         0.0531441           -0.531441
0.07              0.04965853          0.04782969          -0.4782969
0.08              0.044932896         0.043046721         -0.43046721
0.09              0.040656966         0.038742049         -0.387420489
0.1               0.036787944         0.034867844         -0.34867844
0.11              0.033287108         0.03138106          -0.313810596
```

TABLE 8.5C.

8.6 DISCHARGING CAPACITOR II (RC2)

Lesson Characteristics:

ENGINEERING LEVEL   college, introductory

MATHEMATICS BACKGROUND REQUIRED   analytical geometry

PEDAGOGY   computer learning and simulation

PROBLEM APPROACH   numerical method

STUDENT PARTICIPATION   assists in program writing

PROGRAMMING SKILLS   introductory BASIC

TIME OF STUDENT INVOLVEMENT   in class—10 minutes, out of class—30 minutes
(based upon understanding of Section 8.5)

Lesson Description: The tenat of Section 8.5 remains the same for this section. A dramatic improvement over the results of Section 8.5 result from the use of the improved Euler's or second order Runge-Kutta method, by making a relatively easy change to Program 8.5B.

Background and Theory: The simple Euler Method of the last section was satisfactory for demonstration of basic principles, but the accuracy was not as good as could be plotted by hand. The method of this section is a substantial improvement and is often called a second order Runge-Kutta method. The Runge-Kutta method described in Chapter Five was a fourth order method and will be easily understood after investigating this problem.

The Runge-Kutta methods utilize a weighted average for the slope of the curve, over the interval. The Euler method used the initial slope of each interval as the predictor for the value of the curve at the end of the interval. The improved Euler's method simply averages the initial slope and final slope of the interval, and uses this weighted slope to predict the value of the curve at the end of the interval, i.e.

$$y = mx + b$$

where m is the weighted, average slope over the interval.

Computer Technique: For Program 8.6A, I0 will be the initial slope of the interval, and I1 the slope at the end of the interval. The average slope over the interval is then $I = (I0 + I1)/2$, and the charge at the end of the interval becomes the initial charge, plus the slope (I), times the time increment, i.e.,

$$LET\ Q = Q + I*T1$$

The changes to Program 8.5B are:

140 LET I0 = −Q/(R*C)

150 PRINT T, Q, Q, I0

160 LET I1 = (Q+I0*T1)/(R*C)

170 LET I = (I0+I1)/2

172 LET Q = Q+I*T1

174 LET I0 = −Q/(R*C)

190 PRINT T, Q1, Q, I0

200 IF T+T1 > 10*T1 THEN 220

It was necessary to calculate the initial current (slope) before entering the loop, (statement 140) and again after entering the loop (statement 174) but after calculating the charge (statement 172). This allows the calculation of the corrected initial slope for the next interval. This initial value of current is the instantaneous value rather than the average current over the interval, therefore subscript changes in the print statements were made to be I0 vice, I. The accuracy has been very much improved with

```
100 REM ********************************RC2***************************
110 INPUT E,R,C,T1
120 PRINT"TIME","CHARGE","EULERS","CURRENT"
130 LET Q = E*C
140 LET I0 = -Q/(R*C)
150 PRINT T, Q, Q, I0
160 LET I1 = -(Q + I0*T1)/(R*C)
170 LET I = (I0 + I1)/2
172 LET Q = Q + I*T1
174 LET I0 = -Q/(R*C)
180 LET T = T + T1
182 LET Q1 = E*C*EXP(-T/(R*C))
190 PRINT T, Q1, Q, I0
200 IF T + T1>10*T1 THEN 220
210 GOTO 160
220 STOP
```

PROGRAM 8.6A.   Improved Euler (or Second order Runge Kutta)

this method, making it very difficult, if not impossible, to tell the difference on the graph of Figure 8.5C from the theoretical value.

Comments About the Computer Program: Computer Program 8.6A is still a relatively simple program having only minor changes to Program 8.5B. Line 120 could just as correctly had the word "EULERS" replaced by; "2ND RUNGE," as a title for the numerical method of calculating charge.

Discussion of Computer Results: Table 8.6A shows considerable improvement in the results as compared to the values in Table 8.5C. The accuracy is within slide-rule limits and therefore adequate for most engineering applications. Note, particularly, the comparison of values after one time constant, 0.1 seconds. The student should become familiar with the basic engineering principles if he is able to program, run, observe and interpret the results of this type of program.

It is interesting to note that if ΔT, $(T1)$, had been selected as .1 seconds for the Program 8.5B, the value of Q at the end of the first iteration would have been zero. However, using the method of Program 8.6A, the value would have been:

$$Q_0 = .1$$
$$I_0 = -1$$
$$I_1 = -(Q_0 + I_0 T)/(RC) = (-.1 + .1)/10 = 0$$
$$I = (-1 + 0)/2 = -.5 \text{ (average over the interval)}$$

and

$$Q_1 = .1 - .5 \times .1 = .05$$

This value is much closer to the true value, .0368, than it is to zero. The smaller the time interval the closer the numerical answer will be to the analytical answer. It would be helpful for the student to make several iterations for a time interval equal to the "time-constant" of the circuit.

? 10,? 10,? .01,? .01

TIME	CHARGE	EULERS	CURRENT
0	0.1	0.1	-1
0.01	0.090483742	0.0905	-0.905
0.02	0.081873075	0.0819025	-0.819025
0.03	0.074081822	0.074121762	-0.741217625
0.04	0.067032005	0.067080195	-0.670801951
0.05	0.060653066	0.060707577	-0.607075765
0.06	0.054881164	0.054940357	-0.549403568
0.07	0.04965853	0.049721023	-0.497210229
0.08	0.044932896	0.044997526	-0.449975257
0.09	0.040656966	0.040722761	-0.407227608
0.1	0.036787944	0.036854098	-0.368540985

TABLE 8.6A.

Close inspection of the last line of data in Tables 8.5C and 8.6A will reveal that Program 8.6A stopped after 10 iterations, while Program 8.5B stopped after 11 iterations. Statement 200 has been changed in Program 8.6A to read

200 IF T+T1>10*T1 THEN 220 vice

200 IF T>=10*T1 THEN 220 of Program 8.5B.

This was caused by T being slightly less than 0.1 seconds on the 10th iteration of summing T in statement 180. This error is called the "round-off" error, because decimal notation of most fractions becomes a continuing binary fraction. The computer simply carries the binary fraction to as many significant figures as possible, and then, rounds it off. Therefore, when adding 0.01 seconds many times, the sum becomes something slightly less than an integer times 0.01 seconds. Statement 200 of Program 8.6A protects the decision from this round off error.

In other programs where the accuracy of the results could be affected, the round off error is avoided by using the integer (INT) command, e.g., if T+T1 is greater than an integer times T, then T+.5 is given the INT command, i.e.,

LET T=INT(T+.5).

In case T is less than a whole number of seconds, the command is:

LET T=INT(J*T+.5)/J

where J is a number, specified by the programmer, which is large enough to make the temporary number, J*T, greater than (or approximately) one. Dividing by the J puts the time back to the correct decimal place again. This correction will be made in future programs when required.

8.7 DISCHARGING CAPACITOR III

Lesson Characteristics:

ENGINEERING LEVEL   college, intermediate

MATHEMATICS BACKGROUND REQUIRED   analytical geometry

PEDAGOGY   computer learning and simulation

PROBLEM APPROACH   numerical method

STUDENT PARTICIPATION   assists in program writing

PROGRAMMING SKILLS   introductory BASIC

TIME OF STUDENT INVOLVEMENT   in class—20 minutes, out of class—45 minutes

RECOMMENDED READING   Same as Section 8.5

Lesson Description: The last two sections show progressively more accurate numerical solutions to the exponential process. This section demonstrates the third and fourth order Runge-Kutta methods of solving this type of problem. The fourth order Runge-Kutta is a powerful method which can be used: (1) on more complex problems, (2) with an assurance that basic principles and definitions will be reinforced, and (3) to show a dramatic improvement in accuracy over the methods used in Sections 8.5 and 8.6.

Background and Theory: The second order Runge-Kutta method used the average slope of the initial and final slope over an interval. The third order Runge-Kutta uses the slope at the beginning, the end, and at the mid-time point, to weight the average slope over the interval. The slope at the mid-point is weighted by a factor of four, while the slope at the beginning and end of each interval is weighted once each. The fourth order Runge-Kutta is the same as the third order except it takes two slopes at the mid-point, one based upon the initial slope, and the other based upon the predicted value of the slope previously calculated. A pictoral diagram of this procedure is shown in Figures 5.2 and 6.5A on the discussion of the Runge-Kutta methods. The fourth order Runge-Kutta reduces to the third order Runge-Kutta if the variable is only dependent upon time (Figure 6.5B). In the present problem, the slope is dependent upon the value of charge, making it possible to demonstrate both the third and fourth order Runge-Kutta methods.

Computer Technique: The strategy will be to use as much of Program 8.6A as possible. In the previous program, I0 and I1 were calculated in order to find the average current over the interval. In this case, I1, I2, (the mid-time slopes) will be calculated in addition to I_0 and I_3 (the slopes at the beginning and end of the time interval). The initial slope, I0, and charge Q0, will remain the same. The changes will be:

160 LET I1 = $-$ (Q+I0*T1/2)/(R*C)   (Start of Loop)

164 LET I2 = $-$ (Q+I1*T1/2)/(R*C)

166 LET I3 = $-$ (Q+I2*T1)/(R*C)

170 LET I = (I0+2*I1+2*I2+I2)/6

172 LET Q = Q+I*T1   (Start of Loop)

174 LET I0 = $-$ Q/(R*C)   (Start of Loop)

Comments About the Computer Program: Program 8.7A, (RC4) shows the changes to Program 8.6A in statements 160 through 174. In order to change Program 8.7A into a third order Runge-Kutta Program 8.7B, it is necessary to delete I2 in statement 164, replace I2 in statement 166 with I1, and multiply I1 by four in statement 170, i.e.,

166 LET I3 = $-$ (Q+I1*T1)/(R*C)

170 LET I = (I0+4*I1+I3)/6

```
100 REM *************************RC4************************
110 INPUT E,R,C,T1
120 PRINT"TIME","CHARGE","4TH RUNGE","CURRENT"
130 LET Q = E*C
140 LET I0 = -Q/(R*C)
150 PRINT T, Q4 Q, I0
160 LET I1 = -(Q + I0*T1/2)/(R*C)
164 LET I2 = -(Q + I1*T1/2)/(R*C)
166 LET I3 = -(Q + I2*T1)/(R*C)
170 LET I = (I0 +2*I1 + 2*I2 + I3)/6
172 LET Q = Q + I*T1
174 LET I0 = -Q/(R*C)
180 LET T = T + T1
182 LET Q1 = E*C*EXP(-T/(R*C))
190 PRINT T, Q1, Q, I0
200 IF T + T1>10*T1 THEN 220
210 GOTO 160
220 STOP
```

PROGRAM 8.7A.   Fourth order Runge Kutta

Discussion of Computer Results: A comparison between Tables 8.6A, 8.7A, and 8.7B reveals the steady progression of accuracy from the second, third and fourth order Runge-Kutta methods. It is interesting to note that the accuracy of the fourth order Runge-Kutta method taken with a time increment of one time constant, (.1 second), is almost as good as the improved Euler method taken with 10 intervals between one time-constant, (Table 8.6A and 8.7B).

The method of programming has been to emphasize clarity at the cost of speed and efficiency. The simplicity of the methods will encourage students and teachers to try their hand at a computer solution. Some of the things that could be done to improve program efficiency and utility are shown in Program 8.7C, which is a fourth order Runge-Kutta method. There, the print interval is selectable as long as it is an integer times the time increment. It also precomputes all of the constants utilized in the loop, making many fewer calculations during the loop. Time is corrected for round-off error prior to each print cycle, instructions are given on how to enter data, and the data is read in from a data list instead of being inputed at the time of program execution. The error is also calculated and the data

```
100 REM *************************RC3************************
110 INPUT E,R,C,T1
120 PRINT"TIME","CHARGE","3RD RUNGE","CURRENT"
130 LET Q = E*C
140 LET I0 = -Q/(R*C)
150 PRINT T, Q4 Q, I0
160 LET I1 = -(Q + I0*T1/2)/(R*C)
166 LET I3 = -(Q + I1*T1)/(R*C)
170 LET I = (I0 + 4*I1 + I3)/6
172 LET Q = Q + I*T1
174 LET I0 = -Q/(R*C)
180 LET T = T + T1
182 LET Q1 = E*C*EXP(-T/(R*C))
190 PRINT T, Q1, Q4 I0
200 IF T + T1>10*T1 THEN 220
210 GOTO 160
220 STOP
```

PROGRAM 8.7B.   Third order Runge Kutta.

```
100 REM ****************DISCHARGING CAPACITOR 4***********************
110 GOTO 490
120 READ E, R, C, T1, C9
130 IF C9<T1 THEN 470
140 LET T2 = T1*.5
150 LET T3 = -1/(R*C)
160 LET T4 = .166666667*T1
170 IF T1>-1/T3 THEN 440
180 LET Q0 = E*C
190 LET Q0 = E*C
200 PRINT
210 PRINT"TIME","CHARGE","4TH RUNGE","ERROR"
220 PRINT
240 LET J = 1
250 LET Q = Q0
260 PRINT T, Q, Q, 0
270 LET P0 = Q*T3
280 LET P1 = (Q+T2*P0)*T3
290 LET P2 = (Q+T2*P1)*T3
300 LET P3 = (Q+T1*P2)*T3
310 LET Q = Q+T4*(P0+2*P1+2*P2+P3)
320 LET T = T+T1
330 IF T+T1>=J*C9 THEN 350
340 GOTO 270
350 LET T = INT(T/C9+.5)*C9
360 LET J = J+1
370 LET Q1 = Q0*EXP(T*T3)
380 LET E9 = (Q1-Q)/Q1
390 PRINT T, Q1, Q, E9
400 IF T>-4/T3 THEN 420
410 GOTO 270
420 PRINT"YOU HAVE CALCULATED THROUGH 4 TIME CONSTANTS."
430 STOP
440 PRINT
450 PRINT"DELTA T IS GREATER THAN ONE TIME CONSTANT. TRY ANOTHER."
460 STOP
470 PRINT"PRINT INTERVAL LESS THAN DELTA T. TRY ANOTHER."
480 STOP
490 PRINT
500 PRINT"USE DATA AS FOLLOWS:"
510 PRINT"110 DATA E,R,C,T1(DELTA T),C9(TIME PRINT INTERVAL)"
520 END
```

PROGRAM 8.7C. Fourth order Runge Kutta with diagnostics

? 10,? 10,? .01,? .01

TIME	CHARGE	4TH RUNGE	CURRENT
0	0.1	0.1	-1
0.01	0.090483742	0.09048375	-0.9048375
0.02	0.081873075	0.08187309	-0.818730901
0.03	0.074081822	0.074081842	-0.740818422
0.04	0.067032005	0.067032029	-0.670320289
0.05	0.060653066	0.060653093	-0.606530934
0.06	0.054881164	0.054881193	-0.548811934
0.07	0.04965853	0.049658562	-0.496585619
0.08	0.044932896	0.044932929	-0.44932929
0.09	0.040656966	0.040656999	-0.406569991
0.1	0.036787944	0.036787977	-0.367879774

TABLE 8.7A.

? 1∅,? 1∅,? .∅1,? .∅1

TIME	CHARGE	3RD RUNGE	CURRENT
∅	∅.1	∅.1	-1
∅.∅1	∅.∅9∅483742	∅.∅9∅491667	-∅.9∅4916667
∅.∅2	∅.∅81873∅75	∅.∅81887417	-∅.818874174
∅.∅3	∅.∅74∅81822	∅.∅741∅1289	-∅.741∅12888
∅.∅4	∅.∅67∅32∅∅5	∅.∅67∅55491	-∅.67∅554912
∅.∅5	∅.∅6∅653∅66	∅.∅6∅679632	-∅.6∅6796316
∅.∅6	∅.∅54881164	∅.∅5491∅∅1	-∅.5491∅∅1
∅.∅7	∅.∅4965853	∅.∅49688983	-∅.496889832
∅.∅8	∅.∅44932896	∅.∅44964389	-∅.44964389
∅.∅9	∅.∅4∅656966	∅.∅4∅689∅25	-∅.4∅689∅25
∅.1	∅.∅36787944	∅.∅3682∅177	-∅.3682∅1769

TABLE 8.7B.

shows the closeness of the solution between the analytical and numerical solution. The procedure for entering the data is shown in Table 8.7C, and the program is run twice to demonstrate how the program holds the data once it is entered.

USE DATA AS FOLLOWS:
110 DATA E,R,C,T1(DELTA T),C9(TIME PRINT INTERVAL)

>110 DATA 10, 10, .01, .01, .1
>RUN

TIME	CHARGE	4TH RUNGE	ERROR
0	0.1	0.1	0
0.1	0.036787944	0.036787977	-9.03748072E-07
0.2	0.013533528	0.013533553	-1.80746867E-06
0.3	4.97870684E-03	4.97872033E-03	-2.71120483E-06
0.4	1.83156389E-03	1.83157051E-03	-3.61493998E-06

YOU HAVE CALCULATED THROUGH 4 TIME CONSTANTS.

>RUN

TIME	CHARGE	4TH RUNGE	ERROR
0	0.1	0.1	0
0.1	0.036787944	0.036787977	-9.03748072E-07
0.2	0.013533528	0.013533553	-1.80746867E-06
0.3	4.97870684E-03	4.97872033E-03	-2.71120483E-06
0.4	1.83156389E-03	1.83157051E-03	-3.61493998E-06

YOU HAVE CALCULATED THROUGH 4 TIME CONSTANTS.

TABLE 8.7C.

8.8 CHARGING CAPACITOR

Lesson Characteristics:

ENGINEERING LEVEL   college, intermediate

MATHEMATICS BACKGROUND REQUIRED   analytical geometry

PEDAGOGY   computer learning and simulation

PROBLEM APPROACH   numerical method

STUDENT PARTICIPATION   assists in program writing

PROGRAMMING SKILLS   introductory BASIC

TIME OF STUDENT INVOLVEMENT   in class—5 minutes, out of class—30 minutes

RECOMMENDED READING   Same as Section 8.5

Lesson Description: This lesson demonstrates a slightly different and more difficult problem than those presented in the previous three sections. Both the simple Euler and fourth order Runge-Kutta are shown as well as a simple plot subroutine for plotting instead of printing the results.

Background and Theory: The theory presented in Sections 8.5 through 8.7 is applicable to this problem. The student could easily be given this problem as a homework assignment after having learned the methods of any of the previously mentioned sections.

The charging capacitor problem (Figure 8.8A), is more difficult to analyze than the discharging capacitor, in that there is now a driving function, E_b, in the circuit during the time the analysis is being done. The initial conditions at the instant the switch is thrown are:

$$Q_0 = 0$$

$$I_0 = E_b/R$$

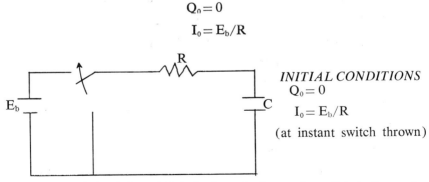

INITIAL CONDITIONS
$$Q_0 = 0$$
$$I_0 = E_b/R$$
(at instant switch thrown)

FIG. 8.8A Initially discharged RC circuit at the instant the switch is thrown for charging. $I_0 = E/R$.

The Kirchoff voltage equation is:

$$E_b = IR + Q/C \qquad (8.8-1)$$

The basic definitions are the same as they were for the discharging capacitor, and the Equation (8.8–1) could be written as:

$$I = E_b/R = Q/RC$$

$$\text{LET } I = E/R - Q/(R*C) \qquad (8.8-2)$$

The charge on the capacitor will increase (instead of decrease), or change, each time increment:

$$Q_{n+1} = Q_n + I \ t$$

$$\text{LET } Q = Q + I*T1$$

In this problem, the plot of charge and current appear as opposites, the current will start out large, and end up small, and the charge will start out small and end up large.

Computer Technique: The following changes will be made to Program 8.5B, in order to demonstrate the Euler method:

130 LET Q=0   (This statement can be deleted, since most computers set all variables to zero before running.)

140 LET I=E/R   (Prior to Loop)

170 LET I=E/R−Q/(R*C)   (Equation 8.8–2)

182 LET Q1=E*C*(1-EXP(−T/(R*C)))
                  (Analytical Solution)

Program 8.8A will allow similar calculations to made by the Euler method as were made for the discharging capacitor (Program 8.5B). To plot the data instead of printing it, add the following:

112 PRINT" Q=0," "TO", "MAX OF" E*C

114 PRINT" I="0 "TO", "MAX OF" E/R

116 LET Q9=55/(E*C)   (Scale Factor)

118 LET I9=55/(E*R)   (Scale Factor)

120 PRINT   "— — — — — — — — — — — —"

190 GOSUB 300

300 LET Q8=Q*Q9   (Scaled Charge)

310 LET I8=I*I9   (Scaled Current)

320 IF Q8<I8 THEN 350

330 PRINT T; TAB (I8); "I"; TAB(Q8); "Q"

```
100 REM ***************************RC5******************************
110 INPUT E,R,C,T1
120 PRINT"TIME","CHARGE","EULERS","CURRENT"
130 LET Q = 0
140 LET I = E/R
150 PRINT T, Q, Q, I
160 LET Q = Q + I*T1
170 LET I = E/R - Q/(R*C)
180 LET T = T + T1
182 LET Q1 = E*C*(1-EXP(-T/(R*C)))
190 PRINT T, Q1, Q, I
200 IF T + T1 > 10*T1 THEN 220
210 GOTO 160
220 STOP
```

PROGRAM 8.8A. Simple Euler (Charging capacitor)

340 RETURN

350 PRINT T; TAB (Q8); "Q"; TAB(I8); "I"

360 RETURN

Comments About the Computer Programs: Statements 300 to 360 are written as a plotting subroutine (Program 8.8B). A subroutine is most useful when it can be used in several different programs. The only changes to Program 8.8A needed to make it plot are the heading to the plot, and the scale factors. The statement number 190 is then replaced by the GOSUB command in order to plot. (Program 8.8C) The plot subroutine would be much simpler if only one variable were to be plotted.

In order to make Program 8.8C fit the fourth order Runge-Kutta, the following changes were made to Program 8.7A:

140 LET $I0 = E/R$

160 LET $I1 = E/R - (Q+I0*T1/2)/(R*C)$

164 LET $I2 = E/R - (Q+I1*T1/2)/(R*C)$

166 LET $I3 = E/R - (Q+I2*T1)/(R*C)$

174 LET $I0 = E/R - Q/(R*C)$

As in the discharge case, the initial slope is important in the analysis of this type of circuit. If three time-constants of data are plotted, the asymp-

```
300 LET Q8 = INT(Q*Q9) + 5
310 LET I8 = INT(I*I9 + 5
320 IF Q8 < I8 THEN 350
330 PRINT T; TAB(I8); "I"; TAB(Q8); "Q"
340 RETURN
350 PRINT T; TAB(Q8); "Q"; TAB(I8); "I"
360 RETURN
```

PROGRAM 8.8B. Plotting subroutine

```
100 REM **********************************RC5*******************************
110 INPUT E,R,C,T1
112 PRINT"Q = 0", "TO",,"MAX OF"E*C
114 PRINT"I = 0","TO",,"MAX OF"E/R
116 LET Q9 = 72/(E*C)
118 LET I9 = 72/(E/R)
120 PRINT"----------------------------------------------------------"
130 LET Q = 0
140 LET I = E/R
150 GOSUB 300
160 LET Q = Q + I*T1
170 LET I = E/R - Q/(R*C)
180 LET T = T + T1
182 LET Q1 = E*C*(1-EXP(-T/(R*C)))
190 GOSUB 300
200 IF T + T1 > 10*T1 THEN 220
210 GOTO 160
220 STOP
```

PROGRAM 8.8C.   Simple Euler using plot subroutine

totic value can be predicted. In the present problem the initial and final values are easily found without plotting the data.

Discussion of Computer Results: The error of the Euler Method is the same as for the discharging case. This is easiest to detect by comparing the current (I) values of Table 8.8A to Table 8.5C. The Program 8.8D was increased to 15 iterations in order to plot more than one time constant and show the need for displaying data. A close investigation of the plotting method described here should enable a plot of most anything desired.

```
100 REM **********************************RC6P******************************
110 INPUT E, R, C, T1
112 PRINT "Q = 0 ",,"TO","MAX OF"E*C
114 PRINT "I = 0",,"TO","MAX OF"E/R
116 LET Q9 = 55/(E*C)
118 LET I9 = 55/(E/R)
120 PRINT"   ----------------------------------------------------------"
130 LET I = E/R
140 LET I0 = E/R
150 GOSUB 300
160 LET I1 = E/R - (Q + I0*T1/2)/(R*C)
164 LET I2 = E/R - (Q + I1*T1/2)/(R*C)
166 LET I3 = E/R - (Q + I2*T1)/(R*C)
170 LET I = (I0 + 2*I1 + 2*I2 + I3)/6
172 LET Q = Q + I*T1
174 LET I0 = E/R - Q/(R*C)
180 LET T = T + T1
190 GOSUB 300
200 IF T + T1 > 15*T1 THEN 220
210 GOTO 160
220 STOP
```

PROGRAM 8.8D.   Fourth order Runge Kutta using Plot subroutine

```
10,? 10,? .01,? .01
Q = 0                TO                      MAX OF 0.1
I = 0                TO                      MAX OF 1
----------------------------------------------------------
 0 Q                                                        I
 0.01  Q                                                 I
 0.02      Q                                         I
 0.03          Q                                 I
 0.04            Q                           I
 0.05               Q                    I
 0.06                 Q    I
 0.07                I   Q
 0.08             I        Q
 0.09          I               Q
 0.1       I                      Q
```

Figure 8.8B.

```
? 10,? 10,? .01,? .01

Q = 0                        TO              MAX OF 0.1
I = 0                        TO              MAX OF 1
------------------------------------------------------------
 0   Q                                                        I
 0.01    Q                                                 I
 0.02       Q                                          I
 0.03          Q                                   I
 0.04            Q                             I
 0.05              Q                       I
 0.06                Q        I
 0.07               QI
 0.08            I     Q
 0.09          I         Q
 0.1        I              Q
 0.11      I                 Q
 0.12     I                    Q
 0.13    I                       Q
 0.14   I                          Q
 0.15  I                             Q
```

Figure 8.8C.

```
RUN
? 10,? 10,? .01,? .01
```

TIME	CHARGE	EULERS	CURRENT
0	0	0	1
0.01	0.009516258	0.01	0.9
0.02	0.018126925	0.019	0.81
0.03	0.025918178	0.0271	0.729
0.04	0.032967995	0.03439	0.6561
0.05	0.039346934	0.0409951	0.59049
0.06	0.045118836	0.0468559	0.531441
0.07	0.05034147	0.05217031	0.4782969
0.08	0.055067104	0.056953279	0.43046721
0.09	0.059343034	0.061257951	0.387420489
0.1	0.063212056	0.065132156	0.34867844

TABLE 8.8A.

8.9 DISCHARGING INDUCTIVE-RESISTIVE CIRCUITS

Lesson Characteristics:

ENGINEERING LEVEL   college, intermediate

MATHEMATICS BACKGROUND REQUIRED   analytical geometry

PEDAGOGY   computer learning and simulation

PROBLEM APPROACH   numerical method

STUDENT PARTICIPATION   assists in program writing

PROGRAMMING SKILLS   introductory BASIC

TIME OF STUDENT INVOLVEMENT   in class—10 minutes, out of class—30 minutes

RECOMMENDED READING   (18) Sections 7.1, 7.2, and 7.5
(19) Chapter 12, Sections 9–11

Lesson Description: This lesson demonstrates still another application of the exponential process and compares the analytical, Euler and fourth order Runge-Kutta methods of solution. If the student has a good understanding of the previous capacitor-resistor problems, this problem could be given as a homework assignment with a minimum of instructions. The problems of harmonic motion, i.e., damped, under damped, critically damped, forced, etc. can be studied as a continuation of this same type of problem solution method. Section 8.11 is an example of the more advanced problem.

Background and Theory: The analysis of the resistor-inductor circuit is similar to the resistor-capacitor circuit of the previous sections. The basic definition for the potential measured across an inductor is the inductance, L, times the rate of change of current through it. The increment form is:

$$E = L(\Delta I/\Delta T) \qquad (8.9\text{--}1)$$

In the case when the current is not changing; $\Delta I/\Delta T = 0$, at this time there will be no potential across the inductor. The rate at which current can change depends upon the circuit elements of the circuit. A large inductance with a rapid change of current, can cause a high value of potential across the inductor. Figure 8.9A is the circuit to be analyzed in this section. The current prior to throwing the switch is:

$$I = E/2R$$

$$\text{LET } I = E/(2*R) \text{ (The steady state value)} \qquad (8.9\text{--}2)$$

The current through the inductor immediately after throwing the switch must remain the same as that prior to throwing the switch. The terminology for the instant of throwing the switch is: Use a $(0-)$ for prior values and a $(0+)$ for values just after throwing the switch, e.g.,

$$I(0+)=I(0-) \qquad (8.9-3)$$

By Kirchoff's law, the potential values around the circuit for time, (0^+), are:

$$RI+L\ (\Delta I/\Delta T)=0 \qquad (8.9-4)$$

Solving for $\Delta I/\Delta T$;

$$\Delta I/\Delta T=-I\ R/L \qquad (8.9-5)$$

Therefore, the slope of the circuit current depends upon the value of current at any particular instant of time. In Program 8.9A, the instantaneous value of current will be compared by three methods:

$$I=I_0 e^{-tR/L}$$

$$I=I0*EXP(-T*R/L) \qquad \text{(Analytical)}$$

$$I1=\text{Simple Euler Method}$$

$$I2=\text{fourth order Runge-Kutta Method.}$$

Computer Technique: The symbol, P, will be used for the value of slope for both the Euler and Runge-Kutta methods. In computer terminology, Equation (8.9–4) becomes:

142 LET $PO=-I1*R/L$
(Slope at beginning of time interval)   (8.9–5)

The current, by Euler's method is:

160 LET $I1=I1+PO*T1 \qquad (8.9-6)$

(Current at beginning of the interval plus the slope times time is equal to the current at the end of the interval.)

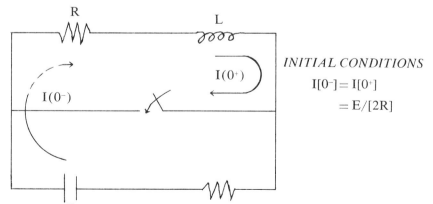

Figure 8.9A̧E RL circuit with an initial cuᏒent flow of E/2R shown at the instant of throwing switch for discharge.

RUNGE-KUTTA METHOD.

Four slopes for current are needed in this method. The first slope is the same for Euler and Runge Kutta on the first iteration only. After that, the value will be different: (Refer to Figure 6.5A)

140 LET I2 = I1   (Prior to iteration loop)

170 LET P0 = −I2*R/L   (Initial Slope)

172 LET P1 = −(I2+P0*T1/2)*R/L
                         (Slope at T1/2 based on P0)

174 LET P2 = −(I2+P1*T1/2)*R/L
                         (Slope at T1/2 based on P1)

176 LET P3 = −(I2+P2*T1)*R/L
                         (Slope at T1 based on P2)

178 LET P = (P0+2*P1+2*P2+P3)/6
                         (Average Slope over T1)

182 LET I2 = I2+P*T1   (8.9–6)

(Instantaneous value of current at time, $T + T1$, at the end of the interval.)

Commments About the Computer Programs: Statement 130 computes the initial current value from Equation (8.9–2). Statement 142 computes the initial value of slope for the Euler method. Statement 160 is the start of the iteration loop, computing the current using the Euler method. Statements 170 through 178, plus 182 are the fourth order Runge-Kutta method, and statement 180 resets P0 for the Euler method. The analytical value is calculated in statement 186, and all values printed in statement 190. The TAB statement is demonstrated to indicate output format under program control.

```
100 REM ************************RL1********************************
110 INPUT E, R, L, T1
120 PRINT"TIME"TAB(10)"CURRENT"TAB(25)"EULER"TAB(40)"4TH RUNGE"
130 LET I1 = E/(2*R)
140 LET I2 = I1
142 LET P0 = -I1*R/L
150 PRINT T;TAB(10);I1;TAB(25);I1;TAB(40);I2
160 LET I1 = I1 + P0*T1
170 LET P0 = -I2*R/L
172 LET P1 = -(I2 + P0*T1/2)*R/L
174 LET P2 = -(I2 + P1*T1/2)*R/L
176 LET P3 = -(I2 + P2*T1)*R/L
178 LET P = (P0 + 2*P1 + 2*P2 + P3)/6
180 LET P0 = -I1*R/L
182 LET I2 = I2 + P*T1
184 LET T = T + T1
186 LET I = (E/(2*R))*EXP(-T*R/L)
190 PRINT T; TAB(10);I;TAB(25);I1;TAB(40);I2
200 IF T + T1 > 10*T1 THEN 220
210 GOTO 160
220 STOP
```

PROGRAM 8.9A.

? 10, 5, 5, .1

TIME	CURRENT	EULER	4TH RUNGE
0	1	1	1
0.1	0.904837418	0.9	0.9048375
0.2	0.818730753	0.81	0.818730901
0.3	0.740818221	0.729	0.740818422
0.4	0.670320046	0.6561	0.670320289
0.5	0.60653066	0.59049	0.606530934
0.6	0.548811636	0.531441	0.548811934
0.7	0.496585304	0.4782969	0.496585619
0.8	0.449328964	0.43046721	0.44932929
0.9	0.40656966	0.387420489	0.406569991
1	0.367879441	0.34867844	0.367879774

TABLE 8.9A.

Discussion of Computer Results: The Runge-Kutta method shows very close agreement to the analytical results, (Table 8.9A) and should be used instead of the Euler method. The Runge-Kutta method will require a deeper understanding of the slopes generated in the problem solution if the student is able to set up his own program. The values of $E(R)$ and $E(L)$ could easily have been plotted in a student problem from the tabu-

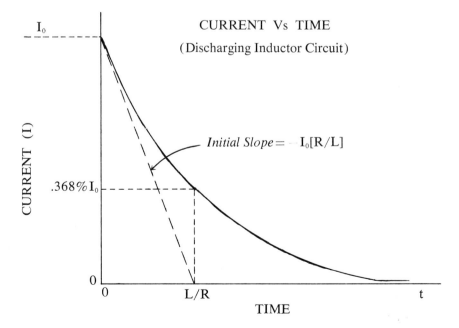

FIG. 8.9B   Discharging Inductor Plot, indicating time-constant from initial slope, L/R

lated values of current, and slope. The student could also adapt this program to obtain inductor potential from the Runge-Kutta value of P:

188 LET E1 = P*L   (Potential Across Inductor)

To plot, the subroutine of Program 8.8B could have been adapted using E8 for scaled inductor potential. A student labeled plot similar to Figure 8.9B is essential to increased student understanding of exponential circuits by relating circuit values to time and current.

8.10 WORK IN A THERMODYNAMIC CYCLE

Lesson Characteristics:

ENGINEERING LEVEL   college, intermediate

MATHEMATICS BACKGROUND REQUIRED   calculus

PEDAGOGY   computer learning

PROBLEM APPROACH   numerical solution

STUDENT PARTICIPATION   assists in program writing

PROGRAMMING SKILLS   none

TIME OF STUDENT INVOLVEMENT   in class—1 hour, in laboratory—1 hour

RECOMMENDED READING   (2) Chapter 25, (20) Chapter 3

Lesson Description: The engineering student finds that solving integral equations becomes a way of life. This lesson describes a thermodynamics problem for the determination of work. The computer solution makes use of Simpson's rule (See Section 5.4) and assumes no knowledge of higher mathematics.

The thermodynamic process considered is an isotropic (constant temperature) expansion and/or compression. The student should be required to write a similar program for an adiabatic process and compare the results to the analytical solution.

Background and Theory: In almost all areas of applied science one encounters problems that require the evaluation of integrals between limits. In the ideal cases with good geometry and imaginary media, it is possible to find a solution of the integral in closed-form. For example, this could be a formula expressed as simple algebra or a transcendental function that can be evaluated between limits to give the numerical value of the integral.

In a real problem the evaluation of integrals seldom leads to an analytical formula due to the complexity of the expression. In numerical integration one begins with the definition of an integral as the limit of a sum of areas under the curve. Various techniques of numerical integration differ basically in the proper approximation of the incremental areas under the curve.

For this problem consider a gas cylindrical container with a movable piston. Initially the gas is in equilibrium with the environment (cylinder walls) and has a pressure P1 and a volume V1. This gaseous system can absorb or loose heat through the cylindrical walls, and work can be done by moving the piston.

How much work is done if the gas expands from P1 to P2 by changing volume from V1 to V2? The work done is by definition,

$$\Delta W = F \,\Delta S \qquad (8.10\text{--}1)$$

that is,

Increment of Work = (*constant force*) * (*increment of displacement*).

In this case, the force over a small increment of distance is

$$F = P \, A \qquad (8.10\text{--}2)$$

Force = (*pressure*) × (*area*)

Therefore,

$$\Delta W = P \, A \Delta S. \qquad (8.10\text{--}3)$$

However,

$$A \, \Delta S = \Delta V \qquad (8.10\text{--}4)$$

(area) (change in displacement) = (change in volume) and Equation 8.10–3 becomes,

$$\Delta W = P \, \Delta V. \qquad (8.10\text{--}5)$$

To obtain the total work W done on the displaced piston by the gas, one must add all the increments of work, ΔW, or in other words, one must integrate. The pressure and volume both change as the gas expands, but at each point the gas is described by the equation of state of a gas,

$$PV = NRT$$

$$\text{LET } P*V - N*R*T, \qquad (8.10\text{--}6)$$

where N is the number of moles of the gas at temperature, T, and R is the universal gas constant. The expansion being considered will be at constant temperature.

Computer Techniques: Figure 8.10A illustrates the geometric interpretation of the problem of numerical integration. This pressure versus volume diagram will be used as an introductory example

of integration since Work = $\int_{V1}^{V2} P \cdot dV$. If the

V2 is divided into N equal spaces, the size of each increment will be, $H = (V2 - V1)/N$. The area under the element of the total curve would be

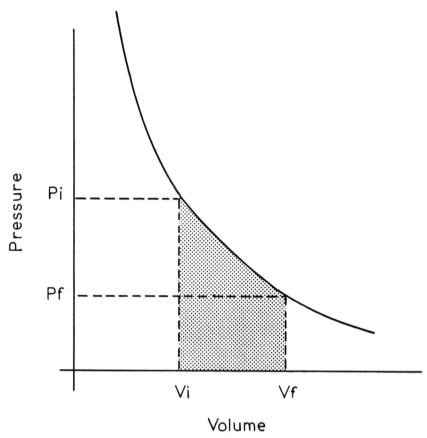

Figure 8.10   The shaded area represents the work done by a quantity of gas in expanding from V_i to V_f with the temperature fixed.

equal to the area of the rectangle, A B′ C D plus the area of the triangle
B′ B C. Or in terms of the x and y coordinates, the area of the trapezoid
will be:

$$\text{LET } A(X) = P(X+1)*H + (P(X) - P(X+1))*H/2$$
$$\text{LET } A(X) = H/2*(P(X) + P(X+1)).$$

For the total area, one would want to add all the incremental areas starting
with A(X0) and ending with A(XN). When a number of these are done,
observe what happens:

$$\begin{aligned}
A(\text{TOTAL}) &= A(X0) + A(X1) + A(X2) \ldots\ldots A(XN)\\
&= H/2\ (P(0) + P(1)) + H/2\ (P(1) + P(2)) \ldots\\
&\qquad\qquad\qquad\qquad\qquad\quad H/2(P(N-1) + P(N))
\end{aligned}$$

$$A(\text{TOTAL}) = H/2(P(0) + 2\ P(1) + 2P(2) \ldots 2P(N-1) + P(N)).$$

This is the trapezoidal rule, so-called because it approximates the integral
by the sum of N trapezoids.

In the trapezoidal method a straight line is assumed between incremental points on the curve. A better approximation can be made by using a parabola to join the three ordinates of two adjacent intervals. This is Simpson's rule and it is based on the idea of replacing the curve $Y=P(X)$ between X0 and X2 by the parabola,

$$Y = AX^2 + BX + C.$$

The area under the parabola depends only on the values of $f(X)$ at the three points, X0, X1, and X2. Thus,

$$\int_{X1}^{X1+2H} P(X)dx = H/3[P(X1) + 4P(X1+H) + P(X1+2H)]$$

where $P(X) = A X^2 + B X + C$.

$$\text{LET } P(X) = A*X\uparrow2 + B*X + C$$

Therefore, if the interval from V1 to V2 is divided into N subintervals by the points $V = X1, X2, X3, \ldots XN$ each of width, H, then the integral can be approximated by

$$\int_{V1}^{V2} P(X)dX = \left(\frac{P(X1) + 4P(X2) + P(X3)}{3}\right) + H(P(X3) +$$

$$\frac{4*P(X4) + P(X5)}{3}\right) + H\left(\frac{P(X5) + 4*P(X6) + P(X7)}{3}\right)$$

etc.

or

$$= \frac{H}{3}[P(X1) + 4P(X2) + P(X3) + 4P(X4) \text{ etc. } P(XN)]$$

$$(8.10-7)$$

Equation 8.10–7 will be calculated by the computer by dividing the total interval, V2−V1, into many small elements.

Comments About Computer Program: The DATA statement of Program 8.10 indicates that the gas will be expanded from 10 m^{-3} to 30 m^{-3} at a temperature of 390 degrees centigrade. Notice that the conditions of the problem are printed out in statements 130 and 140. The interval V2−V1 is divided into N equal increments by statement 170.

From Equation 8.10–7 one can see that it will be necessary to instruct the computer to add all the odd values, $P(X1) + P(X3) + P(X5) \ldots$ etc., and to multiply by four the sum of all the even values of the function, $4(P(X2) + P(X4) + P(X6) \ldots$ etc.). In statement 210 through 240, the even values are added. In the loop beginning at statement 250, all the odd values are added.

The work in expanding the gas is calculated in statements 300 and 310 by adding all the increments of area in Figure 8.10A. Statement 320

```
100 REM******* CALCULATION OF WORK IN THERMODYNAMIC CYCLE ********
110 READ V1, V2, T, N
120 DATA 10, 30, 390, 100
130 PRINT "INITIAL VOLUME OF GAS ="V1"CUBIC METERS"
140 PRINT "FINAL VOLUME OF GAS ="V2"CUBIC METERS."
150 PRINT
160 PRINT
170 LET H = (V2 - V1)/N
180 LET S2 = S4 = 0
190 LET S4=0
200 LET V = V1 + H
210 FOR I = 1 TO N-1 STEP 2
220 LET S4 = S4 + 8.314*T/V
230 LET V = V + 2*H
240 NEXT I
250 LET V = V1 + 2*H
260 FOR I = 2 TO N-2 STEP 2
270 LET S2 = S2 + 8.314*T/V
280 LET V = V + 2*H
290 NEXT I
300 LET W = 8.314*T/V1 + 2*S2 + 4*S4 + 8.314*T/V2
310 LET W = H/3*W
320 LET W1 = 8.314*T*LOG(V2/V1)
330 IF V1 < V2 THEN 360
340 PRINT "WORK DONE IN COMPRESSING GAS FROM V1 TO V2 ="W"JOULES/MOLE."
350 GO TO 370
360 PRINT "WORK DONE IN EXPANDING GAS FROM V1 TO V2 ="W"JOULES/MOLE."
370 PRINT "EXACT SOLUTION.   W ="W1"JOULES/MOLE."
380 END
```

PROGRAM 8.10.   Calculation of Work in a Thermodynamic Cycle

determines the work by the closed-form analytical solution. The results are finally printed in statements 340 through 370.

Discussion of Computer Results: Two runs of this program (See Table 8.10) indicate close agreement between the numerical and analytical solution of the integral equation. The student should be encouraged to design a program to determine the integral value of other thermodynamic processes. This particular numerical method has the obvious limitation

```
INITIAL VOLUME OF GAS = 10 CUBIC METERS
FINAL VOLUME OF GAS = 30 CUBIC METERS.
TEMPERATURE OF ISOTHERMAL PROCESS = 390 DEGREES KELVIN


WORK DONE IN EXPANDING GAS FROM V1 TO V2 = 3562.21 JOULES/MOLE.
EXACT SOLUTION.   W = 3562.21 JOULES/MOLE.




INITIAL VOLUME OF GAS = 30 CUBIC METERS
FINAL VOLUME OF GAS = 10 CUBIC METERS.
TEMPERATURE OF ISOTHERMAL PROCESS = 390 DEGREES KELVIN


WORK DONE IN COMPRESSING GAS FROM V1 TO V2 =-3562.21 JOULES/MOLE.
EXACT SOLUTION.   W =-3562.21 JOULES/MOLE.
```

TABLE 8.10   Thermodynamic Work in Compression and Expansion.

of requiring known boundary conditions thus obviating the indefinite integral.

8.11 FORCED HARMONIC MOTION WITH DAMPING

Lesson Characteristics:

ENGINEERING LEVEL   college, advanced

MATHEMATICS BACKGROUND REQUIRED   analytic geometry

PEDAGOGY   computer learning and simulation

PROBLEM APPROACH   numerical solution

STUDENT PARTICIPATION   assists in program writing

PROGRAMMING SKILLS   intermediate BASIC

TIME OF STUDENT INVOLVEMENT   in class—2 hours, out of class—5 hours

RECOMMENDED READING   (2) Chapter 15, (6) Chapter 12

Lesson Description: A system acted upon by several forces simultaneously is common in engineering design. When the forces are all different and act independently, the problem can be difficult. This lesson demonstrates a computer solution of the equation of motion for a mass acted upon by a spring force, a driven oscillatory force, and a damping force (See Figure 8.11A). The student is introduced to the subject matter in class and then required to develop a computer program that will allow design decisions. He must understand the forces involved in this problem and should be encouraged to explore the effect of the driving frequency on the natural frequency of the spring-mass system. The computer solution depends upon the fourth order Runge-Kutta for approximate values of the displacement and velocity. Calculation of the Runge coefficients is described in detail.

Background and Theory: The first step in the solution of this problem is to describe the forces acting on the block of mass M1. The spring force is

$$\text{Force}(1) = -ky, \qquad (8.11\text{--}1)$$

where k is the spring constant and y is the displacement in the y-direction. The eccentric mass (m_2) causes a force of

$$\text{Force}(2) = m_2 w^2 r \cos(wt)$$

$$\text{LET } F(2) = M2*W\uparrow2*R*COS(W*T) \qquad (8.11\text{--}2)$$

where r is the radius of the wheel turning at an angular velocity of w.

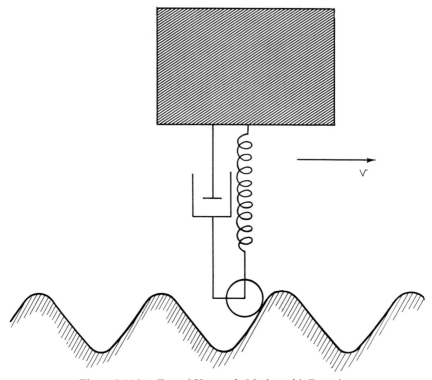

Figure 8.11A.   Forced Harmonic Motion with Damping

The damping force $(-b)$, is assumed to be proportional to the velocity of the block (v), thus

$$\text{Force}(3) = -bv$$
$$\text{LET } F(3) = -B*V \qquad (8.11\text{--}3)$$

Since the sum of the (Forces) = (Mass) times (Acceleration),

$$-ky - bv + m_2w^2r \cos(wt) = m_1a \qquad (8.11\text{--}4)$$

Equation 8.11–4 is the equation of motion of the block under the influence of the three forces. The problem is to describe the motion of the block by calculating the Y-displacement at any time, t, after the wheel begins to spin.

Computer Techniques: Dividing Equation 8.11–4 by M1 and re-arranging the terms yields,

$$\text{LET } A = M2*W\uparrow2*R*COS(W*T) - K/M1*Y - B/M1*V$$
$$(8.11\text{--}5)$$

and remembering the definition of acceleration and velocity,

$$\Delta v/\Delta t = a \qquad (8.11\text{--}6)$$
$$\Delta y/\Delta t = v \qquad (8.11\text{--}7)$$

These equations are approximate values of the acceleration and velocity (more exact as Δt approaches zero). From these equations, one can estimate values of the displacement and velocity by (assuming that initial values are known),

$$\text{LET } Y = Y + V*D \qquad (8.11\text{--}8)$$

$$\text{LET } V = V + A*D \qquad (8.11\text{--}9)$$

where D=Δt, or a small increment of time. V and A represent the best estimate of the velocity and acceleration during the time increment, D. In this problem the initial conditions are at Time, T=0,

$$Y = 0 \text{ m}$$

$$V = 0 \text{ m/s}$$

There are several computer methods for obtaining a good estimate of the velocity and acceleration during the time increment, D. In this lesson the fourth order Runge-Kutta will be used (see Section 5.3).

Comments About the Computer Program: The Runge-Kutta slopes are determined as follows (see Figure 5.3).

(*a*) *initial values,*

420 LET Y1 = Y

430 LET V1 = V

440 LET A1 = C1*COS(W*T)+C2*Y+C3*V

Notice that C1, C2,and C3 were defined in the Program 8.11A in statements 260, 270, and 280.

(*b*) *first midtime estimate,*

450 LET Y2 = Y1+V1*D/2

460 LET V2 = V1+A1*D/2

470 LET A2 = C1*COS(W*(T+D/2))+C2*Y2+C3*V2

The midtime is used, D/2 (See Figure 5.3).

(*c*) *second midpoint estimate,*

480 LET Y3 = Y1+V2*D/2

490 LET V3 = V1+A2*D/2

500 LET A3 = C1*COS(W*(T+D/2))+C2*Y3+C3*V3

(*d*) *estimate at the end of the time interval,*

510 LET Y4 = Y1+V3*D

520 LET V4 = V1+V3*D

530 LET A4 = C1*COS(W*(T+D))+C2*Y4+C3*V4)

The new values of displacement, Y, and velocity, V, can be found by Equations 8.11 and 8.11–9

(a) *displacement,*

$$Y = Y + V*D$$

thus

540 LET Y = Y + (V1+2*V2+2*V3+V4)*D/6

(b) *velocity,*

$$V = V + A*D$$

thus

550 LET V = V + (A1+2*A2+2*A3+A4)*D/6

Time is incremented by

560 LET T = T + D

and the new acceleration is,

570 LET A = C1*COS(W*T)+C2*Y+C3*V.

This concludes the actual calculating portion of Program 8.11. The computer is instructed to do these steps 40 times by the statement.

400 LET = Z + 1

410 IF Z = 41 THEN 540.

Each time through the loop, the value of Z is increased by one until Z = 41 and the program stops.

In statements 200 through 240, the computer is instructed to print out the initial conditions and known parameters of the problem. (This is normally good practice since the general conditions of the problem are thus checked and recorded with each output.)

Discussion of Computer Results: Figure 8.11B shows the results of a poorly damped unstable system. A change in one of the parameters as shown in Figure 8.11C where the angular velocity of the wheel has been doubled demonstrates how the motion can become well-behaved. Likewise, when the damping coefficient of this figure is doubled, the new results are demonstrated and are shown in Figure 8.11D. Notice that the motion can be experimentally designed by proper choice of input parameters.

Students will be able to grasp the simple relationship used in the computer approach to this problem. The program then simulates a real system and should be used by the student to explore the effects of changes in input parameters (i.e., damping coefficient, frequency, etc.) on the final motion of the block.

```
100 REM********** FORCED HARMONIC MOTION WITH DAMPING **********
110 READ K, D, VO, TO, YO
120 DATA 2.8, .1, 0, 0, 0
130 READ M
140 DATA .5
150 READ W
160 DATA 60
170 READ R, M2, M3, B, M4
180 DATA .5, .01, .1, .4, .05
190 LET M1 = M + M2 + M3 + M4
200 PRINT "SPRING CONSTANT ="K"NEWTONS/METER"
210 PRINT "MASS OF BLOCK PLUS WHEEL PLUS DAMPER ="M1"KILOGRAMS"
220 PRINT "ANGULAR VELOCITY OF THE WHEEL ="W"RADIANS/SEC"
230 PRINT "ECCENTRIC MASS ON WHEEL ="M2"KILOGRAMS"
240 PRINT "DAMPING COEFFICIENT ="B"NEWTONS/METER/SEC"
250 LET C1=M2/M1*W*W*R
260 LET C2=-K/M1
270 LET C3=-B/M1
280 LET Y=YO
290 LET T=TO
300 LET Z = 0
310 SETDIGITS(4)
320 LET V=VO
330 PRINT
340 PRINT "                    Y - DISPLACEMENT IN METERS"
350 PRINT "TIME ---------------------------- 0 ------------";
360 PRINT "---------------"
370 PRINT "SECONDS"
380 LET Y1 = INT(4*Y + .5) + 36
390 PRINT T; TAB(Y1); "*"
400 LET Z = Z + 1
410 IF Z = 41 THEN 540
420 LET MO=V
430 LET KO = C1*COS(W*T) + C2*Y + C3*V
440 LET M1=V+KO*D/2
450 LET K1 = C1*COS(W*T) + C2*(Y + MO*D/2) + C3*(V + KO*D/2)
460 LET M2=V+K1*D/2
470 LET K2 = C1*COS(W*T) + C2*(Y + M1*D/2) + C3*(V + K1*D/2)
480 LET M3=V+K2*D
490 LET K3 = C1*COS(W*T) + C2*(Y + M2*D) + C3*(V + K2*D)
500 LET Y = Y + (MO + 2*M1 + 2*M2 + M3)*D/6
510 LET V = V + (KO + 2*K1 + 2*K2 + K3)*D/6
520 LET T = T + D
530 GO TO 380
540 END
```

PROGRAM 8.11. Forced Harmonic Motion with Damping

```
SPRING CONSTANT = 2.8 NEWTONS/METER
MASS OF BLOCK PLUS WHEEL PLUS DAMPER = .66 KILOGRAMS
ANGULAR VELOCITY OF THE WHEEL = 60 RADIANS/SEC
ECCENTRIC MASS ON WHEEL = .01 KILOGRAMS
DAMPING COEFFICIENT = .4 NEWTONS/METER/SEC

                       Y - DISPLACEMENT IN METERS
TIME ---------------------------------- 0 ---------------------------
SECONDS
  0                                      *
  .1                                     *
  .2                                      *
  .3                                        *
  .4                                          *
  .5                                            *
  .6                                              *
  .7                                                *
  .8                                                  *
  .9                                                 *
 1.                                                 *
 1.1                                            *
 1.2                                          *
 1.3                                     *
 1.4                                  *
 1.5                               *
 1.6                           *
 1.7                         *
 1.8                       *
 1.9                     *
 2                      *
 2.1                     *
 2.2                        *
 2.3                          *
 2.4                              *
 2.5                                 *
 2.6                                      *
 2.7                                          *
 2.8                                             *
 2.9                                                *
 3.                                                   *
 3.1                                                    *
 3.2                                                     *
 3.3                                                    *
 3.4                                                *
 3.5                                             *
 3.6                                          *
 3.7                                    *
 3.8                               *
 3.9                            *
 4.                          *
```

Figure 8.11B. Forced Harmonic Motion with Damping: The y-displacement is computer graphed at equal intervals of 0.1 seconds. The wheel is spinning at 60 radians/second

```
PRING CONSTANT = 2.8 NEWTONS/METER
MASS OF BLOCK PLUS WHEEL PLUS DAMPER = .66 KILOGRAMS
ANGULAR VELOCITY OF THE WHEEL = 120 RADIANS/SEC
ECCENTRIC MASS ON WHEEL = .01 KILOGRAMS
DAMPING COEFFICIENT = .4 NEWTONS/METER/SEC

                        Y - DISPLACEMENT IN METERS
TIME ----------------------------- 0 ---------------------------
SECONDS
  0                                *
  .1                                *
  .2                                      *
  .3                                          *
  .4                                              *
  .5                                                  *
  .6                                                  *
  .7                                              *
  .8                                        *
  .9                                 *
 1.                            *
 1.1                     *
 1.2                  *
 1.3                   *
 1.4                      *
 1.5                          *
 1.6                            *
 1.7                             *
 1.8                           *
 1.9                       *
 2                      *
 2.1                 *
 2.2               *
 2.3                *
 2.4                  *
 2.5                      *
 2.6                            *
 2.7                               *
 2.8                                *
 2.9                               *
 3.                            *
 3.1                          *
 3.2                      *
 3.3                 *
 3.4                *
 3.5                      *
 3.6                          *
 3.7                             *
 3.8                               *
 3.9                                *
 4.                               *
```

Figure 8.11C.   Forced Harmonic Motion with Damping: The y-displacement is computer graphed at equal intervals of 0.1 seconds. The wheel is spinning at 120 radians/second

```
PRING CONSTANT = 2.8 NEWTONS/METER
MASS OF BLOCK PLUS WHEEL PLUS DAMPER = .66 KILOGRAMS
ANGULAR VELOCITY OF THE WHEEL = 120 RADIANS/SEC
ECCENTRIC MASS ON WHEEL = .01 KILOGRAMS
DAMPING COEFFICIENT = 10 NEWTONS/METER/SEC

                      Y - DISPLACEMENT IN METERS
TIME ----------------------------- 0 ---------------------------
SECONDS
  0                               *
  .1                              *
  .2                                *
  .3                                *
  .4                                 *
  .5                                *
  .6                               *
  .7                              *
  .8                             *
  .9                           *
 1.                            *
 1.1                           *
 1.2                             *
 1.3                              *
 1.4                               *
 1.5                                *
 1.6                               *
 1.7                              *
 1.8                             *
 1.9                           *
 2.                          *
 2.1                         *
 2.2                          *
 2.3                           *
 2.4                            *
 2.5                             *
 2.6                             *
 2.7                             *
 2.8                            *
 2.9                          *
 3.                          *
 3.1                        *
 3.2                        *
 3.3                        *
 3.4                         *
 3.5                          *
 3.6                           *
 3.7                            *
 3.8                            *
 3.9                           *
 4.                          *
```

Figure 8.11D. Forced Harmonic Motion with Damping: The y-displacement is computer graphed at equal intervals of 0.1 seconds. The damping coefficient is equal to 10 newtons/meter/second

SPRING CONSTANT = 2.8 NEWTONS/METER
MASS OF BLOCK PLUS WHEEL PLUS DAMPER = .66 KILOGRAMS
ANGULAR VELOCITY OF THE WHEEL = 120 RADIANS/SEC
ECCENTRIC MASS ON WHEEL = .01 KILOGRAMS
DAMPING COEFFICIENT = 10 NEWTONS/METER/SEC

TIME (SECS.)	Y-DISPLACEMENT (METERS)	VELOCITY (METERS/SEC.)
0	0	0
.1	.3724	5.219
.2	.9309	5.689
.3	1.348	3.508
.4	1.448	-2.692E-2
.5	1.188	-3.642
.6	.6414	-6.161
.7	-2.277E-2	-6.784
.8	-.6002	-5.313
.9	-.9129	-2.205
1.	-.8653	1.57
1.1	-.4745	4.834
1.2	.1355	6.568
1.3	.7722	6.231
1.4	1.235	3.929
1.5	1.377	.3815
1.6	1.152	-3.303
1.7	.6294	-5.974
1.8	-3.019E-2	-6.796
1.9	-.6222	-5.513
2	-.9635	-2.524
2.1	-.9489	1.238
2.2	-.5847	4.598
2.3	1.402E-2	6.507
2.4	.6587	6.369
2.5	1.147	4.229
2.6	1.324	.7543
2.7	1.134	-2.969
2.8	.6353	-5.778
2.9	-1.851E-2	-6.795
3.	-.6241	-5.702
3.1	-.9935	-2.84
3.2	-1.012	.8971
3.3	-.6764	4.343
3.4	-.0911	6.422
3.5	.5594	6.485
3.6	1.071	4.512
3.7	1.283	1.121
3.8	1.128	-2.631
3.9	.6536	-5.57
4.	7.079E-3	-6.779

TABLE 8.11. The y-displacement and velocity of the block is tabulated at time intervals equal to 0.1 seconds. The angular velocity of the wheel is 120 radians/second

8.12   HEAT TRANSFER I

Lesson Characteristics:

ENGINEERING LEVEL   college, intermediate

MATHEMATICS BACKGROUND REQUIRED   algebra and trigonometry

PEDAGOGY   computer learning

PROBLEM APPROACH   numerical solution

STUDENT PARTICIPATION   assists in program writing

PROGRAMMING SKILLS   introductory BASIC

TIME OF STUDENT INVOLVEMENT   in class—1 hour
                                                        out of class—4 hours

RECOMMENDED READING   (21) Chapter 8

Lesson Description: Heat flows from regions of high temperature to regions of low temperature by conduction. This lesson describes a computer technique for determining the temperature distribution and also the heat flow throughout a heat-conducting object. The technique, called numerical relaxation, has the advantage of applicability to any geometry.

After a brief introduction to the heat transfer equations, the reader learns how to choose the 'points' on the heat-conducting object (in this case a cylindrical fin) about which certain heat-balance equations can be written. The relaxation method is based upon the assumption that, at any point, the algebraic sum of the heat flow in, plus the heat flow out, plus the heat generated, must be zero. This lesson describes the computer 'guessing' method which slowly 'relaxes' the heat-balance equations of each point to zero.

The student should be encouraged to write a similar program either with more points (more accuracy) or with a different geometry, for instance a triangular, heat-conducting fin could be investigated.

Background and Theory: Prior to applying the relaxation method to any physical problem described by a differential equation, some preliminary work is necessary. It is necessary to approximate the differential equations and the boundary conditions by a set of algebraic equations. This is most easily accomplished by choosing a pattern of discrete points within the region of the differential equation. Then one can make finite-difference approximations between the points. Depending upon the accuracy desired, if N points are chosen, a set of N algebraic equations can be written.

Figure 8.12 shows a cylindrical, heat-conducting surface divided into discrete points for a relaxation solution. Each point represents part of the total volume of the circular rod and it is assumed that the characteristics (temperature, conductivity, etc.) of the subvolumes are represented by the

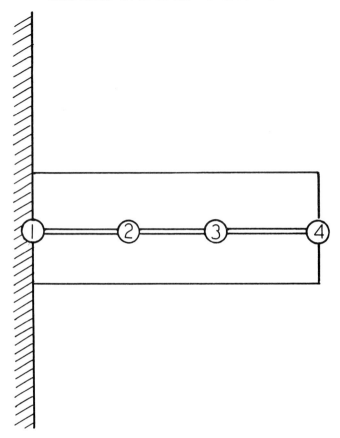

Figure 8.12   A cylindrical, heat-conducting surface is shown divided into discrete elements.

points. Heat will flow from one nodal point to the next nodal point and in the absence of any heat sources or sinks within the system, the rate of heat flow toward each nodal point must equal the rate of heat flow away from the nodal point in the steady state. The heat-balance equation for each interior nodal point is the same but the nodal points at the base and at the tip require special treatment.

Consider point 1 at the base of the circular rod. The temperature at this nodal point is constant and equal to the wall temperature of 100° F. A certain amount of heat enters the subvolume from the wall, a certain amount of heat is gained (or lost) by conduction to subvolume 2, and finally a certain amount of heat is gained (or lost) by convection to the environment (assume ambient temperature is 68° F). The heat-balance-equation becomes

$$Q1 \; = \; X + H/2(T0 - T1) + K/2(T2 - T1) \qquad (8.12 - 1)$$

Where

X = *heat flow from the wall*

H = (*convective heat-transfer coefficient*) × (*area exposed*)

K = (*thermal conductivity*) × (*area*) / (*length of subvolume*)

In this case ½ appears in two terms due to the fact that the first subvolume is ½ as long as the interior subvolumes. Q1 is called a residual and must be reduced to zero by the proper choice of temperature values.

The heat-balance equation at nodal point 2, which is an interior nodal point, would be as follows:

$$Q2 = K(T1-T2) + H(T0-T2) + K(T3-T2).$$

All other interior points will have a similar form.

The heat-balance equation at nodal point 4 differs in that heat is lost by convection at the end of the rod. This is:

$$Q4 = \frac{K}{2}(T3-T4) + H/2(T0-T4) + H1(T0-T4)$$

where

$H1$ = (*convective heat-transfer coefficient*) × (*cross-sectional area*).

Writing all the equations and their residuals yields,

LET Q_1 = X+H/2*(T0−T1)+K/2*(T2−T1)

LET Q_2 = K*(T1−T2)+H*(T0−T2)+K*(T3−T2)

LET Q_3 = K*(T2−T3)+H*(T0−T3)+K*(T4−T3)

LET Q_4 = K/2*(T3−T4)+H/2*(T0−T4)+H*R/2/D*(T0−T4)

If TO = 0, all temperatures can be measured relative to this ambient temperature (room), the equation can be re-written as follows:

LET Q1 = X+K/2*T2−(H/2+K/2)*T1   (8.12−2)

LET Q2 = K*T1+K*T3−(2K+H)*T2   (8.12−3)

LET Q3 = K*T2+K*T4−(2K+H)*T2   (8.12−4)

LET Q4 = K/2*T3−(K/2+H/2+H*R/2/D)T4   (8.12−5)

Q2 through Q4 are called 'residuals'. The objective of the numerical relaxation is to reduce the values of the residuals to as nearly zero as practicable. Those values of T2, T3, and T4 that make the residuals equal to zero are the desired solution to the equations.

The value of T1 is known and is constant throughout the problem. Initial estimates of T2, T3, and T4 can be made with some logic, that is, (100−

$68) > T2 > T3 > T4 > (68-68)$. In this problem it will be assumed that $T2 = 30$, $T3 = 25$, $T4 = 20$.

Comment About Computer Program: The solution of a problem of this complexity normally justifies a well documented computer program, that is, enough descriptive print-out to guide the user. In Program 8.12, the statements 130 through 160 instruct the computer to print out the important parameters of this problem. The initial 'guess' at the temperature distribution is entered by the DATA statement at line 210.

The residuals Q2, Q3, and Q4 are determined in statements 260, 270, and 280 (See Equations 8.12–3, 8.12–4, and 8.12–5 for comparison). In statement 320, the sum of the residuals is checked and if this sum is less than 0.5, the computer stops. If the sum of residuals is larger than 0.5, the computer wants to find the largest residual (statements 330, 340, and 380). When the largest residual is found, the temperature of that residual is changed so as to make the residual zero (See statements 350, 390, and 420). After the temperature has been changed, the computer returns to 260 (Go To 260) and recalculates the residuals. This process continues until the sum of residuals (statement 290) is less than 0.5.

```
100 REM*************** NUMERICAL RELAXATION METHOD ***************
110 READ H1, K1, D, R
120 DATA 20, 10, .1, .05
130 PRINT "THERMAL CONDUCTIVITY ="K1"BTU*FT/HR/F"
140 PRINT "CONVECTIVE HEAT TRANSFER COEFFICIENT ="H1"BTU/HR/F/FT↑2"
150 PRINT "RADIUS OF ROD ="R*12"INCHES"
160 PRINT "LENGTH OF ROD ="3*D*12"INCHES"
170 PRINT
180 PRINT
190 LET P = 3.14159265
200 READ T(1), T(2), T(3), T(4)
210 DATA 20, 32, 30, 25, 20
220 LET K = K1*P*R*R/D
230 LET H = 2*H1*P*R*D
240 LET H2 = H1*P*R*R
250 SETDIGITS(3)
260 LET Q2 = K*T(1) + K*T(3) - (2*K + H)*T(2)
270 LET Q3 = K*T(2) + K*T(4) - (2*K + H)*T(3)
280 LET Q4 = K/2*T(3) - (K/2 + H/2 + H2)*T(4)
290 LET Q = ABS(Q2 + Q3 + Q4)
300 PRINT "TEMPERATURES", T(1), T(2), T(3), T(4)
310 PRINT "RESIDUALS", " ", Q2, Q3, Q4
320 IF Q < .5 THEN 320
330 IF ABS(Q2) < ABS(Q3) THEN 380
340 IF ABS(Q2) < ABS(Q4) THEN 420
350 LET T(2) = T(2) + Q2/(2*K + H)
360 PRINT
370 GO TO 260
380 IF ABS(Q3) < ABS(Q4) THEN 420
390 LET T(3) = T(3) + Q3/(2*K + H)
400 PRINT
410 GO TO 260
420 LET T(4) = T(4) + Q4/(K/2 + H/2 + H2)
430 PRINT
440 GO TO 260
450 END
```

PROGRAM 8.12. One Dimensional Numerical Relaxation

Numerical relaxation can be made more precise by increasing the number of nodal points or by decreasing the cut off value of the sum of residuals (in this case chosen to be 0.5). In most cases there must be a decision made as to how much an increase precision will cost in terms of computer time.

Discussion of Computer Results: In Program 8.12, the computer was instructed to print out the temperature distribution and values of the residuals after each loop. Notice in Table 8.12A, that initially the residual associated with point 2 (temperature = 32) was the largest (absolute value). The

TEMPERATURES	20	32	30	25
RESIDUALS		-31.1	-21.2	-9.82
TEMPERATURES	20	17.9	30	25
RESIDUALS		2.33E-10	-32.3	-9.82
TEMPERATURES	20	17.9	15.3	25
RESIDUALS		-11.5	-4.66E-10	-15.6
TEMPERATURES	20	17.9	15.3	6.96
RESIDUALS		-11.5	-14.2	-1.16E-10
TEMPERATURES	20	17.9	8.86	6.96
RESIDUALS		-16.6	0	-2.53
TEMPERATURES	20	10.3	8.86	6.96
RESIDUALS		-1.16E-10	-5.93	-2.53
TEMPERATURES	20	10.3	6.17	6.96
RESIDUALS		-2.12	0	-3.59
TEMPERATURES	20	10.3	6.17	2.8
RESIDUALS		-2.12	-3.26	-1.46E-11
TEMPERATURES	20	10.3	4.68	2.8
RESIDUALS		-3.28	0	-.583
TEMPERATURES	20	8.82	4.68	2.8
RESIDUALS		0	-1.17	-.583
TEMPERATURES	20	8.82	4.15	2.8
RESIDUALS		-.419	5.82E-11	-.792
TEMPERATURES	20	8.82	4.15	1.89
RESIDUALS		-.419	-.72	-7.28E-12
TEMPERATURES	20	8.82	3.82	1.89
RESIDUALS		-.676	0	-.129
TEMPERATURES	20	8.51	3.82	1.89

HEAT FLOW FROM WALL IS EQUAL TO 17.5 JOULES/SEC

TEMPERATURE DISTRIBUTION
 20

 8.51

 3.82

 1.89

TABLE 8.12A. Numerical Relaxation.

THERMAL CONDUCTIVITY = 10 BTU*FT/HR/F
CONVECTIVE HEAT TRANSFER COEFFICIENT = 20 BTU/HR/F/FT↑2
RADIUS OF ROD = .6 INCHES
LENGTH OF ROD = 3.6 INCHES

TEMPERATURES	20	32	30	25
RESIDUALS		-31.1	-21.2	-9.82
TEMPERATURES	20	17.9	30	25
RESIDUALS		2.33E-10	-32.3	-9.82
TEMPERATURES	20	17.9	15.3	25
RESIDUALS		-11.5	-4.66E-10	-15.6
TEMPERATURES	20	17.9	15.3	6.96
RESIDUALS		-11.5	-14.2	-1.16E-10
TEMPERATURES	20	17.9	8.86	6.96
RESIDUALS		-16.6	0	-2.53
TEMPERATURES	20	10.3	8.86	6.96
RESIDUALS		-1.16E-10	-5.93	-2.53
TEMPERATURES	20	10.3	6.17	6.96
RESIDUALS		-2.12	0	-3.59
TEMPERATURES	20	10.3	6.17	2.8
RESIDUALS		-2.12	-3.26	-1.46E-11
TEMPERATURES	20	10.3	4.68	2.8
RESIDUALS		-3.28	0	-.583
TEMPERATURES	20	8.82	4.68	2.8
RESIDUALS		0	-1.17	-.583
TEMPERATURES	20	8.82	4.15	2.8
RESIDUALS		-.419	5.82E-11	-.792
TEMPERATURES	20	8.82	4.15	1.89
RESIDUALS		-.419	-.72	-7.28E-12
TEMPERATURES	20	8.82	3.82	1.89
RESIDUALS		-.676	0	-.129
TEMPERATURES	20	8.51	3.82	1.89
RESIDUALS		1.16E-10	-.241	-.129

TABLE 8.12B. Numerical Relaxation.

computer obviously chose this residual, changed the temperature from 32 to 17.9 which in turn reduced the residual to 2.33E–10 (close to zero!). This left the residual at point 3 to be the largest. Once more in the third pass through the loop, the temperature at point 3 is changed from 30 to 15.3 which makes the residual there equal to –4.66E–10 (again nearly equal to zero). This process continues until all the residuals are essentially zero (see last set of residuals).

The student should try other initial temperatures to discover that the better the first guess is the quicker the computer will converge on the final answer. Furthermore, other geometrical shapes can be programmed to insure complete understanding of the heat transfer problem.

8.13   HEAT TRANSFER II

Lesson Characteristics:

ENGINEERING LEVEL   college, advanced

MATHEMATICS BACKGROUND REQUIRED   calculus

PEDAGOGY   computer learning

PROBLEM APPROACH   numerical solution

STUDENT PARTICIPATION   assists in program writing

PROGRAMMING SKILLS   intermediate BASIC

TIME OF STUDENT INVOLVEMENT   in class—2 hours
out of class—5 hours

RECOMMENDED READING   (21)   Chapter 8

Lesson Description: Two-dimensional heat transfer problems are quite common in engineering and can be very complex. This lesson is an extension of the method of relaxation discussed in Section 8.12 to include heat flow by conduction in two directions. A square metal plate with unequal temperatures at each edge is described. The temperature of the edges are maintained constant, and a computer solution for the temperature within the plate is demonstrated. Students should be required to solve a similar problem for a rectangular or circular plate. Furthermore, the extension of the relaxation method to three dimensions follows directly from this lesson.

Background and Theory: In Figure 8.13 is shown a square plate which sides are maintained at different temperatures, A, B, C, D. The problem is to find the value of the temperature at any point on the plate. A basic approach to handling numerical relaxation has been shown to be the creation of a grid of points covering the space as shown in Figure 8.13. Only nine nodal points are shown, but for increased accuracy one could easily adjust the discussion to many nodal points.

The assumptions that are being made in this solution can be understood by inspecting one nodal point in detail. Much like Kirchoff's first law for electrical circuits it is assumed that, in the absence of heat sources within the square plate, the algebraic sum of all the heat flowing into nodal point $A(I, J)$ is zero. In equation form this means,

$$K(T(I{-}J,J){-}T(I,J){+}K(T(I,J{-}1){-}T(I,J)){+}K(T(I{+}1,J) \\ {-}T(I,J)){+}K(T(I,J{+}1){-}T(I,J)) \qquad\qquad =0$$

or dividing through by K and re-arranging,

$$Q(I,J) = T(I{-}J,J) + T(I,J{-}1) + T(I{+}1,J) + T(I,J{+}1) - 4 \times T \\ (I,J) \qquad\qquad (8.13{-}1)$$

where $Q(I,J)$ is the residual or remainder at nodal point $A(I,J)$.

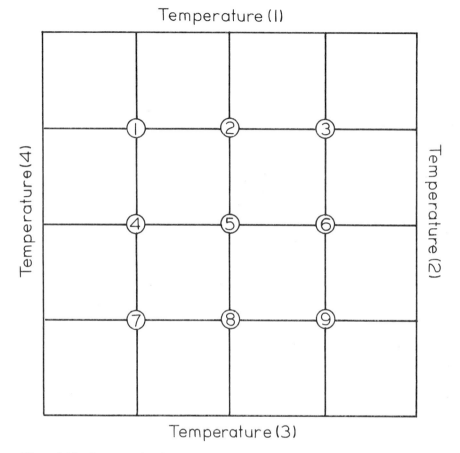

Figure 8.13   A square plate is shown whose sides are maintained at different temperatures.

A different approach to the same problem which emphasizes the use of partial differential equations should be understood at this time. At point $A(I,J)$, the first derivative of the temperature with respect to X can be approximated in two ways.

$$(1) \quad \left(\frac{\partial T}{\partial X}\right) = \frac{T(I+1,J) - T(I,J)}{\Delta X}$$

and

$$(2) \quad \left(\frac{\partial T}{\partial X}\right) = \frac{T(I,J) - T(I-1,J)}{\Delta X}$$

The second derivative of T with respect to X can then be approximated by,

$$\frac{\partial^2 T}{\partial x^2} = \frac{\left(\frac{\partial T}{\partial X}\right)_1 - \left(\frac{\partial T}{\partial X}\right)_2}{\Delta X} = \frac{T(I+1,J) + T(I-1,J) - 2T(I,J)}{\Delta X^2}$$

In a similar manner,

$$\frac{\partial^2 T}{\partial y^2} = \frac{T(I,J-1) + T(I,J+1) - 2T(I,J)}{\Delta X^2}$$

Now if there is no heat source in the square plate, the temperature distribution is defined by the Laplace Equation:

$$\frac{\partial^2 T}{\partial X^2} + \frac{\partial^2 T}{\partial y^2} = 0 \text{ (no heat sources)}$$

Therefore, subtracting and multiplying by ΔX^2, yields

$$Q(I,J) = T(I-1,J) + (T(I,J-1) + T(I+1,J) + T(I,J+1) - 4T(I,J)$$

as was found before (Equation 8.13–1) by heat-balance equations.

Now it is necessary to guess at the possible initial values of the temperatures at all points of the grid and attempt to systematically reduce the residuals at all nodal points to zero. Notice that the temperature at nodal point $A(I,J)$ effects the residual $Q(I,J)$ by a factor 4 times the value of $T(I,J)$. Therefore, at any time $Q(I,J)$ could be reduced to zero by changing the value of $T(I,J)$ as follows:

$$T(I,J) = T(I,J) + Q(I,J)/4. \tag{8.13–2}$$

Of course, changing $T(I,J)$ will affect the residuals of the surrounding points, so they should be adjusted by

$$Q(I-1,J) = Q(I-1,J) + Q(I,J)/4 \tag{8.13–3}$$

$$Q(I,J-1) = Q(I,J-1) + Q(I,J)/4 \tag{8.13–4}$$

$$Q(I+1,J) = Q(I+1,J) + Q(I,J)/4 \tag{8.13–5}$$

And finally,

$$Q(I,J+1) = Q(I,J+1) + Q(I,J)/4. \tag{8.13–6}$$

These steps will be repeated for all nodal points until the residuals at all points are less than some pre-determined value (which is close to zero).

Comments About Computer Program: Program 8.13 begins by DIMensioning two subscripted variables $(Q(15,15), T(15,15))$. As discussed in Chapter 5 this statement is necessary when more than 10 values of the subscripted variable will be required. The temperatures at each of the nodal points on the four edges are initialized in statements 150 through 220. In a double loop, one beginning at statement 250 and the other at statement 260, the inside temperatures of the grid are set to their initial values. In statement 300, the GO SUB 680 command causes the computer to go to line 680 and print the current values of the temperatures of the grid. When this is complete the computer is told to RETURN to the statement following the initial GO SUB command (in this case 310).

The loops beginning with line 310 and 320 are used to calculate the residual at each point. Compare the recursion equation of lines 330 and 340 with Equation 8.13–1. Once the residuals have been calculated, the

```
100 REM*************** PARTIAL DIFFERENTIAL EQUATIONS ***************
110 DIM Q(15,15), T(15,15)
120 READ S, N, A, B, C, D
130 DATA 1, 4, 100, 200, 300, 400
140 FOR I=2 TO N
150 LET T(I,1) = D
160 LET Q(I,1) = 0
170 LET T(1,I) = A
180 LET Q(1,I) = 0
190 LET T(N+1,I) = C
200 LET Q(N+1,I) = 0
210 LET T(I,N+1) = B
220 LET Q(I,N+1) = 0
230 LET Z = Z1 = 0
240 NEXT I
250 FOR I=2 TO N
260 FOR J=2 TO N
270 LET T(I,J) = I*J
280 NEXT J
290 NEXT I
300 GO SUB 680
310 FOR I=2 TO N
320 FOR J=2 TO N
330 LET Q(I,J) = T(I-1,J) + T(I,J-1) + T(I+1,J) + T(I,J+1)
340 LET Q(I,J) = Q(I,J) - 4*T(I,J)
350 NEXT J
360 NEXT I
370 LET L = ABS(Q(2,2))
380 FOR X = 2 TO N
390 FOR Y = 2 TO N
400 IF L > ABS(Q(X,Y)) THEN 440
410 LET L = ABS(Q(X,Y))
420 LET I = X
430 LET J = Y
440 NEXT Y
450 NEXT X
460 LET T(I,J) = T(I,J) + Q(I,J)/4
470 LET Q(I-1,J) = Q(I-1,J) + Q(I,J)/4
480 LET Q(I,J-1) = Q(I,J-1) + Q(I,J)/4
490 LET Q(I+1,J) = Q(I+1,J) + Q(I,J)/4
500 LET Q(I,J+1) = Q(I,J+1) + Q(I,J)/4
510 LET Q(I,J) = T(I-1,J) + T(I,J-1) + T(I+1,J) + T(I,J+1)
520 LET Q(I,J) = Q(I,J) - 4*T(I,J)
530 LET S=0
540 LET Z1 = Z1 + 1
550 LET Z = Z + 1
560 IF Z < 20 THEN 600
570 GO SUB 680
580 LET Z = 0
```

PROGRAM 8.13.   Two Dimensional Numerical Relaxation

computer must be directed to finding the largest residual (each time the largest residual is reduced to zero). Statements 370 through 450 are a sort routine (See Chapter 5) which finds the largest residual. Statement 460 then calculates the value of the temperature at the largest residual which will reduce the residual to zero.

Only the residuals surrounding the nodal point where the temperature has been changed will be effected by this temperature change. Statements 470 through 510 adjust the value of the residuals surrounding the nodal point of the largest residual as found by the sort routine. The values of all the temperatures in the grid are printed out after each 20 iterations of the temperature adjustment by statements 550 and 560.

```
590 PRINT
600 FOR I = 2 TO N
610 FOR J = 2 TO N
620 LET S = S + ABS(Q(I,J))
630 NEXT J
640 NEXT I
650 IF S > 10 THEN 370
660 GO SUB 680
670 GO TO 750
680 PRINT "VALUES OF TEMPERATURES IN GRID"
690 FOR I=1 TO N+1
700 FOR J=1 TO N+1
710 PRINT T(I,J),
720 NEXT J
730 NEXT I
740 RETURN
750 PRINT
760 PRINT
770 PRINT "IN THIS PROBLEM THERE WERE "Z1" ITERATIONS NECESSARY FOR"
780 PRINT
790 PRINT "A SOLUTION CORRECT TO WITHIN ONE PERCENT."
800 END
```

PROGRAM 8.13 (continued)

```
VALUES OF TEMPERATURES IN GRID
0              100          100          100          0
400            4            6            8            200
400            6            9            12           200
400            8            12           16           200
0              300          300          300          0
VALUES OF TEMPERATURES IN GRID
0              100          100          100          0
400            210.879      153.029      140.219      200
400            265.013      161.018      145.68       200
400            288.157      224.309      185.469      200
0              300          300          300          0

VALUES OF TEMPERATURES IN GRID
0              100          100          100          0
400            241.438      181.974      167.941      200
400            295.26       238.163      209.183      200
400            309.158      266.237      238.345      200
0              300          300          300          0

VALUES OF TEMPERATURES IN GRID
0              100          100          100          0
400            246.671      192.511      176.3        200
400            302.696      247.073      216.761      200
400            318.906      278.065      248.146      200
0              300          300          300          0

VALUES OF TEMPERATURES IN GRID
0              100          100          100          0
400            249.411      193.629      177.598      200
400            304.619      248.875      218.741      200
400            320.933      279.114      249.248      200
0              300          300          300          0
```

IN THIS PROBLEM THERE WERE   74   ITERATIONS NECESSARY FOR

A SOLUTION CORRECT TO WITHIN ONE PERCENT.

TABLE 8.13A. Numerical Relaxation.

```
VALUES OF TEMPERATURES IN GRID
0              0               0             0            0
2000           4               6             8            500
2000           6               9             12           500
2000           8               12            16           500
0              1000            1000          1000         0
VALUES OF TEMPERATURES IN GRID
0              0               0             0            0
2000           810.531         410.813       266.066      500
2000           1138.19         566.656       490.962      500
2000           1175.59         843.343       631.125      500
0              1000            1000          1000         0

VALUES OF TEMPERATURES IN GRID
0              0               0             0            0
2000           925.749         528.39        409.284      500
2000           1251.67         836.457       608.744      500
2000           1283.02         957.024       747.165      500
0              1000            1000          1000         0

VALUES OF TEMPERATURES IN GRID
0              0               0             0            0
2000           954.65          557.328       423.753      500
2000           1280.54         865.364       642.503    500
2000           1311.79         985.9         780.896      500
0              1000            1000          1000         0

VALUES OF TEMPERATURES IN GRID
0              0               0             0            0
2000           963.081         565.76        427.367      500
200C           1287.77         872.591       646.117      500
2000           1319.02         993.127       784.51       500
0              1000            1000          1000         0

VALUES OF TEMPERATURES IN GRID
0              0               0             0            0
2000           963.683         566.362       427.969      500
2000           1288.97         873.796       646.719      500
2000           1320.22         994.331       785.112      500
0              1000            1000          1000         0
```

IN THIS PROBLEM THERE WERE   89   ITERATIONS NECESSARY FOR

A SOLUTION CORRECT TO WITHIN ONE PERCENT.

TABLE 8.13B.   Numerical Relaxation.

Next, how does the program instruct the computer when the temperature distribution fits the parameters of the problem, namely, the fixed temperatures at each edge. For Equation 8.13–1 it was shown that the proper temperature in the grid will cause all the residuals to be zero. Consequently, in the double loop, beginning at statement 600, the computer sums all the residuals (absolute value) and compares this sum to 10 in statement 650. If the sum is less than 10, the computer is told to stop (for increased accuracy, the value of the minimum sum of residuals could be reduced).

Program 8.13 demonstrates a method of iteration which basically is a systematic reduction (or relaxation) of the largest residual at each nodal point to zero. Greater precision can be obtained by this numerical relaxation method if the number of nodal points is increased.

Discussion of Computer Results: In Table 8.13A, five print outs of the temperatures of the grid are shown. The first list represents the initial temperature of the grid. The second list represents the temperatures of 20 increments through the relaxation loop, and so on for the third and fourth. The last list of temperatures are those for which the total sum of the residuals is less than 10. The computer counts the number of trips through the relaxation loop and it is seen that 74 iterations were necessary to 'zero in' on an acceptable temperature distribution for the grid.

In Table 8.13B, a more extreme temperature difference was imposed on the edges and, as a consequence, the computer needed 89 iterations to reduce the residuals to zero. Students should be encouraged to graph the resulting temperature distribution to explore areas of equal temperature lines. Furthermore, with this program as a model, the method can be extended to different two- and three-dimensional geometries.

8.14   CHARGE TO MASS RATIO OF THE ELECTRON

Lesson Characteristics:

> ENGINEERING LEVEL   college, intermediate
>
> MATHEMATICS BACKGROUND REQUIRED   analytical geometry
>
> PEDAGOGY   computer data reduction
>
> PROBLEM APPROACH   analytical solution
>
> STUDENT PARTICIPATION   uses prepared program
>
> PROGRAMMING SKILLS   none
>
> TIME OF STUDENT INVOLVEMENT   in laboratory— 10 min., out of laboratory—none

Lesson Description: This lesson demonstrates how the computer can be used to increase the efficiency of the time a student spends in the laboratory. The student will know immediately upon completion of a complicated experiment whether or not he has done it properly. He may re-do the experiment several times so that a meaningful write-up of the experiment can be made by the student.

If the student is working in an advanced laboratory he should investigate the programming techniques of how to use statistical and least-squares-fit routines in the building of a work-saving program. The programming skills would then become intermediate BASIC.

Background and Theory: A Helmholtz coil and a special electron gun and vacuum tube are used to measure the radius of curvature of the electron beam within the magnetic field (B-field) of the Helmholtz coil. (Figure 8.14). The student is required to take five values of coil current, (one for each of five radii used in the vacuum tube) for each of five different values

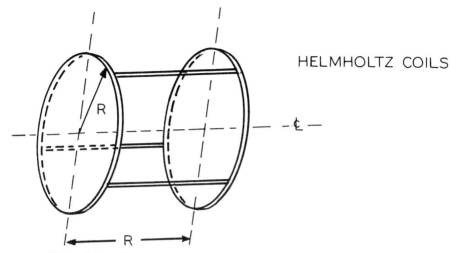

HELMHOLTZ COILS

Figure 8.14   The two coil arrangement which makes up the Helmholtz coils.

of accelerating voltage on the electron gun (giving five different maximum electron velocities).

Knowing the values of coil current (I), and electron accelerating potential (V), the following expression can be derived from the theory: (See Appendix A8.14)

$$i = \frac{R}{8\,\mu_0 N}\sqrt{250V\,\frac{m}{e}}\left(\frac{1}{r}\right) + \frac{\sqrt{125}}{8\,\mu_0}\frac{R}{N}(B_E) \qquad (8.14-1)$$

where:

R = Radius of Helmholtz Coils in Meters

μ_0 = Magnetic Permeability of Free Space

N = Number of Turns of Wire on each Helmholtz Coil

V = Electron Accelerating Potential

B = Earth Magnetic Field

m = Mass of an Electron

e = Charge of an Electron

r = Radius of the Electron Beam in Meters

The unknowns are B, e, and m.

The equation (8.14–1) is seen to be of the form:

$$y = mx + b$$

with $i = y$ and $\dfrac{1}{r} = x$.

```
10  DATA.05770,.05150,.04510,.03875,.03240,.33,72,1.25664E-6
20  FORI=1TO5
24  READ R(I)
26  LET A(I)=1/R(I)
30  NEXTI
50  READ R1, N, U0
100  DATA40,2.17,2.35,2.66,3.12,3.62
101  DATA 50,2.35,2.59,2.92,3.41,4.06
102  DATA 60,2.56,2.86,3.26,3.77,4.4
103  DATA 70,2.73,3.06,3.47,3.98,4.77
104  DATA 80,2.9,3.23,3.71,4.25,5.05
110  FOR K=1 TO5
120  READ V(K)
130  FOR J=1 TO 5
140  READI(J)
150  NEXT J
240  LET R3=0
250  LET I1=0
260  LET X=0
270  LET Y =0
280  FOR J=1 TO 5
290  LET R3=R3+A(J)
300  LET I1=I1+I(J)
310  LET X=X+A(J)*I(J)
312  LET Y=Y+A(J)*A(J)
330  NEXT J
340  LET D=5*Y-R3*R3
350  LET S(K)=(5*X-R3*I1)/D
360  LET B(K)=(250*R1*R1*V(K))/(64*U0*U0*N*N*S(K)*S(K))
370  NEXT K
380  LET E2=0
382  LET E3=0
390  FOR J=1 TO 5
400  LET E2=E2+B(J)
402  NEXT J
403  LET E4=E2/5
404  FOR J=1 TO 5
406  LET E3=E3+(B(J)-E4)↑2
420  NEXT J
440  LET G=SQR(E3/4)
450  LET P=.6745*G
460  PRINT
470  PRINT "POTENTIAL","SLOPE","E/M","1/R"
480  PRINT
490  FOR J=1 TO 5
500  PRINTV(J),S(J),B(J),A(J)
510  NEXT J
520  PRINT
530  PRINT"AVE E/M="E4,"STD DEV="G
532  PRINT
534  PRINT"PROB ERR="P
540  PRINT
999  END
```

PROGRAM 8.14 Charge to mass ratio of the electron using least-squares-fit and statistical routines for treating laboratory data

A plot of i versus $1/r$ would then produce a series of straight lines each with a slope of:

$$s = \left(\frac{R}{8\mu_0 N}\right)\sqrt{250V\,m/e} \qquad (8.14\text{--}2)$$

LET S=R1(8*U0*N)*SQR(250*V*M/E)

which varies only with V, and a common intercept since all values of the intercept of Equation 8.14–1 are constant. A by-product of the experiment could be to calculate the magnetic field of the earth from the intercept value.

Knowing the slope from the experimental data, the ratio of e/m can be solved from Equation (8.14–2):

$$\frac{e}{m} = \frac{250\,R^2}{64\,\mu_0^2 N^2}\left(\frac{V}{S^2}\right) \qquad (8.14\text{--}3)$$

After five calculations of e/m, the values are treated statistically for mean and probable error. Poor results can be immediately investigated and the values re-calculated.

Computer Technique: The formula for finding the slope of a linear set of data by the method of least squares fit is:

$$\text{Balance Slope} = \frac{N\Sigma x_i/y_i - \Sigma x_i\Sigma(x_iy_i)}{(N\Sigma x_i^2 - (\Sigma x_i)^2)} \qquad (8.14\text{--}4)$$

This formula must be done in steps by doing each summation separately, and then finding the slope after the summations have been completed. In terms of this problem, Equation 8.14–4 would be:

$$S = \frac{5\Sigma I/r - \Sigma 1/r\Sigma I/r}{\left(5\Sigma\left(\dfrac{1}{r}\right)^2 - \left(\Sigma\dfrac{1}{r}\right)^2\right)} \qquad (8.14\text{--}5)$$

The separate calculations could be:

    290 LET R3=R3+1/(R(J)) $(\Sigma 1/R)$

    300 LET I1=I1+I(J) (ΣI)

    310 LET X=X+(1/R(J)*I(J)) $(\Sigma I/R)$

    312 LET Y=Y+(I/(R(J))*1/(R(J))) $(\Sigma(1/R)^2)$

The denominator could then be:

    340 LET D=5*Y−R3*R3

and Equation (8.14–5) would become in computer language:

    350 LET S(K)=(5*X–R3*I1)/D

After the slope is known, the value of e/m can be calculated from Equation (8.14–3)

360 LET B(K) = 250*R1↑2*V(K)/(64*U0↑2*N↑2*S(K) ↑2)

This series of computations is made five times, (K=1 to 5) once for each set of data at potential, V.

The mean is then found:

400 LET E2=E2+B(J)   (Σe/m)

403 LET E4=E2/5   (MEAN)

The standard deviation for small samples of data is:

$$\sigma \cong \frac{\sqrt{\Sigma(x_i - \bar{x})^2}}{N-1}$$

In computer language:

406 LET E3 = E3 + (B(J)–E4)↑2   (Σ(B(J)–E4)²)

440 LET G=SQR (E3/4)   (N–1=4)

The probable error is defined as 67.45% of the standard deviation

450 LET P = .6745*G

Comments About the Computer Program: It is more efficient to READ constants into the program than to write LET statements for each constant. A data statement (statement 10) containing the constants followed by appropriate READ statements is more appropriate.

The first READ statement is in a loop and reads each of the pin radii and saves its inverse as A(I).

20 FOR I=1 TO 5

24 READ R

26 LET A(I) = 1/R

30 NEXT I

The remaining constants can be read on one line:

50 READ R1, N, UO

The experimental data is listed with the potential first and each of the five current values obtained at that potential next on the same line. The potential values are read in with the 'K' loop and the current values are read in the first 'J' loop within the 'K' loop. Variables R3, I1, X and Y must be initialized prior to entering the second 'J' loop in order to obtain a correct summation. (These variables would have been zero on the first pass through the loop, but need to be initialized on each subsequent pass.)

The values of slope, (S(K) and e/m, (B(K)) are calculated after the second 'J' loop but prior to 'NEXT K' (statement 370), as shown in the flow chart.

The statistics of five runs are computed in five stages:

(1) 400 LET E2=E2+B(J)   (Σ e/m)

(2) 403 LET E4=E2/5   (Mean e/m)

(3) 406 LET E3 = E3 + (B(J) – E4)↑2   (Deviation Squared)

POTENTIAL	SLOPE	E/M	1/R
40	0•1097	1•7254E+11	17•33102253
50	0•1272	1•6057E+11	19•41747573
60	0•1364	1•6748E+11	22•172949
70	0•1495	1•6271E+11	25•80645161
80	0•1586	1•6513E+11	30•86419753

AVE E/M= 1•6568E+11   STD DEV= 4•6262E+09

PROB ERR= 3•1204E+09

TABLE 8.14A.

(4) 440 LET G = SQR (E3/4)   (Standard Deviation)

(5) 450 LET P = .6745*G   (Probable Error)

Finally, the calculated information is printed in tabular form. The student should still be required to plot the data of I (current) versus 1/r in order to check for poor data points.

Discussion of Computer Results: In the data shown, the typical student error in data taking for this experiment can be shown. Each student was responsible for measuring one set of data, giving each of five students an opportunity to observe and set the electron beam until it is at the proper radius, just striking the pin.

The data of Table 8.14A shows an e/m ratio of approximately 1.66×10^{11} coulombs/kilogram. The actual value is approximately 1.75×10^{11} c/kg. This is normally caused when the electron beam is positioned in too large a circle. The student who made the 40 volt run made the best measurements. Another set of data by each student should give better results, Table 8.14B shows an improved set of data.

```
100 DATA 40,2•1,2•3,2•6,2•95,3•55
101 DATA 50,2•32,2•53,2•88,3•3,3•95
102 DATA 60,2•5,2•8,3•2,3•65,4•3
103 DATA 70,2•68,3•0,3•42,3•92,4•7
104 DATA 80,2•85,3•25,3•7,4•25,5•0
```
TABLE 8.14B.

POTENTIAL	SLOPE	E/M	1/R
40	0•1066	1•8257E+11	17•33102253
50	0•121	1•7743E+11	19•41747573
60	0•1323	1•7798E+11	22•172949
70	0•1482	1•6547E+11	25•80645161
80	0•1572	1•681E+11	30•86419753

AVE E/M= 1•7431E+11   STD DEV= 7•2106E+09

PROB ERR= 4•8635E+09

TABLE 8.14C.

APPENDIX

A8.14

Theory:

A. Helmholtz Coils (Figure 8.14)

The Helmholtz coils are two identical coils mounted on the same axis, separated by a distance equal to the coil radius, R. They have an almost constant magnetic field (B-field) for a significant portion of the distance along the center line between the two coils. This B-field can be calculated from Biot's law, and are therefore useful in experiments which depend upon a constant, known, B-field.

For a coil of radius, R, current, i, and of N turns of wire, the B-field is calculated along the axis to be:

$$B = \frac{\mu_0}{2} \frac{Ni\,R^2}{r^3} \qquad (A8.14-1)$$

In the Helmholtz coils, the B-field at a point midway between the two coils, $(S = R/2)$ is just twice that of Equation $(A8.14-1)$

$$B_{1/2} = \frac{\mu_0 N_i R^2}{r^3} \qquad (A8.14-2)$$

where

$$r = \sqrt{s^2 + R^2} \text{ but } s = R/2$$

Therefore

$$r = \sqrt{R^2/4 + R^2} = \frac{\sqrt{5}}{2} R$$

and

$$r^3 = \frac{5^{3/2}}{8} R^3 = \frac{\sqrt{125}}{8} R^3$$

and Equation A8.14–2 becomes

$$B_{1/2} = \frac{8\mu_0 N_i}{R\sqrt{125}} \qquad (A8.14-3)$$

The B-field of the Helmholtz coils is therefore seen to be directly proportional to the current through coils, a value easily set and read in the laboratory.

B. Electron Kinematics

As long as the accelerating potential is less than 5 kv, the electron is considered non-relativistic and the velocity is seen to be

$$v = \sqrt{2eV/m} \qquad (A8.14-4)$$

(This is obtained from the kinetic energy of an electron, $1/2\ mv^2$ and the charge times the potential, eV. i.e., $1/2\ mv^2 = eV$).

The force on a charged particle is found to be: $F = q(\bar{v} \times \bar{B})$ or in terms of the radial acceleration force:

$$F = m(v^2/r) = qvB_{net} \text{ or in scaler terms with } e = q;$$

$$m(v^2/4) = evB_{net}$$

or

$$mv = eBr$$

and

$$e/m = \frac{v}{(B_{net}r)} \qquad (A8.14\text{--}5)$$

v can be eliminated from Equation A8.14–5 by substitution of Equation A8.14–4.

$$e/m = \frac{1}{B_{net}r}\sqrt{2eV/m}$$

$$(e/m)^2 = \frac{1}{B^2_{net}r^2}(2Ve/m)$$

and finally

$$e/m = \frac{2v}{B^2_{net}r^2} \qquad (A8.14\text{--}6)$$

Now the substitution of the value of B from the Helmholtz coils Equation A8.14–3, could be made if allowance for the magnetic field of the earth was not made. However, if the coils are aligned parallel to and opposite in B-field direction to the earth's B-field, the net field for the experiment would be:

$$B_{coil} = B_{net} + B_{earth} \qquad (A8.14\text{--}7)$$

if the B-field due to the earth is neglected, then Equation A8.14–6 becomes:

$$\frac{e}{m} = \frac{2V\ 125\ R^2}{64\mu_o^2\ N^2_i} = \frac{250\ R^2\ V}{64\mu_o^2\ N^2_i} \qquad (A8.14\text{--}8)$$

To account for the earth's magnetic field substitute in Equation A8.14–7 the value of B_{coil} from Equation A8.14–3 and B_{net} from Equation A8.14–6

$$B_{net} = \sqrt{(m/e)\ 2V\ (l/r)}.$$

$$\frac{8\mu_o\ N_i}{R\sqrt{125}} = \sqrt{2V\ (m/e)\ l/r} + B_{earth}$$

or solving for i in order to obtain an equation of the form:

$$y = mx + b$$

where

$$y = i, \; x = 1/r, \; \text{and} \; B_{earth} = b$$

$$i = \frac{R}{8\mu_o \, N_i} \sqrt{250 \, V(M/e) \, (1/r)} + \frac{R \sqrt{125}}{8\mu_o \, N_i} (B_{earth})$$

The slope, from a plot of i versus $1/r$ is:

$$\text{Slope,} \; S = \frac{R}{8\mu_o \, N_i} \sqrt{250V \, m/e} \qquad \text{(A8.14–9)}$$

and in terms of slope:

$$\frac{e}{m} = \frac{250 \, R^2}{64\mu_o{}^2 \, N^2} \; \frac{V}{S^2} \qquad \text{(A.8.14–10)}$$

Notice the similarity between Equation A8.14–10 and Equation A8.14–8.

REFERENCES

(1) TAYLOR, EDWIN F., *A Skimmable Report on the ELIZA Conversational Tutoring Systems.* Massachusetts Institute of Technology. 1968.

(2) HALLIDAY, D., RESNICK, R., *Physics for Students of Science and Engineering.* John Wiley and Sons, Inc., New York. 1964.

(3) SHORTLEY, G., WILLIAMS, D., *Elements of Physics.* Prentice-Hall, Inc., Englewood Cliffs, New Jersey, 1965.

(4) FEYNMAN, R. P., *Feynman Lectures on Physics.* Addison-Wesley, Cambridge. 1963.

(5) SEARS, F. W., ZEMANSKY, M. W., *University Physics.* Addison-Wesley Publishing Company, Reading, Massachusetts. 1964.

(6) ALONSO, M., FINN, E. J., *Fundamental University Physics.* Addison-Wesley Publishing Company, Reading, Massachusetts. 1967.

(7) SEARS, F. W., *Optics.* Addison-Wesley Publishing Company, Reading, Massachusetts. 1958.

(8) GREGG, D. G., *Principles of Chemistry.* Boston: Allyn and Bacon, Inc., 1958.

(9) METCALFE, H. C., WILLIAMS, J. E. and CASTKA, J. F. *Modern Chemistry.* New York: Holt, Rinehart and Winston, Inc., 1966.

(10) MASTERTON, W. L. and SLOWINSKI, E. J. *Chemical Principles.* Philadelphia: W. B. Saunders Company, 1966.

(11) DANIELS, F. and ALBERTY, R. A. *Physical Chemistry.* New York: John Wiley & Sons, Inc., 1959.

(12) GLASSTONE, S. and LEWIS, D., *Elements of Physical Chemistry.* New York: D. Van Nostrand Company, Inc., 1960.

(13) KUO, S. S., *Numerical Methods and Computers.* Massachusetts: Addison-Wesley Publishing Company, 1966.

(14) FRIEDLANDER, G. and KENNEDY, J. W., *Nuclear and Radiochemistry.* New York: John Wiley & Sons, Inc., 1960.

(15) DANIELS, F., WILLIAMS, J. W., BENDER, P., ALBERTY, R. A. and CORNWELL, C. D., *Experimental Physical Chemistry.* New York: McGraw-Hill Book Company, Inc., 1962.

(16) WEIDNER, R. T. and SELLS, R. L., *Elementary Modern Physics.* Allyn and Bacon, Inc., Boston, Massachusetts. 1964.

(17) CHURCHILL, R. V., *Operational Mathematics*. McGraw-Hill Book Company, Inc., New York. 1958.

(18) CLEMENT, P. R. and JOHNSON, W. C., *Electrical Engineering Science*. McGraw-Hill Book Company, Inc., New York. 1960.

(19) CORCORAN, G. F., *Basic Electrical Engineering*. John Wiley and Sons, Inc., London. 1949.

(20) SEARS, F. W., *Thermodynamics*. Addison-Wesley Publishing Company, Inc., Reading, Massachusetts. 1964.

(21) JAKOB, M., *Heat Transfer*. John Wiley and Sons, Inc., New York. 1949.

APPENDIX A

GLOSSARY OF TERMS OFTEN USED IN COMPUTER SCIENCES

Access, Random

Access to storage under conditions in which the next position from which information is to be obtained is in no way dependent on the previous one.

Access Time

(1) The time interval between the instant at which information is: (a) called for from storage and the instant at which delivery is completed, i.e., the read time; or (b) ready for storage and the instant at which storage is completed, i.e., the write time. (2) The latency plus the word-time.

Accumulator

A device containing a register which stores a quantity; when a second quantity is delivered to the device, it forms the sum of the quantity standing in the register and the second quantity, and stores the result in the register. Frequently, the accumulator is involved in other operations upon a quantity in the register such as sensing, shifting, extracting, complementing, etc. Frequently, the accumulator is only a storage register, the actual electronic arithmetic operations being performed in the adder; this fact is usually of no direct importance to the coder.

Address

A label, name or number which designates a register, a location or a device where information is stored; that part of an instruction which specifies the operand.

Allocate

To assign storage locations to the main routines and sub-routines, thereby fixing the absolute values of any symbolic addresses. In some cases allocation may require segmentation.

Alphanumeric

Characters which may be either letters of the alphabet, numerals, or special symbols.

Analog Computer

A computer which represents numerical quantities as electrical and physical variables. Solutions to mathematical problems are obtained by manipulation of these variables.

Arithmetic Unit

That portion of the hardware of an automatic computer in which arithmetical and logical operations are performed.

Auxiliary Storage

A storage device which is capable of holding (usually) larger amounts of information than the main memory of the computer although with slower access.

Binary

A type of mathematics where the numerical structure utilizes the Base 2 rather than Base 10.

Binary Number

A single digit or group of characters or symbols representing the total, aggregate or amount of units utilizing the base two; usually using only "0" and "1" digits to express quantity.

Bit

A contraction of binary digit.

Buffer Storage

Facilities linked to: (1) An input device in which information is assembled from external or secondary storage and stored ready for transfer to internal storage; (2) An output device into which information is transmitted from internal storage and held for transfer to secondary or external storage. Computation continues while transfers between buffer storage and secondary or external storage or vice versa take place. (3) Any device which stores information temporarily during data transfers.

Call Number

A set of characters identifying a sub-routine and containing information concerning parameters to be inserted in the sub-routine, information to be used in generating the sub-routine, or information related to the operands; a call word when exactly one word is filled.

Card

Heavy, stiff paper of uniform size and shape, adapted for being punched in an intelligent array of holes. The punched holes are sensed electrically by wire brushes or mechanically by metal feelers. One standard card, is 7-3/8 inches long by 3-1/4 inches wide and contains 80 columns in each of which any one of 12 positions may be punched.

Clear

To replace information in a storage device by zero (or blank, in some machines).

Closed Loop

A family of automatic control units linked together with a process to form an endless chain. The effects of control action are constantly measured so that if the process goes off the beam, the control units pitch in to bring it back into line.

Closed-Shop

This is intended to mean that mode of computing machine support wherein the applied programs and utility routines are written by members of a specialized group whose only professional concern is the use of computers.

Closed Sub-Routine

A sub-routine is stored in the main path of the routine. Such a sub-routine is entered by a jump operation and provision is made to return control to the main routine at the end of the operation. The instructions related to the entry and re-entry function constitute a linkage. Also called a linked sub-routine.

Code

A system of symbols and their use in representing rules for handling the flow or processing of information; to actually prepare problems for solution on a specific computer.

Code, Computer

The code representing the operations built into the hardware of the computer.

Code Instruction

An artificial language for describing or expressing the instructions which can be carried out by a digital computer. In automatically sequenced computers, the instruction code is used when describing or expressing sequences of instructions, and each instruction word usually contains a part specifying the operation to be performed and one or more addresses which identify a particular location in storage. Sometimes an address part of an instruction is not intended to specify a location in storage but is used for some other purpose.
If more than one address is used, the code is called a multiple-address code.

Coding

The list, in computer code or in pseudo-code, of the successive computer operations required to solve a given problem.

Coding, Automatic

Any technique in which a computer is used to help bridge the gap between some "easiest" form, intellectually and manually, of describing the steps to be followed in solving a given problem and some "most efficient" final coding of the same problem for a given computer; two basic forms are Routine, complication and Routine, interpretation.

Coding, Numeric

A system of abbreviation used in the preparation of information for machine acceptance by reducing all information to numerical quantities; in contrast to alphabetic coding.

Command

A pulse, signal, or set of signals initiating one step in the performance of a computer operation. See instruction and order.

Compiler

A program making routine, which produces a specific program for a particular problem by determining the intended meaning of an element of information expressed in pseudo-code, selecting or generating the required sub-routine, transforming the sub-routine into specific coding for the specific problem, assigning specific storage registers, etc., and entering it as an element of the problem program, maintaining a record of the sub-routines used and their position in the program and continuing to the next element of information in pseudo-code.

Computer

Any device capable of accepting information, applying prescribed processes to the information, and supplying the results of these processes; sometimes, more specifically, a device for performing sequences of arithmetic and logical operations; sometimes, still more specifically, a stored-program digital computer capable of performing sequences of internally-stored instructions, as opposed to calculators on which the sequence is impressed manually (desk calculator) or from tape or cards (card programmed calculator).

Connector

In flow charting, a symbol used to indicate the interconnection of two points in the flow chart.

Contents

The information stored in any storage medium. Quite prevalently, the symbol (.) is used to indicate "the contents of"; e.g., (m) indicates the contents of the storage location whose address is m; (A) indicates the contents of register A; (T_2) may indicate the contents of the tape on input-output unit two, etc.

Control

(1) Usually, those parts of a digital computer which effect the carrying out of instructions in proper sequence, the interpretation of each instruction, and the application of the proper signals to the arithmetic unit and otherparts in accordance with the interpretation. (2) Frequently, one or more of the components in any mechanism responsible for interpreting and carrying out manually-initiated directions. Sometimes called manual control. (3) In some business application of mathematics, a mathematical check.

Core Storage

A form of high speed storage in which information is represented by the direction of magnetization of ferromagnetic cores.

Counter

A device, register, or storage location for storing integers, permitting these integers to be increased or decreased by unity or by an arbitrary integer, and capable of being reset to zero or to an arbitrary integer.

Counter, Control

A device which records the storage location of the instruction word which is to be operated upon following the instruction word in current use. The control counter may select storage locations in sequence, thus obtaining the next instruction word from the following storage location, unless a transfer or special instruction is encountered.

Cycle

A set of operations repeated as a unit; a non-arithmetic shift in which the digits dropped off at one end of a word are returned at the other end in circular fashion; cycle right and cycle left. To repeat a set of operations a prescribed number of times including, when required, supplying necessary address changes by arithmetic processes or by means of a hardware device such as a B-box or cycle-counter.

Data

A collection of facts, numeric and alphabetical characters etc., which is processed or produced by a computer. Data is properly plural, the singular form being datum but, in common computer usage "data" is taken as plural or singular.

Data Processing

A generic term for all the operations carried out on data according to precise rules of procedure; a generic term for computing in general as applied to business situations.

Debugging

The process of determining the correctness of a computer routine, locating any errors in it, and correcting them. Also the detection and correction of malfunctions in the computer itself.

Decade

A group or assembly of ten units, e.g., a decade counter counts to ten in one column.

Decimal, Coded, Binary

Decimal notation in which the individual decimal digits are represented by some binary code, e.g., in the 8–4–2–1 coded decimal notation, the number twelve is represented as 0001 0010 for 1 and 2, respectively. Whereas in pure binary notation, it is represented as 1100. Other coded decimal notations are known as: 5–4–2–1, excess three, 2–4–2–1, etc.

Decision

The computer operation of determining if a certain relationship exists regarding words in memory or registers, and taking alternative courses of action. Effected by conditional jumps.

Decode

To ascertain the intended meaning of the individual characters or groups of characters in the pseudo-coded program.

Density Packing

A number of units of useful information contained within a given linear dimension, usually expressed in units per inch, e.g., the number of binary digital magnetic pulses stored on tape or drum per linear inch on a single track by a single head.

Digit

One of the n symbols of integral value ranging from 0 to n-1 inclusive in a scale of numbering of base n, e.g., one of the ten decimal digits, 0, 1, 2, 3, 4, 5, 6, 7, 8, 9.

Digit, Binary

A whole number in the binary scale of notation; this digit may be only 0 (zero) or 1 (one). It may be equivalent to an "on" or "off" condition, a "yes" or a "no," etc.

Digit, Decimal Coded

One of ten arbitrarily-selected patterns of ones and zeros used to represent the decimal digits.

Digital

The quality of utilizing numbers in a given scale of notation to represent all the quantities that occur in a problem or a calculation.

Digital Computer

A computer in which information is represented in discrete form, such as by one of two directions of magnetization of a magnetic core, or by the presence or absence of an electrical pulse at a certain point in time.

Double-Precision (Quantity)

A quantity having twice as many digits as are normally carried in a specific computer word. Often called double-length.

Down-Time

The period during which a computer is malfunctioning or not operating correctly due to machine failures; contrasted with available time, idle time or standby time.

Dummy

An artificial address, instruction, or other unit of information inserted solely to fulfill prescribed conditions (such as word-length or block-length) without affecting operations.

Edit

To rearrange information. Editing may involve the deletion of unwanted data, the selection of pertinent data, the insertion of invariant symbols such as page numbers and typewriter characters, and the application of standard processes such as zero-suppression.

Electronic

Pertaining to the application of that branch of science which deals with the motion, emmission and behavior of currents of free electrons, especially in vaccum, gas or phototubes and special conductors or semi-conductors. Contrasted with electric which pertains to the flow of large currents in wires only.

Erase

To replace all the binary digits in a storage device by binary zeros. In a binary computer, erasing is equivalent to clearing, while in a coded decimal computer where the pulse code for decimal zero may contain binary ones, clearing leaves decimal zero while erasing leaves all zero pulse codes.

Eternal Storage

Storage facilities removable from the computer itself but holding information in a form acceptable to the computer (magnetic tape, punched cards, etc.)

Execution

Of an instruction; the set of elementary steps carried out by the computer to produce the result specified by the operation code of the instruction.

Exchange

To interchange the contents of two storage devices or locations.

Field

A set of one or more characters (not necessarily all lying on the same word) which is treated as a whole; a set of one or more columns on a punched card consistently used to record similiar information.

File

A collection of records; an organized collection of information directed toward some purpose. The records in a file may or may not be sequenced according to a key contained in each record.

File Maintenance

The processing of a master file required to handle the non-periodic changes in it. Examples: Changes in number of dependents in a payroll file, the addition of new checking accounts in a bank.

Fixed-Point

A notation or system of arithmetic in which all numeric quantities are expressed by a predetermined number of digits with the point implicitly located at some predetermined position; contrasted with floating-point.

Flip-Flop

A bi-stable device; a device capable of assuming two stable states; a bi-stable device which may assume a given stable state depending upon the pulse history of one or more input points and having one or more output points. The device is capable of storing a bit of information; controlling gates, etc.; a toggle.

Floating Point

A form of number representation in which quantities are represented by one number multiplied by a power of the number base. For instance, in floating decimal, 127.6 might be represented as $1.276 \cdot 10^2$. Most useful in engineering and scientific computers where it is often difficult to predict the size of computer quantities.

Flow-Chart

A graphical representation of a sequence of operations, using symbols to represent the operations such as compute, substitute, compare, jump, copy, read, write, etc. A flow chart is a more detailed representation than a diagram.

Format

The predetermined arrangement of characters, fields, lines, page numbers, punctuation marks, etc. Refers to input, output and files.

Function-Table

Two or more sets of information so arranged that an entry in one set selects one or more entries in the remaining sets; a dictionary; a device constructed of hardware, or a sub-routine, which can either (a) decode multiple inputs into a single output or (b) encode a single input into multiple outputs; a tabulation of the values of a function for a set of values of the variable.

Garbage

Unwanted and meaningless information in memory or on tape. Also called hash.

Generate

To produce a needed sub-routine from parameters and skeletal coding.

Hard Copy

A document produced at the same time that information is transcribed to a form not easily readable by human beings.

Hardware

The mechanical, magnetic, electronic and electrical devices from which a computer is fabricated; the assembly of material forming a computer.

Housekeeping

Operations in a routine which do not directly contribute to the solution of the problem at hand, but which are made necessary by the method of operation of the computer. Examples: Loop testing, tape sentinels, record grouping. Also called red tape operations.

Index Register

A register which contains a quantity which may be used to automatically modify addresses (and for other purposes) under direction of the control section of the computer.

Information

(Used in specialized sense in computing). A collection of facts, data, numerical and alphanumerical characters, etc., which is processed or produced by a computer.

Input

The information which is transferred from external storage into the internal storage; a modifier designating the device performing this function.

Instruction

A set of characters which defines an operation together with one or more addresses (or no addresses) and which, as a unit, causes the computer to operate accordingly on the indicated quantities. The term "instruction" is preferable to the terms "command" and "order"; command is reserved for electronic signals; order is reserved for "the order of the characters" (implying sequence) or "the order of the interpolation," etc.

Internal Storage

Storage facilities forming an integral physical part of the computer, from which instructions may be executed.

Interpret

(1) Refers to an interpretive routine. See Below. (2) To print at the top of a punched card the information punched in it, using a machine called an interpreter.

Key

The field or fields of information by which a record in a file is identified, and/or controlled.

Language, Machine

Information recorded in a form which may be made available to a computer, e.g. punched paper tape may contain information available to a machine, whereas the same information in the form of printed characters on a page is not available to a machine; information which can be sensed by a machine.

Left-Hand Justified

A number (decimal, binary, etc.) which exists in a memory cell, location or register possessing no left-hand zeros; i.e. $\boxed{3|9|2|7|6|4|0|0|5|0}$, is considered to be left-hand justified.

Library

An organized collection of standard and proven routines and subroutines, which may be incorporated into larger routines.

Logic

The science that deals with the canons and criteria of validity in thought and demonstration; the science of the formal principles of reasoning; the basic principles and applications of

Logic, Symbolic

Exact reasoning about relations using symbols that are efficient in calculation. A branch of this subject known as Boolean algebra has been of considerable assistance in the logical design of computing circuits.

Loop

A coding technique whereby a group of instructions is repeated with modification of some of the instructions in the group and/or with modification of the data being operated upon. Usually consists of the following steps: (1) Loop Initialization—The instructions immediately prior to a loop proper which set addresses, counters, and/or data to their desired initial values. (2) Loop Computing—Those instructions of a loop which actually perform the primary function of the loop, as distinguished from loop initialization, modification and testing, which are housekeeping operations. (3) Loop Modification—Those instructions of a loop which alter instruction addresses, counters or data. (4) Loop Testing—Those instructions of a loop which determine when the loop function has been completed.

Master File

A file of semi-permanent information, which is usually updated periodically.

Memory Register

A register which is involved in all transfers of data and instructions in either direction between memory and the arithmetic and control registers. It may be addressed in some machines. Also called Distributer, Exchange Register, High Speed Bus.

Merge

To produce a single sequence of items, ordered according to some rule (i.e. arranged in some orderly sequence), from two or more sequences previously ordered according to the same rule, without changing the items in size, structure, or total number. Merging is a special case of collation.

Message

A group of words, variable in length, transported as a unit; a transported item of information.

Microsecond

One-millionth of a second.

Millisecond

One-thousandth of a second.

Mnemonic

Assisting or intended to assist, memory; of or pertaining to memory; mnemonics is the art of improving the efficiency of the memory (in computer storage).

Modify

To alter in an instruction the address of the operand; to alter a subroutine according to a defined parameter.

Octal

Pertaining to the number base of eight, e.g., in octal notation, octal 214 is 2 times 64 plus 1 times 8 plus 4 times 1 equals decimal 140; octal 214 is binary 010, 001, 100.

Off-Line (Adjective)

Operation of input/output and other devices not under direct computer control; most commonly used to designate the transfer of information between magnetic tapes and other media.

On-Line (Adjective)

Operation of an input/output device as a component of the computer, under computer control.

Operation Code

That part of an instruction designating the operation to be performed.

Operation, Real-Time, On-Line, Simulated

The processing of data in synchronism with a physical process in such a fashion that the results of the data-processing are useful to the physical operation.

Operator

The person who actually manipulates the computer controls, places information media into the input devices, removes the output, presses the start button, etc.; a mathematical symbol which represents a mathematical process to be performed on an associated function.

Output

Information transferred from the internal storage of a computer to output devices or external storage.

Overflow

In an arithmetic operation, the generation of a quantity beyond the capacity of the registor or location which is to receive the result; over capacity; the information contained in an item of information which is in excess of a given amount.

Overlay

A technique for bringing routines into high speed memory from some other form of storage during processing, so that several routines will occupy the same storage locations at different times; used when the total memory requirements for instructions exceed the available high speed memory.

Precision

The degree of exactness with which a quantity is stated; a relative term often based on the number of significant digits in a measurements.

Program

A plan for the solution of a problem. A complete program includes plans for the transcription of data, coding for the computer and plans for the absorption of the results into the system. The list of codes instructions is called a routine; to plan a computation or process from the asking of a question to the delivery of the results, including the integration of the operation into an existing system. This programming consists of planning and coding, including numerical analysis, systems analysis, specification of printing formats, and any other functions necessary to the integration of a computer in a system.

Programmer

A person who prepares instruction sequences without necessarily converting them into the detailed codes.

Punched Card

A piece of lightweight cardboard on which information is represented by holes punched in specific positions.

Random Access Storage

A storage technique in which the time required to obtain information is independent of the location.

Raw Data

Data which has not been processed; may or may not be in machine-sensible form.

Read

To copy, usually from one form of storage to another, particularly from external or secondary storage to internal storage; to sense the meaning of arrangements of hardware; to sense the presence of information on a recording medium.

Reader, Magnetic Tape

A device capable of restoring to a train or sequence of electrical pulses, information recorded on a magnetic tape in the form of a series of magnetized sports, usually for the purpose of transferring the information to some other storage medium.

Reader, Paper Tape

A device capable of restoring to a train or sequence of electrical pulses, information punched on paper tape in the form of a series of holes, usually for the purpose of transferring the information to some other storage medium.

Reading, Rate of

Number of characters, words, fields, blocks or cards sensed by an input sensing device per unit of time.

Real-Time

The performance of a computation during the actual time that the related physical process transpires in order that results of the computations are useful in guiding the physical process.

Record

A collection of fields; the information relating to one area of activity in a data processing activity; files are made up of records. Sometimes called item.

Rerun

To repeat all or part of a program on a computer.

Restore

To return a cycle index, a variable address, or other computer word to its initial or preselected value; periodic regeneration of charge, especially in volatile, condenser-action storage systems.

Return

To go back to a specific, planned point in a program, usually when an error is detected, for the purpose of a rerunning the program. Rerun points are usually three to five minutes apart to avoid long periods of lost computer time. Information pertinent to a rerun is available in standby registers from point to point.

Routine

A set of coded instructions arranged in proper sequence to direct the computer to perform a desired operation or series of operations.

Run

One performance of a program on a computer; performance of one routine, or several routines automatically linked so that they form an operating unit, during which manual manipulations are not required of the computer operator.

Sign

The symbol which distinguishes positive from negative numbers.

Sort

To arrange items of information according to rules dependent upon a key or field contained in the items.

Storage Buffer

A synchronizing element between two different forms of storage, usually between internal and external; an input device in which information is assembled from external or secondary storage and stored ready for transfer to internal storage; an output device into which information is copied from internal storage and held for transfer to secondary or external storage. Computation continues while transfers between buffer storage and secondary or internal storage or vice versa take place.

Sub-Routine

The set of instructions necessary to direct the computer to carry out a well defined mathematical or logical operation; a sub-unit of a routine. A sub-routine is often written in relative or symbolic coding even when the routine to which it belongs is not.

Symbolic Coding

Broadly, any coding system in which symbols other than machine addresses are used. The term is used, unfortunately perhaps, to refer to two rather different types of coding: (1) A relative coding system in which machine instructions are written, but in a much freer form than actual instructions. (2) A method of coding in which addresses are represented by arbitrary symbols which bear no absolute or relative relationship to actual memory locations; in fact, the coding itself may bear little resemblance to machine language.

System

(1) An assembly of components united by some form of regulated interaction to form an organized whole. (2) A collection of operations and procedures men and machines, by which business activity is carried on.

Systems Approach

Looking at the overall situation rather than the narrow implications of the task at hand; particularly, looking for inter-relationships between the task at hand and other functions which relate to it.

Temporary Storage

An area of working storage not reserved for one use only but used by many sections of a program at different times.

Transmit

To reproduce information in a new location replacing whatever was previously stored and clearing or erasing the source of the information.

Word

A set of characters which occupies one storage location and is treated by the computer circuits as a unit and transported as such. Ordinarily a word is treated by the control unit as an instruction.

A SUMMARY OF BASIC STATEMENTS

The form of each statement is given with the parameters in italics. An example of the statement follows.

1. Arithmetic Statements

DIM *letter (integer)*
or
DIM *letter (integer, integer)*

100   DIM A(100)

100   DIM A(10,20)

LET *variable = expression*

100   LET X1=X↑2*(P−2)/D+6

2. Control Statements

100   END

GO TO *line number*

100   GO TO 17

IF *expression relation expression* THEN *line number*

100   IF X>=Y THEN 32

100   STOP

3. Identifying Statements

DATA *number, number, ... , number*

100   DATA 7,0,−2,237.3,6E−3

REM *any string of characters*

100   REM SUMMARY OF BASIC STATEMENTS

4. Input/Output Statements

INPUT

100   INPUT X,Y1,Z

PRINT *"characters,"* *variables* or PRINT *"characters"* or PRINT *variables*

        100   PRINT "X=" X,

        100   PRINT "THE ANSWER IS:"

        100   PRINT X

        READ *variable, variable,* . . . . , *variable*

        100   READ X,Y1,Z

5. Loop Statements

FOR *unsubscripted variable=expression* TO *expression* STEP *expression*

        100   FOR X1=P+2 TO N STEP 5

        100   FOR X1=1 TO 100

        NEXT *unsubscripted variable*

        100   NEXT X1

STATISTICAL PROGRAMS: THE CALCULATION OF THE T-SCORE DISTRIBUTION IS SHOWN WITH AN EXPLANATION INCLUDED IN THE PROGRAM

```
100 REM********** CALCULATION OF T - SCORE DISTRIBUTION ***********
110 REM
120 REM      THIS PROGRAM CALCULATES THE T - SCORE GIVEN THE FREQUENCY
130 REM OF RAW SCORES IN A 50-QUESTION EXAMINATION.  WITH MINOR CHANGES
140 REM THE PROGRAM CAN BE USED FOR ANY SIZE EXAMINATION.  THE DATA
150 REM MUST BE ENTERED AS FOLLOWS:
160 REM IN LINE NUMBER 330, ENTER THE NUMBER OF STUDENTS TAKING THE
170 REM EXAMINATION.
180 REM STARTING IN LINE NUMBER 340, ENTER THE NUMBER OF STUDENTS THAT
190 REM SCORED ONE PROBLEM CORRECT, TWO PROBLEMS CORRECT, THREE PROBLEMS
200 REM CORRECT, ETC., ETC., AND SO ON UNTIL YOU HAVE THE NUMBER OF
210 REM STUDENTS THAT SCORED FIFTY PROBLEMS CORRECT.  AS AN EXAMPLE,
220 REM CHECK THE SAMPLE DATA NOW IN LINES 340, 350, AND 360.  YOU
230 REM MUST ENTER FIFTY FREQUENCIES EVEN IF SOME ARE ZERO.......
240 DIM S(100), F(100), P(150), A(100), C(100), X(100), L(150)
250 PRINT"SCORE","FREQ","CUM FREQ","PERCENTILE","T-SCORE"
260 READ N
270 FOR I = 1 TO 50
280 LET S(I) = 2*I
290 NEXT I
300 FOR J = 1 TO 50
310 READ F(J)
320 NEXT J
330 DATA 640
340 DATA 0,0,0,0,0,0,0,0,1,2,0,2,4,2,5,4,5,10,10,15,20,18,20,25,26
350 DATA 30,30,38,40,45,40,38,30,25,20,25,18,16,15,10,10,8,8,10,5,
360 DATA 4,3,2,1,0,
370 LET Y=0
380 LET F(0)=0
390 FOR K=1 TO 50
400 LET J=K-1
410 LET Y=Y+F(J)
420 LET A(J)=Y
430 LET C(K)=A(J) + (1/2)*F(K)
440 LET P(K)=C(K)/N*100
450 NEXT K
460 FOR M= 1 TO 126
470 READ L(M)
480 NEXT M
490 DATA .08,.10,.11,.15,.16,.21,.22,.29,.3,.39,.4,.53,.54,.7,.71,
500 DATA .93,.94,1.21,1.22,1.57,1.58,2.01,2.02,2.55,2.56,3.21,3.22
510 DATA 4,4.01,4.94,4.95,6.05,6.06,7.34,7.35,8.84,8.85,10.55,10.56
520 DATA 12.5,12.51,14.68,14.69,17.1,17.11,19.76,19.77,22.65
530 DATA 22.66,25.77,25.78,29.11,29.12,32.63,32.64,36.31,36.32,
540 DATA 40.12,40.13,44.03,44.04,48.00,48.01,51.99,52,55.96,55.97
```

```
550 DATA59.87,59.88,63.68,63.69,67.36,67.37,70.88,70.89,74.22,74.23
560 DATA77.34,77.35,80.23,80.24,82.89,82.9,85.31,85.32,87.49,87.5,
570 DATA 89.44,89.45,91.15,91.16,92.65,92.66,93.04,03.95,95.05
580 DATA 95.06,95.99,96.96.78,96.79,97.44,97.45,97.98,97.99,98.42,
590 DATA 98.43,98.78,98.79,99.06,99.07,99.29,99.3,99.46,99.47,99.6,
600 DATA 99.61,99.7,99.71,99.78,99.79,98.84,99.85,99.89,99.9,99.99
610 LET R=1
620 LET Q=1
630 LET J = R
640 LET M = 0
650 IF J>=51 THEN 830
660 IF M>=127 THEN 830
670 IF P(J)>=L(M) THEN 720
680 LET X(J) = 18
690 GO TO 810
700 LET R = J+1
710 GO TO 630
720 IF P(J)<=L(M+1) THEN 760
730 LET Q=M+1
740 GO TO 640
750 IF P(J)<=L(M+1) THEN 760
760 LET X(J) = 18 + (M+1)/2
770 GO TO 810
780 GO TO 700
790 GO TO 630
800 IF M>= 126 THEN 830
810 PRINT S(J), F(J), C(J), P(J), X(J)
820 GO TO 700
830 END
```

SCORE	FREQ	CUM FREQ	PERCENTILE	T-SCORE
2	0	0	0	18
4	0	0	0	18
6	0	0	0	18
8	0	0	0	18
10	0	0	0	18
12	0	0	0	18
14	0	0	0	18
16	0	0	0	18
18	1	.5	.078125	18
20	2	2	.3125	23
22	0	3	.46875	24
24	2	4	.625	25
26	4	7	1.09375	27
28	2	10	1.5625	28
30	5	13.5	2.10938	30
32	4	18	2.8125	31
34	5	22.5	3.51563	32
36	10	30	4.6875	33
38	10	40	6.25	35
40	15	52.5	8.20313	36
42	20	70	10.9375	38
44	18	89	13.9063	39
46	20	108	16.875	40
48	25	130.5	20.3906	42
50	26	156	24.375	43
52	30	184	28.75	44
54	30	214	33.4375	46
56	38	248	38.75	47
58	40	287	44.8438	49
60	45	329.5	51.4844	50
62	40	372	58.125	52
64	38	411	64.2188	54
66	30	445	69.5313	55
68	25	472.5	73.8281	56
70	20	495	77.3438	57.5
72	25	517.5	80.8594	59
74	18	539	84.2188	60
76	16	556	86.875	61
78	15	571.5	89.2969	62
80	10	584	91.25	64
82	10	594	92.8125	65
84	8	603	94.2188	66
86	8	611	95.4688	67
88	10	620	96.875	69
90	5	627.5	98.0469	71
92	4	632	98.75	72
94	3	635.5	99.2969	74.5
96	2	638	99.6875	77
98	1	639.5	99.9219	81

APPENDIX D

ADDITIONAL SUGGESTED READINGS

I. Educational Theory

BRUNER, J. S., *Toward a Theory of Instruction.* Harvard University Press, Cambridge, Massachusetts. 1966

GARNER, W. L., *Programmed Instruction.* Center for Applied Research in Education, Inc., New York. 1966

LOUGHARY, J. W., *Man-Machine Systems in Education.* Harper and Row Publishers, New York. 1966

SKINNER, B. F., *The Technology of Teaching.* Appleton-Century-Crofts, New York. 1968

II. Computer Science

FARINA, M. V., *Programming in BASIC.* Prentice Hall, Inc., Englewood Cliffs, New Jersey. 1968

HASSETT, A., *Computer Programming and Computer Systems.* Academic Press, New York. 1967

KARPLUS, W. J., *On-Line Computing.* McGraw-Hill Book Company, New York. 1967

ZIEGLER, J. R., *Time-sharing Data Processing Systems.* Prentice Hall, Inc., Englewood Cliffs, New Jersey. 1967.

Computers in Higher Education: Report of the President's Science Advisory Committee. The White House, Washington, D.C., 1967. (available from the U.S. Government Printing Office)

III. Numerical Computer Methods

HAMMING, R. W., *Numerical Methods for Scientists and Engineers.* McGraw-Hill Book Company, Inc., New York. 1962

MACON, N., *Numerical Analysis.* John Wiley & Sons, Inc., New York. 1962

STANTON, R. G., *Numerical Methods for Science and Engineering.* Prentice-Hall, Inc., Englewood Cliffs, New Jersey. 1961

VAJDA, S., *Mathematical Programming.* Addison-Wesley Publishing Company, Inc., Reading, Massachusetts. 1961

365

Index